W9-BMX-934

COLLECTED WORKS OF JOHN STUART MILL

VOLUME V

Essays on
Economics and Society

by JOHN STUART MILL

1850–1879

Introduction by
LORD ROBBINS

Textual Editor
J. M. ROBSON
Associate Professor of English,
Victoria College, University of Toronto

Liberty Fund
Indianapolis

This book is published by Liberty Fund, Inc., a foundation established to encourage study of the ideal of a society of free and responsible individuals.

The cuneiform inscription that serves as our logo and as the design motif for our endpapers is the earliest-known written appearance of the word "freedom" (*amagi*), or "liberty." It is taken from a clay document written about 2300 B.C. in the Sumerian city-state of Lagash.

This Liberty Fund paperback edition of 2006 is a reprint from the original edition published by The University of Toronto Press in 1967.
© 1967 The University of Toronto Press.

06 07 08 09 10 P 5 4 3 2 1

Library of Congress Cataloging-in-Publication Data
Mill, John Stuart, 1806–1873.
[Works. 2006]
The collected works / of John Stuart Mill
p.   cm.
Reprint. Originally published: Toronto, Ont.; Buffalo, N.Y.: University of Toronto Press, 1965–1981.
Includes bibliographical references and index.
ISBN-13: 978-0-86597-658-0   (8-vol. set: alk. paper: pbk.)   ISBN-10: 0-86597-658-9
ISBN-13: 978-0-86597-654-2   (vol. 5: alk. paper: pbk.)   ISBN-10: 0-86597-654-6
ISBN-13: 978-0-86597-691-7   (2-vol. pbk. set, vols. 4–5)   ISBN-10: 0-86597-691-0
1. Philosophy. 2. Political science. 3. Economics. I. Title.
B1602.A2   2006
192—dc22   2005044313

The text of this book was set in Times Roman, a typeface designed by Stanley Morison for the *Times* of London and introduced by that newspaper in 1932. Also used for book work throughout the world, Times Roman is among the most important type designs of the twentieth century.

Printed on paper that is acid-free and meets the requirements of the American National Standard for Permanence of Paper for Printed Library Materials, Z39.48-1992. ♾

Cover design by Erin Kirk New, Watkinsville, Georgia
Printed and bound by The University of Toronto Press Inc.

Liberty Fund, Inc.
8335 Allison Pointe Trail, Suite 300
Indianapolis, Indiana 46250-1684

Contents

1850–1879

ESSAYS ON ECONOMICS AND SOCIETY

1850–1879

THE SAVINGS OF THE MIDDLE AND WORKING CLASSES

1850

EDITOR'S NOTE

Parliamentary Papers, 1850, XIX, 253–66. Not republished. Original heading: "*John Stuart Mill*, Esq., called in; and Examined." Running heads: "Minutes of Evidence *taken before* Select Committee/On Savings of Middle and Working Classes." The evidence was taken on 6 June, 1850, with R. A. Slaney in the Chair, and the following members of the Committee present: John Ellis, William Ewart (whose name is omitted from the list in *Parliamentary Papers*), Thomas Greene, Frederick Peel, John Abel Smith, and Lord James Stuart. Identified in JSM's bibliography as " 'Evidence before the Select Committee of the House of Commons on Investments for the Savings of the Middle and Working Classes' printed with their Report, forming No. 508 of the papers of the Session of 1850" (MacMinn, 75). No copy in Somerville College.

JSM's examination includes questions 835 to 961 of the evidence before the Committee.

The Savings of the Middle and Working Classes

R. A. SLANEY: *You are the Author of a work on Political Economy?*[*] I am.

In that work you have directed your attention to the improvement of the condition of all classes? The working classes more particularly.

Have you considered any of the obstacles that you think may arise from the present laws of partnership?[†] The laws of partnership oppose obstacles of various kinds to the improvement of the working classes; but perhaps the most important is the obstacle which they throw in the way of combinations among the workmen engaged in any particular branch of industry, for the purpose of carrying on that industry co-operatively, either with their own capital or with capital which they borrow.

With respect, first of all, to capital to be invested in industrial enterprises, every person, by the present law of partnership, who advances any portion of the capital, is liable to the whole amount of his fortune, is he not? Except in the case of chartered companies; I believe there is no other exception.

Do you think that such liability prevents many persons of prudence and caution, who would otherwise be willing to advance capital to a certain limited amount, from making such advances? I have no means of answering that question from personal experience, but from the reason of the thing, I think it must oppose a very great obstacle.

Another obstacle is the difficulty there is in parties combining together for industrial purposes, to prevent fraud among themselves, is it not? That I have understood is the most serious difficulty at present, a still more serious one than that arising from unlimited liability. With respect to the sort of combinations that I speak of, I am not sure that limited liability, so far as regards the working classes themselves, would make much difference; if they invest anything we may be pretty sure that they invest nearly all they have, and if they lose that they lose everything; but I am

[*Principles of Political Economy* (1848; 2nd ed., 1849), in *Collected Works*, II and III. Toronto: University of Toronto Press, 1965.]

[†7 & 8 Victoria, c.110; amended, largely as a result of this Committee's work, by 15 & 16 Victoria, c.31.]

quite aware from what I have heard stated by members of the working classes, and by persons active and anxious for the improvement of their condition, that they feel very great difficulty in establishing a proper control over one another, and over the managers; and they ascribe to that the failure of such enterprises hitherto, in the cases in which they have failed.

At present, if any one of those humbler persons who join together in partnership to carry on an industrial enterprise acts fraudulently, there is no summary mode of punishing him, is there? I presume there is hardly any certain mode of punishing a partner for almost any frauds, for he is considered to be making use of his own property. The recent fraud on the Globe Insurance Company affords a striking example of that.

Another thing that these industrious persons desire, is to be enabled to enforce the rules made among themselves, before a magistrate, in a summary manner, without going to the Court of Chancery? Exactly. That I understand to be a very great inconvenience in the law of partnership, even when there are but a few partners concerned. It is hardly possible for them to obtain any decision of questions arising between themselves, unless they consent to break up the partnership, and even then only by the extremely expensive process of a proceeding in the Court of Chancery.

Do not the difficulties which exist render it quite impracticable for the humbler classes to join together for such purposes? I imagine they do so at a very great risk. And with regard to the permanence of any association consisting of great numbers, where the members cannot know one another, nor have a sufficient guarantee for each other's integrity and good sense, it can be hardly possible for any association to keep together long without providing some easy means of obtaining a settlement of their disputes and of preventing frauds.

Do not you think it would be politic and wise to afford them some such facilities as we have spoken of, with regard to preventing fraud between themselves, and summarily enforcing the rules made by them? I have no doubt that it would be of the greatest value, both in regard to such associations and many others.

Putting aside all consideration of the law of partnership as to limited liability, because you have stated that possibly that might not be necessary, would it not be just and politic to give to those working people associating together facilities, in the first instance, for preventing fraud among themselves, by summary jurisdiction before a magistrate; and, secondly, that of enforcing the rules before a magistrate also? I should think that hardly anything which the Legislature could do, in the present state of society, and the present state of the feelings of the working classes, would be more useful than that.

Both those powers are given by the Friendly Societies Acts[*] *to certain*
[*See 9 & 10 Victoria, c.27]

associations enrolled under those Acts, are they not? I am not particularly acquainted with the provisions of those Acts; but I have always understood that there are peculiar facilities afforded, and that there is a Government referee in the case of those societies, who is a judge in some degree, I do not know with what powers, as to the rules which they establish, and which they are governed by; so that he is in some measure both adviser and judge how far the regulations of the societies are conducive to the objects they have in view.

Would it be advantageous to the classes that have been referred to, to give them facilities for enrolling themselves under the Friendly Societies Acts, or to give them similar powers, without giving them any peculiar advantage except that facility which the law gives? I think it would be very useful. A limitation of the responsibility, so far as relates to the working classes themselves, might not be essential; but still I think that an alteration of the law in regard to the responsibility of partners would be of great importance to those associations, not for the sake of the responsibility of the operatives who may be members of such associations, but in order to induce persons of capital to advance it to them for those purposes. I think that the great value of a limitation of responsiblity, as relates to the working classes, would be not so much to facilitate the investment of their savings, not so much to enable the poor to lend to those who are rich, as to enable the rich to lend to those who are poor.

Do not you think that if such limited liability were introduced, under reasonable safeguards, many benevolent persons, or persons desirous of giving facilities to improve the condition of the working classes, would be willing to lend moderate sums, say from 100l. to 200l. or 300l. to put them in action? I have not the least doubt that many persons would do so.

At present if they do so they have no security, for if they take any share of the profits they become liable to the whole amount of their fortunes? They do. It is true they might save themselves from unlimited liability by advancing the money in the form of loans: but that would not be of nearly so much use to the borrowers; because those who advanced the money as loans would come in as creditors in common with all other creditors, and therefore would diminish instead of increasing the amount of credit to which the association is entitled; but if they came in as *commandite* partners, that would enable the association to benefit, not only by the capital advanced, but by the credit which that capital would give them, and which would be equivalent to so much more capital.

Do you think from what you have heard among the intelligent members of the working classes and others friendly to them, that some such regulations as those which have been mentioned would go far to promote contentment amongst them, and to remove causes of discontent? I think it would promote contentment in a very great degree, and that it ought to do so; it would remove one great cause of discontent, and a very just cause.

Do you not think, even supposing that the industrial combinations referred to should not succeed, that it would be judicious to allow them to try the experiment, and to undeceive themselves supposing they should be disappointed in the expectations they had formed? I think even if it were quite certain that they would not succeed, it would be of the greatest importance that they should be allowed to try the experiment, and that they should have every facility given to them, to convince those who were trying the experiment, that it was tried fairly. Besides, even if such experiments failed, the attempt to make them succeed would be a very important matter in the way of education to the working classes, both intellectually and morally. I may add that I see no reason why they should not succeed; they are under some disadvantages, but they have other advantages, and it is quite a question whether the advantages do not preponderate. I think it is a matter which experience can alone ascertain.

Are you aware that amongst a portion of the more intelligent of the working classes, an opinion prevails that the present laws are unjust and unequal, and prevent them having fair play in the use of their small capitals, and which they think is afforded to persons possessing greater wealth? Yes, and I certainly see great reason in that. The advantages which the possession of large capital gives, which are very great, and which are growing greater and greater inasmuch as it is the tendency of business more and more to be conducted on a large scale; these advantages are at present, not from any intention of the Legislature, but arising from things into which intention does not enter at all, to a great degree a monopoly in the hands of the rich, and it is natural that the poor should desire to obtain those same advantages by association, the only way in which they can do so. Perhaps I may add this also: I think there is no way in which the working classes can make so beneficial a use of their savings both to themselves and to society, as by the formation of associations to carry on the business with which they are acquainted, and in which they are themselves engaged as workpeople, provided always that experience should show that these associations can keep together. If the experiment should succeed, I think there is much more advantage to be gained to the working classes by this than by any other mode of investing their savings. I do not speak of political or social considerations, but in a purely economical sense. When it has happened to any one, as it must have happened to most people, to have inquired or to have known in particular cases what portion of the price paid at a shop for an article really goes to the person who made it, and forms his remuneration, I think any one who has had occasion to make inquiries into that fact, must often have been astonished to find how small it is, and how much less a proportion the remuneration of the real labourer bears to the whole price than would be supposed beforehand; and it is of great importance to consider what is the cause of this. Now one thing is very important to remember in itself, and it is important that the working classes should be aware of it; and that is, that this does not arise from the extravagant remuneration of capital. Capital, when the security is good, can be borrowed in any quantity at little more than three per cent., and I imagine there is no co-operative association of working-people who would find it their interest to allow less than that remuneration, as an inducement to any of their members who, instead of consuming their share of the proceeds, might choose to save it, and add it to the capital of the association. Therefore it is not from the remuneration of capital that the evil proceeds. I think it proceeds from two causes: one of them (which does not fall strictly within the limits of the inquiry which the Committee is carrying on) is the very great, I may say, extravagant portion of the whole produce of the community that now goes to mere distributors; the immense amount that is taken up by the different classes of dealers, and especially by retailers. Competition no doubt has some tendency to reduce this rate of remuneration; still I am afraid that in most cases, looking at it on the whole, the effect of competition is, as in the case of the fees of professional people, rather to divide the amount among a larger number, and so diminish the share of each, than to lower the scale of what is obtained by the class generally. Another cause, more immediately connected with the present inquiry, is the difference between interest which is low, and profits which are high. Writers have very often set down all which is not interest, all that portion of profit which is in excess of interest, as the wages of superintendence, as Adam Smith terms it, and, in one point of view, it is properly called so. But then it should be added, that the wages of the labour of superintendence are not regulated like other wages by demand and supply, but are in reality the subject of a sort of monopoly; because the management of capital is a thing which no person can command except the person who has capital of his own, and therefore he is able, if he has a large capital, to obtain, in addition to interest, often a very large profit, for one-tenth part of which he could, and very often does, engage the services of some competent person to transact the whole of the labour of management, which would otherwise devolve upon himself. I do not say that this is unjust in the present state of society, for it is a necessary consequence of the law of property, and must exist while that law exists in its present form; but it is very natural that the working classes should wish to try whether they could not contrive to get this portion of the produce of their labour for themselves, so that the whole of the proceeds of an enterprize in which they were engaged might be theirs, after deducting the real remuneration of the capital they may require from others, which we know does not in general, when the security is good, much exceed three per cent. This seems to be an extremely legitimate purpose on the part of the working classes, and one that it would be desirable to carry out, if it could be effected; so that the enterprizes in which they would be engaged would not be conducted, as they are now, by a capitalist, hiring labourers as he wants them, but by the labourers themselves, mental as well as manual, hiring the capital they require at the market rate.

You think, under the circumstances you have referred to, that at all events the more intelligent of the working classes fully believe that it would be a great advantage to them to be enabled to carry out this experiment? They certainly do.

And that it would be but just and politic to allow them, under reasonable safeguards, to do so, that if they are right they may receive the benefit, and if they are wrong they may be undeceived in their unreasonable expectations? Certainly; and there would be this great advantage, that supposing those associations embraced only a small part of the working classes, they would have almost the same salutary effect on their minds as if they embraced the whole; because if a number of those associations were in existence, and they were found to be able to maintain their ground, and to compete well or tolerably, or to compete under great disadvantages even, with individual capitalists, still the whole of the working classes would see that all such disadvantages arose not from the law, but from the nature of the case, or from the absence of the necessary qualities in them; therefore those who might continue to be receivers of wages in the service of individual capitalists, would then feel that they were not doing so from compulsion but from choice, and that taking all the circumstances into consideration their condition appeared to them preferable as receivers of wages.

Putting aside the question as to the unlimited liability of partners, but supposing that capital was found by any parties willing to lend it, what the working classes would desire then would be simply to have laws to prevent fraud amongst themselves, and to enforce the rules which they might make in a simple and inexpensive manner? Those would be the primary objects which I think they would chiefly desire.

w. EWART: *Are the Committee to understand you to say, that the effect of this co-operation on the part of the working classes would be to cut off the cost of the intermediate agency between the producer and the consumer?* Exactly. I may mention that as long ago as the years 1837 and 1838 I have heard intelligent leaders of the working classes speak of this state of the law as one of the greatest grievances which the working classes had to endure.

F. PEEL: *But the share that falls to the retail dealer must vary very much in a small town and in a large town?* No doubt, estimated by the ordinary rule of per centage, the profits where the market was small must be greater in order to afford any remuneration whatever for trouble.

Would the effect of those associations be to reduce the cost of commodities? Associations of workpeople for the purpose of co-operative production would not necessarily have much effect in diminishing the amount of the produce which now goes to the distributors; there might, however, be co-operative shops or bazaars, and in that way the function of distribution might be reduced to the employing of a much smaller number of persons than at present. The greater the number of productive labourers, the greater, in general, is the produce: but an increased number of mere distributors has no tendency to increase the quantity of wealth to be distributed, but only quarters an additional number of persons upon it. For this reason, some of the writers and thinkers of the co-operative school have thought it desirable that distribution should be, as it were, a public function; in which case the distributors might be reduced to a very small number; as the whole of the distribution, that is, the buying and selling, which is required for a village for instance, or a small town, might be performed at one office by very few people. These speculations are not immediately applicable to practice in present circumstances, but still they are not altogether from the purpose.

J. ELLIS: *Have you any good reason to suppose, that if these facilities were offered, money could be borrowed at 3, or 3½ per cent., or 4 per cent.; can you cite any case?* I think it probable, certainly, that it could not at present, or perhaps for a long time, be borrowed at such a rate as that, because there would not be sufficient confidence in the security.

R. A. SLANEY: *If by any alteration of the law there was sufficient confidence felt in the security, do you think then that it might be borrowed at some such rate as that?* We know that when the security is good, that is the ordinary rate of interest now, and anything more than that is compensation for risk, or for some peculiar disadvantage. I suppose that money could be obtained at that rate if the security were considered good, and if these associations did as much business as a tradesman in good credit, or as merchants with a similar amount of capital do now, they could borrow at the same rate in time.

Supposing the interest of the money to be gauged by the interest paid in the public funds, then every increase of interest above that is in some sort an insurance interest? Yes; I only mentioned that rate of interest to show that it was not the extravagant remuneration of capital, properly so called, which is the reason why less than is desirable goes to the actual producer; because it is impossible to say, when capital can be borrowed, as we know it can, at such a rate as that, and in almost any quantity, that that is too great a remuneration for the abstinence exercised in saving.

J. ELLIS: *Are you aware that 4 and 4½ per cent. is now very freely given, when the security is very ample indeed, for very large sums of money?* I am quite aware that the rates vary. I have understood that when the lender can get his capital back again upon short notice, it may sometimes be borrowed at as low an interest as 2 per cent.

R. A. SLANEY: *Do you not think it possible, without stating a confident opinion, that for any of the industrial enterprises which we have spoken of, and to which we have contemplated that facilities might be given in the mode mentioned, if the intelligent minds of the working classes were directed to such objects, that very likely there might be discoveries of economical improvements where they had to manage their own affairs, such as we have not yet seen, and which might produce considerable benefits?* I should think so.

Is it not well known that most of the many inventions for the improvement of machinery from time to time have been made by the workmen themselves? I believe they have very often.

Do you not think it is likely that the intelligence of those men directed to the management of their own affairs would from time to time suggest improvements in the objects to which their attention was directed? I think we can hardly set limits to the consequences that might arise in the way of improvements, from the feeling that would be diffused through the whole of the persons employed in an undertaking, of personal interest in its success.

At the present time, however, existing circumstances prevent that taking place? To a great degree.

W. EWART: *Have you had the advantage of the experience of any such co-operative societies in America or Holland, or in other countries on the Continent?* There exist many such in several countries, especially in France; but I believe they are of too recent origin to afford much experience of their success; we shall probably have to wait some years before the experiment can be considered as conclusive.

In the United States of America have such experiments been tried, to your knowledge? I understand your question as applying to associations of workpeople, and I believe there are in America a considerable number of manufacturing associations in which all the workpeople have an interest; I have understood that that is the case with many manufacturing establishments in New England; that they are held in shares, and that the operatives are almost all shareholders, and all may expect to become so.

T. GREENE: *With limited liability?* I believe so.

R. A. SLANEY: *In page 324 of your work, volume 2,*[*] *you refer to the co-operative principle of capitalists and workmen as prevailing in American trading ships, and among the Cornish miners also?* Yes; I am not particu-

[*Principles, 1st ed., 1848; in Collected Works, III, pp. 769–70.]

larly acquainted with the circumstances as to the Cornish miners; I mentioned them as instances of the advantage which was ascertained by experience to arise from allowing an interest in the undertaking to all the persons employed; I do not know that they are partners in all those cases, but they have an interest, and that varies with the success.

You think under such circumstances that would be likely to stimulate their activity and intelligence? It could not fail to do so; I believe that the working people are generally found to be particularly intelligent and zealous under such circumstances, and that has been always remarked of the Cornish miners.

You have quoted in your work[*] Mr. Babbage's example of the fishermen on the south coast, and other examples, to show how applicable, under certain circumstances, the same principle would be to manufactures? Yes.

That it would be quite practicable to give a moderate interest to the workmen in such a way as to stimulate their good conduct and their industry? A very interesting pamphlet has been published by a French employer of labour, a house-painter, named Leclaire;[†] and I understand his experiment still goes on, and goes on with great success. He speaks very strongly of the moral improvement which it produced in his workmen; an improvement in their conduct both when at work and even at other times; they seemed to have assumed quite a different character, through the feeling that they were not merely working for some one else but for themselves. It seemed to raise them in their own estimation, and induced them to cultivate careful habits of all sorts.

You have also stated in a passage in page 459, "the industrial economy which divides society absolutely into two portions, the payers of wages and the receivers, the first counted by thousands and the last by millions, is not fit for indefinite duration."[‡] Is that the opinion you still entertain? I do.

You think that improvements may be made in those respects by carrying out some of the plans that we have spoken of in such a way as, without endangering property, would give greater contentment to many of those persons? I think that the remuneration of capital, properly so called, would not be felt under those circumstances by the intelligent among the working people to be a grievance. And speaking generally, I do not think that they feel so much, either in this country or in others, the inequality of property, considered in itself, as they do the inequality consequent upon it, which unhappily exists now, namely, that those who already have property have

[*Ibid., p. 770.]

[†Leclaire, Edmé-Jean. *Des améliorations qu'il serait possible d'apporter dans le sort des ouvriers peintres en bâtiments.* Paris: Bouchard-Huzard, n.d. See Mill, *Collected Works,* III, pp. 770–2.]

[‡*Principles,* 1st ed., II; in *Collected Works,* III, p. 896.]

so much greater facilities for getting more, than those who have it not, have for acquiring it.

At pages 469 and 470[*] *of your work you have given the example of the good working of the system in New England, and have enumerated the benefits received from it as many and lasting, and amongst those advantages you particularly mention that the workmen consider this principle as a sort of stepping stones to enable them to raise their condition, by little and little, according to their industry and intelligence, and that it goes far to content them with their humble situation?* No doubt; because it makes their situation not a humble one.

W. EWART: *You think that the possession of power by the working classes to co-operate in the way you have mentioned, would satisfy them, at all events, if the results did not equal their expectations?* I think if the experiment failed, they would see that it failed from some defect either in the principle or in their qualifications for carrying out the experiment.

Have you ever inquired into that association conducted on the co-operative principle, called the "People's Mill," at Leeds? I have heard of it; but I am not particularly acquainted with it.

J. A. SMITH: *Are the Committee to understand you to suggest as one of the most useful things in reference to these co-operative societies, an alteration in the law, which may be called an alteration in the law of partnership as affecting them, and should you advise that generally, or confine it specially to the working classes?* I think such an alteration particularly important as regards the working classes at present, but I would make it universal.

If there were a limitation, could you give the Committee any mode of ascertaining to what extent the principle might practically be carried in reference to those particular views at once? I think it would be difficult; at any rate I have not considered that point, because I have never seen a necessity for any limitation.

With regard to the limitation, is there any mode of arriving at that by limiting the objects to which you would apply the co-operation? It would be very difficult, I think, to draw any line, and to say that the principle is fit for some objects and not for others; I do not see any object for which it is unfit, though it may be more necessary for some than for others.

In reference to the results in an economical point of view, if I understand you rightly, you imagine that if it were generally adopted it would very much limit the number of retail dealers? It is uncertain whether any such effect would be produced at first, since the co-operative associations of workpeople are associations for carrying on production rather than distribution; still I do not doubt that retail dealing might be carried on by

[*Principles, 1st ed., II; in Collected Works, III, pp. 904–5.]

associations of shopmen and clerks without the assistance of great capitalists.

Do not these societies, as far as we have any experience of them, combine production and distribution? Some of them do.

If they do combine distribution and production, that would tend very considerably to limit the number of distributors, would it not? No doubt.

Should you consider that desirable, or the reverse? I should consider it desirable, provided it were done without the assistance of any restrictive laws or privileges.

Why should you consider it advantageous? On the same principle on which it is advantageous to suppress any useless intermediate steps in the process of production. If any of those who are employed in the production of wealth can be rendered unnecessary by any new discovery, it is thought an advantage to do so. If the business of distribution, which now employs, taking the different classes of dealers and their families, perhaps more than a million of the inhabitants of this country—and that is a very large draught upon the total wealth of the country—if all that they do could be done by a hundred thousand people, I should think the other nine hundred thousand could be dispensed with, and that would be the same sort of advantage as dispensing with labour by any improvement in production.

W. EWART: *Would not this illustrate your principle: In the town of Liverpool formerly the consumers were supplied from shops; a few years ago large markets were established in that town, and on a very splendid scale. The consumers did not go any longer to the intermediate distributors, but went to the markets, and therefore there was in that instance, by the operation of improvement, a cutting off of the intermediate agents between the producers and the consumers, of course with much greater cheapness to the consumers than formerly?* Exactly. I understand that there are many branches of trade in which certain grades and classes of middlemen have been dispensed with, a more direct communication being established between either the wholesale dealers and the consumers, or the wholesale dealers and some particular class of retailers. I believe there was a much greater number of factors, brokers, and such intermediate agents between the different classes of dealers, formerly than there are now.

J. A. SMITH: *You do not mean that it was an undecided question whether the number of retail dealers or distributors would be diminished or not, and that it was possible by this mode of co-operation that production would take place at a less cost, and therefore consumption be largely increased?* I think that is an undecided question, certainly; there is a good deal to be said in the way of probabilities on both sides, but it could be clearly ascertained by the common law of competition. If this mode of production was found more advantageous and economical, it would undersell the others of course, and if not it would be undersold.

Generally speaking, you think, as an economical question, that it would be desirable to encourage associations of this co-operative character? Decidedly.

R. A. SLANEY: *To give them fair play, at all events?* To give them all possible facilities, but no premium.

J. A. SMITH: *But it is to a certain degree an experiment, if the law of partnership, as affecting them, is much to differ from the law of partnership as affecting the community at large?* Yes, that enters into the question, whether the law as respects the community at large should not be altered.

W. EWART: *Do you think it would be advisable to make a special law, in fact, for any particular class without considering the expediency of altering the whole law with regard to partnership?* If it were not possible to alter the law of partnership generally, altering it in favour of a particular class would be, I will not say objectionable, but it would be a serious argument against it.

J. A. SMITH: *Would any alteration of the law of partnership, inter se, affecting the large transactions in the commercial world in England necessarily involve a machinery of expense and delay, bearing in mind, that however it might be simplified, it could hardly be made applicable to small enterprises, such as those which have been spoken of?* It would give the smaller enterprises an advantage, certainly; but I am not aware that that advantage would be greater than what arises from any arrangement for the administration of justice, or the decision of disputes by tribunals or by arbitrators.

Are you not rather looking to a tribunal of less authority and less weight and less importance, in reference to the disputes of these workmen amongst themselves when associated together co-operatively, than to a tribunal of a higher order, with greater knowledge and experience, and greater weight, which would be necessary to decide the various difficult questions arising out of partnerships engaged in large transactions in commerce? I have understood that there is great difficulty and inconvenience felt in the case of ordinary partnerships for want of a tribunal. If there were a tribunal properly constituted, and adequate to decide such questions, which are often, and necessarily so, of a very complicated nature, I should think that this class of associations would rather be under a disadvantage than an advantage in consequence of their great numbers.

There might be a more expensive tribunal than those people could afford to go to? If it were made a general measure, probably it would be thought that the State ought to supply the tribunal, as it does in all other cases.

The State when it does give in other cases a tribunal of justice manages to make it tolerably onerous? Yes, it does; but many people, of whom I am one, think that one of the great defects in the present institutions of all countries.

R. A. SLANEY: *Would it be equal justice that a tribunal for the decision of disputes between partners should be so costly that it would be utterly impossible for the working men to go into it at all; and do not you think that where the existing law is such as that humble persons joining together as small capitalists are utterly deprived of any tribunal, that is an unjust state of things?* I think so.

J. A. SMITH: *Inasmuch as that question as to the expense of law is of very great importance, and an extensive question, which must involve long consideration and long time in its settlement, would it not be expedient, at all events in the meantime, that some means, even if it were temporary, should be given to the working classes to settle disputes amongst themselves in an easy, effectual, and cheap manner, by reference to a tribunal to be appointed for that special purpose?* Perhaps so. It takes so long to frame, and so much longer to carry, a general measure of improvement in the law, that it is sometimes desirable to have a temporary measure applicable to particular classes of cases.

Do you think there is anything in the present tone and temper of the working classes which would make it now desirable to give attention to this subject? I think there is at this moment more than there has ever been before, and there is likely to be more and more, a feeling on their part, against all the inequalities which exist in society. There is a very growing feeling of that kind, and the only way of mitigating that feeling is to remove all inequalities that can be removed without preponderant disadvantages.

R. A. SLANEY: *At all events, by that means you could give them facilities for trying industrial associations, without giving them privileges, but merely those facilities which you think would be politic?* Certainly.

W. EWART: *Do not tribunals exist in France, self-formed among the working classes, called, "Société de Prud'hommes"?* The "Conseils de Prud'hommes" are public institutions for the purpose of arbitrating in disputes between the masters and the workpeople. Before the February revolution they consisted entirely of masters; but by a law subsequently enacted, they have been constituted on a different footing, and are now composed of masters and workmen in equal numbers; including among workmen the *Chefs d'Ateliers.*

R. A. SLANEY: *Do they work pretty well?* I have not much knowledge of that; the law has not existed very long.

W. EWART: *With regard to the Tribunal of Commerce, that is constituted, is it not, of persons conversant in trade?* Yes, the judges are elected by the merchants of Paris.

J. A. SMITH: *Have they anything to do with the settlement of disputes?*

They are an established court of justice in commercial cases; I do not know whether in all such cases, or only in some. It is one of the principles of that branch of French law that questions of mercantile law should be decided on by merchants, and not by lawyers; the parties plead their own cause.

Do you think that is a sound principle? I think that still better tribunals might be devised.

R. A. SLANEY: *Without speaking of those industrial associations, but with reference to the general law of partnership, and to some alteration of the law of unlimited liability, do you not think that the existing law of unlimited liability has a tendency to prevent persons of prudence and position in their respective neighbourhoods from taking shares in any local enterprises of moderate risk, on account of their being liable to the whole amount of their properties?* I should think it must have that tendency.

Are you aware with reference to the proposition which was made in this metropolis for the purpose of establishing model lodging-houses, which were intended for the improvement of the condition of the working classes, to be carried on by joint shares, and in which many noblemen and gentlemen took shares, that the first thing that prevented its being carried out was the law of unlimited liability? I have heard so.

And that they were obliged to apply for a charter? Yes.

And that the charter cost upwards of 1,000 l.? I have heard that it did, but I do not know that personally.

Supposing that the cost of obtaining a charter is what I have stated, do not you think that, and the law of unlimited liability, two circumstances almost sufficient to prevent any parties from embarking in such undertakings? We see that they do embark in them very often; but I have no doubt they are often prevented by the circumstances that you mention.

Do not you think that in many of the large towns in this country it is probable that persons, if they had facilities given them of taking shares with limited liability for local enterprises of public benefit, would be willing to do so? Many persons no doubt would.

Are you aware that application has been already made from eight or ten large towns to have the shelter of the charter given to this society for improving the dwellings of the humble classes in London? I have heard it mentioned.

Do you not think that if such advantages were conceded, either by limited liability confined possibly to such enterprises, or by means of limited liability given by a charter, without expense and delay, that it would give great encouragement to such enterprises being carried out in those large towns? There are two questions of limitation of liability; one is that of allowing *commandite* partnerships, under which the managing and acting partners are under unlimited liability; and the liability that is limited is only as to those who advance capital, but do not take part in the management. The other is the question of allowing perfect freedom of forming joint-stock companies with unlimited liability; and that is a question much more difficult than the other. It there were a general law, by which persons might form themselves into joint-stock companies with limited liability whenever they pleased, I think you ought to allow individuals also to limit their liability, giving due notice; in order that the competition might be equal. It would be a very great alteration in the present state of the law, but one to which general principles are favourable. On general principles, one sees no sufficient reason why people should not be allowed to employ their capital and labour on any terms that they please, and to deal with others on any terms that they please, provided those terms are known, and that they do not give themselves out for what they are not. Still that is a more difficult question than the question of *commandite* partnerships; and it is very possible that in the case of joint-stock companies with unlimited liability, it might be better to consider each particular case on its own merits; to facilitate the obtaining of a charter where the purpose was of public utility, and to take away the expense in cases where the public advantage was recognised.

Supposing in the law of partnership, either for particular enterprises or generally, there were introduced limited liability, are there any safeguards which you think it would be right to introduce against fraud; as, for instance, that the shares should be paid up, that the names of the shareholders should be known, that there should be a public audit, that the accounts should be open, and that the interest upon the shares should be limited, or any such conditions as those which I have mentioned? Does the question relate to companies with unlimited responsibility of partners, or to *commandite* partnerships?

Either to one or the other, as you may think it right to apply the limitation. In the case of *commandite* partnership there does not seem to be a necessity for anything like the same amount of precautions that might be necessary in the other case, but generally speaking I should say that any security that could be taken for complete publicity would be desirable; anything tending to prevent the terms of the business from being held forth as different from what they really were.

Anything to prevent fraud upon the public, in short? Anything to prevent people from being misled as to what they had to expect.

Do not you think that some kind of precaution to prevent uneducated or incautious persons from being induced by the plausible representations of projectors from entertaining too high an opinion of the speculation that shall be entered into (for instance, as to the amount of capital to be *divided), might be advantageous?* The reason that you suggest, the danger that persons might be deceived by projectors, is the same reason which was long given for maintaining the Usury Laws;[*] and it seems to me that the prohibition of *commandite* partnership belongs to the same kind of legislation as the Usury Laws. It belongs to the idea that the law ought to regulate the terms on which money shall be permitted to be lent, under the supposition that the lenders are not capable of taking care of themselves. I look upon *commandite* partnerships as a mode of lending. So long as it was the principle of the law that you ought to prevent people from lending at more than a limited rate of interest, it was necessary to prevent them from evading the prohibition, and doing the same thing in an indirect way; but that principle the law appears to have given up, with a single exception, for which reasons other than those of public utility may be assigned; the case of contracts relating to land. I think it an inconsistency to say that people are free to lend money in the ordinary way at any rates they like, but that there shall be one particular mode of lending from which they are interdicted, namely, lending at a rate of interest varying with the profits of a concern; which is the only difference between *commandite* partnerships and any other loan, except one other difference, which is greatly to the advantage of all parties, namely, that the loan by *commandite* increases the security of all the other creditors instead of diminishing it, because all the other creditors must be paid out of the capital of the *commanditaire* before he can recover anything.

Do you think, on the whole, that the introduction of the law of commandite, *with such safeguards, or regulations, or limitations as the wisdom of the Legislature might introduce, would be advisable?* I see no reason against it.

Do you think that if it were introduced, with such regulations and such safeguards, it would give additional facility for enterprises directed by intelligence, and create additional facilities for the investments of the middle and working classes? I think it would do both these things; and above all, which is very important, it would enable personal qualities to obtain in a greater degree than they can now the advantages which the use and aid of capital affords. It would enable persons of recognised integrity and capacity for business to obtain credit, and to share more freely in the advantages which are now confined in a great degree to those who have capital of their own.

J. A. SMITH: *You do not think that in this country any enterprise that offers a chance of more than an ordinary rate of profit is ever stopped by want of capital?* It is difficult to say; I think one can never tell while a restrictive law exists, what number of useful things it prevents. In the case

[*See 2 & 3 Victoria, c.37.]

of the duties which have been taken off, a number of minor articles in the tariff, nobody could have told before the duties were taken off whether they prevented much commerce or not; I believe in many cases that branches of trade have risen up since which promise to be of great importance. In the same manner I do not think anybody can now appreciate the degree in which the existence of restrictions on partnerships may prevent persons of capacity for business from obtaining credit and the use of capital which would be advantageous to the public and to them.

Does it seem an unreasonable inference from the existence of so many enterprises of a very speculative and wild character, that no reasonable enterprise has failed from want of capital? Perhaps, with regard to the very same people who encourage rash enterprises, the same imperfection of judgment might make them reject beneficial ones.

That would not arise from reluctance to embark capital, but from a want of discretion in the selection of the mode of embarking it? It might arise from this: there might be the promise of more brilliant success in the enterprises they undertook, than in those which they rejected. There may be many cases in which the promise of possible benefit is not so tempting, but in which the chances of profit would on the whole be better.

The danger of responsibility is not the motive or the reason why they reject a sound scheme? It is possible that rash people now do advance capital, and that the prudent do not in the same degree.

R. A. SLANEY: *Do not you think that the existing law has rather a tendency to give advantage to persons possessing large amounts of capital, and disadvantage to those possessing small amounts of capital?* I think that is the tendency of the present law of partnership.

Do not you also think the unlimited liability of partnerships has a tendency to keep out of partnerships persons of cautious and prudent habits, who would be the very persons likely to direct many local enterprises? I think it must have a great tendency to induce prudent people, when they are no longer able to give personal attention to business, to take their capital out of such enterprises.

And to abstain from investing it in them? Yes.

Are not enterprises guided by prudent and cautious persons, the very enterprises one should seek for, for the investments of the middle and industrious classes? In the case of persons of very small means, no doubt security is the primary consideration, much more than profit, but in the case of the middle classes very often the advantage to them would be great of having a tolerably safe investment for their savings, which would at the same time promise them a higher degree of interest than the means which they must have recourse to at present.

Do you think that such local enterprises would be more cautiously and properly guided, if limited liability were introduced in them, so that more cautious persons would be willing to embark in them? I should think so; I have not very specially considered that part of the subject.

J. A. SMITH: *Do not you think that the existence of limited liability would render it probable that enterprizes would be undertaken with even less scrutiny and less examination than under the present law?* I do not see that. At present it is in the power of anybody to commence these businesses with borrowed capital. Now the same person who has sufficient confidence in the undertaking to risk money *en commandite* upon it, would probably advance the same amount on loan; which would be a less advantageous mode both to the borrower and to all persons with whom he might deal, because the lender would come into competition with the other creditors in the event of failure, instead of supplying funds out of which their claims might be satisfied. The Legislature does not think it necessary to restrict people from carrying on business with borrowed money, lest it should give a stimulus to speculation; and there seems no reason why, when it permits borrowing in every other mode, it should select for prohibition the one mode which is at the same time the most useful to the borrower, and the most advantageous to the security of all other creditors. A person to whom 5,000 *l.* have been advanced in *commandite,* is in exactly the same position with regard to those who have transactions with him as if he had inherited, or acquired that sum in his own right.

You give an unqualified opinion in favour of commandite *partnership, and an undecided opinion with respect to joint-stock companies with limited liability?* Yes.

Is it easy to distinguish between a large commandite *partnership and a joint-stock company?* The distinction in principle is clear enough, because where the law of *commandite* exists no person whose responsibility is limited is allowed to do any act whatever as a partner; he may inspect the accounts and give his opinion and that opinion will have weight, but he cannot act towards any third party as a partner, nor even as an agent, nor can his name appear in the firm, nor can be he held forth as a party concerned; so that he is in reality merely a creditor; but he is a creditor on peculiar terms; that is to say, he receives nothing at all unless the concern is profitable; if it fails he is the last satisfied, and may lose all, when no other creditor loses anything.

You consider that the great distinguishing feature and merit of the commandite *system is the unlimited liability, the complete responsibility of the managers?* And the facilities for publicity: though even without publicity, I see no greater objection to *commandite* than to any other mode of carrying on business with borrowed money. As long as a person in business can borrow at all, persons may deal with him under a supposition that the capital with which he is trading is his, when in point of fact it may all have been borrowed. Still the case of *commandite* partnership affords facilities for giving publicity, which are taken advantage of in the American and French law. Both in the law of New York and in the French law the amount of the sum advanced *en commandite* must be registered, and the number of persons from whom it comes; and the fact that the amount is registered enables persons dealing with that firm to be acquainted with the resources of the firm much more than with those of any other firm whatever.

R. A. SLANEY: *You think on the whole that the law of* commandite, *with such improvements as might be suggested upon deliberation, would be advantageous?* Very advantageous.

Do you think that it works well in Holland and America; and I believe it prevails also in France and in Germany? I am not informed as to its working anywhere but in France and in America. I believe the general opinion there is, that it works very well.

J. A. SMITH: *In reference to the economical interests of the middle and industrious classes, do you conceive it is desirable that in choosing their investments they should think more of perfect security or of a high rate of profit?* In the case of the working classes no doubt security is the main object, and in the case generally of all those whose savings are small.

Agreeing with you mainly in that view myself, would it not influence you in your decision as to presenting this temptation or encouragement to the working classes to engage in trade? In regard to the working classes it could make very little difference; I think it would be neither an encouragement nor a discouragement; the savings of those classes are seldom so large as that they have much more to lose, if they lose what they have invested.

Does not that make it still more important to them to keep what they have? Only, if they are to invest it at all, they are equally liable to lose it whether *commandite* is permitted or not; if they had unlimited liability, it would be just the same.

My question meant this, would it not be a thing to be desired, for instance, that they should rather put their savings into the Three per cent. Consols than avail themselves of almost any other devisable means of investment? With certain exceptions; for instance, the associations referred to, the associations by the working classes to carry on, as their own capitalists, their own employment. I think those have very great advantages over any other investments for the working classes. Those associations are on a very different footing in point of security for good management from joint-stock associations generally. Ordinary joint-stock management is management by directors only and the directors are very often not chosen with the necessary degree of discrimination, and are not sufficiently superintended, because the shareholders have other occupations, and their attention is otherwise taken up, and the sum they have invested is probably but a small portion of what they have; but in the case of these associations, in which the capital would be employed in carrying on a business with which all the persons concerned are alike familiar, which they know better than anything else, and which they are daily occupied about, their whole attention being given to it, they would be likely to keep a much better control over the managers, and to be much better judges of who would be the best managers.

Would it not almost follow from that, that you would not wish, as far as your desires went, to see the lower and working classes engaged in such enterprises as the Honourable Chairman has alluded to, such as bridges or roads? It is not very likely that they would engage in them. The means for carrying on such enterprises would be more likely to be supplied from the savings of the middle classes, and from sums which the higher classes could spare, and which they would willingly invest, though they would not willingly incur larger responsibility.

Have you any suggestions to make with regard to the working of savings banks in reference to the mode of investments for the poorer classes as now existing? I think it would be very useful to make the nation responsible for the amount deposited. Certainly the general opinion among the depositors hitherto was, that the nation was responsible; they were not aware that they had only the responsibility of the trustees to rely upon.

Are you aware that the Bill now before Parliament accomplishes that object? I am not aware to what extent it accomplishes it.

R. A. SLANEY: *Would it be advisable to devise some mode by which the working classes might be enabled from their high gains at one period of the year to provide against the time when they might be out of work?* It would be very useful.

Are you not aware that at the present time they have no safe investments into which they can put such a fund so as to be able, from what they gain at one period of the year, to make an allowance to those out of work at another period of the year? I am not aware how far the law of Benefit Societies affords them any advantages for that purpose.

J. A. SMITH: *Are the Committee to understand you to mean that the savings banks offer a mode of investment to those who, while in the receipt of high wages, are willing to deny themselves and to save money against the time when they may be out of employment, or when wages may be much reduced; but that there ought to be greater facilities afforded for establishing mutual insurance funds amongst the men for the purpose of guarding against the contingencies arising from the chances of trade, sickness, and other accidents to which they may be liable?* There is an association now projected, and I believe some progress has been made in it, under the name of the Tailors' Guild, which has that object among others.

R. A. SLANEY: *Do you think that additional facilities should be afforded for bodies of workmen under proper regulations to join together for the purpose of insuring to those parties who are out of work an allowance from their aggregated capital, or fund, laid together when they are in work?* I do.

Do you think that that would be useful, not merely referable to the fluctuations of the demand for labour arising from the fluctuations in commerce, but also from the changes of season in particular works? Yes, and from changes of fashion.

The changes of seasons with regard to bricklayers and several trades have the effect in the winter months of rendering the demand for their services slacker than at other periods? In the case of those periodical slacknesses of work, as they all undergo them nearly equally, in the long run it must be from the individual's own savings that he makes up that loss. But even as individuals they might be induced to practise greater economy, by forming themselves into an association and coming under engagements to one another; as is found in the case of the temperance societies, which *primâ facie* have the air of an absurdity, being associations not for the purpose of doing, but of not doing something; yet they are found very effectual in promoting their object.

Is not the principle of co-operation a very popular one among the working classes, and one which they are very desirous to carry out? It appears to be so.

Would it not be useful to direct that to good purposes? Even in the case of personal conduct the fact of being associated is felt as a sort of pledge that they will adhere to certain rules.

In the case of friendly societies, it seems to be carried out very effectually in providing against illness, does it not? Yes.

J. A. SMITH: *On the other hand, has not the spirit of union amongst the working classes, or rather the expectation of benefit to be received from the trades unions, very much diminished of late years?* I am not aware how far that has diminished of late years; but we so seldom hear of strikes now, that I should think that is the case. I have found that the intelligent members of the working classes have ceased to place the confidence in the effect of strikes which they did formerly, and which it was natural they should do as long as the Combination Laws were unrepealed, and even for some time after. The repeal of the Combination Laws[*] was I think one of the most useful things in its effect on the minds of the working classes, and on the soundness of their judgment, that the Legislature ever did.

R. A. SLANEY: *You are aware generally that the proceedings regarding the title and conveyance of real property are very complex and expensive?* Every one is aware of that.

Do you not think that that has the effect, as regards the middle and

[*5 George IV, c.95.]

working classes, of excluding that species of investment in a great measure from their means? I think almost entirely, and perhaps that is one reason why there is so little of that taste among the poor for investments in land, which is so universal in other countries.

Would it not be a great advantage if it were practicable to give facilities for a simpler and less expensive mode of conveyance, and the purchase of small portions of either real property, or divisions of charges upon real property, in the way of mortgage? No doubt it would be of great importance to do both. In regard to the last, that has been found to be of great importance practically. In Germany, one of the safest and most usual investments for small sums is in a kind of land debentures. My information is derived from reading a report by an officer who was sent by the French Government into Germany to study the laws and practice of the different States there, with a view of introducing improvements into the French law of *crédit foncier*, which has long been a great object in France, but has not yet been accomplished. This report was published, and contained a full account of the whole system of the laws of mortgage in the different States of Germany, from which it appeared that by a combination of the different landed proprietors, making their joint security available for each individual, a very convenient mode had been provided of raising money on mortgages, but which were always temporary; there was always a provision for redemption at the end of a certain time. Those mortgages were divided into shares, and the documents which conveyed the right to those shares, which attested the fact of the holder's being a mortgagee to a certain amount, were very generally in use as an investment by all classes, and were found very convenient, and increased very much the facilities of mortgaging land for its value.

J. A. SMITH: *And also increased the value of land?* Undoubtedly, they must have had that effect.

You are also perhaps aware that an experiment with these land debentures is about to be made in Ireland; you would be highly favourable to that probably? Very much so.

Those debentures, sufficiently subdivided in amount, might give to the lower classes a degree of interest in the land susceptible of no question on the ground of subdivision? There could be no possible objections of an economical nature to that kind of subdivision.

It would not meet all the results that you think follow to the landowner by the possession of land? It would be a safe investment for small savings, and no doubt would interest the possessor in the security of landed tenure.

But it would not have the same effect upon his character and self-esteem as the actual possession of the land? I think it would operate in quite a different way; I do not think it would have any other moral effect than the possession of the same sum in a savings bank might have.

R. A. SLANEY: *Do not you think that affording facilities to the middle and humbler classes, without interfering with the rights of property, for obtaining moderate portions of land, would also be of great advantage?* Yes, in many ways.

As under the existing laws referable to landed property the title is so complex, and the difficulties connected with it are so great as that the middle and humble classes are almost entirely precluded from such investments, is it not the more necessary to give them facilities for investments in other ways? The difficulty is always greatest in investing small sums, and therefore the facilities are most necessary in the case of small amounts.

THE REGULATION OF THE LONDON WATER SUPPLY

1851

EDITOR'S NOTE

Public Agency v. Trading Companies: The Economical and Administrative Principles of Water-Supply for the Metropolis. Correspondence between John Stuart Mill, Esq., Author of "Principles of Political Economy," and the Metropolitan Sanitary Association on the Proper Agency for Regulating the Water-Supply for the Metropolis, as a Question of Economical and Administrative Principle. London: Metropolitan Sanitary Association, [1851,] 19–23. Not republished. Headed "Letter by John Stuart Mill, Esq.," dated 15 February, 1851, and addressed "To the Honorary Secretaries of the Metropolitan Sanitary Association" (M. W. Lusignan and Adolphus Barnett). Identified in JSM's bibliography as "A letter to the Metropolitan Sanitary Association, in answer to an application for my opinion on the Water supply of the Metropolis—dated 15 February 1851 and printed by the Association in a pamphlet entitled 'Memorials on Sanitary Reform' " (MacMinn, 76). No corrections or variants in Somerville College copy. The pamphlet consists of a "Memorial" addressed to Lord John Russell, the Prime Minister, and Sir George Grey, the Home Secretary, by the Honorary Secretaries of the Association; a letter covering the Memorial; the letter asking for JSM's opinion; his letter, with a postscript by the Secretaries; and two Appendixes.

In a letter to Edwin Chadwick, dated only "Thursday", JSM says in part: "I shall not give the Assn a *long* answer. If they want me as an authority against the nonsense of the Economist &c. they will get what they want." (Letter in University College, London.)

The Regulation of the
London Water Supply

GENTLEMEN,—The subject on which the Committee of the Metropolitan Sanitary Association has done me the honour of asking my opinion is a question of general policy rather than of political economy.

The water supply of London may be provided in three modes:—By trading companies, as at present; by a functionary, or a board of functionaries, appointed by Government; or by some local or municipal authority. Each of these modes of supply has its advocates.

The defenders, on principle, of the existing system, rely mainly on general arguments against the interference of public authority in operations which can be adequately performed by the free agency of individuals. They contend, that the supply of water is no more a fit subject for Government interference, than the supply of food, and should be left, as that is, to the ordinary operations of industry.

The maxim, that the supply of the physical wants of the community should be left to private agency is, like other general maxims, liable to mislead, if applied without consideration of the reasons on which it is grounded. The policy of depending on individuals for the supply of the markets, assumes the existence of competition. If the supply be in the hands of an individual secured against competition, he will best promote his interest and his ease by making the article dear and bad; and there will be no escape from these influences but by laying on him a legal obligation, that is, by making him a public functionary.

Now, in the case of water-supply, there is virtually no competition. Even the possibility of it is limited to a very small number of individuals or companies, whose interest prompts them, except during occasional short periods, not to compete but to combine. In such a case, the system of private supply loses all that, in other cases, forms its recommendation. The article being one of indispensable necessity, the arrangement between the companies and the consumer is as much compulsory as if the rate were imposed by Government; and the only security for the efficient performance by the companies of what they undertake, is public opinion, a check which would operate much more effectually on a public board.

To establish the alleged parity between the supply of water and that of food, it would be necessary to suppose, that food could only be brought to London at so great an expense, and by arrangements on so large a scale, as to limit the supply to seven or eight associations. Were these the necessary conditions of the supply of food, the public would certainly require that either the article should be supplied, or the terms of its supply fixed and controlled, by a public authority. The question is not between free trade and a Government monopoly. The case is one of those in which a practical monopoly is unavoidable; and the possession of the monopoly by individuals constitutes not freedom but slavery; it delivers over the public to the mercy of those individuals.

The cases to which the water-supply of towns bears most analogy, are such as the making of roads and bridges, the paving, lighting, and cleansing of streets. The nearest analogy of all is the drainage of towns, with which the supply of water has a natural connexion. Of all these operations it may reasonably be affirmed to be the duty of Government, not necessarily to perform them itself, but to ensure their being adequately performed. I do not say that it ought not to be lawful to build a house without proper drainage and a proper water-supply; but assuredly every one who owns or builds houses in a town should have the means of effectual drainage and water-supply put in his power, at the smallest practicable expense.

The principle, therefore, of Government regulations, I conceive to be indisputable. But it remains to be considered whether the Government may best discharge this function by itself undertaking the operations for the supply of water, or by controlling the operations of others.

It is quite possible, especially when private companies have long since established themselves, and have taken possession of the supply, that the most eligible mode of proceeding might be to leave the operations in the hands of the companies; prescribing such conditions as to quantity and quality of water, convenience of supply, and rate of charge, as to ensure the best provision at the cheapest rate which local facilities and the state of science and engineering may admit of.

If the saving to be obtained by a consolidation of establishments and of works be a sufficient reason against keeping up a plurality of companies, it might be expedient to entrust the whole to a single company, giving the preference to that which would undertake to conform to the prescribed conditions at the lowest rates of charge.

It does not, however, appear to me that this last plan would have any real advantage over that (for instance) of a board elected by the ratepayers. Individuals acting for their own pecuniary interests are likely to be in general more careful and economical than a public board; but the Directors of a Joint Stock Company are not acting for their own pecuniary interests, but for those of their constituents. The management of a company is representative management, as much as that of an elective public board, and experience shows that it is quite as liable to be corrupt or negligent.

Whether the operations are actually conducted or merely controlled in behalf of the public, an officer or officers would be required for the purpose. It is, then, to be next considered, whether these should be state or municipal officers; whether they should be appointed by, and responsible to, the general government, or the local government of the town.

In the case of London, unfortunately, this question is not at present a practical one. There is no local government of London. There is a very badly constituted and badly administered local government of one section of London. Beyond this there are only parochial authorities.

The municipal administration of a town, whether great or small, ought to be undivided. Most of the matters of business which belong to local administration concern the whole town, not the separate parts of it, and must be all taken in at one view, to enable any part to be well managed. Such are the drainage, the water-supply, the police, the management of the markets, and of the port. Besides, the administration of an entire town, being a larger object, attracts more attention, excites more discussion, and is carried on under greater responsibility to public opinion; while, for the same reason, it will naturally be sought by a far superior class of persons. Were there a General Council, or Board of Administration for all London, invested with power over every branch of its local affairs, a place in that Council or Board would, like a place in the Municipal Commission of Paris, be sought and diligently filled by persons of high character and standing, as men not only of business capacity, but of general instruction and cultivation. The contrast between such persons and those who usually compose parish vestries, or the Common Council and Court of Aldermen, is too obvious to require comment.

Were such a body in existence, I should have no hesitation in expressing an opinion, that to it and not to Parliament or the general government should be given the charge of the operations for the water-supply of the capital. The jealousy which prevails in this country of any extension of the coercive and compulsory powers of the general government I conceive to be, though not always wisely directed, and often acting the most strongly in the wrong places, yet, on the whole, a most salutary sentiment, and one to which this country owes the chief points of superiority which its government possesses over those of the Continent. Nor does it appear to me that a government agency is by any means peculiarly suited for conducting business of this character. A Government board is an excellent organ for giving the first start to an improved system. The time when an improvement is introduced is always a time when much attention is directed to the subject; and the interest felt in it by the public and by the Government insures, in the first choice of officers, a certain degree of attention to superior qualifications, and on the part of the officers themselves a considerable amount of zeal and activity. In ordinary times such boards are apt to become indifferent and inactive; and little being required of them, those who appoint them soon think that anybody is good enough for the office, and it becomes a mere job for personal connexions or Parliamentary adherents. No doubt, the same tendency exists, and perhaps to as great an extent, in appointments by municipal authorities; but the mischief of local jobbing does not extend much beyond the matter immediately concerned; while jobbing by a minister or a political party helps to give undue influence in the legislature. Besides, a body popularly elected for local business only is likely to be held by the opinion of its constituents (if sufficiently numerous and intelligent) to a stricter responsibility for the due performance of its one business, than will usually be felt by the general government, for what can after all be only one of its minor occupations.

While, however, it appears to me preferable on the whole that the Government should not habitually conduct the operations for local purposes, there is no similar reason against its appointing persons to watch and advise those who do. I consider no municipal government to be complete without an accredited representative on the part of the general government. I conceive it to be one of the duties of the general government to hold the local government to the performance of its duties. There are two modes in which the general government might exercise this superintendance. It might have an officer attached to each municipal corporation or county board, who, like the préfect in France, but without his compulsory powers, might give advice and suggestions to the local body in all things pertaining to its functions; and if it failed of the due performance of them, might report to Parliament, that the necessary means might be taken to compel performance. Or, instead of a functionary attached to each local corporation, and taking cognizance of all subjects, there might be a board for each distinct subject, corresponding on that subject with all the corporations. There might be a Drainage Board, a Waterworks Board, and so forth; or, rather, for the sake of undivided responsibility, a General Commissioner of Waterworks or of Drainage, whose business should be to make himself master of his particular subject; to communicate his best ideas and information on that subject to the various local elective bodies; to give his opinion on all their plans; to suggest plans to them when they proposed none of their own; and to report annually to Parliament the state of that particular branch of local administration throughout the country.

This functionary should, I think, have no power of over-ruling the decisions of the local bodies, but he might recommend to Parliament to do so, if he saw need.

This would, I conceive, be in itself the best mode of providing for questions of local administration, similar to that of water-supply; and when a local body, such as I have described, shall exist in London, I am of opinion that the water arrangements should, under some such securities as I have suggested, be delivered up to its charge. For the present it seems to me that the authority to which the work may most fittingly be entrusted is a Commissioner, appointed by the Government, and responsible to Parliament like the Commissioners of Poor Laws.[*] Whether this officer should reform the water system of London by the formation of new arrangements, or by employing, under a rigid system of controul, the existing water companies is a question, not of principle, but of practical expediency, which can only be decided on by those who are accurately acquainted with the matters of fact on which it depends.

[*See 4 & 5 William IV, c.76.]

NEWMAN'S POLITICAL ECONOMY

1851

EDITOR'S NOTE

Westminster Review, LVI (Oct., 1851), 83–101. Unsigned; not republished. Originally headed: "Art. IV.—*Lectures on Political Economy*. By Francis William Newman, formerly Fellow of Balliol College, Oxford.—London: [Chapman,] 1851." Running head: "Newman's Political Economy." Identified in JSM's bibliography as "A review of Newman's Lectures on Political Economy in the Westminster Review for October 1851" (MacMinn, 76). W. E. Hickson, the editor of the *Westminster*, suggested the subject to JSM in June, 1851, and he agreed to write on it on 20 July; after its publication, he wrote to Hickson (15 Oct., 1851), saying in part: "The article on Newman is spoilt by printer's punctuation & typographical errors." (Letters in the Huntington Library.)

The substantive corrections and variants indicated in ink by JSM in the Somerville College copy (an offprint paged 1–19, but otherwise unaltered) are given in the text below. JSM also added nine commas and deleted one; these alterations are accepted silently. His correction of the typographical error at 457.20 is noted in the Textual Introduction, as is the error at 451.24, which he did not correct.

Newman's Political Economy

A NEW TREATISE on Political Economy, whether professedly scientific, or, like the one before us, discursive and popular, is now opened and read with very different expectations from what would have been felt even a few years ago. At that time, however polemical might be the performance, and however great the author's notion of the importance of what he had to say, the reader might feel certain beforehand that all the leading principles of the existing structure of European and even of English society would be assumed, not discussed: or if occasionally a writer, to satisfy his ideas of scientific completeness or didactic symmetry, gave a place in his book to a few remarks in justification, for example, of the institution of private property, there was a slightness in the texture of his argument—an air of carelessness and ^aroutine^a in the ^bselection^b and treatment of his topics, showing plainly that the contest was but a sham fight, with no serious adversary. Now, however, in this, as in many other respects, there is a change perceptible, at least in the higher regions of political and moral discussion. The days of taking for granted are passing away: doctrines and principles, which were lately deemed an infallible standard for the decision of disputed questions, are now required to produce their own credentials. The minds of thinkers and readers have become unsettled, and there is a growing conviction that they have to be disturbed still more before they can be again settled on any firm basis. The value of a treatise on social subjects now principally depends on the worth of its treatment of precisely those topics which, but recently, were not even made subjects of discussion.

It is under this aspect, then, that we shall first consider Mr. Newman's book; these being also the topics on which he first enters, and forming the principal subject of several of the thirteen lectures into which the work is divided.

The business and relations of life, within the province of political economy, are mainly constituted on the basis of private property and competition. Another practical principle, commonly called association or

^{a-a}[*altered from* venture *in Somerville College copy*]
^{b-b}[*altered from* solution *in Somerville College copy*]

co-operation, also rules within certain limits, which, as society advances, are progressively widening. Many eminent reformers, being forcibly impressed with the mass of physical and moral evils which are not only consistent with, but directly grow out of the facts of competition and individual property, have adopted the opinion, that these facts, so full of deplorable consequences, should cease—that individual ownership, at least in the instruments of production, should no more be suffered, but that all who are capable of work, should form themselves into co-operative associations, work for the common account, and share the produce with each other and with those unable to work, not by competition, but on a prearranged principle of justice. Opinions are not unanimous as to what this principle should be; according to some, equality; others say that each should receive according to his or her wants and requirements; others, again, hold that quantity and quality of services should be considered, and that those who do most for society should receive most from it. There is also a great variety in the means proposed for holding the members of the association to the fulfilment of its conditions. All the supporters of association, as opposed to competition, however they may differ respecting the rules of association, call themselves, or are called, Socialists.

In this controversy, Mr. Newman takes part with things as they are; he dislikes socialism, and is in favour of private property and competition. He does not defend all the applications which are made of the idea of property, nor deny that there are evils and injustice in the present economical order of society, and that a great part of these may be remedied; but his position is, on the whole, that of an apologist for the existing social system.

His defence of private property and competition, against socialist attacks, is not at all calculated to convince an opponent, or to remove doubts or difficulties in the mind of a sincere inquirer. Some just and valid reasons he of course brings forward. The benefits that flow from private property and competition are, like the evils, too obvious to be missed; and there is so much exaggeration, and often radical misconception, in a great part of what is said on the other side, that no advocate of private property against its opponents can help being often in the right; but when Mr. Newman steps, even for an instant, out of the veriest commonplaces of his subject, what he finds to say always admits of a very obvious reply.

For example, an argument on which he lays great stress, is, that the idea of property is not created by law, but exists anterior to law, which only recognizes, sanctions, and in certain cases, limits it [pp. 29ff.]. From the beginning, he argues, people have a sense that what they have called into existence by their skill and labour is their own, and that they are wronged when they are deprived of it. The fact is historically and psychologically true. A socialist, however, might say that it is of small consequence what are a savage's ideas of justice; that if a savage thinks he has a property in the weapon or the ornament which he has fashioned, he is, as Mr. Newman admits, persuaded that he has a property as unquestionable and as unlimited in human ᶜbeings;ᶜ in the captives whom he has taken in war. Socialists, however, can afford to admit the right of the savage to the produce of his own industry, and they do so with perfect ᵈconsistency. Theyᵈ are the last who can be accused of undervaluing the right of those who work, as against those who take without ᵉworking. Theirᵉ quarrel with existing arrangements is precisely because *that* right is not, as they contend, respected ᶠsufficiently. Butᶠ they do not deny that until mankind have adopted a just rule for sharing the produce of their combined labour, each should be protected in the fruits of his own; that it is unjust to take from any one when he has, without also giving to him when he has not; that so long as the individual cannot look to society to compensate him for his bad chances, it is just to leave him the benefit of the good. This is not, in the smallest degree, inconsistent with desiring to do away with dependence ᵍonᵍ chance, and make reward depend on exertion alone; and this socialists assert to be possible.

Mr. Newman thinks it a sufficient argument against socialism that property is of natural right. It would be necessary to settle, in the first instance, what this expression ʰmeans. Weʰ apprehend that what is called natural right, would be more properly described as a first appearance of right; it is a perception of fitness, grounded on some of the more obvious circumstances of the case, and requires, quite as much as any other first impression, to be corrected or controlled by the considerate judgment. So partial and imperfect are these supposed natural impressions of justice, that almost every disputed moral or social question affords them on both sides. Mr. Newman appeals to a natural feeling of the right of a person to what he has made; socialists appeal to a natural feeling of the right of every one who is born, to be born to as advantageous a lot as every other human being. The question is a very complex one, into which the not offending these supposed instincts about rights, may be allowed to enter as one consideration, but not a principal one, of the many involved. The ultimate standard is the tendency of things to promote or impede human happiness, and to this even Mr. Newman is obliged to resort, though like others of his school, he tries to show that he only does it when his other standards fail him. Thus he says, that expediency must decide whether persons shall have power by will to tie up their property to particular uses, because "by nature, whatever property a man possesses, is his to keep or to give away;

ᶜ⁻ᶜ[*altered from* beings and *in Somerville College copy*]
ᵈ⁻ᵈ[*altered from* consistency; they *in Somerville College copy*]
ᵉ⁻ᵉ[*altered from* working; their *in Somerville College copy*]
ᶠ⁻ᶠ[*altered from* sufficiently, but *in Somerville College copy*]
ᵍ⁻ᵍ[*altered from* or *in Somerville College copy*]
ʰ⁻ʰ[*altered from* means; we *in Somerville College copy*]

and therefore, by his last will, he may give it to whomsoever he pleases, but he has no natural power or right to give it away under limitations." [P. 32.] This restriction of his assumed "natural right" is very arbitrary. If, by nature, he can give the thing to whomsoever he pleases, absolutely and unconditionally, why can he not, in the exercise of the same right, give it on condition of a promise? and that admitted, everything else follows, even to an entail in perpetuity. If the question is to be argued as one of natural right, Mr. Newman would find it difficult to reply to the many moralists and jurists who have said that there is no natural right whatever to bestow property by *i*will. One*i* can only give (it may be said), what one has; after death the thing has passed out of the possession of the person who was the owner, and he can exercise no power over it. Bad as this argument is, and deserving no better name than that of a lawyer's quibble, it is yet preferable to Mr. Newman's.

i It appears to us that nothing valid can be said against socialism in principle; and that the attempts to assail it, or to defend private property, on the ground of justice, must inevitably fail. The distinction between rich and poor, so slightly connected as it is with merit and demerit, or even with exertion and want of exertion in the individual, is obviously unjust; such a feature could not be put into the rudest imaginings of a perfectly just state of society; the present capricious distribution of the means of life and enjoyment, could only be defended as an admitted imperfection, submitted to as an effect of causes in other respects beneficial. Again, the moral objection to competition, as arming one human being against another, making the good of each depend upon evil to others, making all who have anything to gain or lose, live as in the midst of enemies, by no means deserves the disdain with which it is treated by some of the adversaries of socialism, and among the rest, by Mr. Newman. Socialism, as long as it attacks the existing individualism, is easily triumphant; its weakness hitherto is in what it proposes to *k*substitute. The*k* reasonable objections to socialism are altogether practical, consisting in difficulties to be surmounted, and in the insufficiency of any scheme yet promulgated to provide against them; their removal must be a work of thought and discussion, aided by progressive experiments, and by the general moral improvement of mankind, through good government and education.

The following paragraph contains Mr. Newman's summary of his criticisms on socialism:—

Their errors I would classify as moral, political, and economical. *Moral:*— 1st, In speaking as though my duties were equal towards all mankind; which is

i–i[*altered from* will; one *in Somerville College copy*]
i[*new paragraph indicated in Somerville College copy*]
k–k[*altered from* substitute; the *in Somerville College copy*]

untrue. To have any but a very secondary care for those who are unconnected with me in the relations of life, would be a hurtful Quixotism. 2nd, In wonderfully undervaluing the difficulty of subduing a ruinous selfishness in a community that lived on common property. *Political*:—In imagining that such a community, if men were allowed to choose their own occupations, would not presently break in pieces from the rival preferences; or that if it were subjected to the despotism of a single mind, it would fail to degenerate into apathetic stupidity. But my peculiar business is with the *Economic* error, which consists in blindness to the fact, that there can be no such thing as price, except through the influence of competition; and that if they mean to allow exchanges between community and community, they ought to abandon this declamation against competition. (Pp. 10–11.)

Of these objections, the second alone touches a really vulnerable point. The other three appear to us inconsistent with any just conception of the subject, or any knowledge of the opinions of socialists; and the first "moral objection," in point of moral judgment and feeling, thoroughly vulgar minded. To regard impartially the interests of all—to be concerned in any but a very trifling degree for those who are not in some special relation with self, is termed Quixotism! a word invented to hold up to contempt any nobleness and generosity beyond the conception of the common herd. With respect to "duties;" if at present our duties are not "equal towards all mankind," this is only true as a consequence of the institutions which it is adduced to justify. The duty meant is, of course, that of beneficence; for the duty of justice *is* "equal towards all mankind." If, then, we are more bound to good offices towards certain persons than towards others, it can only be because those persons are by position more dependent upon our good offices. The argument therefore is in a circle. It is this—the system of private property and insulated families, causes a certain group of persons to have only each other to look to for help and sacrifice; therefore they are more bound towards each other than towards other people; therefore it would be wrong to take away the exclusive dependence, because, to do so, would abolish the exclusive obligation!

As well might it be said, If I am a soldier, I am bound to fight against those with whom my government is at war, therefore there ought to be soldiers and war. If there is an established clergy, they are bound to teach the doctrines of their church, therefore there ought to be an established church. If the decisions of the judges ought to be according to the laws as they are, therefore the laws ought to be as they are. The answer is, that bad as well as good institutions create moral obligations; but to erect these into a moral argument against changing the institutions, is as bad morality as it is bad reasoning.

The "political" objection is, that the socialist community would break in pieces if the members were allowed to choose their own occupations, and stagnate if a single mind chose for them. It shows a great lack, either of invention or of candour, to see only this alternative, and admit no choice in human affairs between no government at all, and the despotism of one. A teacher of political economy, writing against socialism, should have known something of what has been proposed by socialists, for getting over the difficulty. According to Owen, the able-bodied would share by turns all kind of necessary labour; the community deciding in general assembly, or by its elected officers, what labours *are* necessary. According to Fourier, each would select his or her own occupations; but if some employments were chosen by too many persons, and others by too few, the remuneration of the former would be lowered, and of the latter raised, so as to restore the balance. Socialists may be over-confident, but they are no such fools as Mr. Newman takes them for; they have foreseen many more objections than he tells them of; and if there are others which they have not foreseen, or have not effectually provided against, his criticisms do not reach the depth even of *ltheir*l failures.

There remains the "economic" error: "blindness to the fact, that there can be no such thing as price, except through the influence of competition;" nor, therefore, without competition, can there be any exchanges between community and community. Socialists would reply, that they propose that exchanges between community and community should be at cost price. If it were asked how the cost price is to be ascertained, they would answer, that in the operations of communities, every element of cost would be a matter of public record; *m* that every dealer, on the private system, is required and able to ascertain what price will remunerate him for his goods, and the agents of the communities would only be required to do the same thing. This would be, no doubt, one of the practical difficulties, and we think it somewhat undervalued by them; but the difficulty cannot be insurmountable.

The following is one of Mr. Newman's arguments for competition:—

The truth is really plain, but needs to be enforced, that competition, though, like all the laws of nature, often severe, is yet a beneficial, as well as a necessary process. If I desire to get my garden dug, and am about to pay a man 4s. for his day's work, merely because I have been accustomed to pay that sum; but before I have agreed with him, another man offers to do the same work for 3s. 6d., the presumption is, that the latter is in greater need, and, unless I am in some previous moral relation to the former, which ought to be respected, I shall do a more humane act by employing the one at 3s. 6d. than the other at 4s. (P. 12.)

Humanity may be a reason for employing the man who will take 3s. 6d., but not for paying him only 3s. 6d. Humanity dictates giving the preference

l–l[*altered from* these *in Somerville College copy*]
m[*so* cancelled *in Somerville College copy*]

to the most necessitous, but does it dictate taking advantage of his necessities? Would not any person, in a right moral state, pay to the necessitous as much as he would have paid to the man who needed it less? If 4s. are the fit and proper wages for a day's digging, it is an evil that competition should reduce wages below that amount. Mr. Newman may say that there is no mode of deciding what are the fit and proper wages; but he cannot pretend that competition decides it. The question, then, is resolved into the possibility of determining by law, what wages society can afford to give to those who do its work. Now, what there is to be said as to the difficulty of deciding this, or of enforcing the decision, does not apply to socialists; in their communities no such difficulties would exist; there would be no doubt either what could be given, or that it would be given. Socialists do not say that competition can be dispensed with in society as it is. But they say it is a great defect in the constitution of society, that it can only work by such an instrument.

As we are not on the present occasion discussing socialism, but Mr. Newman's book, these examples of his treatment of that subject may suffice.

As a treatise on political economy, in the narrower sense—an exposition of the working of existing economical laws, of the causes by which the amount and distribution of the produce of labour are determined under the conditions of the present social organization, Mr. Newman's book does not afford much to be said, either in commendation or in dispraise. He has followed, in general, the best previous authors; not implicitly, but his deviations from them in ⁿourⁿ opinion are seldom improvements. Not a few of his criticisms on them are evidently grounded on imperfect acquaintance with their works. For example, speaking of what is called the Ricardo theory of rent, which he in the main agrees with, though a number of his pages are employed in combating it in detail, he says, "it assumes that wheat is the only agricultural product, and that the value of land is to be measured by capacity of producing it." (P. 153.) This is a complete misapprehension. Ricardo's numerical illustrations are expressed in quarters of wheat; but any one, who will take the trouble, can adapt the theory to all other products of land; his successors have partially done so. Mr. Newman's other objections to the doctrine, as a practical representation of the facts, have reference chiefly to the allowance which must be made in this as in all other theories of political economy, for disturbing causes, and especially for fixed habits, and the difficulty of removing capital to another employment, which difficulty he deems peculiarly great in the case of agriculture. We believe it would be more correct to say, that as far as regards rent the influence of this disturbing cause is particularly small. A farmer either has a lease, and in that case he makes his contract so as to be repaid

ⁿ⁻ⁿ[altered from an in Somerville College copy]

during the currency of his lease for the sacrifice of that portion of his capital which he cannot remove; or he has no lease, and in that case, if he has ordinary prudence, he does not sink his capital, but keeps it in a form to be capable of removal at six months' notice. The only remark of Mr. Newman, tending to a correction of the Ricardo theory, to which we can allow any value (and that remark has been made by others before him) is, that there are many small capitalist farmers, whose position, in respect of rent, is analogous to the peasant farmers of Ireland, inasmuch as they cultivate for subsistence, not for trading profit; and as long as they can live by their farms, never think of changing their occupation, however their profits may be reduced. If such persons, therefore, are numerous, habit may keep up their rent, or competition may raise it, beyond what would be the value of their farm on any mercantile principle.

A doctrine respecting price continually recurs in the book, apparently without any knowledge of its being disputable, which a more careful reading of former writers would have corrected. It is used (p. 25) as an argument against protectionists, but is not the less, in our opinion, erroneous; it is, that price (the price of food, for instance), can only be raised by diminishing the supply. We apprehend it is quite possible that the supply may be as great at a high as at a low price. We grant, that if there were no *power* of diminishing the supply, the price would not rise; but it is not necessary that the power should be exercised; and even if it be exercised, the diminution of supply will not necessarily be more than temporary. As much will be produced at the increased price as can find a market at that price: there will be no permanent diminution of quantity, unless the heightened price has placed the article beyond the means or the inclination of some of the consumers. In the case of an article of necessity like food, it might easily happen that as much might be demanded and as much consequently produced after the rise of price as before. The inconvenience to the consumers would then consist in the privation of something else, a greater part than before of their means of expenditure being required for food.

The operation of tithes is discussed (pp. 165–175) without any apparent knowledge of the view taken of it by the best writers since Ricardo— namely, that a tax of a fixed proportion of the gross produce raises the price of the produce in that proportion. The author displays, with the minuteness of numerical examples, what he supposes to be the effect of a tithe in discouraging improvement; tacitly supposing, that when the farmer is taxed one-tenth of his produce, he obtains no higher price than before for the remaining nine-tenths. If the price rises in proportion to the tithe, all his conclusions are vitiated. A tithe undoubtedly prevents many improvements, which would be made if there were the same price without any tithe to pay; but all those which would be profitable if there were no tithe, and the price of produce were a tenth lower, will be profitable in spite of the tithe.

On the population doctrine of Malthus, Mr. Newman's opinion is, that "when stated as an abstract theory," it is "undeniably true; but that every practical application, which either Malthus or his followers have given it, is deplorably and perniciously false." [P. 107.]

One of the "practical applications" which he seems to have in view, is the objection at first made by Mr. Malthus against poor laws: thus far, however, he is fighting shadows, since no Malthusian now condemns poor laws when so administered as not to take away the inducement to self-support. It is difficult to see, from any of Mr. Newman's explanations, in what consists the "Malthusianism" which he objects to. He says "it is impossible for any poor man to hope that his individual prudence in the delay or renunciation of marriage, will ever be remunerated by a higher rate of wages. He knows that others will swamp his market with *their* children if *he* live childless. If the good alone are Malthusians, the bad families will outbreed them." (Pp. 109–10). *o* This is perfectly true: what is wanted is, not that the good should abstain in order that the selfish may indulge, but such a state of opinion as may deter the selfish from this kind of intemperance by stamping it as disgraceful. He next says (p. 111) "it does not appear that Malthus, or any of his followers, have given us any test by which we may ascertain that we are actually suffering under redundancy of population." They have given the only possible test: they say that population is excessive when, in a country in which labour is tolerably productive, wages are too low. "The only intelligible test," according to the author, of general over-population, "is that propounded by Mr. Lawson[*] —viz., a people is *then* beginning to press on the limits of its subsistence, when a larger and larger portion of its entire power is needed to raise the food of the community." [P. 111.] *p* Independently of all other objections to this criterion, it does not show whether the pressure on the means of subsistence is too great, but only whether it is increasing. No Malthusian, we believe, thinks that the pressure of population is greater, relatively to the means of subsistence, than it was thirty years ago. No one can think so who believes that there has been any moral or mental improvement in the people. The complaint is, not that there is no improvement, but that there is not improvement enough—that wages which, with greater restraint on population, might be as high as in America, are kept down by too rapid multiplication. Malthusians would deplore that the advancement constantly

[*Lawson, James A. *Five Lectures on Political Economy*. London: Parker, 1844, pp. 52ff.]

o[*paragraph division removed in Somerville College copy*]
p[*paragraph division removed in Somerville College copy*]

450   ESSAYS ON ECONOMICS AND SOCIETY

taking place in the arts of life, and the good which may be expected from improved social institutions, and a better distribution of the fruits of labour, should be nullified for practical purposes, by serving, as such things have always hitherto done, to increase the numbers of the labouring class much more than to improve their condition.

The part of these lectures to which we can give most praise, is that which treats of the limitations to the right of property, and especially of property in land. We agree fully with Mr. Newman in the doctrine that there can be, morally speaking, only a qualified property in things not produced by labour, such as the raw material of the earth. We might go further, and say, that there is only a qualified property in anything not made by the individual's own labour; but we confine ourselves at present to property in land. We think this subject so important, and so usefully (though not altogether unexceptionably) treated by the author, that we shall make a rather long extract from his observations:—

If a solitary family land on the shores of an empty continent, like Australia, and occupy a plot of desert land, prior occupation would confer on them a right superior to that of any other claimant. After they had cultivated it ten years, if a stranger tried to drive them off, all bystanders would call it an invasion of right. Let him take a portion of the unoccupied land if he please, but not eject them from that which they have made their own by usage and by improvement. . . . . .

If the stranger, on considering the labour which it will cost him to clear copses, to make fences, to dig drains or wells, to build outhouses, to make roads, or execute other works, to say nothing of the dwelling-house, chooses to offer a price to the pioneers of civilization for their improvements, on condition of their yielding up the farm to him, it needs no proof that they are able to make over to him the whole of their right, and that the price which they receive will have been honestly earned. But thereby they abandon all further claim to it.

Should he not be rich enough to pay down what they regard as a fair compensation for their labour, the contract may take the form of a yearly payment on his part, which may perhaps be called a rent. But supposing it to be intended as a remuneration for the trouble which they have taken with the estate, the payment will, in fact, be a return of profit to the capital sunk, exactly as in a common house rent. . . . . . .

Let me alter my supposition. After the colonist has held his land for some years, he removes and occupies a different spot. A new colonist comes in, and seats himself on the vacated ground. Can we imagine the first occupant hereupon to send him word, not to intrude on his private property, but to go elsewhither? I think not. The new comer would reply, that empty ground is open to all; that the first was free to use, to occupy, to keep; but what he has left he cannot keep. At the utmost he might hope to receive some thankoffering from the new comer, as soon as it proved convenient, as an acknowledgment of the advantage derived from his predecessor's labours. But any claim on his part to be regarded as the owner of the soil would be treated with contempt. 'What!' the stranger would reply, 'did you create the earth? or why is it yours? You used it while convenient, you abandoned it when convenient; and it is now mine as much as it then was yours.' . . . . . .

But what if a settler were to forbid a stranger to occupy land within a mile of that which the former was cultivating, saying that he wished to keep this for galloping and hunting ground, or that he expected it would be useful to his children twenty years hence? This surely would be greedy usurpation, not to be defended by the plea that he had set up marks, or run a light trench, to denote the extent of his intended park, or of his children's future estate. Where land is so abundant and so equally convenient, that each may exercise his caprice without inconvenience to others, even caprices might be respected; but none would be justified in thus excluding their neighbours from valuable sites. If any one who pleases is allowed to carve out a park in the wilderness, yet he cannot be allowed to take the river-side for it, so as to shut others out from its conveniences. Over land that has never been subdued and improved by labour, no individual has any moral claim. Being wild, it is public.

Let me suppose that the English Crown, while it was the legal owner of vast tracts in interior America, gave away an estate ten miles square to some British subject, who succeeded in planting colonists on it, from whom he received some trifling rent. This rent they are willing to pay, in order to get security from molestation. Time goes on, and a political revolution overthrows all power of England in those districts. The increase of population and the industry of the farmers has gradually improved the farms; a new generation has succeeded; and now the representative of the first grantee, calling himself the owner of the soil by gift of the King of England, claims to raise the rents of the farmers, because of the increased value of the farms. Is this conceivable? In England, undoubtedly such things are done: but if not enacted by a most peculiar state of law, it certainly would never suggest itself as right. In America such a claim would be a signal to the farmers to pay no more rent. They would say, this man, who calls himself landowner, has done nothing for the soil. By favour of an old king, his predecessor was once invested with a nominal right over it; that right was worth something at the time, and it was paid for: it is worth nothing now, and we will pay no longer. (Pp. 134–9.)

The conclusion is, that property in land is essentially subordinate to public convenience; that the rights of the landed proprietor ought to be construed strictly; that the law should not merely, as in the case of moveable property, forbid him from using it to the injury of others, but should compel him to allow to others all such use as is not incompatible with the purposes for which he is permitted to exercise dominion over it; and, finally, that it may at any time, if the public interest requires, be taken by the legislature, on payment of compensation.

Imagine a continent like America to be gradually covered by tenant freeholders, each of whom is recognized, for the present, as absolute owner of the soil which he cultivates. You will yet see that an increase of human population might hereafter take place, so great that the law must refuse any longer to admit the right of the freeholders to be absolute. For to allow anything to become a complete private property it must either be needless to human life, as jewels; or practically unlimited in quantity, as water; or brought into existence by human labour, as the most important kinds of food; and it is rather as a result of experience and wisdom than by direct moral perception that we forbid all invasion of private property in food, even to alleviate public famine. Now, as water, which is ordinarily allowed to be private, becomes public property in time of siege, so soon as its quantity is painfully limited; and as the possessors of wells would then be indemnified for the expense of their well only and not for water, so if at any time land becomes needed *to live upon*, the right of private possessors to withhold it comes to an end, and the State has merely to secure that they be liberally indemnified for their actual expenses, and for any fixed capital which they are made to yield up. (Pp. 140–1.)

The concluding sentence is ambiguous, and if the writer means that landowners have no claim to indemnity for the market value of their land, but only for the capital which has been laid out on it, we cannot admit that he awards full justice to them. It is true the original claim to hold land as private property, was only valid in so far as it was grounded on past, or conceded with a view to future, expenditure of labour and capital. But when the law has given more than this—has allowed the original powers of the soil to be permanently appropriated, and to pass by purchase and sale to those who have paid full value for it in things produced by labour— this property is no more a fit subject of confiscation than any other. Society has no right to seize upon one particular kind of property, and on the ground of a moral defect in the first title, a thousand years ago, turn out the possessors with no compensation except for actual expenses. For the sake of great public reforms, sacrifices may have to be imposed on the possessors of property, but not on one class or description of property peculiarly, no more than on one individual; and the most proper time for demanding such sacrifices is on the occasion of succession by death, that being the mode which least interferes with the habits and expectations which have grown up under the sanction of law.*

*A pamphlet of some ability lately published under the title of "Rent no Robbery, an Examination of some Erroneous Doctrines respecting Property in Land, by George Makgill, Esq.," [Edinburgh: Blackwood, 1851,] maintains the contrary thesis to that of Mr. Newman, chiefly in reply to Mr. J. S. Mill, who, in his "Principles of Political Economy," [*Collected Works*, II, pp. 226ff.,] had affirmed the essentially limited and merely provisional character, in an ethical point of view, of property in land, as distinguished from property in things produced by labour. Mr. Makgill disputes the distinction mainly on two grounds. First, that every kind of property, and not land alone, may be taken by the state in case of public necessity [p. 12]. Granted; but until the state does take it, the owner of moveable property is its absolute master, and may wholly exclude other persons from its use and enjoyment; which it is contended he ought not to be permitted to do with land, as, for example, to stop up roads, or to eject the inhabitants *en masse*. Secondly, all rent, according to Mr. Makgill, is the result of capital laid out in improvements; so small a portion only as to be scarcely worth computation being due to original fertility or natural advantages of situation [pp. 18ff.]. This assertion he supports not by proof, but by conjectural statistics, though the most positive statistical evidence in support of such a proposition would prove nothing except its own fallacy; so contradictory is the statement to reason and common observation. There are lands, no doubt, for

The last two lectures relate to "Remedies for Pauperism," distinguished without much precision into "Public" and "Economical." Most of these "remedies" have no peculiar reference to pauperism, but apply generally to what the author considers as evils in the present state of society; with his conception of which, though we think at least as ill of the present state of society as he does, we can by no means agree.

Mr. Newman considers as the great evil in society, that it is, what he calls, morally "disorganized;" that it is "relapsing into a disorganization similar to that of primitive barbarism." [P. 292.] Many other writers have said the same thing; it has been said, especially by the various socialist schools of the continent, but they said it in a different and a far deeper sense than his. They meant by it the gradual wearing out of belief in the old creeds and doctrines, and the sort of interregnum which precedes the growth and general acceptance of other and higher convictions. This, however, is not what Mr. Newman means by moral disorganization. His complaint is, virtually, that the old doctrines and old institutions do not continue. He complains that human beings are not bound together into fixed groups by an irrevocable bond; that hardly any of the relations of life are permanent; that people do not always hire the same labourers, buy and sell with the same persons, work for the same employers, and so forth; which he not only thinks it desirable they should do, but would have them permitted and encouraged to bind themselves to do by a legal engagement.

He who buys once at a shop, or in a fair, enters into no permanent moral relation with the seller nor conceives any particular interest in his welfare; but if we, every day of our lives, see the same street-sweeper at the same crossing, the repeated sight gives him some kind of lodgment in our good will and good wishes. . . We all know that the sanctity of marriage depends upon its

---

instance some of the fen districts, of which the fertility is all artificial, and the rent may not be more than a moderate profit on the expenditure incurred in bringing the land into its present condition: but there are other lands as fertile naturally as these are artificially, and which were brought into cultivation at an expense comparatively trifling; and there are others of which the value is chiefly derived from situation, and the income from which is constantly increasing without any expenditure at all. No one will pretend that the high rents of the garden grounds in the neighbourhood of London are a remuneration for the landlord's outlay of capital, or that the Marquis of Westminster and Lord Portman have given full value for the wealth they derive from their London estates; wealth becoming still more gigantic as leases fall in, and houses built by capital not their own lapse to the accidental inheritors of a few hundred acres of land in the west and north-west of the metropolis. Even when the fertility of land is the effect of capital laid out, it is in a great, if not the greatest number of cases, the capital of the tenant, of which, when the lease expires, the landlord reaps the permanent benefit: to him as unearned and gratuitous as if it had been the gift of nature.

permanence, and the same is true of all other relations. But nearly all of these are apt to be dissolved by change of place, hence a flitting population loses internal coherence. The masses which meet externally in large towns have lost all organization. They work at certain trades, or for certain masters, and sell to certain shops, or in the open market or street; but they have no fixed moral unions with any part of the community, except the narrowest ties of family life. . . . Marriage, with the kinsmanship arising out of it, is fast becoming the only permanent relation in cultivated England, so grievously disorganized are we, so deplorably has the temporal power forgot its moral mission. (Pp. 291–2.)

Thus, while the thinking minds of Europe are tending more and more to the opinion that the enforced adherence to a choice once made, the irrevocability of an error once committed, is a vice and an immorality in the institution of marriage, Mr. Newman, on the contrary, makes the indissolubility of marriage the type of what he thinks desirable in social relations generally. He would have labourers encouraged (pp. 322–3) to bind themselves by what he terms "labour-leases," [p. 327] to the same employer for long periods; and he would re-establish the relation of patrons and clients (by a ceremoney at church!) between domestic servants and their masters.

In the Hebrew law, if a servant loved his master and his family, and desired to serve for ever, the master performed a symbolic act by which the servant became nailed to the house as a permanent part of it, and the same result would everywhere be a wholesome consummation. Our difficulty is that custom needs to grow up as a guide to law before enactments can be wise and profitable, while, in fact, custom has long been moving in the opposite direction, making the union of master and servant, as of buyer and seller, more and more transient. In ancient times religion did for a nation what law could not do, and so it might be with us if we would wink at some of our differences, and if the ministers of religion were not bound in iron fetters. Else, if I had a servant whom I esteemed, and who trusted me, why might I not come forward with him before the Church and exchange solemn pledges with him; I, declaring that I take him as my client, and promise to him a kindly protection and care for his welfare; and he, avowing that he takes me as his patron, and promises to me honour and respect? After such a mutual public recognition, a neglect of duty on either side would incur moral censure. Precedent would grow up, indicating and limiting the rights of the parties, and it would ultimately appear whether the sanction of legislation was also desirable. By the institution of clientship, every family rich enough to have servants would be brought into nearer contact with a number of poorer families. For when a client married, or on other grounds left the patron's house, the bond would not be broken; and that result would in part be brought about, which is so very desirable in large towns, a definite relation between certain richer and certain poorer men. (Pp. 304–6.)

Permanence in human relations is not a good, *per* [q]*se.* Permanence[q] when it is unforced, spontaneous, when the relation is permanent not because the persons concerned cannot, but because they will not change,

[q–q][*altered from se;* permanence *in Somerville College copy*]

is a proof or a presumption that the relation has been found good by experience, and when thus voluntary, it doubtless excites in the persons concerned a much greater degree of reciprocal interest in the well-being of each other, than arises from a relation known and intended on both sides to be transient. But because these are the natural effects of a permanent connexion when it is permanent because it is preferred, and when every month or year that it continues affords additional proof of voluntary preference; this is no ground for expecting that the same benefits will arise from making the connexion permanent whether preferred or not. The only "moral relation" which there is any certainty of establishing by such means, is one of moral obligation, which in itself, and independently of the purposes for which it exists, cannot be accounted a good. Ties are not desirable merely because they are ties; duties ought not to be created merely that they may be fulfilled; the only ties which are desirable in themselves are those of love and attachment, and we are very sceptical respecting the attachment to a position which is engendered by not being able to get out of it. If the attachment would not exist without compulsion, patience and resignation would be its more suitable epithets. There is such a thing as making a virtue of necessity, but that is no reason for creating as much necessity as possible, in order that there may be the more virtue.

Mr. Newman seems to be under an historical delusion on the subject of permanent union. He thinks that human beings began by being solitary and isolated; that the first step out of barbarism was marriage, and that every advance in civilization was marked by the greater number and closeness of permanent ties. Accordingly the tendency which he now perceives in a direction contrary to permanence, presents itself to his mind as a relapse into barbarism. We find no warrant for this doctrine in history. Whether there was ever a time when human beings lived in a state of entire isolation, we have no means of knowing: but the rudest men of whom we have any knowledge, either in past or in present times, were bound by ties of great strength and permanency, either to their family in the patriarchal ʳsenseʳ, or, like North American Indians, to their tribe: and in the earliest known nations which had industry and laws, men were bound even to their hereditary occupations. There is a period doubtless in the upward growth of society, during which there is a tendency to bring every individual into permanent relations with some other or others. The reason is that permanence is the earliest contrivance for the tempering of oppression. When there is no law capable of restraining the tyranny of a powerful man, his weaker neighbours consent to become his vassals, that he may have an inducement to protect them against all tyrants but himself, and that the degree of interest which he may feel in them as his dependents,

ʳ⁻ʳ[altered from tents in Somerville College copy]

may serve (instead of conscience or humanity) as a motive to confine his own tyranny within some bounds.*

This particular phasis of social progress attained its greatest development in the middle ages, which according to Mr. Newman's theory, should be the type of perfection in social life; since there was no one, the king excepted, who was not bound by an indissoluble relation to some superior, and no one save the lowest of serfs who was not tied by some reciprocal obligation to a host of inferiors. When this social organization had reached its height, all subsequent improvements assisted in the gradual decomposition of it. As society emerged from a state of mere compromise with lawlessness, and came to some extent under the authority of impartial laws, each step in advance has set free a less or greater part of the community from enforced ties. The workman no longer needing the protection of his guild, is no longer tied to it; the labourer has ceased to be the serf of any seigneur; the nation is no longer entailed by hereditary right on a particular line of rulers. These "permanent moral unions" have been dissolved, because in themselves they were an evil, when the exigencies which alone rendered them useful had ceased to exist. And since such exigencies are not likely to return, it may safely be predicted, that whatever permanence is to be looked for as the consequence of future improvement, will be the effect of reason and free choice, not of irrevocable engagements;—will be voluntary, and not in any shape compulsory.

Even putting compulsion out of the question, such fixity of relations as Mr. Newman aims at, is inconsistent with a rapidly progressive state of society and life. By his theory on this subject, he is an apostle of Conservatism. His ideal could only be realised in an age of standing still. The spirit of progress, the best and only hope of the world, is incompatible with shutting the door, first here, then there, against change for the better. Even physical progress, improvement in the material arts of life, is not consistent with his system. If customers were always to adhere to the same

*Even in the case of marriage, the permanence, so far as it existed for any good purpose, had no other origin. It is being wholly the dupe of words to speak of marriage, in the sense of a "permanent relation," as "that with which all civilization begins"—to be without which "is to be lower than the lowest savages now known," [p. 292] merely because savages have something which they call, or which somebody chooses to call, marriage. In early ages marriage is only permanent as against the woman—she, being the man's property, cannot leave him; but he can part with her as he can with any other property. It was the first stage out of slavery, to the woman, when it was made impossible for the man to shake her off; just as it was the first stage out of slavery, to agricultural slaves, when they were made *adscripti glebæ*. The earliest state of human relations is all liberty on one side, all obligation on the other: the next step is into reciprocity of obligation, but it does not therefore follow that the final step may not be into equality of freedom; and this is the final destiny of the institution of marriage.

dealer as long as they found him honest, it would doubtless be an encouragement to honesty, but a great discouragement to improvement. To whom could the producer or dealer who supplied better goods at lower prices, look for his remuneration? Fixed personal relations, as a general rule, can only belong to a fixed state of society. Until Mr. Newman or somebody else can point out any existing state of society which it is desirable to have stereotyped for perpetual use, we must regard as an evil, all restraint put upon the spirit which never yet since society existed has been in excess— that which bids us "try all things" as the only means by which with knowledge and assurance we can "hold fast to that which is good."[*]

Some of the measures of political improvement which Mr. Newman advocates, we recognize as useful, though not always for the reasons he assigns. He insists much on the value of provincial legislatures, to transact the local business now performed by private Acts of Parliament, together with much other business not now performed at all. We are of the same opinion; not however for the sake of remedying what he deplores, "the loss of local patriotism;" [p. 293] for the provincial spirit, in every country where it exists, is a mere hindrance to improvement. In the United States, which Mr. Newman justly holds up as a model of local self-government, the local institutions do not engender local, but general patriotism; or (to call it by a better name, because unconnected with ideas of narrowness,) public spirit, and intelligent interest in public affairs.

The concluding chapters contain some useful observations in favour of small landed properties, of *commandite* partnerships, of giving the labourers a joint interest in the profits of the capitalist, and other matters of considerable, though secondary importance, of which the limits already attained by this article, forbid any more particular notice.

[*I Thessalonians, 5:21.]

THE LAW OF PARTNERSHIP

1851

EDITOR'S NOTE

"Appendix to the Report from the Select Committee on the Law of Partnership," *Parliamentary Papers*, 1851, XVIII, 182. Signed; not republished. Original heading: "1.—Reply to Queries by J. Stuart Mill, Esq." Not mentioned in JSM's bibliography or *Autobiography*. No copy in Somerville College.

JSM's reply was to the following "Form of Queries" (*ibid.*, 181), which was sent to twelve respondents in all:

"It has been proposed to limit the liability of partners to the amount of their respective subscription in certain companies or partnerships duly registered.

It has been thought by some persons that such a measure, properly guarded by regulations to prevent fraud and rash speculation, may assist useful investments for the combination of capital of the middle classes, and aid useful local enterprises.

It is proposed that this measure should not extend to banking, insurance, or other employments for capital of a very speculative nature.

Such partnerships of limited liability, under certain rules, are established in France, Germany, Holland, and the United States of America.

It is desired by some parties that such partnerships should be introduced here.

Your opinion is requested on this subject, with such suggestions as you may think useful."

The Law of Partnership

THE LIBERTY of entering into partnerships of limited liability, similar to the *commandite* partnerships of France and other countries, appears to me an important element in the general freedom of commercial transactions, and in many cases a valuable aid to undertakings of general usefulness.

I do not see any weight in the reasons which have been given for confining the principle to certain kinds of business, or for making certain employments an exception from it. The prohibition of *commandite* is, I conceive, only tenable on the principles of the usury laws, and may reasonably be abandoned since those principles have been given up. *Commandite* partnership is merely one of the modes of lending money, viz., at an interest dependent on, and varying with, the profits of the concern; and subject to the condition, in case of failure, of receiving nothing until other creditors have been paid in full. This mode of lending capital is evidently more advantageous than any other mode to all persons with whom the concern may have dealings; and to retain restrictions on this mode after having abandoned them on all others, appear to me inconsistent and inexpedient.

The only regulations on the subject of limited partnerships which seem to me desirable, are such as may secure the public from falling into error, by being led to believe that partners who have only a limited responsiblity, are liable to the whole extent of their property. For this purpose, it would probably be expedient, that the names of the limited partners, with the amount for which each was responsible, should be recorded in a register, accessible to all persons; and it might also be recorded, whether the whole, or if not, what portion of the amount, had been paid up.

If these particulars were made generally accessible, concerns in which there were limited partners would present in some respects a greater security to the public than private firms now afford; since there are at present no means of ascertaining what portion of the funds with which a firm carries on business may consist of borrowed capital.

No one, I think, can consistently condemn these partnerships without being prepared to maintain that it is desirable that no one should carry on business with borrowed capital; in other words, that the profits of business should be wholly monopolized by those who have had time to accumulate, or the good fortune to inherit capital: a proposition, in the present state of commerce and industry, evidently absurd.

THE INCOME AND PROPERTY TAX

1852

EDITOR'S NOTE

Parliamentary Papers, 1852, IX, 780–91, and 794–820. Not republished. Original headings: "John Stuart Mill, Esq., called in; and Examined," and "John Stuart Mill, Esq. called in; and further Examined." Running heads: "Minutes of Evidence taken before the/Select Committee on Income and Property Tax." The evidence was taken on 17 and 20 May, 1852, with Joseph Hume in the Chair, and the following members of the Committee present on the 17th: Sir Francis Baring, Joseph Henley, Charles Newdegate, John Lewis Ricardo, Harry Vane, Thomas Vesey, and Sir Charles Wood. On the 20th the same members were present, except Baring, Newdegate, and Vane, and in addition Benjamin Disraeli (Chancellor of the Exchequer), Edward Horsman, T. Sotheron Estcourt, and James Wilson. Identified in JSM's bibliography as "Evidence before the Select Committee of the House of Commons on the Income Tax, printed with their Report, forming Vol. IX of the papers of the Session of 1852" (MacMinn, 77). No copy in Somerville College.

On 17 May, JSM's examination includes questions 5222 to 5269 of the evidence before the Committee; on 20 May, questions 5277 to 5447.

The Income and Property Tax

J. HUME: *You have given considerable attention to the subject of taxation, and have published your opinions upon the income and property tax? On* the general principles of the income and property tax.[*]

What is your opinion of the present income tax,[†] *as regards its fairness and equality to the different interests affected by it?* It seems to me to be the chief defect of the present tax, that it does not make any distinction between permanent and temporary incomes, or between precarious and certain incomes. I should not however be inclined to make so great a distinction in either of those cases as is contended for by many. The most popular of the plans for remedying the inequality or injustice of the present tax in making no distinction between permanent and temporary incomes, is the plan of capitalizing, as it is called, the income, and taxing each income at what would be its selling value at the moment when the tax is levied. Now this appears to me to involve an arithmetical fallacy. Suppose, for instance, there were two incomes, each of 1,000*l.* a year, the one a permanent income, and the other an income for 10 years, or what is equivalent, a life income, the life being supposed to be worth 10 years' purchase. Supposing that the permanent income would sell for 20 years' purchase, it would be double the value of the other, and, according to the maxim of taxing all persons in proportion to their means without consideration of anything else, all would admit that an income which is worth only half as much as another income, should pay only half as much. Under cover, however, of this principle, it is contended that an income of 1,000*l.* a year which is to last for only 10 years, should be considered as equivalent to an income of 500*l.* a year to last for ever, and should be taxed at only the same rate at which a perpetual annuity of 500*l.* would be taxed. This appears to me to be fallacious: because, after converting an income of 1,000*l.* a year for 10 years into an equivalent value in perpetuity, that is to say, into 500*l.* a year in perpetuity, you do not tax it in perpetuity, which you would do if it were really a permanent income of that value,

[*See *Principles,* in *Collected Works,* II, pp. 807–72.]
[†5 & 6 Victoria, c. 35.]

but you tax it only for 10 years. The fallacy lies in capitalizing the income without at the same time capitalizing the tax. It appears to me that you ought to do both, or neither. The point might be illustrated in this way. Supposing the tax were to be paid only once, and assuming, as before, that a perpetual income is worth 20 years' purchase, it would be fair to take from a perpetual income of 1,000*l*. a year exactly twice as much as you take from an income of 1,000*l*. a year for 10 years; that is to say, an income of 1,000*l*. in perpetuity being worth 20,000*l*., an income of 1,000*l*. a year for life at 10 years' purchase, would be worth only 10,000*l*., and therefore ought to pay half as much as the other. Now supposing the tax were levied once for all, and that it were a tax of five per cent., the one income would pay 1,000*l*. once, and the other income would pay 500*l*. once, because the one would be worth 20,000*l*., and the other only 10,000*l*.; that everybody would allow to be fair, the one being half the selling value of the other. As that would be fair if the tax was to be levied only once, I apprehend that it would be fair in whatever mode the tax was levied; the one ought to pay what is equivalent to 1,000*l*., and the other to pay what is equivalent to 500*l*. But it is proposed that an income of 1,000*l*. a year for 10 years only, should be taxed as if it were an income of 500*l*. a year, that it should be taxed therefore only 25*l*. a year, and should pay that for only 10 years. So that where the perpetual income pays a perpetual tax equal in value to 1,000*l*., the terminable income pays a terminable tax equivalent only to 250*l*., and consequently pays a fourth, instead of a half, what the other pays. This, I conceive, is not consistent with the principle of paying in proportion to means, which is the principle of the tax as at present levied. At the same time, I do not consider that to be the right principle of taxation. I do not conceive that the tax should be in proportion to the means only, but that it should take into consideration the means, and also the wants. I would therefore tax temporary or precarious incomes at a lower scale than permanent or certain incomes, not because of their having a less selling value, but because the possessors of those incomes have one want, which those who possess permanent incomes have not; they are liable to be called upon in most cases to save something out of that income to provide for their own future years, or to provide for others who are dependent upon them; while those who possess permanent incomes can spend the whole, and still leave the property to their descendants or others. It is for this reason that I would tax a temporary income at a lower rate than a permanent income.

When you speak of temporary incomes, you include professional incomes? Yes.

You say that in the case of temporary incomes, not only the means but the wants should be taken into consideration in levying the tax. Are you able to point out what those wants are, in regard to any particular class of incomes, or to lay down a rule upon the subject? It is impossible to lay down a rule with precision, and entirely impossible to take into consideration the special circumstances of individual cases; but it may be said generally of both classes of incomes, that is, temporary and precarious, that the possessors will be unable prudently to spend the whole of the incomes, as possessors of permanent incomes might do. I think that this difference between those classes of persons and persons having permanent incomes is a ground for making a distinction between them in taxation. The true principle of the equality of taxation, I conceive to be, not that it shall be equal in proportion to means, but that it shall, as far as possible, demand an equal sacrifice from all. If two persons have equal incomes, and one of them can afford to spend the whole of that income, while the other is called upon to make a certain reserve to meet future wants, to demand from these two persons the same annual sum, is to require from them not an equal, but an unequal sacrifice.

You consider that there would be an equality in the tax if the allowance which you have now stated were made? I am only stating now what appears to me to be the principal objection to the present tax, namely, that it does not make any distinction between permanent and temporary incomes. The distinction which I think it ought to make, would be to leave untaxed such a proportion of the temporary income as it might reasonably be expected that the individual possessing it should save. Of course you cannot consider individual cases, you must consider classes of cases, and obtain as good an average as you can.

In what manner would you be able to ascertain what those wants were? It must be done to a considerable degree arbitrarily. No rule that can be adopted is perfectly just, because no two persons are in the same circumstances as to wants and means, but you may adopt a sort of general standard. It seems to me that the suggestion of taxing incomes in proportion to their capitalized value is a great deal too favourable to temporary incomes. If you convert an income of 1,000*l.* a year for 10 years into a permanent income of an equivalent value, which we will suppose to be 500*l.* a year, and tax the income as if it were 500*l.*, you leave untaxed 500*l.* out of 1,000*l.* According to the view I take, this would be only justifiable if it was reasonable and just to suppose that the person enjoying that income would save 500*l.* out of the 1,000*l.* as a provision for future years or for his descendants, or any persons in whom he is interested. Now this is much more than the owners of life incomes generally do save, or can reasonably be expected to save. If a person having an income of 1,000*l.* a year which he has to work for, and which therefore depends on his life, were to put by as much as would convert this into a perpetual income of an unvarying amount, that is to say, on the present supposition, 500*l.* a year, he would leave to his posterity as large an income in perpetuity without work, as he allowed himself out of the produce of his labour, which is a very exaggerated view of the obligations or the probabilities of saving.

You think that an allowance should be made in all those cases according to the prudential views of what it is necessary to lay by in order to provide for the old age of the individual, or to provide for the family which he may have? I do not think you could establish any minute classification, but you might take an average of what those whose incomes are for life, or for a shorter period than life, might be reasonably expected to save, and that may, perhaps, be taken to be one-fourth. I say one-fourth, without much consideration, and without much means of judging, but you can only strike a general average. It might, I think, be assumed, that on the average persons with temporary incomes may prudently expend three-fourths and save the other fourth; if that were a fair calculation I would tax them on three-fourths and leave a fourth untaxed.

If I rightly understood you, what you mean is this, that supposing A from landed property received 400l. a year and B from professional income received 400l. a year, you would tax the one on 400l., and you would tax the other on 300l. a year? Exactly.

That you put as the average, without being able mathematically to arrive at the correct result, because the parties enjoying those incomes in each class will require, in order to act with prudence, to lay by a portion of their incomes to meet future wants? Of course it is a general average, but it does not seem to me objectionable to take it as such an average.

Would you apply that to salaries and all temporary incomes? I would apply it to all temporary incomes. But in the case of professional incomes, or incomes derived from trade or business, where, in addition to being only temporary, they are precarious, I would make a further distinction in favour of them. A precarious or variable sum which averages 1,000*l.* a year is not to any one's feelings of so great value as 1,000*l.* a year of certain income. It would therefore be fair that incomes of the precarious class should be taxed on a somewhat lower scale, in addition to the exemption of one-fourth, or whatever other proportion were adopted, on the score of its being a temporary income. This would not apply to salaries, or any incomes of a fixed character, but only to those which are precarious; to all incomes from commerce, for instance.

On that view, probably half in a trade where considerable risk existed, your proportion might go up to a half, whilst other incomes were charged upon the three-fourths? To a certain extent regard is paid to that consideration in the present system, by allowing losses to be deducted, but it is not provided for completely, because under the present system all losses are not allowed to be deducted; it is only the loss in a particular year which is deducted. If for several years in succession there has been a loss in business, though no tax is levied in those years, yet nothing is given back; therefore it is not, in the present mode of levying the tax, correct to say that losses are allowed for; they are only partially allowed for.

SIR C. WOOD: *Is not loss allowed for in each and every year?* If in one year there is 1,000*l.* gained and 500*l.* lost, the tax is levied on 500*l.*, but if in the succeeding year the profits are 500*l.* and the losses are 1,000*l.* the State is content with levying no tax in that year, but it does not refund to the taxpayer, as I conceive in justice it ought to do.

That is to say, the State does not indemnify a man for the loss of income in any one year, by paying him a certain sum in that year, although it received the tax from him in the year when he made a profit? Precisely so; he has paid the tax in those years in which there was a profit, but in those in which there was a loss he has not received anything back, therefore taking a series of years he has paid the tax on more than the surplus of his profits above his losses.

J. HUME: *You are aware that under Schedule (A.) for losses arising from repairs, or other circumstances attending the management of real property, no allowance is made. Do you consider that just?* On principle I should say it is not just; but I have not considered the subject very particularly.

Then we understand you to speak of net income after making the allowances which under each class might fairly be made? Yes. There is something further which I think is not strictly just with reference to losses. In consequence of the classification of the sources of income in the return that each person makes under Schedule (D.), the whole of the losses are not allowed for, even in the same year. As I understand the matter, if under some of the heads he has received profits, and under others he has sustained losses, the losses under one head are not allowed to be deducted from the profits under another. For instance, supposing a person in Schedule (D.) makes a return that he has lost 500*l.* by his business, but that he has gained during that year 500*l.* by the sale of railway shares, he is called upon to pay on the 500*l.* he has gained on railway shares, taking no account of the 500*l.* which he has lost in his regular business; but I apprehend, in the case supposed, he ought to pay nothing.

You would require each individual under Schedule (D.) to place his whole receipts and his whole losses, so that he should pay only on the net balance, if it was a profit? Exactly, and that I conceive must have been the intention of the Legislature, but I believe it is not the practice.

C. NEWDEGATE: *You have stated that it would be just in the case of temporary incomes, and more especially in the case of professional incomes, to allow for a reserve, and that amount allowed for a reserve should be exempt from the tax; would not that be equally just under Schedule (A.), in the case of estates, where at certain periods buildings are required to be renewed as well as repaired?* I think so, on the principle that people ought to be taxed only on their net receipts; on the income they receive after deducting all the charges necessarily connected with it. They ought to be taxed on that portion of the year's income which they can afford to spend upon themselves. That is the principle on which all my remarks have been founded.

Making allowance in all cases for a necessary reserve? Yes.

Have you ever considered the case of the owners of mineral property who receive what is termed a royalty, which includes rent for the use of the mines and also the whole of their share of the coal or minerals in each year? I have not considered that case particularly.

Is it not the case that those parties pay the tax upon their whole share of the coal sold in each year, that coal being absolutely disposed of, and, in fact, being so much capital? I apprehend that they ought only to pay upon the surplus of their receipts beyond expenses, like other people.

The case I put is this: under Schedule (A.) the coal-owner is taxed upon the whole royalty which he receives, that royalty includes the sale of a certain portion of his coal, which is so much capital; is it just that he should be taxed upon the whole value of that sale? I can only conceive that question to arise in contemplation of the ultimate exhaustion of the coal mines, but as that must be at so very distant a period, it does not seem to me that any deduction which could be reasonably made with reference to that contingency, could make any material difference.

Would you, then, tax the royalty, which includes the value of the coal sold, at the same rate as you would tax rent, which is only an annual payment for the user of the land? As far as I can see at present, without much consideration, I should; but in regard to precarious incomes, such as profits of trade, or professional incomes, which cease altogether with the life of the person, and are liable to fluctuate from illness, or varying success, or from a hundred other circumstances, I think the tax is doubly unjust to the holders of those incomes. In the first place, it taxes them on the whole of their receipts, but does not deduct the whole of their losses. In the second place, I conceive that even if you deduct the whole of their losses you will not do full justice to them. Supposing a variable income which averages 1,000*l.* a year after all losses were deducted, but which might cease altogether any day, though on a series of years the income might be the same as that of a person who had 1,000*l.* year from land, still it would not be just to tax it on the same scale, because it is not the same to any one's feelings. A permanent income of the same amount is of more value to any man's feelings than an uncertain income, averaging that amount, but which may at any time dwindle to nothing. On that account, if all losses were allowed to be deducted, and justice done in that respect, still some additional consideration would, I think, be due to the possessor of a precarious income.

J. HUME: *Though you do not agree entirely in the principle that the State should levy the tax by capitalizing the different incomes, still you come to the conclusion that those who have precarious incomes should not be taxed, as they now are, at the same rate with those who have permanent incomes?* Not only so, but I would make a double distinction: in the first place, as regards those whose incomes are temporary, I would tax only such a proportion of their income as it may be reasonably supposed they can afford to spend upon themselves, and leave untaxed that portion which they are bound, or may be reasonably expected to save. In addition to that, where incomes were precarious, I would tax even that reserved portion at a somewhat lower rate. For instance, supposing that permanent incomes were taxed as at present, 7*d.* in the pound, then in the case of temporary incomes I would levy 7*d.* in the pound only upon three-fourths of the income; and in the case of precarious or uncertain incomes, such as those derived from professions and trades, I would take, perhaps, only 6*d.* in the pound upon the three-fourths.

Do you think that those classes could be so arranged as to enable the officers who were employed to levy the tax to collect it with fairness? I do not think it would be possible to make nice distinctions in particular cases, but it seems to me that there would be more justice in drawing the line a little arbitrarily than in not drawing any line at all.

Though you could not draw the line quite correctly in all cases, you are of opinion that it would be better to attempt it than to continue the present system, which you consider unjust? Decidedly.

C. NEWDEGATE: *You stated in reference to the principle of taxation, that means only should not be considered but wants also to a certain degree, including under the term "wants" the necessity for making a reserve in the case of persons who have limited interests. Is there not also this further consideration, viz., the advantages derived by each from the state, which are not the same in all cases; for instance, are not professional incomes much more dependent upon the good order and permanent condition of society than incomes derived from land?* It seems to me that all incomes are essentially dependent upon the protection of government.

But are not professional incomes more so than the incomes derived from land? Supposing society to be sufficiently ill governed, no property whatever would be safe.

But would not professional men, in the case of society not being well governed, suffer more than the owners of real property? It seems to me very disputable whether they would, but supposing they did, I do not conceive that to be a consideration on which a principle of taxation can be grounded. The just principle of taxation, I conceive to be, to impose as far as possible an equal sacrifice on all.

According to their means? Yes.

Then, after all, the distinction you have established resolves itself into the principle of taxation according to a person's means? Taxation in proportion to means, but with an allowance in certain cases where the payment of the same proportion would be an equal sacrifice.

Without a consideration of the necessities of the enjoyment, or the advantages derived? If you could ascertain the particular necessities of every individual, which you cannot do, and if you could also distinguish the necessities he brings upon himself by imprudence from those which are inherent in his position, I think justice would require that you should do so. But as that is clearly impossible, all you can do is to consider classes of cases; and if you can in any particular class of cases distinctly see that there is a necessity which does not exist in another class of cases, and that if you took the same proportion of income from both, it would impose a greater sacrifice upon the one than upon the other, I think this should be avoided.

You admit that wants are to be taken into consideration in fixing the tax, and that the tax is to be regulated according to certain classes which you would establish? Yes.

Without consideration of the advantages derived by each class from the institutions of the country? Exactly.

J. HUME: *I understood you to have said that taxation is raised for the protection of all parties in the State; will you explain the words you have now used, "equal sacrifice." You say there ought to be an equal sacrifice, but you do not look to the sacrifice which each individual has to make, but you take it in classes?* I hardly know how to give any better explanation than is implied in the words themselves. If the object was to raise from a number of persons a contribution for some common object, the natural course would be not to take exactly the same sum from each, because they can afford it in unequal degrees; and by taking, not the same sum, but the same proportion, you would still take from them what they could not afford in equal degrees. I would make an allowance for that circumstance, and I would endeavour so to regulate the sum taken from each, that each should be required to give up an equal share, not of their means, but of their enjoyments.

J. L. RICARDO: *That each should make an equal sacrifice?* Yes.

J. HUME: *You would not look altogether to the property possessed, but to other circumstances connected with the situation of the property?* The amount of the property is one of the principal circumstances to be looked to, but not the only one.

In a former answer you stated that you would make a certain allowance to all; what do you mean by an allowance; is it for necessaries, not luxuries? In order to answer that question, I must enter into another part of the subject, which is, the expediency of leaving a certain portion of all income untaxed. It seems to me right to exempt from income tax, and from all taxes as far as you can, the amount of income required for the necessaries of life. If, for instance, 50*l.* a year would provide an individual and an average family, or rather a family just sufficient to keep up the population, with necessaries of life, so much should be left untaxed.

For rich and poor? Yes. I would not leave incomes of 50*l.* untaxed, and tax incomes of 60*l.* upon the whole 60*l.*; I would tax them on the surplus above 50*l.*, in order to take a certain proportion of the surplus, and not a certain proportion of the whole income.

Is it your view that all property, and all incomes should be taxed, subject to the exception you have now stated? If the income tax was the only tax, and the whole national revenue was raised by means of it, I should say so, certainly; but as circumstances are now, one part of the revenue system must be considered with reference to other parts. If I were laying on an income tax to supply the whole of the national expenditure, I would tax all incomes that yield more than the necessaries of life, and tax them on the surplus above what would yield the necessaries of life. But under the present system of taxation, it is right to consider whether the remaining taxes do not press more on the smaller than on the larger incomes. I conceive that they do, and that this justifies the present exemption from the income tax of incomes under 150*l.* a year. The excise and customs, and our indirect taxes in general, are levied mostly on commodities of very general consumption, other articles being seldom worth the expense of levying a tax: and thus the great mass of our revenue is derived from the articles consumed by the middle and lower classes. The consequence is, that probably the people in this country who are most heavily taxed in proportion to their incomes, are those receiving incomes of between 50*l.* and 150*l.* a year, because all articles of general consumption are consumed in a greater proportion by that class than by the rich.

C. NEWDEGATE: *You consider that under the present system of taxation, what may be termed luxuries are, in a great measure, exempt?* The luxuries of those whose incomes are small, are taxed much more heavily than those of the rich; and that is carried so far, that the same amount of tax is often levied on the lower qualities of the same articles as on the highest qualities.

If I understand you, the luxuries of the comparatively poorer classes are more heavily taxed, under the present system, than the luxuries of the richer classes? Yes; what I mean to say is this, that if there were no tax but an income tax, it would be fair to commence at as small a sum as 50*l.*, which would cover the necessaries of life, and to tax in all cases the excess above 50*l.*, but under present circumstances it is justifiable to begin as high as 150*l.* The class between 50*l.* and 150*l.* now pay a disproportionate share of our indirect taxes, inasmuch as the articles upon which those taxes principally fall, are articles upon which a larger proportion of small incomes than of large incomes is expended.

SIR C. WOOD: *Is not this what you mean, that you justify the exemption of the lower incomes from the income tax, because in your opinion the indirect taxation presses more heavily upon persons of smaller incomes than upon persons of larger incomes?* Yes.

C. NEWDEGATE: *If I understand you rightly, you would recommend the abolition of the exemption from the taxes upon incomes under 150l. a year, if you were not of opinion that the other taxes of the country pressed so heavily upon them; but you think the incomes which are most heavily taxed, according to the present system, are the incomes between 50l. a year and 150l.?* Yes.

J. L. RICARDO: *Most heavily taxed by indirect taxation?* Yes; and in order to re-establish the balance, as the other taxes press more heavily upon the small incomes, it is just that the income tax should exclusively upon the larger incomes.

You mean that the pressure upon the lower incomes is not from direct but from indirect taxation? Exactly.

J. HUME: *Would you recommend a graduated scale in the plan which has been recommended by Archdeacon Paley,*[*] *increasing the tax as the amount of income increased, and as Mr. Pitt did in the first Act of his?*[†] I should not be favourable to taking a larger per centage from the higher incomes than from the lower incomes.

Do we understand you to say that before the present income tax on any class of the community can be fairly imposed, you must take into view the general amount of taxation, and how far those who have smaller incomes pay a larger proportion of their incomes under indirect taxation than others who have larger incomes? Yes.

And therefore the absolute money payment from individuals in the middle and lower classes of society does not indicate the pressure of taxation on those classes? No, and an income tax which would not in itself be

[*Paley, William. *The Principles of Moral and Political Philosophy*. 15th ed., London: Faulder, 1804, II, p. 429 ff.]
[†39 George III, c. 13.]

just, may be rendered just by the necessity of compensating for the undue pressure of other taxation.

[*]*You were asked your opinion as to taxing property on a graduated scale; you stated that you did not think that would be advisable. Do the same objections, in your opinion, apply to taxing land or realized property?* I think there are the strongest objections to an income or property tax exclusively on realized property. The objections are that, in the first place, it is taxing people upon what they save, and leaving them untaxed upon what they spend; and, further than that, it appears to me to be taxing only the present owners of land or securities. By realized property, I presume, is understood not property engaged in business, but property which has been taken out of business if it was ever in business, and invested in some permanent form. I am using the term "realized" in the sense in which it is generally used by those who contend for a tax on realized property only. Now, it seems to me that it is absolutely impossible for the Legislature, by any income tax, to tax future realizations. They can only tax present realizations. The imposition of a tax on incomes from realized property, from which tax other incomes were exempted, would lower the price of all realized property of land and all securities, and all who hereafter bought such property would buy it at a reduced price; so that they would escape the tax, and it would be levied exclusively on those who at present hold land or securities. The present holders would continue to pay the tax after they had parted with the property, because they would have had to sell it at a lower price. I conceive therefore that the tax would be simple confiscation of a certain proportion of their property.

You stated that you would not make any exemption from charge in the case of realized property? Yes.

Does the same rule apply to professional and variable incomes? With reference to variable incomes, it appears to me that some allowance may properly be made not only for their temporary nature, but also for their precariousness.

SIR C. WOOD: *Would you apply your rule of taxing three-fourths only of the income to temporary incomes derived from realized property, as well as to other temporary incomes?* Yes.

J. HUME: *Supposing the exemption to be made, to what amount would you descend of income, both as regards income from landed property and income from professional exertions?* If there were no other tax than an income tax, I would make that tax descend to the amount which might be considered sufficient for necessaries. I mean necessaries not very strictly interpreted, and not necessaries for the individual only who is assessed to the tax, but for the whole of the existing population. At that point, whatever

[*The evidence of 20 May begins here.]

it is, the income tax should commence, if there were no other tax whatever; but when there are other taxes existing, it is necessary to consider the incidence of those taxes, and if they fall, as I think they do, with a much greater proportional pressure on the smaller than on the larger incomes, it is a fair compensation that the income tax should fall only on the larger incomes. On that account I think the present limit of 150*l.* is defensible.

We understand you to say, that in order to call for an equal sacrifice from all parties, not the income tax only, but the other items of taxation bearing on the different classes of the community, ought to be taken into consideration before a judgment can be pronounced as to what would be a fair and equal rate of taxation upon all classes? Certainly.

The plan you have stated you do not consider to be perfect justice, but you consider it the nearest approximation to justice, and much better than the present system? Certainly much better than the present system. But in order to do complete justice, it seems to me, though it is not a principle generally recognised, that the income tax ought to exempt all that portion of income which is saved. I express this opinion not solely on grounds of policy or expediency, with a view to encourage savings, but as a simple question of arithmetic. If that portion of income which is laid by is charged with income tax, it pays the income tax twice; first on the capital, and then on the interest derived from it. For instance, suppose that in one year I save 100*l.*: if I did not save that 100*l.* I should have to pay 3*l.* to the State, which would leave me 97*l.* to expend on luxuries or indulgences: but if, instead of spending, I save the 100*l.*, I should not save it to lock it up, but to invest it; and I should immediately begin to pay income tax on the income derived from it, which would be equivalent to paying the tax on the 100*l.* If I spend the 100*l.* I pay 3*l.* to the State, and have 97*l.* for my own use; if I save it, I pay 3*l.* to the State, which reduces my future income from it in the same proportion, and I also pay three per cent. on this diminished income; so that, in reality, I pay the income tax twice, first on the capital, and then on the interest. This could only be just, on the supposition that I had the use and benefit both of the capital and of the income; but I have not. If I have the use of the capital I derive no income from it; and if I have the income, it is because I abstain from using the capital.

SIR C. WOOD: *Your principle is this: if I had an income of 50,000l. a year, and spent the whole of that income, I ought to pay income tax upon the 50,000l.; but if I were a great miser, and lived on 1,000l. a year, and saved 49,000l. I ought to pay the tax upon the 1,000l. a year, leaving the 49,000l. untaxed?* The reason for exempting the 49,000*l.* is, that it will hereafter pay the tax when invested. Instead of paying 7*d.* in the pound at once, it will pay an annuity of 7*d.* in the pound on the interest, the present value of which annuity would be exactly equal to 7*d*. in the pound upon the 49,000*l*. At present, the 49,000*l*., if spent, only pays the tax once, but if saved, it pays it twice, although the person to whom it belongs has not the use of it twice, but only once.

Is not the future tax upon the interest derived from the investment of the capital which is so saved? Yes, but the interest is all the benefit that by the supposition is derived from the investment by the owner. The benefit of the capital is obtained by the labouring class whom he employs, or who are employed by the person to whom he lends the money.

Do you think that the opinion which you have now expressed in favour of exempting from the income tax all monies saved is consistent with the opinion which you formerly gave,[*] *that the wants of parties ought to be considered as well as their means, in apportioning the income tax?* The consideration which ought to be given to wants, in modification of the rule of taxing persons in proportion to their means, seems to me quite compatible with interpreting that general rule in the mode which appears to me arithmetically correct. If the portion of income which is saved pays twice as much tax as that which is spent, this is not equal taxation in proportion to means. The principle of making allowance for wants, does not require that the same portion of income should pay the tax twice when employed in one way, while if employed in another way it would pay it only once.

J. WILSON: *When you say it is taxed twice, you mean that first of all it is taxed as income in the year when the income arises, and that afterwards it is not taxed once only, but annually, as the interest of that capital accrues?* Yes, that is equivalent to being taxed twice; first of all, it pays three per cent., supposing that to be the amount of the income tax, and afterwards it pays in a perpetual annuity, what is equivalent to another three per cent., so that in fact it pays as much as if it had had to pay six per cent. at once.

SIR C. WOOD: *Is not the principle for which you contend of exempting savings from incomes, equally applicable to increases of all capital in the country derived from gradual accumulation?* Certainly; but if that portion of the income which was saved was exempted from the tax, it would still be called upon to pay income tax in proportion as it came to be expended and used for the benefit of the owner.

Therefore all additions to incomes derived from the investment of savings ought, in your opinion, to be exempt from income tax? I am not entering into the question of what is now practicable, but what would be necessary to make an income tax a strictly just tax.

Is it your principle that, in strict justice, all income derived from the investment of accumulated savings ought to be exempted from the income

[*See p. 466 above.]

tax? I would tax the income; what I would exempt would be the investment itself. I would not tax the investment and then the income derived from it; in fact, I would make the tax a tax upon expenditure, and not upon income.

J. WILSON: *You would only tax the portion of the income which the man expended, and not the income which he actually made?* Yes; and if he saved any portion of his income, and afterwards derived income from it, I would tax that income according as it came into use by expenditure.

SIR C. WOOD: *Would you call upon every person under Schedule (D.) to make a return, not of his income, but of his expenditure?* That is a question of expediency and practicability, and depends on the reliance to be placed on conscience. I do not think that such a mode of levying the tax would be practicable; but it is necessary to keep in view the requisites of exact justice, whether they can be completely realized or not, in order that we may at least approach as near to them as we can.

J. HUME: *But you state that you do not think it would be practicable?* I do not see any means by which you can secure the correctness of such returns, especially if it is borne in mind, that if a person saves a certain sum in one year, that same sum may be squandered in the next year, and it would not be possible in such a case to take back the boon which had been conceded.

SIR C. WOOD: *However just the tax would be, you do not regard it as being very practicable?* That is a question for persons of greater experience of details than myself, but I do not see how it would be practicable.

E. HORSMAN: *After all you have said, does it not resolve itself into this, that a person pays a higher tax because he is a richer man from his accumulation?* He would equally pay a higher tax because he was richer if the distinction which I propose were made. In consequence of his savings, he would have a greater income next year than this year; and he would be taxed on the whole of that greater income except any part of it which he saved in that year.

SIR C. WOOD: *In the case of the miser, who saved 49,000l., you would never get the additional tax from him, however rich he might be?* That, no doubt, as far as it goes, is an objection to what I suggest; but the less he paid, the more would be paid by those who succeeded to his accumulations.

If the tax is at all imposed in proportion to the advantage derived from the State in the shape of protection, is it not fair that this party should pay in proportion to that which is protected? That is an objection which if it exist applies to all taxes on expenditure, and therefore to all existing taxation.

All taxes are not imposed on the same principle as income tax? No; on the opposite principle, I conceive.

Is not the general principle of income or property tax, that a person should pay in proportion to the property which he has, and which derives protection from the State? I would rather say that the equitable principle of taxation is to require from each the same proportional sacrifice of his enjoyments.

Is not the principle which you have laid down, that each person should be taxed to the income tax according to the amount of his expenditure? Yes.

J. WILSON: *The principle which you lay down with regard to income tax you consider to be exactly analogous to indirect taxes upon articles of consumption; you would substitute an income tax for Customs and Excise taxes and all other indirect taxes, and tax a man in proportion to his expenditure and not in proportion to his income; and your idea is that that would make the income tax analogous in its operations to indirect taxation?* Yes; except that it would be a tax on all expenditure, and not a tax on expenditure of some particular kind.

SIR C. WOOD: *Do you remember whether a tax on expenditure was the principle of Mr. Pitt's original scheme?* I rather think it was.

Do you remember what the result of that was? No, but I should be quite prepared to find that it was a complete failure.

Are you not aware that the principle of a tax upon expenditure was abandoned in consequence of its being an utter failure, and the tax on income substituted as the only means of getting a fair amount of tax? It is very probable, and I never expressed an opinion how far that mode of levying the income tax would be practicable; but it seems to me the fairest mode if it were practicable, and therefore any approach to it in practice would be desirable.

J. HUME: *You have, in your publication, expressed an opinion as to how far you consider the land tax should be reckoned at the present moment as a tax paid to the State?* As far as I am acquainted with the nature of the land tax, it seems to me simply a reserve made by the State of a certain portion of the rent of the land, which never properly belonged to the present owners. They or their predecessors were liable to feudal obligations which, if fairly commuted, would have required from them a payment of a much greater amount than the present land tax.

Do you consider that Mr. Pitt, in making the land tax perpetual,[*] laid it on the land as a substitute for all the feudal charges which had existed on the land before that time? Undoubtedly he did not, because the feudal charges had been taken away previously; but they had been taken away without commutation, which I think was a gross injustice; to abolish charges upon land which had been previously held subject to those obligations, and to render it free of those obligations.

At what period do you consider those feudal charges on land to have been abolished? The last of them were abolished in the time of Charles

[*38 George III, c. 60.]

the Second, therefore only a short time before the first imposition of the land tax,[*] the proportion of which was larger than it is now, having been since reduced.

SIR CHARLES WOOD: *Has not the land tax varied from time to time in amount?* Yes, but chiefly in the way of reduction.

J. HENLEY: *You say that the feudal charges would have been heavier than the existing land tax; what per centage do you apprehend the feudal charges would have been?* I am not competent to say.

How, then, do you form your opinion that they would have been higher than the present land tax? Because the land tax bears a very small ratio to the value of the land: and as the land was granted for the purpose of feudal service, it cannot well be supposed that the burthen of that service was only a twentieth or a thirtieth part of the value of the land.

What do you suppose to be the amount of the land tax? I have not the facts in my memory at the present moment, and therefore I cannot say.

You neither know the amount of the land tax, nor have you formed an estimate of the amount of the feudal charges? No, I am not in a position to form any estimate upon the subject; I did formerly make estimates upon the subject, but what they were I cannot at this moment say.

Do you give that opinion from an examination of estimates formed upon the subject, or is it merely a general opinion? I give the opinion upon general grounds, and upon details which I do not now recollect; but I have formerly read many discussions on the subject of the land tax.

Feudal charges were applicable to all lands held from the Crown by military service? Yes.

Many lands in the country were not so held? Not very many.

There were some, were there not? In this country there were very few; there were more in other countries.

Do you mean to assert that there were no lands held in England except on terms of military service? No, I do not mean to say that; but the general rule in this country was a feudal tenure; there was scarcely any allodial tenure remaining in this country in the middle ages, though in still earlier times tenure was allodial here as elsewhere.

If the imposition of the land tax was, as you state, in substitution of feudal tenures, how happens it that it was not imposed equally over the whole kingdom? It is very difficult to say, without a minute investigation of the history of taxation, what is the explanation of the caprices of taxation that have existed in this as in all other countries. There have been many more such irregularities in all countries than are justifiable on any good grounds.

Have you ever seen any estimate of what the cost of those feudal charges

[*1 William & Mary, c. 20.]

was in the time of Charles the First? I imagine in the time of Charles the First they were already very much diminished, but I cannot offer any particular estimate; any estimates that may have been made must in a great measure have been conjectural.

The whole of this matter is very conjectural, is it not? Yes.

Were there, as well as burdens, any privileges which the lands enjoyed formerly under the feudal system which they have since lost? I am not aware of any which they have since lost; the possession of land has always been a source of importance and power.

Take, for instance, manorial rights; were there not many manorial rights dependent upon the feudal tenures, which were very much more valuable at the time that those tenures existed than they are now? I should doubt very much whether any of that description of rights were more valuable in a poor state of society than in a rich one. Manorial rights have generally become limited in the course of time, by customs of different kinds, by which indefinite obligations were exchanged for definite ones, but I do not think that on the whole it can be supposed that the value of manorial rights has diminished with the growth of society.

Have any rights been wholly swept away? I dare say some have.

Wardship for instance? Wardship was a privilege to the vassal, with regard to sub-vassals; but a burden to the tenants *in capite*, in relation to the Crown.

Do you consider that, on the whole, it was a gain or a loss to the landed interest when that was done away? I am unable to say.

You have not looked into that part of the subject? I have not looked into any part of the subject for several years.

Do you consider that there are any other rights analogous to wardship which have been swept away? It is possible there may have been.

You have, then, given a general opinion, without having looked into the subject in all its bearings? I cannot say whether or not I have considered it in all its bearings, but I think it would be very difficult for any one to maintain that the whole of the feudal obligations, taking those to which the tenants and sub-tenants of the Crown were liable, did not amount to fully as much as the land tax now amounts to.

Then, having given that opinion to the Committee, have you taken all those elements into consideration? I have not entered into the minutiæ of the subject very accurately. I have gone on general probabilities and presumptions.

Do you know what the land tax is in the county of Lancaster, and what it is in some of the Southern and Midland counties in England? I cannot say particularly.

If you heard that, in the Midland counties, the land tax was 1s. in the pound upon the rental, and that in Lancashire it was not 1d. in the pound, should you say that it was a tax imposed as a substitution for military service, equally applicable to both counties? I never said that it was imposed as a substitute for military service; I said that the fact of these lands having been subject to military service would have justified the tax being imposed; and, therefore, when the land tax was afterwards imposed, it appears to me just on the principle of substitution, even though there were no coincidence in point of time, or in the amount of the tax.

According to your view, to make it just, it would be necessary to equalise it? I should not be prepared to admit that consequence. I should rather regard it as a deduction from the rent of the land, which might be considered as having been reserved by the Government. I would put it on the ground of prescription. If an express commutation had been made, there probably would not have been the great inequality which there is now; still, that inequality existing, I should not be inclined to increase the amount on the lands which are most lightly taxed.

You would regard it as prescriptive, although its origin is statutory and known? I would; it does not appear to me that its origin being statutory makes any difference in that respect.

Not in the use of the word "prescription"? In the legal use of the word "prescription" it may make a difference, but not, I conceive, in the moral sense of that word.

Why not? Because it seems to me that prescription in regard to property consists in allowing that to continue in possession which has been very long held, and under reasonable expectation of being held permanently.

Without reference to its origin? With reference to its origin only in so far as that might affect the reasonableness of the expectation that it would be continued.

Then if the origin was clearly known, and was of a nature adverse to that view, your reasoning would not hold good? That would be matter of opinion in each case.

It would wholly depend in your opinion upon the ground of the origin justifying the conclusion that you had come to? Yes.

If the origin was entirely adverse, all the superstructure you had raised upon it would fall to the ground? Of course it would.

Do you know at all the history of the alterations of the land tax from time to time? I know that the tax has been several times reduced, but at what precise times I am not aware; I know that at one time it was as high as 4s. in the pound, and that afterwards it was reduced to 1s. in the pound.

Do you happen to know what it was at its origin? I did know those facts, but I have not got them in my recollection.

Was it originally put on at more or less than 4s. in the pound? At less, I believe.

Then it has been subject to increases as well as decreases? Yes.

According to your belief now, is it at 1s. in the pound? It is extremely variable; it is very unequal in different situations.

It was always irregular; that irregularity depending upon the amount of the charge, and not upon the amount in the pound to be raised upon the assessment? I am not sufficiently acquainted with the facts to be able to answer any questions with certainty upon the subject; but the total amount at any time which has been raised by means of the land tax, if it were distributed equally over all the lands of the kingdom, would certainly be a small equivalent for the feudal obligations upon those lands in respect of military service.

But not being so distributed, it may press very heavily upon some lands, and amount to 2s. in the pound upon their rack rents? I should consider the case to be very similar to the commutation of tithes. It may appear hard that some persons should have to pay a larger amount as commutation of tithes than other persons of equal income have to pay, but it does not at all follow that what they have to pay is unjust. The question is, whether they can be considered to have been ever entitled to the tithes; and in the present case, to have been ever entitled to that portion of the rent of the land which is taken from them by the land tax.

In the case of title it is a prescriptive payment, of which we do not know the origin, but in the case of the land tax it is a statutory payment, of which we know the origin and the circumstances? The origin was statutory, but it may be considered to have been, at the time it was imposed, morally, though not legally, an equivalent, or a partial equivalent, for the obligations to which the land was previously subjected; and in that view, even if some lands were dealt with more leniently than others, still if that comparative lenity has continued for generations, it does not appear to me that it can be made a subject of complaint now.

Then the justice of your comparison would depend altogether upon the identity of the origin, would it not? The only way in which it could be affected would be, if the land tax now levied on the land of the community, or on any portion of that land, could be considered as more than a fair equivalent for the obligation of military service, and for whatever other feudal obligations of an expensive nature the land was subject to.

What you mean to contend for is this, that if A. B. were taxed ever so highly to the land tax, and could not show that that was more than he ought to have paid for military service, he would have no right to complaint? It appears questionable whether it would be just to impose on the present generation an increased charge as land tax, on the ground that the present land tax was an insufficient equivalent for the burthens which the land of their forefathers was subject to. After a certain duration of such an arrangement, even though made by statute; after the property has passed through several generations, and the expectations of families have been founded upon the arrangement, it appears to me that the Government could not equitably take advantage of a defect in the origin of it, for the purpose of laying on upon that ground any higher tax.

However unjustly the tax may bear at a particular time on particular parties, on account of the length of the time for which it has existed, and the change of circumstances, whatever they may be, that have taken place, in your opinion it would be unjust now to make an alteration in the tax? Yes. I might illustrate my meaning by saying that it is my opinion, and the opinion of many other persons, that it was an exceedingly improper act of Hen. 8th to give away the lands of the monasteries to individuals, whose successors now possess those lands; but I conceive it would be now unjust to take those lands, or any portion of them, from the present possessors.

How do you establish an analogy between a grant of the Crown and a tax upon the subject, which has always varied and been dealt with from time to time according to the circumstance of the State? It is a question of degree, in my view of the matter. In proportion as the State has adhered to a particular mode of taxation, as in the case of the land tax, and made no alteration in it for a long period, just in that proportion the arrangement of landed property which has grown out of that system of taxation, approximates more and more in its character to the case of property held under direct gift. It seems to me, though I would not lay down any fixed principle on the subject, that the same principles are to a certain degree applicable to the two cases.

SIR C. WOOD: *May not a tax which has been unjust in its first imposition become just in the case of the person succeeding to the property as far as regards the subsequent holders?* Certainly; it may become just as regards subsequent buyers, because if the land is under any disadvantage it tells on the price for which the land is sold.

J. HENLEY: *But in the case of the present holders it would not be just?* All you have to consider in the case of those who have inherited property and not acquired it, is the reasonable expectations which they were justified in forming, and those expectations necessarily depend upon the state of the law. It is not to be supposed by a person who inherits land that he is to have the land altogether, free from the burdens to which his ancestors who held that land were subject.

If a tax of that sort by the State has continued for a considerable length of time, you think that that class has no right to complain of that tax or to consider it a hardship? After a tax has existed for a considerable time, so as to be attached to a particular property, and to be considered in all settlements and all bequests of that property, and in all sales of it, though it may be on the ground of policy expedient and desirable to make an alteration in the tax, it has been never contended for on the ground of justice to the possessors of the property.

You consider that that applies to every species of taxation? Every species of taxation that is of the same nature as this. I can never suppose that taking away the malt tax, or the tax on any other commodity, is required by justice to the particular class that immediately pay it, though it may be advisable on grounds of policy.

You apply that to municipal taxes as well as imperial? I apply it to all taxes which fall upon particular kinds of property, and which have been for some time imposed; it can never be said that on the ground of justice to the possessors of those particular kinds of property, it is necessary to take the tax off.

J. WILSON: *I understand you to say in your answers, that whatever irregularities may exist in the tax where it is first imposed, as the property is dealt with in reference to the tax which is so imposed, the subsequent holders of the property have no right to complain?* I think so.

There was an answer which you made with reference to direct taxes, that a new tax imposed upon realized capital in any shape or form would not be just, because it would be an act of confiscation, the present owners of that capital only paying the tax and not the future owners? Yes.

Would not the same objection apply to any tax which is imposed now for the first time; take for instance the house tax?[*] If a tax were imposed on one description of property and no other, I think it would be liable to that objection. I apprehend that according to all received opinions, the imposition of a tax on one particular description of property, is only just supposing the general system of taxation to tax other kinds of property in a proportionate degree.

The same observation would apply to taxing capital, if all realized property were taxed in whatever shape it was found. You described it as an act of confiscation, because the tax would be paid by the existing owner, the future owner paying less for the property in consideration of its being subject to that tax? Yes.

That would apply whether it was general or partial? I apprehend not if the possessors of all property paid equally, and not merely the possessors of land and securities. Supposing, for instance, property engaged in trade paid the same tax as land and securities, a person would not subject

[*See 14 & 15 Victoria, c. 36.]

himself to any peculiar tax by buying land and securities, and therefore there would be no reason why he should give a less price for them.

That would be a reason for saying that the owner of the property for the time being would not suffer from the tax; but the argument you put forward was, that the present holder of the property would pay the tax, and that the future holder of it would pay no tax? I do not conceive that would be the case if the tax were imposed upon all property; because as all property would stand in the same situation, the buyer of any particular description of property would not pay a lower price for it in consideration of the tax. If a person by buying land subjects himself to a particular tax, he will pay so much less for the land; but if he subjects himself, by buying the land, to no further tax than he would have to pay if he derived income from the purchase money in any other manner, the tax would constitute no reason why he should pay a less price for the land.

Your remark with regard to confiscation applied to the case of the tax being imposed partially and not generally? Yes.

J. HUME: *You were asked to give your grounds for the opinion you have held; have you not published your opinions on the principles of general taxation; and did you not, before publishing those opinions, have the whole question of the several taxes of this country before you in order to enable you to judge?* In the book which I published,[*] my object was to give my view of the general principles of taxation, and to enter into the consideration of hypothetical taxes rather than into the complication of the taxes of any particular country, and I do not consider myself bound by the opinions which I have expressed on such details, in the same degree as on the general principles, because opinions upon particular taxes are liable to vary.

Does not the land tax form one of the points on which you have given a decided opinion, that opinion being founded on researches made at the time? It was founded on general considerations rather than on the special details of the case, but certainly with a full conviction of its justice.

You have been asked with reference to the origin of the land tax; are you aware that Mr. Pitt, on the general valuation of the land in England, fixed the quota for each county? I have no doubt that was so, but I cannot say that I remember the facts with respect to the history of the land tax, except in a very general way.

You are not aware that Mr. Pitt's valuation, and the quota which was fixed for each county, were with reference to the rent of cultivated land at the time, and that all wild lands were excluded? I was not aware of that.

You have not been able to account for the irregularity of the tax as laid on property, which is now of great value, by the circumstance of its being in a wild and unproductive state at the time the tax was fixed? That, I

[*Principles of Political Economy.]

conceive, is only one of a great number of inequalities which must necessarily grow up in any such case. If, for example, a tax is laid on in reference
to the value of land at the time, and the tax is not afterwards altered, but
the land afterwards changes from being employed in cultivation to being
employed in building, the tax must necessarily become unequal.

*Are you aware that the whole of Marylebone parish, and various parts
round the metropolis, do not pay one twentieth of a penny land tax, while
there are portions in the city and in the country which pay several shillings
in the pound to the land tax?* I am aware that there are great inequalities,
as great as those which you mention, but in what particular cases they
occur I do not know.

SIR C. WOOD: *Is not the present inequality of the tax mainly, if not
entirely, owing to the changes which have taken place in the value of land in
different parts of the country at the present moment, as compared with the
value at the time the tax was imposed?* Yes; it is owing to the fact that the
tax was imposed on a fixed assessment, which was not altered with the
subsequent increase in the value of the land.

J. WILSON: *The inequality is precisely similar to the inequalities which
have arisen, and which will further arise in the commutation of tithes?* No
doubt it is.

J. HUME: *You have stated your opinion respecting taxing incomes. Have
you formed any opinion as to how far what may be called unproductive
capital, such as pictures, jewels, coins, or any other matters, which may
be of great value but produce no income, should be subject to a fixed
taxation?* Though I have not very much considered the subject, it seems to
me that there is no reason why expenditure on durable articles should be
taxed in preference to expenditure on articles of daily consumption. On
the contrary, I should say that it is more desirable to encourage people to
expend money on things which last, and which will be of benefit to future
generations, than to expend it on articles which are consumed by the person
himself, and from which no other person derives any benefit. Buildings,
paintings, sculptures, and other matters of that kind, have an indefinite
duration, and money so expended gives pleasure to others as well as to
the individual concerned; and it appears to me that such expenditure ought
rather to be encouraged than to be subjected to any peculiar tax.

*Do we understand you to say that capital invested in such articles ought
to be altogether without taxation, or more lightly taxed than any other
capital?* I conceive that the tax should in all cases be levied on income, and
not on the capital from which the income proceeds; property which does
not yield an income being exempt. The income expended in the purchase
of those articles will have paid its share of the taxation when it was received.

In fact, the tax should be on income and not on property? Certainly.

Are you able to state upon what amount of capital the income tax in this country has been assessed? I have read various estimates of the amount, but, as I was not aware that I should be questioned on the subject, I am not able to say anything about it. One thing, however, has always struck me in looking at the estimates, viz., the very small amount of capital which pays income tax under Schedule (D.). This seems to me a strong proof of the evasion of the tax. In a country like this, where trade is carried on to so large an extent, it is difficult to believe that there is not a much larger amount of income derived from professions and trades than the amount shown under that schedule.

You are aware that the amount, according to the Parliamentary papers before us, upon which the tax is assessed, is 193,000,000l.,[*] *including all the schedules. Do you consider that a small amount?* No; I was speaking of the proportion which the income assessed under Schedule (D.) bears to the other schedules, and which I presume to be much less than the true proportion of those incomes in this country.

The tax is assessed under Schedule (D.) upon the amount of 58,000,000l. out of 193,000,000l.; and your opinion is that that is a small proportion? Yes; I have no particular knowledge upon the subject, but I think it must appear to any one to be a small proportion.

In speaking of the fairness of this tax, do you not consider that if the Government would make the income tax and the property tax more equitable and just, that would remove many of the objections that now exist to that tax being made a permanent tax? Undoubtedly it would remove a large class of objections.

In speaking of the present system as being palpably unjust, are you able to state what particular parts strike you, besides those that you have mentioned, with regard to permanent and variable incomes? I believe I have mentioned all the points which I consider decidedly unjust in the present income tax.

Those objections you mentioned in the first part of the evidence which you gave.[†] *If those objections were removed in the way you suggest, you think that the tax would be more equitable to the payer, and would be collected with less dissatisfaction?* It would certainly be much more equitable, but whether it would be collected with less dissatisfaction I am not sure; especially as a number of those who are of the same opinion with me, that the tax at present presses unjustly on temporary and professional incomes, carry that opinion much further than I do, and contend for a much greater distinction in favour of temporary incomes than I advocate. There would probably remain a considerable amount of dissatisfaction, in whatever way the tax might be regulated.

[*See, e.g., "Appendix No. 10," *Parliamentary Papers*, 1852, IX, p. 964 n.]
[†See pp. 465 ff. above.]

You were asked a question respecting the tax on houses. Do you consider the tax at present levied on houses to be fair, on the principle you have advocated of each class being called upon to make an equal sacrifice towards the support of the State? I conceive that the house tax justly assessed is a very fair tax. No tax is exactly fair in all cases; but what a person spends in house rent is generally a fair criterion of what he can afford to spend altogether. But in order to make it just, it appears to me that a different rule from the present should be adopted with reference to houses not let, but retained in the hands of the proprietor, including some of the largest and most valuable houses in the country. Those houses are considerably under-taxed when they are taxed, as they are under the present house tax, on the rent which they might be supposed to let for, because that would bear no proportion to what they cost to the proprietor. I am not aware what may be the practical difficulties in making a fair assessment of such houses, but I imagine that they could not be great.

In reference to the equal sacrifice which every individual ought to be called upon to make for the support of the State, take the houses in Hanover-square and the houses in Hoxton-square; in the one case they may average 150l. a year, and in the other they may average 25l. a year. Do you consider that the parties occupying those houses pay an equal rent in proportion to their several incomes? Of course there can be no exact correspondence, but I think there would be a nearer correspondence than in most of the other modes that could be adopted of taxing expenditure.

Supposing house rent in St. George's parish to be on the average 150l., and that no person could occupy any house there with an income of less than 1,500l., paying therefore one-tenth of the income in house rent, are you not aware that persons occupying houses in the surrounding districts pay 20l. or 25l. a year rent for those houses, which is equal to paying one-seventh or one-eighth of their incomes instead of one-tenth; and would it not be unjust in your view to tax both parties equally? I should conceive that persons generally expend in house rent something bearing a more equal proportion to their general means of expenditure than almost any other criterion that can be selected.

Are you not aware that many persons living on from 150l. to 200l. a year live in houses of 20l. and 25l. a year, and is not that, generally speaking, in this metropolis a much larger proportion of rent to income than rich men pay? But rich men have very often more than one house, which makes a sort of equivalent.

You consider that the liability of the rich man elsewhere to the same tax, may be regarded as an equivalent? Yes.

Have you expressed any opinion as to how far the house tax should be continued, and whether any exemption should be made, as at present, of houses under 20l.? I have not particularly considered whether in the present state of our general taxation, I would make any exemption of low-rented houses.

In offering the opinion which you have offered, as to the principles of an income tax, do you consider it necessary, according to your principle of an equal sacrifice by all classes for the support of the State, that the whole question of indirect as well as of direct taxation should be considered by Parliament? I certainly think that the justice of any one tax can only be estimated as part of the general financial system of the country; because that which might be unjust if it were the only tax, might be a just compensation for other inequalities in the general taxes.

Seeing that the taxes of this country have been from time to time levied according to particular emergencies, do you consider that before a tax, such as the income or property tax as now levied, ought to be made permanent, the whole system of our indirect and direct taxation, as well as the facility of collection, and the mode of collection, and other matters, ought to be considered? Decidedly.

You have expressed the opinion very decidedly that it is the duty of the Government to act upon the principle of requiring an equal sacrifice from all parties? Yes.

In fact, the Government cannot, in your opinion, do justice to its subjects paying taxes, without having before it the other taxes, in addition to the income tax, as bearing upon each class of the community? Without that they cannot, in my opinion, form any rational opinion of the fairness of any particular tax.

It is on that principle that, in the early part of your evidence,[*] *when you were asked whether an income tax was a fair tax upon particular classes, you said that you could not offer an opinion unless you considered all the other taxes and burdens which each class had to pay?* I said, that any opinion which I should express would be dependent upon what other taxes are retained, and that if you retain the indirect taxes which bear more heavily upon the smaller incomes than upon the larger ones, it would be just to exempt those smaller incomes from the income tax, although it would not be just under other circumstances.

The opinion you have expressed is, that the tax should upon the net income, allowance being made in each class for the necessary deduction in producing that income? Certainly.

You think that that would be better than making it a tax on property, instead of making it a tax on income? A tax on property, as distinguished from a tax on income, I should say, is only just under certain circumstances. It seems to me not just or politic to make a distinction between property saved from income obtained by personal exertions, and that which is spent

[*See pp. 473–5 above.]

as income, and not converted into property; that it is not just, in fact, to tax persons on property saved from their personal exertions, which would remain untaxed if they expended it on their own indulgences. But I think it is just to make a distinction between property acquired by exertion and that which is inherited, and I would make that distinction very broadly by imposing a tax on inheritance and bequest.

You would draw a distinction between savings handed down by a person's ancestor and savings by a person living? Yes, and especially if the savings were of a great amount. The principle of graduation I do not think is just as applied to incomes derived from personal exertions, or to the savings from incomes derived from personal exertions; but I do not think that the same objection holds good to the principle of graduation when applied to inherited property.

Ought not the principle of taxation to be the same, whether the property is large or small, agreeably to your former evidence, or would you draw the line, and say that the tax should be graduated in the case of large property, and not of small? In the income tax you cannot make any distinction, and I would not attempt to make it; but that degree of distinction which I think ought in justice to be made between inherited property, and property acquired by personal exertions, may be made by means of a tax on succession.

Would you make any distinction whether it was real or personal property? No, I would not make any distinction; whatever might be the kind of property transmitted by succession, I would tax it all; but I should be inclined to make a distinction by imposing higher rates on larger than on smaller inheritances.

Why would you make that distinction? On the principle that it is much more important to spare small inheritances than large ones. There are not by any means the same reasons against peculiar taxation on property acquired by gift or bequest, that there are in reference to property which people earn by their own exertions. It is unjust to tax a person because, by his own savings, he acquires a large fortune, and to tax him in a larger proportion than if he had squandered more and saved less; but there is no injustice in taxing persons who have not acquired what they have by their own exertions, but have had it bestowed them in free gift; and there are no reasons of justice or policy against taxing enormously large inheritances more highly than smaller inheritances.

SIR C. WOOD: *You would impose in point of fact a graduated succession tax as a legacy duty?* I would do so to the utmost extent to which the means could be found for imposing it without its being frustrated. The larger the sum demanded by the tax, the more would people try to evade it; but that is the only limitation I would apply to the principle.

J. HUME: *Having expressed a decided opinion that a graduated income tax on the man who earned that income is unjust, you say that a graduated tax on property acquired by succession would not be equally injust?* A graduated legacy duty would not be unjust in my opinion.

In that case do you consider that properties, though not likely to be productive of profit, such as pictures, cabinets, and other valuable matters, ought to be subject to legacy duty? Certainly.

Your opinion is, that all property exempted from the present legacy tax ought in that way to be brought in? All property which could be sold for money should pay legacy duty in proportion to its present value.

J. HENLEY: *I understood you to say that you would not tax a man, and that you do not think he ought to be taxed for capital that he saved?* I have expressed the opinion that, if possible, savings for investment should be exempted from income tax, and that the tax should only be levied on the proceeds of the investment when made; but that is not the particular point in question now.

But with reference to the point now in question, do I understand you rightly, that you would not tax a man during his lifetime upon the amount of his savings? I have said that in assessing an income tax it would be just to exempt savings altogether. But a graduated property tax, in so far as it bears on property acquired by a man's own exertions, does the extreme contrary; it imposes an extra tax on savings. If a person is taxed a fifth of his income because he has increased that income by saving, while he would have been taxed only a tenth if he had not saved, it seems to me that the extra tenth so imposed upon him is a penalty on saving.

You would not tax a man upon his savings? Strict justice would require that he should not be taxed at all on his savings: but the plan under consideration now, namely, a graduated property tax, does much more than tax his savings: it lays a heavier tax on what he saves than on what he spends.

Will you be good enough to answer the question, whether you would tax a man at all upon that property which he saves out of his own exertions? I have already said, that I do not think it would be practicable, though I do think it would be just that the portion of a person's income which he saved should be exempt from taxation. But even assuming that he ought to be taxed on that which he saves exactly as if he spent it, a graduated property tax not only taxes him upon what he saves, but makes his savings a reason for taxing him in a higher proportion.

I cannot collect from you whether I have rightly understood or not that your proposal is that the amount which a man saves from his industrial exertions should not be liable to taxation according to your view of justice?

According to my view of strict justice it ought not, but according to my view of expediency it probably ought.

Though you would not tax those savings during the lifetime of the man who saved them, you would, by means of the tax on succession, tax the man who succeeded him? Yes.

Consequently you would mulct the son for the virtues of the father? I do not conceive that it is mulcting the son. It is not mulcting him to prevent him from receiving what he has not exerted himself to earn. If you were to retain the property, and not allow him to receive it as a free gift from another, you would not do any injustice to him; if there were any injustice, it would be an injustice to the giver, by limiting him in his right of property.

You would deduct from the son by means of a succession tax, that amount which you did not levy from the father? Yes; I would make taxation bear upon that which people acquire without exertion and talent, rather than upon that which they acquire by exertion and talent.

Do you conceive it is an advantage for the State that a miser should put by money, or that he should spend what he has? It depends upon the mode of spending. There are ways of spending money which are more useful than saving it. But if people invest their money in some mode in which it is rendered productive, it is more useful than if they spent it upon themselves. If 1,000*l.* a year were expended even in alms, it would be soon spent, and the benefit of it would remain only so long as it lasted; but if the same sum were employed productively, by being lent to a manufacturer or an agriculturist, it would become a fund in perpetuity for maintaining labour; so that the miser, when he invests money, employs it usefully. But there are methods of expending this 1,000*l.* which would be still more useful than saving it.

When I used the term "miser's savings," I did not suppose that you would understand me as referring to a man laying out his money in manufactures, or any other useful employment that does not ordinarily come within the notion of savings, but is the employment of capital in industrial pursuits. Whatever any one saves, unless it is locked up, is, generally speaking, employed in industrial pursuits. If he buys securities, the person who has sold those securities lends the money to some one else for productive employment; in fact, all, or almost all savings, go into productive employment and become a permanent source of employment for labour.

Then we are to understand that you are of opinion, that a man who saves money and invests it in any security, does more benefit to the country than the man who spends that money? Yes, than the man who spends that money on his own enjoyments. But there are many ways of spending the money which are still more beneficial to the public. If, for example, he endowed a school, with proper precautions for its being useful, I think the money would be still more usefully employed than by being saved and employed productively.

To what degree would you carry that proposition? To this degree: if the money is spent on the man's personal indulgences, the most that it can do, even on the most favourable supposition, is to support those who derive employment from it, while it lasts; whereas, if it is invested and employed productively, it reproduces itself, and becomes a means of supporting a number of persons in perpetual succession.

Do you think that the consideration of the natural benefit derived from such investment requires that it should go to a quarter, or half, or three-fourths, or to what proportion of a man's income? I do not consider it a duty to save for those purposes; all I would say is that, ordinarily speaking, a person does a work of public utility who saves money to employ it productively.

To increase the capital of the country? Yes.

You have expressed an opinion with regard to the taxation of money which is saved which is acquired by a man's own industrial pursuits; but with regard to the capital which a man inherits, you propose that that should be taxed upon the succession; do you apply the same principle to the further taxation upon that after it has been so taxed upon succession; do you put it in the same category as capital saved by industrial exertions? I certainly think it is the income of capital, and not the capital itself that should be taxed. I do not clearly understand what principle you speak of when you ask whether I would apply the same principle to inherited capital.

I have understood you to say, that in the case where a man saves out of his industrial occupation, you would not subject it to taxation till the succession? I would not tax the capital, but I would tax the income which he derives from the capital.

In both cases? Yes.

Then we misunderstand you; you would not impose a tax on realized saved capital? All I said was, that if it were possible, it would be just to exempt from taxation that portion of income which a man saves; and if he saved it, and invested it, and derived an income from it, I would tax that income, except again such portion as he saved. And I would apply that same principle to inherited capital; that is, having taxed it on the inheritance when it came into the possession of the inheritor, I would afterwards tax only such part of the income as the possessor did not save.

Whatever principle you applied to savings of a man from his industrial earnings, you would apply to the savings of a man from inherited property; in the same proportion as you taxed the one you would tax the other? Yes; savings from whatever source derived.

T. VESEY: *Would you capitalize income derived from land and tax that capital in the case of inheritance?* In the case of land, in the same way as with any other saleable property, whatever tax is levied I would levy on the saleable value; the mode of estimating different kinds of property might be different, but what it would sell for I would tax.

With regard to inherited property, you would tax all that property at the marketable value? Yes.

SIR C. WOOD: *Did I rightly understand you in the former part of your evidence to say, "That you did not think that the claim to taxation on the part of the State was owing only to the protection which it afforded"?*[*] I do not think that the proper test by which to determine the proportional amount of taxation to be paid by different persons. It seems to me to have nothing definite in it. It is not possible to say that one person derives more benefit than another from the protection of the Government; it is necessary for all.

Did I understand you to say that the claim of the State to support by means of taxation was not in return for the protection afforded by the State to the different classes? It is in return for good government, which includes that and much beyond it.

What do you include beyond the protection of person and property which the State gives to parties? In answering that question it would be necessary to enter into a large consideration of what the Government can do for the benefit of those subject to it, and that is a very wide question, on which people may differ.

Will you state what, in your opinion, that includes? I should say that it includes the improvement and benefit of the community in all ways in which those objects can be promoted by legislation.

Will you state any instances so as to make clear what you mean? For example, the establishment of schools and universities; that cannot be called the protection of person or property; it is not in all cases a thing which I think the Government should do; but in many cases it is. It seems to me a matter of judicious discrimination in each case, what the Government can do for the benefit of the community. Whatever it can do usefully, which will be different in different circumstances, it ought to do.

E. HORSMAN: *With reference to what you said about Schedule (D.), you seemed to think that the returns under Schedule (D.) were very much less than they ought to be?* I have no very good means of judging of that, but they do seem to me very much less than I should have expected them to be.

You followed that up by saying, that most probably there were very great evasions under the schedule? Yes; and that appears to be a very great objection, and the only great objection that cannot be got rid of, to an income tax. It seems impossible, without a degree of inquisitorialness which

[*See pp. 471–2 ff. above.]

no free community will submit to, to dispense with relying mainly upon the returns made by individuals; and those returns, even in the most honourable community which has ever yet existed, could not be implicitly relied upon.

That is the result of secrecy in making the returns? No doubt if there were not secrecy there would be a greater check, but the check would not be complete even then.

It is the secrecy which is observed which gives the facility to evasion? Yes.

Therefore the correctness of the return depends, to a great extent, upon the man's own conscience? Yes.

It becomes a tax on conscience rather than on income? Yes, and that appears to me to be a very great objection to the income tax in any case. It seems the only objection which it is impossible to get rid of. Whether it is such an objection as to render the income tax inadvisable in a country which has to raise by taxation so large a sum as this country has to raise, I should not venture to give an opinion upon. There are many worse taxes than the income tax, but there are many better.

But would you say that the income tax was the fairest of all taxes, provided you could carry it out justly? I should say that the house tax was a much fairer tax than the income tax, because the house tax makes its own allowances, which must be made artificially in the case of the income tax. The house tax, being proportioned to an item of expenditure which approximates to a correct measure of the general scale of a person's expenses, has the advantage that what he saves is spontaneously and naturally excluded, and you are not obliged to exclude it by special regulations.

In the case of a man with 1,000l. a year, the proportion of expenditure which his house costs him is very much larger than in the case of a man with an income of 50,000l. a year? That would be the case; but then a person with 50,000l. a year has usually several houses; and if you include the whole sum which his houses cost him in taxation, together with the grounds attached to them, and suppose an equitable assessment of the house tax, which does not exist at present, it would probably make up the difference.

Your view is, that the objection arising from the income tax is to be attributed to the secrecy? Not exactly that, because, in the first place, publicity, if there were publicity, would be an additional objection, and even if there were publicity it would not altogether check the evasion. It would do so to a certain extent; but if there were publicity the objection that people have to the inquisitorial nature of the tax would be necessarily increased.

J. L. RICARDO: *Do I understand you to say, that you hold the doctrine of direct taxation is the true principle of taxation?* Not in that unqualified manner, certainly.

Can you state what qualification you would place upon that doctrine? It seems to me that all direct taxation must necessarily recognise some limit; that is, you must leave a certain amount of income untaxed, on the supposition that that income is required for necessaries. Now it is quite possible, when a liberal allowance is made for necessaries, that some part of it may be applied to indulgences instead of necessaries. I would not restrict the allowance to that which was just sufficient to prevent starvation. If, for instance, you began to impose the tax at 50*l.*, which you might suppose, on a liberal allowance, to be the sum required for necessaries, it is quite possible that a portion of that might be expended on indulgences, and not used for the purpose for which the exemption was intended, and in that case I think it is just that those indulgences should be taxed.

I understand you that your proposition was that there should be a certain limit calculated upon the amount required to procure the necessaries of life; and that with that exception you would consider that direct taxation was the proper mode of raising the revenue of the country? I am not aware that I gave any general opinion that direct taxation was the proper mode of raising the whole of our large revenue.

Do you consider it the fairest and most equitable mode? I should hardly say that; for a house or income tax, or any other tax, however imposed, has inequalities which are inevitable; and since there are inequalities in all taxes, it seems to me desirable to have several different modes of taxation, in order that the inequalities of taxation may not all fall in the same place.

Your proposal was, that the direct taxation should not bear on the poorer classes? Yes, because the articles which are taxed by indirect taxation are consumed in larger proportions by the poorer classes than by the richer classes.

Would you hold the doctrine that all direct taxation should be coupled with a graduated scale? I should say not. I would have no graduated scale on any kind of direct taxes, except taxes on succession. It seems to me that the just claims to graduation are sufficiently satisfied by taxing only the surplus above the minimum allowance to cover necessaries. No doubt, supposing 150*l.* to be the minimum allowance, those who have an income of 160*l.*, if they are taxed on the whole of that, have an injustice to complain of; but if they were taxed only on 10*l.* they would have nothing to complain of.

Did I not understand you, a short time ago, to state that you consider that the property tax should be a graduated tax? I was speaking of taxes on succession.

You made a distinction, if I understood you rightly, between capital inherited and capital realized from personal exertions? Yes.

It is only on capital inherited that you consider that there should be a graduated scale of taxation? Yes; and for this reason, that if there is a graduated scale of taxation on capital acquired by saving, people are taxed more heavily for saving than they are for squandering.

Under the present system the capital realized by personal exertions is taxed, not merely upon the interest it produces but upon the capital itself, before it is actually put aside? Yes; and that, as I have already said, if you can prevent it, appears to me not just.

J. HUME: *Have you any other observations to make?* I do not remember anything further.

THE BANK ACTS

1857

EDITOR'S NOTE

Parliamentary Papers, 1857 (Session 2), X.i., 189–218. Not republished. Original heading: "John Stuart Mill, Esq., called in; and Examined." Running heads: "Minutes of Evidence taken before the/Select Committee on the Bank Acts." The evidence was taken on 12 June, 1857, with Sir George Cornwall Lewis, the Chancellor of the Exchequer, in the Chair, and the following members of the Committee present: Edward Ball, Sir Francis Baring, Peter Blackburn, Benjamin Disraeli, John Fergus, George G. Glyn, Sir James Graham, Thomson Hankey, Robert Hildyard, Hope Johnstone, Christopher Puller, Martin Smith, Richard Spooner, William Tite, John Vance, Thomas Weguelin, James Wilson, and Sir Charles Wood. Not mentioned in JSM's bibliography or *Autobiography*. No copy in Somerville College.

JSM's examination includes questions 2010 to 2318 of the evidence before the Committee.

The Bank Acts

SIR G. C. LEWIS: *Have you had occasion to consider the provisions and the operation of the Bank Act of 1844?*[*] As much so as any person can do who has no practical acquaintance with commercial business, and knows only at second hand facts which are known at first hand by those concerned in business.

In the first place, what is your opinion as to the policy of imposing by law any restriction upon the Directors of the Bank of England with respect to the issue of notes? My opinion is that there should not be any restriction by law, except that of convertibility, which appears to me to be sufficient for all the purposes for which restriction is intended.

Are you aware of the nature of the limit which Mr. Tooke has proposed in his book[†] *with respect to the bullion reserve of the Bank?* Mr. Tooke, I believe, proposes what cannot possibly be imposed by law, namely, a limit which should consist in the Bank's retaining a much larger average reserve than it has hitherto done, an average reserve of 12,000,000*l*. Public opinion might enforce a restriction of that sort, but it is incapable in its terms of being enforced by law.

Does not he recommend that it should be made to depend upon an agreement with the Government, that they should have a discretion as to relaxing the limit, if they thought fit? I was not aware that he had recommended that there should be any positive minimum, but I know he recommends that the Bank should keep an average reserve of 12,000,000*l*., which of course would be kept for the purpose of being allowed partially to run out when necessary. Now, the difficulty would be, how to bind the Bank otherwise than by general considerations of policy.

If the Bank were in any way bound to keep an average amount of bullion, would not the effect be that if the reserve was below that average in certain times, it would be necessary that the Bank should keep more than the average at certain other times? Yes; there might be an honourable

[*7 & 8 Victoria, c.32.]
[†Tooke, Thomas. *On the Bank Charter Act of 1844.* London: Longman, Brown, Green, and Longmans, 1856, p. 105.]

understanding to that effect, but I do not see how it could be anything more.

Would there be any advantage in a rule, which required the Bank to keep more than was necessary at certain times, because it had kept less than was desirable at other times? It is desirable, I think, that the Bank should keep a larger reserve than the average at some times, as well as a smaller at others, in order to prevent the Bank, at times when there is a tendency to over-speculation, from encouraging that tendency by making loans at a much lower rate of interest than the average rate. I am not prepared to say that I would impose on the Bank any compulsory rule in respect to the amount of its reserve. It might probably be better done by fixing a rate of interest below which they should not be permitted to lend. I am not giving an opinion in favour of any restriction, but if any were necessary, I think that would be the best restriction to impose.

At present, the Bank of England are not required by law to keep any fixed amount of bullion? The Bank is not required to keep any fixed amount of bullion. The only restriction is, that the Bank cannot issue notes beyond a certain amount, except on bullion; therefore, under the Act, for all the notes which they issue beyond that amount, they have a corresponding quantity of bullion in their coffers.

Under the present law, if the circulation of the Bank did not exceed 14,500,000l., it would not be required to keep a single sovereign in its reserve? No.

Therefore, a limit such as Mr. Tooke proposes, would tie up the hands of the Bank much more than the limit fixed by the existing law, would it not? I do not know whether it would tie them up more or less, but it would tie them up more usefully, and less hurtfully.

Then your opinion is, that if a limit is to be fixed by law, it would be better to fix it on some such principle as that proposed by Mr. Tooke than on the principle embodied in the present Act? Decidedly.

Have you observed the operation of the present Act in such a manner as to enable you to form any opinion whether the mode of fixing the limit which the Act prescribes has worked well, or in a mischievous manner in practice? I think it has worked well in one particular case only; viz., in a certain stage of a period of over speculation and over trading. At all other times I think it has either had no effect at all, or a bad effect.

Do you believe that the effect of the present law has been to induce the Bank Directors to keep a larger reserve of bullion than they would otherwise have kept? To give any answer to that question which would be of use, it would be necessary to enter into particulars. It would be necessary first to distinguish between the two departments of the Bank, the issue and the banking department.

But taking the bullion of both departments as a whole, do you think that the Bank has kept a larger reserve of bullion since 1844 than it would have kept if the Act of that year had not passed? Taking both branches together, I would not undertake to say; but this I will undertake to say, that under the Act the Bank has kept a much less reserve of bullion than the Act makes necessary, because I think it can be shown that in order to prevent the Act from operating very perniciously in certain cases, it would be necessary that the banking department alone should keep as large a reserve as, but for the Act, need have been kept in both departments together.

Will you be so good as to cast your eye over that Table (Paper No. 19, Appendix),[*] and to say whether, comparing the greatest and the least of the average amounts of bullion in the 10 years before 1844 and in the years since 1844, it does not appear probable that the operation of the Act has been such as to induce the Bank to keep a larger bullion reserve than it would have kept if the Act had not been in existence? This Table leaves no doubt that they have kept a much larger reserve than they kept previously to 1844; but whether larger than they would have kept, in consequence of the increased knowledge of the subject which now exists, if the Act had never existed, I cannot say. I think the tendency of the opinion of competent persons of late years has been in favour of the necessity of keeping a much larger reserve than was formerly thought necessary; and the circumstances of trade have really required a larger amount of reserve, because the great increase in the magnitude of transactions, and particularly the unexampled drains of bullion which have occurred, have rendered it necessary to keep a larger reserve in order to meet those drains.

If the change in the practice of the Bank had taken place in consequence of a change of opinion on the part of the Bank Directors, in the exercise of their discretion, would it not have been likely that the change would have been gradual, whereas it appears from that Table that the change was sudden, and took place exactly in the year 1844? In the years 1844 and 1845 there was a great quantity of gold coming into this country, therefore there would naturally have been a much larger quantity of bullion in the Bank at that time than there was before; and after 1847 the change of opinion had begun, because the drain of that year was such as had never been known before.

Then your opinion is that, as respects the total amount of bullion found in the Bank, in both branches, its quantity has not been affected to any considerable amount by the operation of the Act of 1844? I do not give any opinion on that subject; I am not prepared to say either that it has or that it has not.

You expressed an opinion that the operation of the Act of 1844 had

[*Parliamentary Papers, 1857 (Sess. 2), X. ii, pp. 156–60.]

been detrimental in causing the Bank to keep an unnecessary large amount of bullion in the banking department? Not in causing them to do so. If it had really caused them to do so, I think the Act would not have been so mischievous as it has been. It is precisely because, to make their position safe under the Act, or to make the Act work well, it would have been necessary for them to keep a much larger reserve than they did, that I think the Act has worked mischievously. Those who framed the Act do not seem to have adverted to what may be called the double action of drains. They provided against drains, just as if drains acted upon the issue department only. Now every drain, as a general rule, is drawn from the deposits. Therefore, when the two departments are separated, the drain comes first on the deposits. Notes are drawn out of the deposits, and those notes are presented to the issue department to obtain bullion for exportation. The consequence is, that supposing there is a drain of 3,000,000*l.* only, the effect on the Bank previously to the Act would have been that of a drain of 3,000,000*l.*; but now, when the two departments are separated, and neither of them can in the most extreme case help the other, the effect on the Bank is the same as if there were a drain of 6,000,000*l.*, because the banking reserve is diminished 3,000,000*l.*, and the issue department has parted with 3,000,000*l.* of gold from its reserve also. Now, it appears to me that one convertible currency differs from another mainly in the degree in which it tends to produce frequent and violent revulsions of credit; and inasmuch as all the circumstances which lead to revulsions of credit, operate upon the banking department of the Bank of England before they can get to the issue department, the violence of the shock is almost always first felt by the amount of reserve available to meet the demands on the banking department. If, therefore, the Bank cannot help its banking department by sending notes or gold from its issue department, it must either keep in the banking department as great a reserve as it would otherwise be requisite to keep for both departments together; or if not, having a much smaller reserve available to meet the demands on the banking department, it must necessarily, the moment there is the smallest drain, contract its discounts and raise its rate of interest. It thus appears to me that the effect of the Act is, that whenever any drain, however small or temporary, commences, the Bank will be likely, with its present reserve in the banking department, at once to contract its discounts, or to sell securities, in a manner which, if the Act had not existed, it would only do in the case of a very considerable drain.

Are you of opinion that the separation of the two departments has an influence upon the Bank's rate of interest? A very great influence. I should think that it produces much more violent and frequent fluctuations in the rate of discount; and there is no doubt that the variations have been much more frequent, in point of fact, than they were before.

Do you hold that the Bank rate of discount determines the general rate of discount in the market? No; not that it determines it, but it is certainly a very important element in determining it, because the Bank is so large an establishment, and its loans form so large a portion of the total amount of loans.

C. PULLER: *Do you say that the variations have been in the Bank rate of discount, or in the general rate of discount?* In the Bank rate of discount.

SIR G. C. LEWIS: *Is it your opinion that the separation of the two departments, created by the Act of 1844, is prejudicial, as well as the fixing a limit upon the issues?* Yes; I think the separation of the two departments is the most prejudicial part of the whole. I think the fixing a limit to the issues is also prejudicial; but I may perhaps be permitted to explain what I said on this point in answer to a former question.[*] I do not think the effect prejudicial in all cases; I think it useful in one particular case; I think it is useful at a certain stage in the progress of a revulsion of credit which has been the effect of a previous over extension of it.

In what way do you think it operates well in those circumstances? In this way. One particular kind of commercial crisis, and perhaps the worst kind, is occasioned by previous over speculation and over trading, which is always accompanied by an undue extension of credit, and by a rise of prices of a speculative character, having no sufficient justification in the circumstances of the markets. Now when this is the case, there must necessarily come a revulsion, which is normally brought about by an increase of imports owing to the rise of prices, and by a diminution of exports. That produces a drain of bullion and a collapse of prices, and this collapse of prices is generally brought about by the necessity which the speculators are in of selling in order to fulfil their engagements. Now this speculative rise of prices, I apprehend, is usually attended by an increased quantity of bank notes. It does not follow that it is caused by it, because the speculative purchases generally take place on credit for a certain term; and even if they did not, the transactions between dealers are generally not liquidated by means of bank notes. However, there comes a time in this series of phenomena when the dealers begin to be pressed, when the rise of prices has stopped, but when the speculators do not yet despair of their rising again. At such a time there are generally great applications to bankers for loans, in order to enable the speculators to hold on; and I think the effect of the Act of 1844 is to prevent them from getting those loans to the extent to which they might do but for the Act. And I think that very often the speculative rise of prices is upheld, and has been upheld, as a matter of

[*See p. 502 above.]

history, by loans which the Bank of England and other banks have made to merchants and holders of goods, the effect of which has been to prevent them from being under the necessity of selling so soon as they otherwise must have done. The consequence of this is, that the fall of prices is retarded, that the drain of gold continues longer, and that therefore the reserve of the Bank comes nearer to being exhausted; and when the time comes that they are really alarmed about their reserve, they are obliged to pull up more suddenly, and to make a greater reduction of discounts or a larger sale of securities then they otherwise need do, and thereby produce a greater alarm, sometimes amounting to panic, and a greater destruction of credit in the country, and the whole thing is rendered more calamitous than it otherwise would be. In that case, I think, the provisions of the Act do good, because there is no doubt that before the Act existed, the Bank used often in such cases to make loans by the reissue of notes which had been returned to it in exchange for bullion. This appears to me to be the great advantage of the Act; but against it there are two things to be set. One is, I do not think that this mode of operation is so much required now as it perhaps was at one time, because the commercial public generally, and the Bank Directors, understand much better than they did the nature of a commercial crisis, and the extreme mischief which they do both to themselves and to the public by upholding over speculation, and I do not think that they at all need the provisions of the Act in order to induce them in that case to conduct themselves as the Act would make them. In the next place, I think that if in the first stage of this process the Act operates usefully, it operates exceedingly injuriously in the latter stage; that is to say, when the revulsion has actually come, and when, instead of there being an inflated state of credit, there has been an extraordinary destruction of credit, and there is nothing like the usual amount of credit that there is at other times. At such a time the Bank can hardly lend too much; it can hardly make advances to too great an extent, as long as it is to solvent firms, because its advances only supply the place of the ordinary and wholesome amount of credit, which is then in deficiency. But the Bank, under the operation of the Act, can only make those advances at such a time from their deposits. Now it is very true that the deposits are likely to be large at those times, because at those times people leave their money in deposit; they leave it within call, to be able to have it at any moment when they want it, and therefore the Bank deposits are larger than usual. But still this resource is not sufficient, as was proved in 1847, when the Bank Directors, after doing the very utmost which they could do from their deposits to relieve the distressed state of trade by advances to solvent firms, were obliged to go to the Government to ask for a suspension of the Act, and the Government were obliged to grant it.

Is it your opinion that the measures of the Bank, during the last two years with respect to high rate of discount and the duration of bills, have been more restrictive than was judicious? I think the Bank has acted on the principle which was laid down for them by great authorities at the time when the Act of 1844 was passed, viz., that in the management of their banking department they had nothing whatever to consider but their interest as a bank. I think they have taken that view of their position. They have thought, therefore, that they were not under the necessity of keeping a much larger reserve than ordinary banking principles required. I think they at first began, after the Act of 1844, to act entirely upon that principle; they took the word of Sir Robert Peel, the author of the Act, anything they did as mere bankers, in the management of their deposits, was no concern of the public, but only their own concern. I think that in 1847 that error was, to a great degree, corrected. I think that since that time the Bank have been quite aware, and the public have been aware, that that view of the theory of the Act of 1844 is not sustainable; and that an establishment like the Bank is not like other bankers, who are at liberty to think that their single transactions cannot affect the commercial world generally, and that they have only their own position to consider. The transactions of the Bank necessarily affect the whole transactions of the country, and it is incumbent upon them to do all that a bank can do to prevent or to mitigate a commercial crisis. This being the position of the Bank, and the Bank being much more aware of it since 1847 than they were before, they have not acted so entirely as before on the principle that they had nothing to consider but their own safety. Still, however, as bankers, they have not kept in the banking department the whole reserve necessary to meet a drain, and being obliged, as bankers, to consider the solvency of their banking department, they have been obliged to vary their rates of discount more violently and more frequently than they did before; which, I think, is owing to the Act.

Do not you believe that, although the law requires the accounts of the Bank to be kept in a certain form, and to be exhibited to the public as partly in the banking department and partly in the issue department, the Bank Directors who manage both look at them as a whole, and consider the bullion in both departments as one quantity? I think that if they do so, they commit a very great mistake. They have to consider, on the contrary, that each of their two reserves is now liable to all the demands to which the joint reserve was liable before. The reserve of the Bank can only be acted upon to any great extent by a drain of bullion. When this drain of bullion took place before the Act of 1844, they had a single reserve, and if that reserve was sufficient to meet the drain, it was enough; but now the drain acts doubly, first on the banking reserve, and afterwards on the reserve in the issue department. Therefore, it seems to me that, in order that there might not be more violent fluctuations of credit than before, it would be necessary that they should now have in each department as large a reserve as previously sufficed for both.

Then you believe that the Bank Directors administer the Bank as if the issue and the banking departments were not only legally but practically distinct? Certainly, I think they are practically distinct. I think the fact that under no circumstances can the issue department afford either notes or coin to the banking department, makes them as completely distinct as if they belonged to separate establishments; and it is undoubtedly the intention of the Act that they should be as distinct as if they belonged to separate establishments.

Are you of opinion that if the Act of 1844 had never passed, the Bank rates of discount would have been lower during the last two years than they have actually been? I do not know whether they would have been lower; I think they would have fluctuated less; I think they have been both lower and higher than they would have been but for the Act.

If you compare the rates of discount on the Continent during the last two years, do you not find that they bear a very close resemblance to the rates of discount in this country, and that whatever difference there is between them is in favour of this country, and not against it? The commercial world is so much one world now, that whatever acts upon one country acts upon another.

Then if we find that there is an uniform rate of discount in London and Amsterdam and Paris and Hamburgh, inasmuch as the Bank Act of 1844 is not in force on the Continent, does not that rather raise a presumption that the rate of discount in London is independent of that Act? It does not follow that the Act may not, by operating on so important a market for securities as the London market is, have influenced all the other markets also. In fact, it could not materially affect the English market without affecting in something like a corresponding degree all others, because securities of an equal degree of safety in one country cannot fall below their rate in others without attracting capital to buy them from other countries.

That answer assumes that the Bank of England has very great power over the rate of discount in this country? I do not think that in ordinary times, either the Act or the operations of the Bank have much influence on the rate of interest, but only that under the Act the Bank is obliged to follow the variations in the rate of interest much more closely than it otherwise would do. The occasions on which the operation of the Act seems to me to be decidedly mischievous, are those cases of drain which do not arise from previous over speculation; such as those arising from a great import of corn, or a greatly increased price of raw materials of manufacture, such as cotton, or great foreign remittances by the government, or exportations of capital.

You know that the Act of 1844 imposes a limit upon the issues of all country banks which existed in that year, founded upon an account taken of their circulation, and that it also prohibits the establishment of any new banks of issue in England. Do you approve of that regulation? I do not think it is of very much consequence whether there is one bank of issue or many in the country. It seems to me quite a minor question; but inasmuch as there have always been many, and I believe the local feeling is always in favour of having many, it probably is desirable that there should be.

The Act of 1844 seems to have contemplated the voluntary extinction of country banks of issue in England, does it not? Yes.

Hitherto the operation of the voluntary clause has been but limited; do you think it would be desirable to accelerate its operation by taking stronger measures for either suppressing or diminishing the issues of country notes in England? I see no reason for thinking so.

Does it appear to you that the law at present is in a satisfactory state with regard to country banks of issue in England? Not in a satisfactory state theoretically, certainly, because it is grounded on a principle which it does not carry fully out; but as I think the principle a wrong one, I am not desirous that it should be carried out.

Then you would be in favour of removing the present restriction upon country issues? I would remove it both from the Bank of England and from all other banks.

Does it appear to you desirable that the country banks in England should have a power of issue unlimited by law, and limited merely by the convertibility of the note, and that they should not be required to issue against either securities or bullion to any extent? As far as excess of issues is concerned, I think there is no reason for any restriction. There might be a reason in consequence of the probability of insolvency, which is not to be apprehended in the case of the Bank of England. There have been lately instances of such gross mismanagement and consequent insolvency of banks, that I cannot give a positive opinion against requiring special security to be given for the notes; but I am not inclined to think that it is necessary, now that there are no small notes. As long as there are no notes in England below 5*l.*, the probability is that the holders of 5*l.* notes can as well take care of themselves as the depositors, who have generally been the greatest sufferers by those mismanagements.

Do you think that there would be any advantage in the issue of any denomination of notes under 5l., in England? I think it is much better that there should be no notes below 5*l.*, because this retains a quantity of gold in the country which may be used to replenish the banking reserve in case of necessity, without waiting for the slower process of its importation. Besides, 1*l*. notes are liable to be used in the payment of wages, and a currency which is used in payment of wages is much more liable to produce evils from over issue, than any currency which is only issued to the mercantile public.

Then, on the whole, your opinion is in favour of maintaining the present law with respect to the denomination of bank notes in England? Yes.

What would you say with respect to the expediency of a single bank of issue, either for England or for the whole country? The principal advantage of it would be, that the profit of the issue might be to a great degree secured by the public. I do not think that as to the working of the currency, it would make any material difference whether it came from one issuer or more.

Is it your opinion that the profit to the public of a bank of issue would be considerable, or that there would be any profit at all, assuming that it was a bank of issue and nothing else? Supposing the wants of the country require 30,000,000*l*. of notes, and those were supplied by the public, the public would obtain a loan to that amount without interest; that is the extent of the advantage that the public would gain.

But then you would have to set against that advantage to the public the expense of the establishment and the expense of management? Yes.

Would not the nation be obliged to establish a great number of branch banks? Yes, certainly.

Is it your belief that the expenses of the central establishment in London, together with the expense of a large number of branches in the country, would not be greater than the profit derived from the issue of the paper? It is not so, I presume, in the case of the Bank of England, although that does not supply the whole country.

The Bank of England has a banking business besides its business of issue? Yes; but I presume that it derives profit from its business of issue, and that it would not be in a better position pecuniarily if it were not permitted to issue.

Is it not conceivable that the Bank of England may derive profit from the issue business and the banking business combined, when it might derive no profit from the issue business separate from the banking business? If an establishment which has the power of lending 30,000,000*l*., for which it pays nothing, cannot make that a source of profit, I cannot conceive how money-lending can, under any circumstances, yield a profit.

You are of opinion that the only benefit which the public would derive from having a single bank of issue in the hands of the Government would be the profit of the circulation, and nothing else? Nothing else.

As far as the management and control of the circulation itself is con-

cerned, you think that would be as well left in private hands? Yes. I would add, that if it were thought that there should be only one bank of issue, I do not think that bank of issue should be the Government itself. I think the currency should not be provided by the Government, but by such an establishment as the Bank of England, the public making a bargain with it for so much of the profit as they thought they could reasonably require.

With regard to Scotland and Ireland, you are aware that in Ireland and Scotland the same law prevails as in England with respect to the country banks, but that the banks can issue against bullion in excess of their fixed circulation? In that respect they are in the position of the Bank of England, not in the position of the English country banks.

Only that their limit is fixed upon their average circulation, and they are not required to hold securities against the fixed credit circulation? I have not paid any particular attention to the Scotch and Irish Acts,[*] and I would rather not give any opinion upon them.

Do you approve of the action of the Acts with regard to Ireland and Scotland? I apprehend that the Acts with respect to Ireland and Scotland have for their object and effect to extend to those countries, making allowance for local circumstances, the provisions of the Act of 1844; and as I think that the Act of 1844 is more hurtful than useful with respect to England, I think that the Scotch and Irish Acts are so too.

In Ireland and Scotland there are notes under 5l. circulated; do you approve of allowing 1l. as capital to continue to be circulated in Scotland and Ireland? I believe that in Scotland it is perfectly safe; that there are no failures of banks there, or very rarely, and that if they did happen the notes would probably be taken up by other banks. Therefore I do not believe that there is there that danger of insolvency which constituted so great an evil in the case of the poor holders of 1l. notes when they existed in England. And that being the case I think it very likely that 1l. notes may do more good than harm in Scotland. In Ireland probably it is the reverse, because there are bank failures, sometimes of a very bad kind.

J. VANCE: *Are you not aware that the joint stock banks in Ireland possess a very large capital, and that they are in a high state of solvency at the present moment?* Yes, I believe so; and I believe the same is the case with the joint stock banks in England. At the same time we know that there have been, both in England and in Ireland, very bad cases of insolvency of joint stock banks, and it is to provide against those exceptional cases that it seems to me necessary to have some restriction on 1l. notes.

Do you think you are justified in saying that the Scotch banks are in a higher position of solvency than the Irish ones at the present moment? I do not mean to say that the Irish banks are generally less solvent; but it is the

[*8 & 9 Victoria, cc. 38 and 37.]

fact that nobody has lost anything for a long while, I believe for a century almost, by the non-payment of notes of Scotch banks. I believe that cannot be said to the same degree of the Irish.

What failures do you refer to in Ireland? The Tipperary Bank is the most notorious instance.

Are you aware that the Tipperary Bank was not a bank of issue? I was not aware of that; but I do not know that if it had been a bank of issue, it would have been on that account the less liable to fail, or the less liable to be mismanaged.

Have you a recollection of what bank failure has taken place in Ireland previously to that of the Tipperary Bank? I have no particular recollection on the subject. I know so little about Irish banks, that I would rather not be asked for an opinion upon them. What I said was merely that I might not be supposed to speak of the Irish banks as I did of the Scotch, and not from a wish to say anything against the Irish banks; which I have no ground for doing.

SIR F. BARING: *You stated that you objected to an issue of 1l. notes, because it was more liable to over-issue. What do you mean by over-issue?* In order to explain that, it is necessary to go into some particulars. I think that as long as the Bank confines its advances to merchants and general dealers, to what is called the mercantile public, people who deal in goods but who do not pay wages, its issues never originate a rise of prices, because a dealer only uses notes for the purpose of fulfilling previous engagements. Dealers never make purchases in the first instance with Bank notes; the dealers to whom Bank notes are paid usually either send them into deposit, or pay them to persons who send them into deposit. But the operation is different when advances are made to manufacturers or others who pay wages. When that is the case, the notes do or may get into the hands of labourers and others who expend them for consumption, and in that case the notes do constitute in themselves a demand for commodities, and may for some time tend to promote a rise of prices; and when they do so, and there is not any other cause for that rise of prices than the issue of notes, that constitutes over-issue, that is to say, an issue that will be followed by a revulsion.

In that case the Bank would have been the moving power to raise the prices? The notes would have been the moving power to raise the prices: but that I do not think is ever the case now.

W. TITE: *I understand you to say that you attribute to the operation of the present Bank Act, the sudden and rather violent fluctuations in the rate of interest which have occurred of late years?* I think the natural effect of the Act is to necessitate more frequent and more violent fluctuations in the rate of interest than would otherwise take place.

That in your opinion is due to the division into the issue department and the banking department, and the necessity involved of keeping up two reserves? Yes; there is a double action of drains, which, instead of acting upon the joint reserve, act to their full extent, first upon the one, and then through that upon the other.

Is it your opinion that the Bank should in any manner be limited to a minimum rate of discount according to the practice that existed before the passing of the Act of 1844? I think that since the Act of 1844, the Bank have lowered their rate of interest very unnecessarily and undesirably, at times when they might have foreseen that the low rate of interest would not last, that the then replenished state of their reserve which induced them to lower the rate of discount was only temporary, and that there would soon be a demand on their reserve again. I think the Bank has several times made that mistake. Whether it would be desirable to cut them off from ever lowering their rate of discount below a certain rate, is a question upon which I have not made up my mind.

You are not able to say whether or not they should be fettered in the discretion which an ordinary banker exercises of doing as he pleases with his own money and taking any rate of interest that he thinks fit? I think that the Bank, as being a great public body, exercising public functions, cannot in all respects be properly guided only by its banking interest. Whether it should be subject to restriction by law in this particular I do not know; but I think that it cannot rightly be governed by its pecuniary interest, in circumstances in which a private banker might reasonably be so; that the Directors ought not always, when the market rate of interest is temporarily low, to conform their rate to it, but rather to allow their reserve to accumulate at those times, in order not to minister to a spirit of speculation, which a low rate of interest does.

I understood you to say, that all that you would seek with regard to a change in the law, under which the management of the Bank is now conducted is, that there should be a sort of understanding that the capital of the Bank should range from 10,000,000l. to 12,000,000l. on the average? Something like that.

What would be the enactment you would propose? There is a distinction to be drawn between two kinds of drains. One may be called an unlimited, another a limited drain. A drain occasioned by a revulsion from a state of over-speculation is in its nature unlimited; unless there be something done to stop it, it will go on. If the high state of prices, occasioned by an inflated state of credit, continues, the drain will continue; and it can only be stopped when the high prices have ceased by a diminution of the currency, or a diminution of loans. But the case is different with all other drains; for instance, a drain occasioned by payments for the import of corn, or by foreign payments by Government, or the exportation of capital for foreign investment. That drain stops of itself as soon as the purpose is effected which caused it; and, therefore, it seems to me that the reserve should always be such as may be equal to the probable demand on account of a drain of this sort; and that in the case of such a drain, bullion may be allowed to run out from the reserve, without any violent action on credit to stop it. For that reason it seems to me necessary now, when drains to a large amount are liable to arise from causes of that sort, that the Bank should keep habitually a much larger reserve than it used to keep, in order to meet a drain.

That seems to involve a sort of foreknowledge on the part of the Bank as to how long a drain is to continue; but, with knowing that, surely they must exercise some power of controlling it? Of course they have that power; and they may in any case be obliged at last to contract their discounts; but if they have a large reserve, and if, from the circumstances of the times, and from the knowledge which they have, and which the public have, of the causes producing the drain, they think that the drain that is existing is of the one kind, and not of the other, they will act accordingly. If they find that the drain exceeds their provision for it, notwithstanding their having kept so large a reserve, then they must take measures to replenish their reserve; but the effect of this would only be, that they would be then obliged to bring on the public in a smaller degree, and at a later period, inconveniences which, under the present system, they must bring on at once, and much more frequently, and in a much greater degree.

I understand you to say that you would recommend the Committee to return to the provisions of the law as it was before 1844, only with some understanding as to the amount of the reserve that the Bank should keep? That would be my idea. Although, as I have already stated, I think in the commencement of a revulsion from a state of over speculation the Act at times has operated beneficially, yet I am of opinion that with the experience that we now have, and the principles on which the Bank of England is likely to continue to act, even if the Act were repealed the Directors would probably do spontaneously, in that particular case, what the Act now compels them to do; that is, they would not reissue notes sent back to them in exchange for bullion.

With regard to relieving their reserve by the sale of securities, do you think that much could be done in that way in the event of a drain? It could be done. The effect of it upon the money market would be the same as that of a refusal to make advances, because the money paid by the buyer of those securities would be so much withdrawn from the loan market.

You spoke of an issue of 30,000,000l. of money as being in the nature of a loan. Supposing it were issued by one body, and that body the Bank of England, is it possible to state approximately what the profit of the loan might be; would it be 2 or 2½ per cent., or any other appreciable per-centage? The value of the difference between getting a loan for nothing and having to pay interest upon it, of course depends upon what the rate of interest at the time might be, and it must be different in every different condition of the money market. I think it is fair to take it at the lowest rate; it may perhaps be taken at 3 per cent.

Then the first element of the profit would be the market rate of interest of such a loan, against which would have to be set the expense of the establishment and the machinery necessary for the issuing of the money? Yes, the expense of management.

Three per cent. on 30,000,000l. would be 900,000l.? Yes, which is not a very great object to a great country.

Do you imagine that although these principles are tolerably accurate theoretically, in point of fact there are no disturbing elements in their consideration? There are disturbing elements in almost every question relating to commerce, but what they are in this case I do not exactly see.

In point of fact you do not know what profit the Bank do make out of the issue which is placed in their hands? No.

Does your position in the East India House give you any opportunities of knowing the amount of the exportation of silver which has been going on for some years past to India and China? I am not acquainted with the details; but I have seen a calculation which makes out that for a certain number of years the average export of silver to India has been 6,000,000l. sterling.

That amount of drain is in excess of commodities brought back? Yes; it is a payment for commodities imported from England, and it is probably in a great measure the result of the great gold discoveries; the gold discoveries having raised the price of silver in many countries in Europe beyond the mint valuation as compared with gold; and having thus made gold the standard in those countries, and the medium of payments. For instance, in France gold was always at a premium before the gold discoveries, and therefore silver was practically the standard; but since the gold discoveries, gold has practically been the standard, because it has been cheaper to pay debts in gold. Therefore the gold coinage has immensely increased in France, and has taken the place of silver; which silver having retained its bullion value in reference to commodities, became an advantageous remittance.

What is your notion as to the cause of what is called popularly the drain of silver which has been going on to the extent of 6,000,000l. annually to India? The cause is the great increase of production and exportation from the East, and the habit of the people of India of hoarding. A large portion of whatever increase of wealth comes into the hands of a native of India, he usually either hoards, or if he expends it, he expends it in ornaments, which are generally silver ornaments, and hoards it in that shape. In fact, the reserved funds, similar to those which a person in this country invests at interest, are generally by a native of the East converted into ornaments; and therefore, any increase of money payments, from any other country to India, usually, to a very great extent, takes the form of ornaments; the remainder being mostly hoarded as treasure. Now, as the currency of India is mainly silver, at present they hoard in silver chiefly; but, no doubt, if they had a gold currency, they would be as ready to hoard in gold, and there would still be a considerable swallowing up either of gold or silver in the East, just as there always has been since the beginning of history. The general tendency from the earliest period was a flow of the precious metals towards the East, not from it, on account of this practice of hoarding.

Then this practice of hoarding is no new practice? It is no new practice, but it is a very general practice. Everybody who has the means of hoarding does hoard, and whenever they get more they hoard more.

M. T. SMITH: *Has not the price of the great articles of production in the east risen very much throughout Europe, more particularly sugar, indigo, silk, and spices?* Latterly.

Is not it natural that an increased quantity should be sent to this country on account of the increased price in these markets? Yes, but I think the drain to the East had commenced before this rise of price happened in either sugar or silk.

But not to the extent to which it exists at this moment; not to the extent of 7,000,000l. or 8,000,000l.; but of course the best that goes is from England? It is natural to suppose that the rise of prices must cause a much greater debt to be due to India.

Is not it equally true that the same cause, namely, an increased production of gold in Australia and California, which has caused a rise in the prices of Asiatic goods in this country, has also caused a rise in the price of manufactured goods in this country, and has thereby prevented the same quantity of manufactured goods going back to India in return for the productions imported from India as used to go before? It is so unsettled a point yet, to what extent general prices in this country have been raised by the gold discoveries, that I should hardly feel able to answer that question.

Should you be disposed to attribute the increased efflux of silver from this country to India to the increased production in India, stimulated by the higher prices in this country? Yes, I should think so, or at all events to the increased production, and the greatly increased importation from India; which naturally produces a great balance of trade in favour of India, unless there were an equal demand there for English goods, which there is not.

Is not that, in a great degree, on account of the prices being higher than they used to be? Opinions differ on that subject.

SIR C. WOOD: *Do you conceive that there is a much greater quantity of goods coming from India either to England direct, or to other countries through England, than the quantity which is sent from this country to India; so that there is a balance of trade against this country, which is sent in bullion?* Yes; that is the normal state of affairs between this country and India.

Do you conceive that that has been increased of late years? Yes, I think it has.

Then there has been of late years a necessity for sending a larger quantity of bullion to India than was the case in former years? Yes.

Do you conceive that the demand for expenditure on railways in India has much to do with the necessity of exporting bullion from this country? The export of capital, for the purpose of constructing railways, must have contributed to it.

Do you suppose that that is the case to any great extent? The amount of capital which has gone from this country to India for that purpose is already considerable. Of course that is, so far, an addition to the export of bullion.

Do I rightly understand you to say that you attribute the necessity of sending silver partly to the demand in India for that metal in preference to gold, and partly to the diminished value of gold as compared with silver in Europe? Yes.

Do you suppose that a considerable portion of the export from this country to India, for the purpose of railways, has gone out in iron-work and other materials for the construction of railways, rather than in coin? A great deal of it, no doubt.

Do you suppose that the quantity of coin and bullion sent to India for the purpose of the construction of railways has been of very considerable amount? I am not able to say; I have not made myself acquainted with those particulars; I have no practical acquaintance with that department of Indian affairs, and I have no other knowledge of it than anybody else has.

SIR F. BARING: *You do not know whether the quantity of silver has increased considerably?* It must have increased considerably by the continued import. It is known from the returns that there has been a very great importation of silver into India, but where it goes is only matter of speculation. It is generally supposed to go into hoards; it has not told upon prices there to the degree that might have been expected.

SIR C. WOOD: *Do you recollect the circumstance that at a period of great commercial distress in Madras the natives sent in their silver ornaments to be coined?* I believe such things have happened. Money which goes into the form of ornaments, and is hoarded in that form, is brought out when there is a high rate of interest, and goes back again when the rate of interest falls.

You stated that in your opinion the variations in the rate of interest charged by the Bank of England had been increased by the operation of the Act of 1844. In what way do you attribute that effect to the Act of 1844? In this way. At present all drains operate, in the first place, upon the banking department of the Bank of England. As the private bankers now keep the bulk of their deposits at the Bank of England, the deposits at the Bank of England comprise the bulk of the disposable capital of the country, the bulk of that which is available for exportation in case of a drain of bullion for that purpose. Hence, whenever there is a drain, this drain operates in the first place on the reserve of bullion in the banking department. As long as the banking department and the issue department were one, the whole reserve of the Bank was available to meet these demands on its deposits; and so it would still be, notwithstanding the separation of the departments as a matter of account, if in an extremity the issue department was allowed to come to the assistance of the banking department; because in that case, supposing, for example, that 3,000,000*l.* were drawn out of the reserve of the deposit department, the Bank, instead of selling securities, or contracting its discounts in order to replenish its reserve, would simply transfer the necessary number of millions from the issue department, either in notes or in gold, to the reserve of the banking department; not for the purpose of lending it to the public, but simply to meet the demands of its depositors if they should continue to draw their deposits out. In that case, therefore, the Bank would not be obliged to take immediate means for contracting its credit in order to replenish its reserve; but now it must. The Bank is now exactly in the position, with regard to the solvency of its banking department, that it would be in if the issue department were annihilated altogether. The Bank is obliged to depend for the solvency of its banking department upon what it can do to replenish the reserve in that department; and therefore as soon as it finds that there is any drain in progress, it is obliged to look to the safety of its reserve, and to commence contracting its discounts, or selling securities.

Is not the operation which you contemplate in your answer an issue of notes from the issue department at a time when a drain is going on, and when, if the circulation is to be viewed as a metallic circulation, the quantity of Bank notes ought to be diminished rather than increased? Yes, according to the principle of the Act of 1844; but I think that principle a wrong one.

Would not such an operation as that take place exactly at a time when you stated that you thought the operation of the Act of 1844 had been beneficial, namely, to prevent the continuance of a large circulation of paper, so as to keep up prices when it would be more advantageous that they should fall? I think the operation of the Act is beneficial when the drain arises from one particular cause, viz., previous over speculation. When that is the case, it appears to me desirable not only that the Bank should not re-issue notes that are returned to it, but also that it should take measures moderately and discreetly to reduce its discounts, in order, by action on the rate of interest in a moderate degree, to prevent that violent operation on discounts which would otherwise become inevitable, in order to put a stop to the drain.

Would not an issue of notes from the issue department, in the manner you stated in your last answer but one, operate precisely in contravention of what you stated to be desirable, viz., would it not operate to maintain a rise of prices, originally produced by speculation, after the exchanges had taken an unfavourable turn, when, according to your last answer, the Bank ought to take moderate measures to restrain speculation? It would, or at least it might, and therefore I admit that the Act, in that particular case and stage of drain, is beneficial; but that is not the most usual cause of drain; other causes are much more frequent, namely, unusual foreign payments that have not originated in any undue extension of credit or general rise of prices; and in those cases, I think, it is desirable that the Bank should be able to replenish the reserve of its banking department from its issue department.

Do you think that the Bank can, with sufficient certainty, distinguish between the separate causes of drain, so as to be able to pursue a different course according to the cause which, in their opinion, produces the drain? The causes are matters of public notoriety. Everybody knows whether there has been a bad harvest, or whether the price of cotton has risen in America to a great extent, and generally whether a considerable export of capital is taking place. Then, on the other side of the question, all persons who pay attention to commercial transactions know well when there has been an inflation of credit, and, great speculation going on in goods; therefore, I think, the Bank have very sufficient means of distinguishing between the causes of a drain. The only case in which there can be any difficulty is, when there are causes of both sorts operating; in which case it may be difficult to determine exactly how much of the effect is due to each; but still, even in such a case as that, a course of action founded upon the judgment that experienced men can form upon the subject, seems to me much better than deciding by a mechanical rule that is only applicable to the extreme of one case, and pernicious in every other.

At certain times the Bank of England raises its rate of interest in order to maintain its reserve of notes; and in that case you think the operation of the Act of 1844 has tended to increase the rate of interest charged at certain times? Yes.

Do you think it has had the effect of lowering the rate of interest at other times? It has had that effect in point of fact, but I am not sure that it is fair to charge it upon the Act, because it is rather the effect of the doctrines put forth by the supporters of the Act than of the Act itself. When the Act was introduced, the language usually held by its supporters was, that the Bank in the management of its deposits was no more bound to consider the public interest than any other bank, and that it was to regulate its conduct with a view solely to its own safety; and so far as the Bank have acted upon that opinion, they have no doubt been led by it, not only to contract their discounts when they otherwise might not have been obliged to do so, but also to extend them at periods when probably otherwise they would not have done so; because seeing that they were at liberty, like other bankers, to lend their money to any extent that they thought prudent for their own interest, at the market rate, that they have lent money at less than 4 per cent., and upon some occasions at as little as 2 per cent. But that is not a necessary effect of the Act. The Act does not oblige them to do that, and the Bank may, if they please, abandon the doctrine that they are at liberty to act in the same way as other bankers; and seeing that such a body as the Bank must, in the management of its ordinary banking business, produce so great an effect upon the public interest, they may come to the conclusion that they are bound to consider that, and therefore ought not to lend below 4 per cent. or some such rate.

Then so far as the lowering the rate of interest is concerned, that has been the effect of the course taken by the Bank Directors, rather than any effect produced by the Act itself? I think it is more the effect of the mistaken grounds upon which the Act was first defended, and which have been partly abandoned by its defenders, than any effect of the Act itself.

Are you acquainted with the constitution of the banks of Hamburgh and Amsterdam? I have a general acquaintance with them.

In the case of both of those banks, are not all the notes which they issue represented by bullion actually existing in their coffers? Yes; that was the supposition, but it was found not to be the case in the bank of Amsterdam at the time of the events which followed the French Revolution; the bullion in deposit in the bank of Amsterdam was found to have been deficient.

Was not that supposed to be an accidental circumstance owing to the pressure of the revolutionary war at the time? I think it was supposed that the deficiency had existed long before that time.

But it was a principle in the constitution of those two banks, that all the notes were actually represented by bullion in their coffers? Yes.

Therefore, their circulation must have varied exactly upon the principle which has been laid down in the Act of 1844, viz., that it should vary exactly as a metallic circulation would vary? Yes.

Are you aware whether they were ever unable to afford the requisite accommodation to the trade, either of Hamburgh and its neighbourhood, or of Holland, in consequence of that regulation? I cannot answer that question; I should think it would require a very minute acquaintance with the history of commerce to be able to answer it.

You are not aware of any complaints having been made of want of accommodation, such as we have heard of in this country, in consequence of that state of things? Even if there were no such complaints, it might have been owing to their having never been accustomed to a different system.

Are you at all acquainted with the variations in the rate of interest, either in Holland or at Hamburgh? I cannot say that I am.

You cannot say whether they have been greater or less than the variations in the rate of interest charged by the Bank of England? I should expect that they were less; commercial transactions are now upon so much larger a scale, that we must expect more violent variations.

Do you not suppose that the variations in the rate of interest charged by the Bank of England latterly, are very much due to great influxes of bullion at one time, and an export of it at another, which must have had the effect of making practically a considerable difference in the amount of capital available for discounts at different times? Certainly, but if that were the only cause in operation, there would probably be very few variations, because the gold comes with tolerable regularity. I do not suppose that there are often considerable fluctuations in the rate of interest owing to the arrivals of gold, unless there is an unexpected retardation of an arrival; then of course that may operate for a short time on the money market, but not to any violent degree.

You are in favour of the Bank retaining a large reserve, but without the restriction of the Act of 1844. Would any amount of reserve secure the Bank against the effect of a drain, unless measures were taken by the Bank in reference to the amount of its circulation? The Bank may be driven to such measures ultimately. Even if the Bank has a reserve that is equal to the probable amount of the drain, it may undoubtedly happen that the drain may exceed that probable amount and if so, the Bank will at last be obliged to have recourse to other measures; but it is plain that if the Bank may allow 10,000,000l. of gold to run out without taking measures, it will not be obliged to resort to such violent measures to stop the drain, as if it were necessary to stop it at the beginning.

*Do not you think that earlier measures of a moderate degree may check
an incipient drain, which if suffered to go on, would require much stronger
measures in the end?* Yes, in the case of a drain arising from over speculation; but in the case of a drain arising from no cause affecting prices
generally, it seems to me a great deal better that the drain should be provided for by bullion kept in reserve to meet it, rather than that the bullion
to meet it should be obtained by a violent action on credit or on prices.

Do you recollect the drain of 1839? Yes, I think that was the occasion
on which the Bank was obliged to have recourse to the Bank of France.

*Was not it the fact that that drain of gold, unchecked by any measures
on the part of the Bank, went to such a length that the Bank was saved only
by borrowing 2,000,000l. from the Bank of France?* Yes.

*In point of fact, the ultimate measures that the Bank had to take after
having suffered it to go on for some time, were of a more stringent nature
than anything they had done in former days?* That will naturally be the
case if the Bank does not keep a sufficient reserve.

*Do you recollect whether the reserve of the Bank of England previously
to the commencement of that drain was not of an adequate amount according to the then received notions?* I have not the details in my memory.

Will you look at Paper 19 before the Committee,[*] *and state the amount
of bullion which appears to have been in the Bank in December 1838?*
In Decembeer 1838 it was 9,683,000l.

Will you state in what month in 1839 it was lowest? It appears to have
been lowest in August 1838.

The drain appears to have commenced from December 1838? Yes.

*What was the lowest point to which the bullion was reduced in the
course of 1839?* 2,444,000l., in the month of August.

*Does it not appear that the drain actually went to the extent of
7,000,000l. of bullion, gone from the coffers of the Bank of England?* Yes.

*I understood you to say, that after the experience we have had of the
discretion of the Bank of England, you think it might be thoroughly trusted
not to re-issue notes in cases when they might be called for to strengthen
the banking department?* Not to re-issue notes in cases in which the return
of those notes upon their hands was the effect of previous over-speculation.

*Have not almost all the great drains in this country, the drain in 1847,
the drain in 1849, the drain in 1839, and the drain in 1836 all been, if not
entirely, in a great measure caused by over-speculation previously occurring?* That can hardly be said, I think, in the case of the drain of 1847,
because the over-speculation which there had been at that time was principally in railway shares, which had very little tendency to produce a drain.

Do not you recollect the evidence which was given as to the system of

[*Parliamentary Papers, 1857 (Sess. 2), X.ii, pp. 156–60.]

drawing bills creating fictitious credits to a most inordinate amount, particularly at Manchester and Liverpool? To whatever extent that might be the case, unless it was for the purpose of making speculative purchases in goods, it would have no tendency to produce a drain.

Did not it produce very great discredit, and when the means of paying those bills failed, did not it cause great demands upon the Bank to furnish accommodation to those persons who could not obtain it in any other way? Accommodation in notes, but not necessarily in gold.

W. TITE: *May we take it, that the distinction which you intend to make between the different kinds of drain may be described by the expressions used in the Committee in 1848, namely, "a home drain," and "a foreign drain"?*[*] Yes.

With regard to a foreign drain, would not the state of the exchanges show very much what was operating upon the English market? The state of the exchanges would show whether there was, or whether there was likely to be, a drain; but it would not show from what cause the drain proceeded.

Do you think that the causes operating to produce either a home drain or a foreign drain, may be accurately distinguished? Yes.

With regard to the banks of Hamburgh and Amsterdam, do you know whether they were bound by law to keep bullion equal to their circulation, or whether it was left in the discretion of the Government? I always understood that they were bound by law, or by the constitution of those banks.

But I believe it is an historical fact that at the time of the failure of the Amsterdam bank, at the time of the French Revolution, it was found very deficient? Yes.

You do not know the amount of deficiency? No.

T. WEGUELIN: *In a question that was put to you with regard to the drain in 1839, it was said that it was unchecked by any measures on the part of the Bank. Are you aware that the circulation of the Bank in the hands of the public, which was the only circulation then known, in 1839 was reduced lower than ever it was known before or since in modern times?* I remember that the variations in the circulation in the hands of the public did not at all correspond with the state of the Bank reserve.

Does it not appear that at that time the bullion in December 1838 in the Bank of England was 9,686,000l.? Yes.

The circulation in the hands of the public was then 17,718,750l.? Yes.

In December 1839 the bullion in the Bank of England was 4,139,400l., and the circulation in the hands of the public was 15,823,000l.? Yes.

Then, whatever measures were taken, they had the effect of reducing the circulation in the hands of the public at that period? Yes; it had been from some cause or other reduced.

[*Parliamentary Papers, 1847–8, VIII, i–ii.]

You conceive that the circulation in the hands of the public is not always affected by the measures which the Bank may take? Not always.

Was not the drain of 1839 caused almost entirely by a demand for corn to supply a deficiency in consequence of a bad harvest? I have not the circumstances in my recollection, but I believe that was the main cause.

You state that the Bank, by a low rate of interest, increased their discounts; do you state that as a matter of theory or as a matter of fact? I believe, on the contrary, that as a matter of fact, the discounts are usually greatest when the rate of interest is highest; but that is accounted for by this circumstance, that the Bank's discounts are greatest at times when, in consequence of general commercial distress, there is greatest difficulty in obtaining assistance from other quarters; consequently, at the very time when the rate of interest is highest, the demands on the Bank are the greatest.

Therefore as far as the action of the Bank upon its securities is concerned, it is exactly the opposite to what the theory would induce you to suppose that it would be? It seems to me that the fact just mentioned is perfectly consistent with the theory; because although the Bank, not being the sole lenders, would be likely at the time when they get the lowest rate of interest (the facility of obtaining loans from other quarters being greater) to have a less demand upon them than at other times, and therefore might find it necessary to lower their rate of interest in order to employ their funds at all, still it does not follow that if they were to stop their loans till the rate of interest rose again, it would not have a very considerable effect on the money market generally. I believe that their refusal to lower their rate at such a time would be sufficient to have a very considerable effect on the rate of interest.

Does a reduction of the rate of discount on the part of the Bank necessarily increase the securities? Not necessarily.

Nor does a rise in the rate of discount necessarily diminish the securities? No; but perhaps I may be allowed to say that that does not affect the question about the operation of the Act; because in a time of difficulty when the Bank, in order to replenish their reserve, raise their rate of discount, if that rise in the rate of discount does not suffice to diminish their advances, they must do more, they must actually refuse to make advances; because their object is not to get a greater rate of interest, not to make more of their money, but to increase their reserve, and that is to be done either by their refusing to make advances, or by their selling securities, which will prevent somebody else from making advances to an equal amount.

Does selling securities increase the reserve of the Bank? Selling securities for the purpose of replenishing the reserve would do so.

Does not the reserve of the Bank consist of the notes unemployed? The notes, generally, that the Bank holds for the purpose of meeting the demands of the depositors.

Is not the reserve of the Bank affected only by a diminution of its bullion? The reserve of the Bank may be affected by any drawing out of their deposits.

The purpose of drawing out deposits is to meet a foreign drain, as expressed by a diminution of bullion? Yes.

Therefore any measures which the Bank take must be to increase its stock of bullion? It must be so now, but it need not be so but for the Act.

If the Act did not exist, the whole reserve would be in bullion, and the same effect might take place upon the bullion as does now? The whole reserve, in that sense, would be in bullion, but there would still be virtually a banking reserve that might exceed the amount of the bullion, or the Bank might, independently of the bullion that it kept to meet a foreign drain, keep in reserve notes also to meet the demands of depositors.

Notes unrepresented by bullion? Notes unrepresented by bullion; because the demands of depositors do not necessarily result from a demand for bullion, although they very commonly do.

You are aware that in consequence of the position which the Bank holds, being, as it were, the ultimate resort of all the banking expedients of the country, what it loses on one account it usually gains upon another, and the deposits usually remain pretty nearly equal under all circumstances? In a quiescent state of trade no doubt they do.

The principal fluctuation being in Government accounts, which increase from a certain period of the quarter up to the time of the payment of the dividends? In ordinary times that is the case.

Are you aware that the mode in which the expenditure on railways is conducted in India is by the Indian Government expending what is necessary for labour in India and placing it to the account of the Indian Government on this side? I do not know in what form those advances are made.

And that the amount so debited to the East India House here is between 3,000,000l. and 4,000,000l.? I cannot answer that question.

You stated that a high rate of discount charged in this country, attracts capital from the Continent? Yes.

The rate of discount on the Continent is for bills due upon the Continent? Yes; but I presume it may also be for bills due from this country.

But then there must be a question of exchange entering into it? Yes.

Therefore, when you talk of the rate of discount in London, and of the rate of discount in Paris, it is for two different articles; one is for a bill due in London, the other is for a bill due in Paris? Yes.

Before you can convert the one into the other, there must be an operation on the exchange? Yes; but that operation will very often consist in rectifying a previous operation; that is to say, supposing there was previously an exchange adverse to this country in consequence of foreign payments, a rise in the rate of interest here, by inducing those to whom those payments are due to invest their capital here, will tend to rectify the exchange.

You think that a high rate of discount here will cause investments to be made in this country? Yes.

Investments in permanent securities? Investments in permanent securities certainly, but very often, no doubt, not intended to be held permanently, but intended to be sold again after they have risen in price.

Do you think that a high rate of discount in London would induce bankers to send money over here to be employed in discounts? I think it is very likely to induce such a house as Rothschild's to buy any quantity of securities here.

But not bills? It would come to the same thing, because, if Rothschild bought securities, the sellers of those securities would sell them for the purpose of employing the money here in other modes; they would be very likely to be either themselves discounting or sending their money to bankers, by whom it would be employed in discounts.

Then the operation would be, that foreign capitalists would be attracted by the low price of securities, not by the high rate of discount here? The two always come together.

Does a high rate of discount necessarily accompany a low price of public securities or of commodities, generally speaking? Not necessarily a low price of commodities. It is possible that the prices of commodities might not vary; but in most cases the prices of commodities are ultimately affected. When the low price of securities is owing to commercial difficulties, if those commercial difficulties continue, and there is great difficulty in raising money by discount or otherwise for temporary exigencies, the natural effect is to lower the prices of commodities, because the holders of goods, being unable to get money in any other way, are obliged to sell at a forced reduction of price.

But is it not the fact, that practically the rate of discount in the money market has upon very few occasions had any more than a limited effect upon the price of public securities? I do not imagine how that can possibly be.

The price of consols is now 94, and the rate of discount is 6 per cent. Is there any relation between those two rates that you can trace? Probably Exchequer bills would be a more suitable comparison, because it is generally Exchequer bills that are held by bankers, not consols. Of consols there is a very great proportion held by persons who keep them as permanent holders for the income they yield, and not as a reserve to meet their engagements.

But my question refers to the attraction which the high rate of discount affords to foreign capitalists to send their capital over to this country. You stated that you thought that a high rate of discount necessarily implied a low price of public securities? I am speaking of the high rate of discount that takes place in times of commercial difficulty. I apprehend that when there is a state of commercial difficulty there is always, as one of the features of that state, a considerable fall in the price of securities both private and public, and that all sorts of securities, railway shares for instance, fall very much. That is one of the forms in which these transfers from foreign countries take place; foreigners send over to buy railway shares in this country, or English holders of foreign railway shares sell their foreign railway shares abroad. That is one way in which the transfer takes place, and there is so much transfer of bullion prevented.

You say, that you think that a considerable rise in the rate of discount necessarily causes foreign capitalists to invest in securities in this country, and English capitalists to sell the securities which they hold in foreign countries? I do not say necessarily; I think that it is a probable and natural result, and that by means of this, which is under the circumstances supposed a profitable investment, the necessity of so great an exportation of bullion as would otherwise be required is in some degree saved. I have understood that in 1847 this occurred to a considerable extent.

You think that large investments were made by foreigners in this country in 1847? I believe there were considerable purchases by foreigners, either of English or foreign securities, which were previously held by persons in England.

Do you think they invested in consols much at that time? I should not think they invested much in consols, because consols are always at a much higher price than other securities, and, what is more important, there is not so much to be made by speculating in them, because the prices do not fluctuate so much. Those investments, I suppose, were made on speculation, with a view to sell again afterwards.

In a general way, when the market for securities is going down in this country, does not the market for securities on the Continent go down also? Yes, in some degree it does; but still it does not go down in the same degree. I apprehend that the country in which the cause of the fall originates, is always that in which it is greatest. And when it originates in a great payment of money from this country to foreign countries, it is natural to suppose that so far from the same phenomena taking place in the foreign country, to a certain extent, phenomena of a contrary description may be expected to take place there.

Do you think that the merchants in this country hold many foreign securities? I should think not as a general rule, though they may occasionally, on speculation.

Are those speculations, in your opinion, mainly confined to the capitalists, who upon occasions of commercial distress, are inclined to transfer their capital to foreign countries? There is a large and rich class of bankers and dealers in securities, through whom the equalization of the rate of interest and the equalization of commercial pressure between different countries usually takes place; and when disposable capital is to be transferred from one country to another, it is usually through the agency of these people that the transaction takes place. We know they are always on the look out to buy securities which are likely to rise; therefore if securities have fallen in one country from circumstances leading to an export of bullion, while in other countries bullion is coming in, the place for them to buy securities will be the country which is sending bullion away.

In point of fact the transfer of capital is a speculation in the permanent investments of that country, rather than in the rate of discount? Yes; but I apprehend the rate of discount is always affected by it, because those who buy securities buy them from somebody who previously held them, and who after the sale has the price of them instead, and he has probably sold his securities because he intends to make use of the price in a more profitable manner than the securities afford. This, at such a time, he would be best able to do by employing the money in discounts. Or he perhaps uses it to pay a debt of his own, and in that case the person to whom he pays the debt is probably a monied man, and employs it in discounts.

Of course the whole force of the argument depends upon the amount to which those investments are made in foreign countries. You think they are very large? I always understood that they took place to a very considerable extent in 1847, to a sufficient extent to have relieved the drain considerably.

R. HILDYARD: *I understand you to state that, in your judgment, there ought to be no legislative restriction upon the Bank, but that the Bank Directors ought, as a general principle, to endeavour to keep a large reserve of bullion, amounting to the sum of about 12,000,000l., which you specified?* Yes.

Do you advocate that they should keep that reserve with a view of meeting any sudden emergency that may come upon them, without being obliged to have recourse to extreme measures injurious to the commerce of the country? Just so.

Is the effect, in your opinion, of the Act of 1844 to deprive the Bank of the use of a large portion of the bullion actually in its hands, and to compel it to meet the requirements of the public out of the diminished portion over which they are permitted to have control? I think they are obliged in any case to meet all the demands of the public, or the greater part of those demands, from their banking reserve, and that if they could have recourse to their issue department, either for bullion or for notes, they would often not be obliged to limit their advances from the banking department, when now they are obliged to do so; or if they were obliged, it would not be to the same extent.

Would you illustrate your view by what occurred in 1847. Was it not the fact that the active circulation of the Bank of England during the crisis of 1847 was never below 20,000,000l. sterling? I presume that in 1847 the amount given as the circulation of the Bank of England represents all the notes out of the issue department, and therefore includes the banking reserve of notes. It appears to have been at the lowest, a little below 19,000,000l., in the month of September.

But the crisis did not occur till after September; will you state what the actual circulation was in October? On the 9th of October the circulation is stated to have been 19,182,000l.

Then, subtracting from the active circulation the credit circulation of the Bank, the Act compelled the Bank of England to hold bullion representing the difference between the active circulation and the credit circulation of 14,000,000l.? Yes; the Bank was obliged to retain bullion to represent the surplus of 19,000,000l. above 14,000,000l.; but they might still have been compelled to keep this bullion, and yet the inconvenience might have been prevented if the restriction on the issue of notes had not existed; because they might have made an advance to the banking department of notes from the issue department, which would not necessarily have been lent to the public at all.

But under the Act of Parliament they had no such power as that which you say would have obviated the difficulty? No.

Then were we not near experiencing this phenomena, that the Bank of England might have been compelled to declare its inability to comply with the Act at a time when it had between 6,000,000l. and 7,000,000l. of bullion in its coffers? What it might have been compelled to do would have been to stop payment in its banking department.

If on the Monday following the Saturday when the Chancellor of the Exchequer thought proper to give way, the bankers had chosen to withdraw their deposits, the Bank of England must have stopped payment, although it had at the time 6,000,000l. of bullion in its coffers? Yes; in the case of an internal panic that evil is liable to arise, because there is no knowing how far the panic may reach; the longer it goes on the longer it is likely to go on, because panic creates panic. Any amount of issue of notes which the Bank could possibly make at such a time could not under any circumstances do any harm, because all that people would want them for would be to keep by them; they would never go into circulation.

You stated that in your opinion, in every case but one, the action of the Act of 1844 has been prejudicial; but that in one case you think it is beneficial, that is to say, in the case of a drain resulting from an inflation of credit and over speculation? Yes; and even in that case, I think it is beneficial only in the first stage, and extremely injurious in the last stage.

Are you sure that you are right in saying that any merit exists in the Act of 1844, even in that particular; have not the Bank Directors, from their position, ample means of ascertaining that that over speculation and that inflation of credit is going on? Do not the character of the bills presented to them and their general knowledge of the commercial affairs of the country enable them to arrive at that conclusion? I should say that there never has been a time of over speculation to any great extent, when the fact has not been notorious to persons accustomed to attend to commercial affairs.

Must it not be particularly within the knowledge of the Bank Directors if they are men of intelligence? Undoubtedly.

Then would it not be their duty to check that over speculation by their own spontaneous action, even if they were not compelled to do so by the Act of 1844? I think it would be, and that they would probably do it with their present lights, but they certainly did not always do it.

You have stated that they would have a knowledge of what ought to be done and that they would be able to do it, and you think that now, with the experience they have had, they would do it? Yes.

If they did not do it would it not simply amount to this, that the Bank Direction is not properly constituted, and not that there is any necessity for any legislative enactment to effect it? I think so, certainly.

Therefore the Act of 1844 has really no merit, inasmuch as this one beneficial action which you ascribe to it, might and ought to follow from the intelligence and discretion of the Directors? At the same time I must say, that I am not aware that the Bank Directors have ever been in intelligence of commercial affairs behind the commercial public generally. I think they have always had quite as enlightened views as the bulk of the public had. They have not always had the best views. They had not in the time of the Bank restriction; but then neither had the public. They had improved views quite as soon as the public. When Sir Robert Peel found that the Bank of England had not been observing the requisite caution in checking speculation in its commencement, he might very naturally think that it would be beneficial to compel them to do so. But whether compulsion was required or not at that time, I think that the effect has now been produced. The feeling of the public is now even of an exaggerated kind on the subject of the necessity of checking speculation. The alarm is sounded very early, sometimes earlier than is necessary; and I do not think it is to be apprehended that, under the present constitution, the Bank of England is ever likely to be less alive than the commercial world in general are to that object, so as to require the restraint of the Act.

Therefore you would not recommend the continuance of this Act of 1844 in order to accomplish that beneficial action, which you say it may have produced in certain cases, but which you believe would be effected without the Act by the spontaneous action of the Bank Direction, with the improved intelligence and the experience that they now possess? Decidedly. I think that the degree of enlightenment of the Bank Directors has been constantly progressive; that they have advanced with the public, and are likely still to do so. I think they are now kept back more by the false theory upon which this Act rests, than by anything else; and that they would act in a more judicious way than the Act prescribes, if they had larger discretion entrusted to them.

Is not one mode, if not the only mode, of checking a drain, gradually raising the rate of discounts. Is not that the most important, if not the only engine which they possess for the purpose? And the limitation of their advances.

Do you remember the precise date of the repeal of the Usury Laws?[*] They have been repealed by degrees.

Have not the Bank since the year 1844, by the repeal of the Usury Laws, possessed an engine by which they can check the efflux of bullion and arrest over speculation, which was not possessed by their predecessors during the period that elapsed between 1819 and 1844? The Usury Laws were relaxed, as far as regarded bills of exchange, long before 1844.

That relaxation was confined to bills of exchange? Yes, and to bills of less than three months' date; but those are the bills which the Bank discount, I believe, exclusively.

You have been asked whether larger reserves of bullion have not been held by the Bank in the 10 years subsequent to 1844 than were held in the 10 years previous to 1844. Will you look at the paper[†] *before the Committee and see whether that appears to be a necessary consequence of the Act of 1844, or whether you do not find that the bullion in the Bank had actually risen previously to that Act. What was it in 1844?* In January 1844 it exceeded 14,000,000*l*. In March it exceeded 16,000,000*l*.; then it began to diminish.

But previously to 1844, what was it? During the whole of 1843 it was from 10,000,000*l*. to 13,000,000*l*.; never so much as 13,000,000*l*.

When did the Act itself come into operation? In 1844; and that confirms what I stated, that during those years gold was flowing in in large quantities; therefore the quantity of bullion in the Bank would naturally have been very much greater, even if the Act had never passed.

Is it not evident that that great amount of bullion in 1844 could not by

[*See 2 & 3 Victoria, c.37.]
[†*Parliamentary Papers*, 1857 (Sess. 2), X.ii, pp. 156–60.]

possibility be the effect of the Act of 1844, but must have been the result of previous causes in action? So much so, that in all probability no one would have thought of venturing to separate the reserve into two parts, if it had not been so large. If the reserve had been no more than 7,000,000*l.*, it is highly probable that Parliament would not have thought it safe to enact that only part of it should be available in each department.

It has been stated in this Committee that the supposed reason for adopting 14,000,000l. as the amount of circulation on securities, as fixed by the Act of 1844, was, that the minimum active circulation previously to 1844 was 15,600,000l.; of which 15,600,000l., 1,000,000l. consisted of bank post bills, not under the operation of the Act, and 600,000l. of lost notes which have subsequently been written off. Deducting therefore those two sums from the minimum circulation, we get at the 14,000,000l. which is made the amount of the credit circulation of the Bank. The Legislature, therefore, having regard simply to the then existing amount of the circulation, and not at all to the regulation of the banking department, seems to have assumed, that if they made provision for bullion against every note issued above the lowest amount that had ever been out in active circulation, they had secured convertibility? Yes.

Without asking you whether you agree in that view, but assuming that the minimum circulation since the passing of the Act has not been less than 16,700,000l., exclusive of bank post bills; and there being no amount worth speaking of of lost notes to write off, ought not the Legislature, if it follows the principle of 1844, to make 16,500,000l., or about that amount, the amount of the credit circulation which should be permitted to be issued? It is evident, that proceeding on that principle, if the framers of the Act had been framing it now, they would have fixed the larger amount instead of the smaller.

Upon the same principle they would have said, as we cannot contemplate a lower circulation than 16,500,000l., if we provide bullion for everything beyond that amount we provide for convertibility? That would have been their course probably.

Still, not asking you to pledge yourself to the principle, would not it seem a more rational thing to have the credit circulation expanding according to the wants of the country, as indicated by the minimum active circulation, than to adopt an arbitrary amount of 14,000,000l., as fixed in 1844, although the industrial operations of the country might increase to any extent? I am not sure that it would operate in that way, because the only difference that would exist as compared with the present state of things is, that the Bank would be obliged to hold bullion against 2,000,000*l.* of its circulation, which now it may issue on securities.

If you increased its credit circulation from 14,000,000l. to 16,500,000l., it would dispense with the legislative necessity on the part of the Bank to hold 2,000,000l. of gold? Yes, it would enable the country to part with 2,000,000l. of bullion which now it must hold.

It would therefore so far relax the operation of the Act of 1844? Yes.

If you think that the restriction of the Act of 1844 ought not to exist at all, I imagine you would advocate its relaxation to that extent, as going part of the way that you would propose to go? Provided that this permission to the Bank to issue 2,000,000l. more on securities than they can now do, did not cause their reserve in bullion to be less than what I think requisite for meeting the probable or possible drains.

You have already stated that you think that the principle of the Act of 1844 is defective, because it pays no regard to a drain that will fall upon the banking department (which you say is the first effect of a drain), but simply has reference to the issue department. Now adopting the principle of the Act of 1844, for the sake of the argument (without asking you to acquiesce in it, and to say that it is a right principle), if that principle is to be adopted by Parliament with respect to the legislation we are about to enter upon, ought it not consistently with what was done in 1844, to make this relaxation of 2,000,000l.? On the principle of the Act of 1844, I see no reason whatever against it.

You have been asked whether the Bank at Amsterdam and the Bank at Hamburgh were not bound to hold bullion to the full extent of every note issued; assuming that that was so, and that that was their habit (which you say you believe in the case of the Bank of Amsterdam was not practically their habit), what economy of capital would be gained if every note is represented by bullion? Of course none; the only advantage, then, of the paper currency would be its convenience.

It would be encountering the evils which are urged as objections against a paper currency, namely, liability to forgery and loss without any economy of capital whatever? None whatever.

And no profit resulting to the Bank which had to make the issue? No profit from the issues, of course; only expense.

You say you consider that, having reference simply to the question of circulation, it is a matter of importance whether the issue of notes is from one bank or from several banks; you qualified that remark by saying, "As a question of circulation"?[*] Yes; I consider that it may be of consequence with reference to the probability of forgery; the probability of forgery is, no doubt, greater when the same notes circulate all over the country, than when notes circulate only locally in a small district. At the same time that might possibly, in the case of the Bank of England, be provided against by means of branch banks, and by making the notes of those banks supply the whole local circulation.

Do you believe that, in fact, there are many districts where it would

[*See p. 510 above.]

not answer the purpose of a bank, like the Bank of England, to establish branch banks for the purpose of distributing its notes, and where the notes of private bankers are now circulated, affording great conveniences to the district? Yes; but the notes of branch banks would get distributed too. However, they would probably circulate over a much larger district than the notes of private bankers; and therefore the danger of forgery would be considerably greater.

But do you think that they would of necessity be distributed so conveniently as they now are, assuming that country bankers were prohibited altogether from issuing them? Possibly not.

Do you know the fact that the Bank of England has found it to be inexpedient, as a mercantile operation, to have branch banks even in such places as Norwich and Gloucester, and that they have withdrawn their branch banks from those places? It is not within my knowledge. It is a striking fact, certainly, but it does not follow that the notes of a central bank would not circulate in those districts just as much as if there were branch banks.

Can you not conceive that great practical inconvenience would result to many outlying districts if there were not the conveniences at present afforded by country banks? I think it is very useful to such districts, perhaps to less opulent districts even more than to opulent ones, that there should exist bankers ready to make advances of money on proper security. In some districts it is probable that a bank could not maintain itself by its deposits only, unless it had a profit on its issues also; and so far the inconvenience referred to in the question would certainly be produced, if there were only one bank of issue.

Do you not also know that in practice, if a farmer comes into a country bank and wants to draw 100l. from his deposit, he is asked, "In which will you have them?" and he invariably takes the notes of the district, and prefers them to Bank of England notes? Perhaps he does so only because he is more used to them.

Assuming that he is satisfied of the solvency of the bank, is not the danger of forgery less, in the case of a private note? Unquestionably that is the strongest argument for having private notes.

T. HANKEY: *You said that you considered that it would be injurious to the public interest that the Bank of England should be managed in the same way as other banking establishments?* I think that the operations of the Bank produce much too great and important effects on the general business of the country to admit of its considering, as other bankers may do, only its own safety and pecuniary interest.

You stated that you considered that the deposits of the Bank of England were the reserves of the disposable money, generally, throughout the country, and that that was one of the reasons why you thought it was not desirable that the Bank of England should act as any private banker would do? The private bankers keep all that portion of their reserves, which they do not immediately want, with the Bank of England; the consequence is, that the deposits of the Bank of England are the bulk of all the deposits in the country; and as the deposits of the Bank of England consist of the whole capital that is lying waiting for employment, they necessarily constitute the fund which is drawn upon when bullion is wanted for exportation.

Do you think that that remark applies to any other account of the Bank of England, except the account of the London bankers with the Bank of England? Possibly not; but at the same time the private country bankers are brought very much into connexion with the Bank of England through their London agents. I imagine that there are very few private country bankers that had not a portion of their funds in the hands of London agents.

If we exclude the account of the London bankers at the Bank of England, are not all the other deposits of the Bank of England very much of the same nature as those which are kept in any other banking establishment in London? Except that another London banker does not keep the whole of his reserve by him; he only keeps that portion which he thinks liable to be called for immediately. He keeps the rest with the Bank of England.

But my question is excluding the deposit account of the London banker at the Bank of England; are you aware of any other accounts which require a peculiar action on the part of the Bank of England different from that of any other ordinary well managed bank? I apprehend that the Bank is obliged so to conduct the management of its banking concerns, that it shall always be able to meet from its banking reserve any probable drain of bullion for exportation; because any drain for exportation comes as a general rule upon the banking branch, before it can reach the issue branch; and the Bank being under this obligation, and knowing that whatever drain of bullion takes place from the country will almost all come out of its banking reserve, is obliged to consider the probabilities of drains, and their probable extent, in its banking operations, as well as in its issue operations.

Are you aware whether, when there is a drain of bullion, any other deposit accounts in the Bank of England are withdrawn or diminished, except those which are of the nature to which I have alluded, namely, the deposit accounts of the London bankers? The accounts of the Government certainly are not generally liable to be diminished in that way.

Then it is only those other accounts, which you would not consider the public accounts, which are liable to be diminished by a drain of bullion from abroad? Yes; but there are cases in which the Government accounts also may be liable to be drawn upon, namely, when the Government itself has payments to make abroad.

If I could show you that the accounts at the Bank, other than the public accounts (excluding those of the bankers), have not varied materially with any drain of bullion, you would not perhaps attach so much import-ance to the argument? I imagine that if the deposits of the bankers vary, that is sufficient to make a very great action on the part of the Bank necessary to maintain its reserve.

Excluding the account of the London bankers, can you point out any other account at the Bank of England which is liable to diminution in consequence of a drain for bullion; have you ever observed any indication of any such thing in any accounts that you have seen? If any private merchant or dealer banks with the Bank of England, I apprehend that he may have foreign payments to make, and therefore his deposits may be drawn out in case of a demand for exportation; and I suppose that the public accounts and the bankers' accounts, and the accounts of merchants and dealers, compose nearly the whole of the deposits of the Bank.

At times when the rate of interest was very low, do you imagine that the amount of deposits in the Bank of England, of an ordinary character, was larger or smaller than at other times? I cannot say.

Do you think that the amount of deposits in London is in any way affected by the current rate of interest at which people can employ their money? When the current rate of interest is unusually high, I should expect that, *cæteris paribus*, the deposits would be low; because the very fact of money bearing a high value proves that people want it either to meet their engagements, or because they are able to make unusual profit by the use of it.

Have you observed [*] *that at the time when money was worth 7 per cent., the private deposits in the Bank of England were about 12,600,000l. Will you see what was the amount of private deposits in the Bank of England in the first week of January 1856?* In the first week in January 1856 the public deposits were 5,500,000l.; the other deposits were rather more than 12,500,000l.

Now, will you refer to the amount of deposits on the 1st of January 1852, which is the period when money was extremely abundant? At that time the private deposits were 9,371,000l.

Then, at a time when money was extremely abundant, and the rate of interest very low, and when you would have expected there to have been an unusual amount of money unemployed, it appears from the return of the Bank of England that the deposits were considerably less than they

[*See *Parliamentary Papers*, 1857 (Sess. 2), X.ii, pp. 144–55.]

were at a time when the interest of money was extremely high, and when you would have expected a very considerable diminution of the deposits. Is not that the fact as it appears from the paper? Yes.

Therefore, as far as those facts go, there is no indication that the private deposits have been materially affected by a higher rate of interest? No.

The question is, whether it is true that the deposits generally, otherwise than those of the bankers, are of a nature which require any peculiar action on the part of the Bank of England? The Government deposits do not.

Therefore it is only the private deposits that do? Yes.

And in fact it would apply to no other account than that of the London bankers? Or the London merchants and dealers.

But we have seen from the account before the Committee that the amount of deposits in the Bank of England did not materially vary, according to the scarcity or abundance of money; and does it not follow, therefore, that it can only be the private bankers' accounts at the Bank of England which are of that peculiar nature which requires a different action from that which would be pursued by every other bank? It strikes me, that when bankers withdraw their deposits it is because their customers are likely to withdraw their deposits for the purpose of meeting the demands to which they are liable in the peculiar state of the market.

You stated that you thought that since 1844 the Bank has lent money at lower rates of interest than it did previously? Yes.

And that that was partly caused by the Act of 1844? I said that I did not think the Act could be held responsible for it, because it is rather a circumstance which has accompanied the Act than the direct effect of the Act itself.

You believe it to be a matter of fact? Yes.

Is it not a notorious fact that the Bank of England lent money in 1843, at 1½ per cent.? That must have been under very peculiar circumstances.

Previously to 1844 the Bank never lowered their rate of discount below 4 per cent., but you are aware that the Bank when they had large amounts of money at their disposal made use of it, and were consequently obliged to employ it at the current rates of interest? Yes, they have I know been charged with having almost caused some commercial crises, by the use they have made of their large funds at certain periods of speculation and of consequent revulsion: I mean by the use which they made of extraordinary public deposits which they had for a time.

You think that at a time when the Bank of England has large deposits in its hands, and when the current rate of interest is from any causes below 4 per cent., it is not expedient for the Bank to enter into competition in the money market, or to employ that money at all? I would not lay down any general rule, but I think they are bound not to do it without great consideration of the circumstances; that is to say, not without considering whether there is likely to be a demand on their reserve; in fact, whether their superfluity of reserve is likely to last.

Would it not be rather difficult for the Bank Directors to foresee what may happen two or three months hence? Do you think that the Bank, having a large amount of money which had been paid in from taxation, ought to be prevented from circulating it among the public because the the rate of interest was not 4 per cent? Do you think that would be a wise, a wholesome action on the part of the Bank Directors? I should think that it would be necessary that they should consider a great many circumstances in order to decide that. I do not think any general rule can be laid down.

But without laying down a general rule, do you not think there are many cases which would justify the Bank in lending out money at the current rate of interest? I think they are bound to consider well the disadvantage which would be occasioned, at a time when there was a low rate of interest, by lending a very large sum of money in addition to what had been lent before, which would tend to encourage speculation, and whether that would be a greater evil than leaving a portion of their deposits for a time in their coffers.

You think that in those particular times they ought to depart from such principles of action as would guide any ordinary banking establishment? I think so, because a private banker may fairly think that his operations cannot produce any great effect upon the general circumstances of the money market, and that, therefore, it is enough if he considers himself.

Do you consider that the rates of interest have varied more frequently since the Act of 1844, than they did before? Yes.

Can you refer to any statement which shows that the variations in the rate of interest in London have been greater or more frequent since 1844 than they were previously to 1844? It is matter of notoriety that the variations in the Bank's rates of discount have been much more frequent than they were before.

But seeing that before 1844 the Bank of England never discounted below four per cent., but employed their money in other ways below four per cent., would it be a fair thing to take the Bank's rate of interest at that period as an indication of the value of money, and to found an argument upon it, that the variations in the rates of interest have been more frequent since 1844 than previously to 1844; would it not be more fair to take the current rates of interest in London, as indicated by the rates adopted by the great money dealers, such as Messrs. Overend & Co., whose money is generally employed in discounting bills? I have no doubt that the rate at which Overend & Co. lent would be a very correct indication of what the rate of interest was, but it would not at all show to what extent the general rate had been affected by the circumstance of the Bank lending or not lending at a low rate of interest, which cannot fail to affect it very materially.

The rate to which you are alluding is merely the rate at which the Bank have themselves lent money, having no reference whatever to the current rates of interest in London? Just so; but this distinction is not always important, because everybody feels that the operations of the Bank do very materially affect the general rate of interest in a period of commercial difficulty; and it is in a period of commercial difficulty, brought about by other causes than over speculation, that the restrictions imposed by the Act are particularly noxious. Although the Bank does even in ordinary times vary its rate of interest much more frequently than it did, no doubt it does so, merely following the market rate of interest, and I do not attach any great importance to the effect of what it does then. It is what it does in times of difficulty, that is of importance, and the restrictions under which it is then placed appear to me to be a source of evil.

As there has been a very large increase in the production of gold, which has been principally coined, and has therefore added to that extent to the circulating medium of the world, should you not expect that in the general distribution of the precious metals a great proportion of that increase would find its way to India? Certainly.

Would it not naturally continue to do so until India had received its share in its general distribution? Yes; but I apprehend that it will be found that the export of bullion to the East has been greater in proportion than to other countries.

Is not the alteration in the relative value of gold and silver which has taken place in consequence of the enormous increase in the production of gold, quite sufficient of itself to account for this large export of silver from Europe to India? It would no doubt account for the export of silver to the East to the same proportionate extent as to other places, but not for the greater proportional exportation, which I imagine has taken place to the East, than to other places.

Is it not natural that in this process of equalising the general increase of the precious metals all over the world, that increase should find its way in the shape of silver to the East, where silver alone is used as the circulating medium to a greater degree than to any country where gold and silver are used jointly as the circulating medium? Certainly.

Then it is natural to suppose that the large export of bullion which we have sent to India would have taken place quite irrespectively of any action of trade, or railways, or anything else? Not independently of any action of trade, because it must take place through the medium of that action.

But independently of any extraordinary action, different from the ordinary action of the trade of the country? Yes; but if it had not been for the practice of hoarding in the East, the probability is, that in a country like India, where prices depend much more on the metals than on any of those contrivances of credit which affect them so greatly here, the effect of this influx would have been felt much more upon prices than it has been; and in proportion as it affected prices, it would have diminished the export of the precious metals to India, which it has not done.

w. TITE: *I have now before me the statistics with regard to silver which were given to the Committee in March last,*[*] *from which it appears that the exports of silver to India and China in six years have been 36,530,000l., and the imports from the producing countries have been 25,820,000l., making the amount of silver abstracted from the European stock in the six years 10,700,000l., which is at the rate of about 1,600,000l. in a year. Do you apprehend that that drain of 1,600,000l. from Europe to the East is likely to continue?* I should think that a drain to that extent or more is likely to continue.

Do you know the amount of circulation in France? I have not the figures in my possession, but there has been a great substitution of gold for silver in the French circulation, and a great part of the silver which has gone to the East has come from France.

It was suggested that the circulation of silver in France is about 120,000,000l. sterling? Not now, I think.

Supposing that drain to the East should go on to the extent of 1,500,000l. above the silver imported from the silver producing countries, would the effect be very important upon the commerce of the country, or what effect would it have, in your opinion? The probable effect will be to oblige countries whose standard is now silver to adopt a gold standard. If this took place in India, the effect would be in a great degree to stop the influx of silver, and to substitute an influx of gold.

No other effect? No other effect, that I know of.

R. SPOONER: *Some questions have been put to you about country bankers being required to give securities for their notes; I understood you to say that you do not think that at all necessary as long as the issue of notes is limited to 5l. and upwards?* I hardly think so; I admit that it is a question on which there may be a difference of opinion, but, inasmuch as the amount of deposits is generally greater than the amount of notes, and the holders of notes, when they are confined to 5l. notes, are much the same class of persons as the depositors, there probably is no reason for placing the holders of notes in a different position, or giving them any security which cannot be given to depositors.

Would it not be unjust and unfair towards one creditor of the Bank to give a better security to another creditor of the Bank? Not if it were known beforehand on what security they took the notes or made the deposits.

[*Parliamentary Papers, 1857 (Sess. 2), X.i., p. 15.]

In what way could the security be given; how could it be practically worked out? The banker might be compelled to hold public securities of some description to the amount of his notes, which should not be liable to be taken to pay other debts.

Where should those securities be deposited? They might be entered in the books of the Bank, in such a manner as to secure them against other creditors. Means could easily be provided in some way equivalent to a *distringas* upon stock which is not permitted to be sold.

Suppose that were done, a banker must still keep in his possession a large reserve to meet the daily demands of his customers in respect of those notes? Certainly, he must, and he would hold, besides, a certain amount of securities which would be a pledge for his notes.

Would not that, in point of fact, be requiring the banker to provide for his notes in two places? He would not be required to provide so much for his depositors if his notes were otherwise provided for.

But you mean still to make the banker liable to pay his notes on demand in gold, although he has given security? Certainly.

Then you would make him provide for his notes in two ways, namely, by giving security for them, and by providing for the daily demands which are coming upon him? Yes, undoubtedly he must; but the securities which he was obliged to provide on account of his notes would be bringing him interest.

Would it not be in a time of panic or disturbance that he would require to realise his securities to meet his notes? That might be the case; and it might be necessary that some public officer should have power to authorise sales of the securities that were given for the notes.

At such a time, would not the securities most probably fall very much in value? Yes, undoubtedly they would.

Then while you ask security from the banker, would not you give him indemnity against that possible loss? That is a loss to which bankers are always subject; they are always liable to invest their money in securities when securities are dear, and to have to sell them out when they are cheap.

They change them according to the best of their judgment? Yes; but they invest what they receive in deposit, and the deposits are likely to come in to them in the greatest abundance when there is not much to be made by keeping them.

I understood you to say that your opinion is, that the theory upon which the Act of 1844 was grounded has been proved by experience to be completely erroneous? I think that some parts of the theory have been proved, by practical experience since, to be erroneous, and that they are mostly given up, even by the defenders of the Act.

What part do you say is not proved to be erroneous? I think the whole of the theory erroneous; but I think the part which experience has overset is chiefly that which turned upon inattention to the effects which the Bank produces by its deposits, the importance of which certainly, before 1844, was not sufficiently appreciated either by the Bank Directors or by the public generally.

I understand you to say that you are of opinion that the Act of 1844 has not answered the purposes which its promoters had in view, and that it would be better to repeal it? That is my opinion.

Do not you think that the convertibility of the note might be as well secured, or perhaps better secured, without the Act than under its provisions? I think the convertibility of the note is safe in any case, and Lord Overstone, in his evidence,[*] said as much. He said the Bank can always take care of itself, but it is at the expense of the public. I have no doubt the Bank always would take care of itself.

The convertibility of the note would, in your opinion, be as safe without the Act of 1844 as with it? Yes; while at the same time a much greater evil than the convertibility of the note, namely, suspension of payments by the banking department, is much more possible with the Act than it was before.

C. PULLER: *You stated that, with respect to a drain of gold, since the Act of 1844 every drain had a sort of double action; that in the case of a drain extending, say to 3,000,000l., its first operation is upon the banking department, by drawing out 3,000,000l. of notes; and that then it acts upon the issue department, by the presentation of those notes, in drawing out 3,000,000l. of gold?* Yes.

You went on to add those two sums together, as if they constituted a drain of 6,000,000l. upon the Bank? Yes; what I said was, that the two departments cannot help one another, but the Bank is obliged to take separate measures for the security of both. As to the issue department, the security of that is provided for by the Act; but, in addition, the Bank are now obliged, as the drain would come out of the deposits, to take measures for the security of the deposit department, which can only be done by a contraction of their credit.

Is it fair to add those two sums together, as representing a drain upon the resources of the Bank to the amount of 6,000,000l., the notes being, in fact, certificates of so much gold deposited in the issue department? If it were a question that concerned the solvency of the Bank, I admit that it would only operate to the extent of 3,000,000l.; but in as far as the operation upon the money market is concerned, I apprehend it operates virtually as a drain of 6,000,000l. would do upon the Bank.

[*Loyd, Samuel Jones. "Evidence," *Parliamentary Papers*, 1857 (Sess. 2), X.i., pp. 339–431.]

But the 3,000,000l. of notes that are drawn out of the banking department are, in fact, the same identical portion of the resources of the Bank as the 3,000,000l. of gold which are afterwards drawn out of the issue department to meet those notes? It is as if a man having to lift a weight were restricted from using both hands to do it, and were only allowed to use one hand at a time; in which case it would be necessary that each of his hands should be as strong as the two together.

You say that, since the Act of 1844, the Bank has not kept so large a reserve in their banking department as was necessary? Not so large a reserve as would have been necessary to make the Act innocuous. To have prevented the Act from producing more violent revulsions of credit than would take place without it, it would be necessary for the Bank to keep in the deposit department alone, a reserve sufficient to meet any probable drain.

Was not the intention of the Act to make the circulation fluctuate exactly as a metallic circulation? Yes.

Has not that effect been successfully carried out? That effect has been carried out; but, I apprehend, that effect is not of the smallest consequence.

Do you think that the Act has the effect of causing the Bank to keep a less banking reserve now than it would have kept if we had had a purely metallic circulation at work, and therefore the Bank of England had been a mere bank of deposit? If the Bank had been a mere bank of deposit, and had continued to act as it has acted under the present system, namely, to consider only its own banking interest, it would have done just as it has done.

Therefore, there is nothing in the Act to cause less caution on the part of the Directors than they would have exercised if there had been a purely metallic circulation? Exactly so; but I think, in a system of credit like what we have in this country, you may have a very much more steady currency than a purely metallic currency would be.

But if there has been a less banking reserve kept than was necessary to meet the banking engagements, that result is due, not to the Act of 1844, but to the want of sufficient caution and discretion on the part of the Bank Directors? They have had a sufficient reserve to meet their liabilities; that is, they have always been able to replenish it in time; but they have been able to do so only by selling securities or diminishing their discounts very rapidly and suddenly, because of the insufficiency of their reserve to meet the whole of the drain. Now it appears to me that this is not a necessary evil, but an evil owing to the Act of 1844. By the authors of the Act it is laid down as a broad principle, that the paper currency should conform to a metallic currency. I apprehend the meaning of that is, that the permanent or standard value of the paper currency should be the same as that of a metallic currency; but not that it should have the same fluctuations. It does not follow, because we ought to make the permanent value of the paper currency conform to the value of a metallic currency, that therefore we ought to have the same fluctuations which occur in the value of a metallic currency. The fluctuations to which the value of a convertible currency is subject, depend not upon anything that affects either the metals or the bank notes, but upon general extensions or contractions of credit. The currency which is the least liable to violent contractions of credit, will be the currency with the fewest fluctuations. Therefore, if a convertible paper currency, issued by bankers and not restricted by Act of Parliament, is likely to lead to fewer variations in credit than a metallic currency, it appears to me better than a metallic currency, and better than a paper currency which is obliged to conform to a metallic currency.

Then I understand that the ill effect which you ascribe to the Act of 1844, is by comparing the actual state of things, not with any actual metallic currency, but with some imaginary system which you think would be more perfect? Not exactly so; what I mean is, that no currency can be good of which the permanent average value does not conform to the permanent average value of a metallic currency; but I do not admit the inference that in order to enable it to do this, its fluctuations in value must conform to the fluctuations in the value of a metallic currency; because it appears to me, that fluctuations in value are liable to occur from anything that affects credit; and I think that a metallic currency is liable to more severe revulsions of credit, than a mixed currency, such as ours was before the Act of 1844; and therefore, that a paper currency of the permanent value of a metallic currency, and convertible, but without any other restriction, is liable to less fluctuation than we now have under the Act of 1844 .

I understand your opinion to be, that the great advantage of unrestricted issues, as compared with the existing system, would be this; that in times of great commercial difficulty the Bank might draw upon the additional quantity of bullion which it keeps as a security for its notes for the purpose of sustaining credit in times of panic? I should rather state it in this way, that they will not be obliged to contract credit in cases in which there had been no previous undue expansion of it.

I am supposing the case of a drain in consequence of over speculation; in that case I understood you to say that the advantage of the system of unrestricted issue which you advocated, would be this; that when a panic did come after periods of over speculation, the Bank then would be able to use its whole reserve, consisting of the bullion that is now in its banking department, and so much of the bullion as is now in the issue department, as it would keep under such circumstances; and that it would therefore have a larger fund to draw upon to sustain credit than it has now? I would state it even more strongly; because in the case you are supposing, which is not a case where there is any doubt about the convertibility of the Bank note, the Bank might issue notes to any extent they were asked for, as they did after 1825.

You admit that there might be a very great extension of its issues under those circumstances? I think there ought to be in those circumstances, because there is such a destruction of ordinary credit, that it is necessary that some credit should come in to take the place of what is destroyed, in order to prevent great calamities.

Such extension of issues would increase the total amount of circulation much beyond what it would be, if it were a purely metallic currency? Very much beyond. That is a great advantage, because one of the great inconveniences of a metallic currency is, that it is impossible for it to come to the assistance of a drain in those emergencies.

You do not agree with Mr. Tooke in thinking that a mixed circulation of convertible paper must fluctuate always as a metallic currency? I am not aware that Mr. Tooke thinks that it must fluctuate in quantity as a metallic currency would; I think it is a great advantage of our currency, as it would be without the Act, that it does not fluctuate exactly as a metallic currency would.

In stating the advantages that would be obtained in a time of extreme panic by the system you recommend, you admit that they would be purchased at the expense of a certain disadvantage, namely, that the commercial crisis, when it did come, would be more violent than it would be if it was checked in time, as it is now checked by the operation of the Act of 1844? I think the Act does check it in its earlier stages, when the crisis has proceeded from over speculation. At the same time, I think there is every probability that the Bank would now act in such cases exactly as the Act prescribes, even if the Act did not exist.

Would there not also be this possible great disadvantage, that under a system of unrestricted issues, if notwithstanding the assistance which the Bank rendered to the public they were unable to stop the panic, it would be enormously aggravated by the alarm of every note-holder throughout the country? That is supposing a case that is not likely to happen, unless the country were in possession of a foreign army. I can hardly imagine any other case in which there could be any doubt as to the sufficiency of the notes of the Bank of England to secure anybody who possessed them. We know that at the time of the panic in 1825, there was never a doubt for a single instant about the notes of the Bank of England.

But sometimes a panic is not always governed by reason? No; but in such an extreme case any system of credit or banking must break down.

With respect to a foreign drain, such a drain as is produced by a bad harvest, or by foreign remittances of the Government, of course turns the exchange against this country? Yes.

Must not that amount of drain ultimately be paid for and the exchanges corrected by the operation of the trade of the country? Not necessarily; it may be by mere transactions in securities, by transfers of securities from one country to another.

But as a general rule, would you not say that you must look to the trade of the country? It is of very great consequence, I apprehend, whether the effect is produced through an action on the prices of commodities, or without that action; because that affects a much larger class of persons than could be affected by changes in the price of securities.

You have expressed an opinion that such a drain ought to be met by the reserve of bullion in the Bank rather than by an action on discounts; now, supposing the reserve of bullion to be nearly drained out, would you think that such a state of things ought to be allowed to continue; or is it not desirable that the Bank should have every motive so to act, by contracting its discounts, as to correct the exchanges? It would always have that motive when its reserve got low; it would necessarily be obliged to take such measures; the only difference would be, that it need not take them so violently; because if the drain should be a limited drain, a drain arising from a cause not permanent, of course as to so much of the drain as had already taken place, it would be unnecessary for the Bank to provide for it by restricting its discounts.

Under a system of metallic currency all these matters would be regulated by the natural laws which govern the distribution of the precious metals? Yes.

Do not you think that upon the whole that system is more likely to be safe and right than by entrusting the regulation of them to the discretion of any body of men whatever? It seems to me that natural laws would equally operate in the other case. The course that would naturally be followed in a case of panic, for instance, is exactly the one which the Act prevents, namely, to come to the assistance of trade at a time when there is a great destruction of credit, which the Bank would always do if it were not prevented, but which it cannot do now in those cases, unless the Act is suspended.

You said that you were in favour of allowing country banks, as well as the Bank of England, to issue notes without any other restriction than convertibility,[*] *or, at all events, that you saw no need of restriction from the fear of over-issues; will you state what you mean by "over-issues," because you have already told us that you admit that it is possible that*

[*See p. 509 above.]

issues of paper may be in excess of that which a metallic circulation would supply? By over-issues, I mean such as create undue speculation, or maintain it when it ought to be checked. In any other sense I do not conceive that there can be over-issues so long as convertibility is maintained.

Then your opinion is a theoretical opinion; it is not deduced from the fact that there have been no such issues? It is my interpretation of the facts that have taken place.

Do you remember the case of the American banks in 1835, when the issues rose from about 100,000,000l. to about 150,000,000l. in the course of one year? Yes, but I have always understood that there was not practical convertibility at that time.

They were legally convertible, were they not? The fact was, that either through the influence of the banks, or for some other reason, they were not convertible. In the next place, I admit that in a period of violent speculation, that speculation may be ministered to by banks; not that they do so in the commencement, at least not by means of their notes, but they may prevent speculation from being early checked by the necessity of re-selling goods that had been speculated upon.

T. WEGUELIN: *Has not your examination to-day turned entirely upon the management of the Bank as a bank of deposit?* It seems to me to involve the whole management of the Bank, as far as the currency is affected by it.

Has it not turned mainly upon the management of its deposits? I think it has turned mainly upon the deposits, for this reason, that it is chiefly, in my opinion, by not attending to the management of the deposits that the promoters of the Act have been led to what I consider a wrong conclusion.

THE INCOME AND PROPERTY TAX

1861

EDITOR'S NOTE

Parliamentary Papers, 1861, VII, 244–64. Not republished. Original heading: "John Stuart Mill, Esq., called in; and Examined." Running heads: "Minutes of Evidence taken before the/Select Committee on Income and Property Tax." The evidence was taken on 18 June, 1861, with John Hubbard in the Chair, and the following members of the Committee present: Walter Buchanan, Stephen Cave, William Gladstone (Chancellor of the Exchequer), T. Sotheron Estcourt, Sir William Heathcote, Sir Frederick Heygate, Robert Lowe, Sir Stafford Northcote, James Turner, William Pollard-Urquhart. Not mentioned in JSM's bibliography or *Autobiography*. No copy in Somerville College.

On 19 Sept., 1861 JSM wrote to Leonard Courtney, in answer to the latter's "intelligent objections" to his arguments before the Committee, saying in part: "It so happened that none of my cross-examiners in the Committee took the same view of the subject which you, and the actuaries, take; and their questions, therefore, drew out very little of what I could have said in opposition to that view. I will merely place before you one form of the argument, which appears to me very simple and conclusive. The actuaries argue that income of equal capitalized value should pay equal amounts to the tax. Granted: that is, equal *total* amounts. But if these equal total amounts are to be made up by equal annual payments, it is implied that the payments are of equal duration, and the owner of the terminable income would be required to go on paying his quota to the tax after his income had ceased.

If you will only consider what would be the payments required from the two supposed taxpayers if each of them was required or empowered to redeem the tax by paying down a gross sum once for all, you would, I think, see that the opinion of the actuaries has no ground whatever to stand on." (Letter in the British Library of Political and Economic Science.)

JSM's examination includes questions 3538 to 3804 of the evidence before the Committee.

The Income and Property Tax

J. HUBBARD: *You have given considerable attention, have you not, to the subject of taxation in its different forms?* I have given considerable attention to that subject.

Would you have the kindness to state to the Committee what are the principles upon which you would recommend the construction of a tax of the nature of an income tax, levied for the purpose of providing a portion of the annual supplies of the country, and therefore differing in that respect from a property tax, which is levied upon the corpus *of the property at its change of possessor or transfer?* It seems necessary, I think, to begin by considering what would be the conditions of a perfectly just income tax, although those conditions may not be, and are not, entirely realizable; in order to have a standard of absolute justice before one, which one must endeavour to carry out so far as insuperable practical obstacles do not interfere with it. Unless we set before ourselves an idea of what would be perfectly just, we are unable to make any fair approximation to justice in the practical application. I should say that the first rule is the general rule of taxation, namely, equality; that is to say, taxation in proportion to means. But this does not, I think, necessarily imply taxation in proportion to the whole of a person's receipts; because the whole of his receipts may greatly exceed what he can, with any propriety, expend upon himself. It seems to me, therefore, that two kinds of allowances are necessary; an allowance for small incomes, and an allowance for incomes that are of temporary duration, or precarious; and I think that the present income tax fails of justice under both those heads, though I do not go nearly so far as many people in my estimate of the amount of that injustice.

Would you state what are the special features in the present income tax[*] *which appear to you to conflict with those two principles which you have laid down?* Perhaps I had better begin with the one of the two cases which will take the shortest time to state, and that is the allowance due to small incomes. It seems to be admitted that a just income tax ought never to fall on necessaries; and accordingly all income taxes fix a certain minimum

[*23 Victoria, c. 14.]

up to which no tax is paid. That I think perfectly right; but the present income tax taxes incomes which exceed that minimum on their full amount, and that seems to me not just. Justice, I conceive, requires that any income exceeding the minimum should be taxed only on the excess, and not on the whole amount; because otherwise those who are immediately above the minimum are placed in a worse position than if they were at the minimum. The rule of equality and of fair proportion seems to me to be that people should be taxed in an equal ratio on their superfluities; necessaries being untaxed, and surplus paying in all cases an equal percentage. This satisfies entirely the small amount of justice that there is in the theory of a graduated income tax, which appears to me to be otherwise an entirely unjust mode of taxation, and in fact, a graduated robbery. What gives it plausibility is the fact, that at present the lowest incomes which are taxed at all are overtaxed. If an income above 100*l.* a year, supposing that to be the minimum, as at present, were only taxed upon the excess above 100*l.* a year, I think everybody would see that the ratio was in that case fair, and that the lower incomes were exempted as much as they had any just right to be.

Following out for a moment the last inference which the Committee might draw from your reply, you are aware, are you not, that the objection to taxing upon the excess beyond a certain sum, if applied strictly, would involve the collection of sums so small, and spread over so wide a surface, that they would not be worth collecting; do you think that any adjustment in a middle form might be taken which would reconcile those difficulties; for instance, instead of taxing 101l. at 1l., or 105l. at 5l., a certain minimum, say 60l., should be deducted from incomes of 100l. up to 150l., so as to leave 40l. as the sum which should be assessed? That seems to leave too large a margin. I know that there would be an objection to assessing incomes of 101*l.* upon 1*l.*; the income tax upon 1*l.* would not be worth collecting; but I presume that the income tax upon 5*l.* might be so. A 6*d.* income tax on 1*l.* would be 2*s.* 6*d.*, and I imagine that the tax-gatherer does collect as small sums as that. At any rate that is only a question of degree. You might tax every income on its excess above 100*l.*; that is, you might make the taxable amount the excess above 100*l.*, but might only begin to collect the tax at the point of 105*l.*, or 110*l.* Or if it is thought necessary to begin the actual collection at 100*l.*, you might tax only the excess above 90*l.*, or the excess above 80*l.* But I have no very decided opinion upon that point.

To settle the principle of your remark, it implies that a certain sum would be adjusted as an equivalent for the necessary maintenance, and that above that all should be taxed, releasing then only sums so small as not to be worth collecting? Just so.

Then, passing to the other point of your remark, which was the mode in which the present tax falls upon precarious incomes; in what way would you describe the present inequality of the tax in that respect, and in what way would you propose to remedy it? The injustice of the present tax as it affects permanent and temporary incomes, and fixed and precarious incomes, seems to me to result from this: that incomes which are nominally equal, are not equal for the purpose of expenditure. Those whose income is either temporary or precarious are under obligations, or necessities, one may say, which others are not under, to save a portion of their income; and that I conceive to be the only claim in equity that there is to any remission of taxation in the case of temporary incomes. The plan of capitalising incomes and taxing them on their value as capital, I confess, seems to me to be not merely impracticable, but, even if it were practicable, thoroughly unjust and unequal, and to involve such arithmetical fallacies, that it is to me a matter of astonishment that good arithmeticians should have fallen into them. But what I should lay down as a perfectly unexceptionable and just principle of income tax, if it were capable of being practically realised, would be to exempt all savings; that the portion of an income which was saved, and converted into capital, should be untaxed. I would leave this untaxed, because otherwise, as it pays income tax again after being invested, as it pays income tax on its produce after having paid it on the capital, it really pays twice, whereas the portion of income, which is devoted to personal expenditure, pays only once. By the adoption (if it were practicable) of the principle of not taxing savings, all the claims of justice towards individuals would be included and covered. Inasmuch as the only claim which any income has to be taxed more lightly than others consists in the greater necessity for saving; if you could exempt from taxation what any person does save, you would have done him full justice in that respect, and if he does not actually save it, he has no claim to any exemption. I am laying this down merely as the theory of a perfectly just income tax. I am quite aware that it cannot be fully carried out; that you cannot consider individual cases, and you are therefore obliged to consider, not what people actually do save, but what are their necessities and obligations to save; with merely a general consideration whether, on the average, it is practically the fact that as a class they do it, or not.

In the attempt to carry out that theory, if you are unable to consider individual cases, would you make it a portion of your design to consider classes of incomes, so as to ascertain as nearly as you might, those incomes which are subject to the demands of saving to a greater degree than others? Certainly; and the impossibility of doing full justice in every case would be no good reason with me against doing it whenever I could.

Would you describe to the Committee what characteristics you would *demand in incomes which you would conceive to be entitled to concession in the matter of taxation, seeing that the present law levies the same tax upon all receipts under the shape of income which came into the possession of an individual during the year?* I beg to be understood as speaking positively only on the claims of justice, and the scientific principle on which the tax should rest. On the question of practicability, or of the administrative difficulties which might arise in applying the principle, I must be understood as always speaking under correction from many who are much more competent than I am to judge of those administrative difficulties. But in principle, I would say that all life incomes, with certain exceptions which I could specify, have a claim to some consideration as compared with permanent incomes; and that all precarious incomes, without any exception that I know of, have a claim to some consideration as compared with those which are not precarious, but fixed. Those which, like industrial incomes generally, are both precarious as to amount and also temporary as to duration, having thus a double claim, have the strongest claim of any. By industrial incomes, I mean, as the Honourable Chairman means in his memorandum,[*] professional and trading incomes; but trading have not quite so strong a claim as professional incomes, because traders, at least those who are trading on their own capital, in some degree combine the two characters, and hold an intermediate position between those who depend on property and those who depend on labour.

When you state that you would place life incomes in a different category from permanent incomes, do you state that with regard to the tenure of the owners, and without consideration of the nature of the income itself or of the property which produces it? I state it without any distinction as to the nature of the property from which the income emanates: but I am quite aware that the source from which it emanates makes a great many practical differences, some of which are such as in my opinion ought to exclude some life incomes from the consideration which I would give to them in other cases.

If you look at the schedule[†] *which is in the paper lying before you on the table, you will find that in the scheme which is there presented to the Committee, it is proposed to range in one class only all the incomes derived from property which may be invested; the Committee now, I think, understand you as wishing, if possible, to discriminate between the different tenures under which portions of that income might be held?* As far as possible; as far as is consistent with administrative impracticabilities.

That is to say, that land, or the rental of land, might be held under some

[*Hubbard, John G. "Memorandum submitted by the Chairman," in "Appendix 1 to the Report from the Select Committee on Income and Property Tax," *Parliamentary Papers*, 1861, VII, pp. 315–17.]
[†"Income Tax Schedule," *ibid.*, p. 314.]

charges or tenures to which you would grant an indulgent measure of taxation, while the rental of land held under other tenures you would tax to the full amount which might be imposed? Exactly.

The consequence of the application of that rule would also apply, would it not, to the dividends of funded property, or to any of the products of money invested? Yes. In principle, and as a general rule, I would exempt merely life incomes from a portion of the tax, by taxing them only on a part of their gross amount. But in some cases, I do not think that they possess this claim for exemption: particularly in cases of life incomes derived from settled property. There are a number of interests, which are life interests, one may say, only in name, and in a sense which is quite consistent with the tenant in possession being able to spend the whole of the income without imprudence. For instance, a tenant in possession of settled property, though he may be only a tenant for life, has, I should say, no claim to exemption, because the reason on which I would give an exemption in other cases does not apply to him. It may be fairly presumed that if he has any person whom he is bound to provide for, that is, if he has any children, for that is the only case that can be laid down as a case of obligation, they are probably provided for by the same settlement under which he is a tenant for life. The same reason applies to the next heir, the person who, under the settlement, will come in next. He may have an allowance by the settlement, which is of course liable to income tax, and I do not think that he has any claim to be taxed on less than its entire amount; because as he is to come into the whole property ultimately, he is not obliged to save out of his income, the amount of which, probably, has been adapted to his present needs and expenditure, and nothing else. I do not undertake to say positively how far the exceptions to the rule of partially exempting life incomes should extend. For instance, the case of a widow's jointure is a case in which doubt might arise. But upon the whole, I should say that a widow's jointure is not entitled to any exemption; because in almost every case in which a jointure is settled on a widow, either she has no children, or if she has, they are provided for by the same settlement; and therefore, generally speaking (of course you cannot allow for individual cases) she is under no extraordinary obligation to save anything for children from her jointure. Therefore, taking cases in classes, and without considering individual cases, these are life interests, and yet have no claim. I do not think that the same reasons apply to collaterals. I think that charges for younger children, for instance, though they have not quite so strong a claim as industrial incomes, still have a claim to exemption to a certain extent.

The motive, as I understand, for the concession of which you are now speaking, as desirable for the purpose of carrying out a perfectly just theory of taxation, is the view of the necessity of saving? It is so.

Would you allow to be introduced, with regard to that necessity of saving, other considerations beyond that of mere tenure; for instance, would you allow the introduction of the consideration of whether other property might be held by the person in question, and what children he either had or might have; whether he were married or unmarried, in what degree the relations who were next of kin might stand to him, as influencing his desire of accumulating on their behalf; all those circumstances would, of course, form elements which would weigh upon a man with regard to his disposition to save; are you prepared to admit that those considerations should be ascertained for the purpose of qualifying or establishing the concessions that you think would be desirable? I do not think it would be possible to enter into those minutiæ, or into the particular circumstances of individuals. I think you can only proceed on a general and rough classification of incomes. Besides, if it were possible to enter into those minutiæ, I apprehend that there would be just the same reason for entering into them in the case of industrial incomes, as in that of incomes from land, or the funds.

Then you would, by the concession which you think might be required here, imply a new interpretation of the tenure of the owner? Yes.

Have you at all considered whether, in legal form, that tenure could be so described as to carry out the object which you have in view, without giving rise to doubt or litigation? The only way which has occurred to me (but it is possible that better ways may occur to others) is, that all incomes which are for life, or for terms of years, shall be entitled to exemption, except an enumerated list. The list of exceptions would perhaps comprise three-fourths of all those which are nominally life tenures. For instance; if it were enacted that the case of a tenant in possession of settled property, the case of the future possessor, and the case of widows' jointures, should be excepted cases, to which no exemption should be allowed, these alone would cover, I imagine, the great mass of the nominal life interests in property. Thus a very small list of exceptions would include such a mass of incomes as would make it comparatively unimportant, whether or not you specified all the exceptions that might be with justice made. If you except those great classes of cases in which there could be no claim to exemption, I think an exemption might be allowed in all unmentioned and unenumerated cases of temporary incomes.

Would you allow the same indulgence to take effect upon the execution of a deed of trust by the owner of an estate, as you would in the event of that disposition having become a legal document, and being subject to its legal results; would you, for instance, allow a man of middle age to make by deed a disposition of his property which he would ordinarily make by will, so as to involve the same consequences with regard to a claim for concession in the incidence of the tax? Yes; for instance, if he chose to bind himself to give a provision of so much a year to one of his younger children in his lifetime, instead of postponing it until his death, you have a right to consider that from the time the income is out of his control it belongs to his younger son, and the younger son must be treated like any other life annuitant, I should say, from that time.

Supposing a large landowner of middle age, who holds an estate in fee, of course naturally subject to the incidence of the tax, to make a trust deed, under which he provides for his several children, reserving to himself only a life interest in the estate, and giving to them a contingent reversion in the property in various shares, and supposing that that disposition in no degree fettered the amount of expenditure which he had previously been commanding, do you think that there is anything in the mere legal determination of that property which should exonerate the estate from a portion of its liability to the Exchequer? His power of expenditure is now fettered in a degree in which it was not before, because he has, by a special bond, bound himself legally to make certain allowances to certain people; and has it not in his power to expend that part of his income on anything else. It has become the property of the person to whom he has given it; it has become the income of that person, and is no longer part of his own income. Therefore, in considering how it should be taxed, we ought to consider the circumstances of the person receiving it, and not those of the person paying it.

If, for instance, a person having an estate of 10,000l. a year, with the property tax at the rate of 9d., amounting to 375l. a year, were to place it entirely in trust in that way, he might diminish the liability of the estate by one-half; as regards the income tax, do you think that the circumstances of a family arrangement or a settlement are of such a nature as to justify the relaxation of the Chancellor of the Exchequer in his demand upon the revenues of that estate? If such a rare case should happen as that of a person who, during his life time, legally appropriates the half of his income to another person, it is then no longer his, and the Exchequer has no longer any business to come upon him for it. With regard to those who now have it, it seems to me that they are to be considered each of them as to his own position or his own circumstances. If a parent is in such a position that he ought to save for his younger children, or to give them the means of saving for themselves, it is a thing rather to be rejoiced in than not; that by these family arrangements he is enabled to obtain an allowance from the Exchequer for what is thus saved.

We are assuming that he retains in his own possession the full sum which he wishes to expend, and therefore he does not embarrass his own expenditure, but it is merely that he changes the legal tenure of the property which is to be rated, and so far changes its incidence to the tax? Yes.

Have you considered whether the question of savings should override in the assessment of the rental of property, the rule which has been equally affirmed that all property being protected by the State should, to its full extent, be taxed equally? I do not recognize any rights or obligations as existing in property itself, in things; I recognize them only as existing in persons. All moral rights reside in persons; and all moral obligations are towards persons and I should consider nothing but persons in any question of justice.

But then you would consider those persons not simply in their persons, but with regard to their property, which qualifies them to pay taxes? I should consider it, so far as it constitutes their means of paying the taxes, and the payments ought to be adjusted equitably to those means; but I should not think that anything depends on whether one form of property is more easily accessible than the others, or whether you are more certain of its amount in the case of one person than in the case of another. I should say, in each case ascertain that as you best can, and then tax it with reference to the circumstances of the person, and not with reference to any supposed peculiarity in the thing. I only recognize things as influencing the question of justice in so far as they operate upon the situation and feelings of persons.

Are we to understand you to state that you conceive that the incomes derived from real property should under a perfect theory of taxation be taxed not upon their net amount but upon their amount with regard to the supposed saving in each individual case, as measured by the tenure of the owners? The amount of saving cannot be got at in an individual case; but the presumable savings of classes I think depend more upon the tenure than upon anything else. The saving which you have a right to presume that classes will make, depends on the classification according to the tenure; it depends upon whether the tenure of the property is permanent or temporary, and whether it is of a fixed or of a precarious amount. I would beg to add that whatever claims I may think exist to exemption in the case of some life incomes derived from property (and therefore falling within the first class in the Chairman's memorandum), I can hardly imagine that any of them are so strong as the claims of the second class; because the second class has the double claim of precariousness and of temporariness, whereas incomes from land, though they may be for life only are usually fixed, and the cases of their being at all variable or precarious in amount are very rare. That is one reason. Another reason is because in the great majority of life incomes derived from land or from realized property, the obligation or necessity for saving, though it exists, is of a considerably less binding character. For example, in the case, which is one of the strongest, that of provisions for younger children, I do not think that the necessity of saving in that case is on the average nearly so great as in the case of industrial incomes. In the first place, there is some difference between the case of sons and that of daughters. In the case of daughters, a large proportion of them will probably marry, and of those who marry a large proportion, if they marry in their own class, will not be under the necessity of saving from their separate incomes. Still, they may marry some one to whom their income is of importance, or they may not marry at all, and therefore I do not think that their claim is annihilated; it is only weakened. Then as to younger sons who have life incomes; they have a claim to exemption, but not so strong a one as professional and industrial incomes have; because generally speaking, incomes given to younger sons are not meant to be their sole provision; they are destined to enter into the professional class in some way or other, and what is given them is generally as a help to that rather than a substitute for it. As a matter of fact, I believe those of them who marry do generally acquire more than the incomes so allowed them, and those who do not marry are not obliged to save. As a class, therefore, they have I think, a less strong claim than industrial incomes, but still a real claim to partial exemption.

With regard to incomes in the first class, with regard to which you have described very ably the remissions which you would be glad to see put in force if they were practicable, and upon which I dare say you are aware that there may be considerable doubts, but with regard to the second class you affirm a stronger claim, because there are more of those elements which should influence saving, which you conceive to be the proper test for concession? Yes. In the case of industrial incomes there are all the elements that possibly can be; there is want of permanence, and want of fixity. There is nothing, generally speaking, to fall back upon in the case of those for whom the saving is made, and, if they are not provided for from that source, they are not so at all. That applies in its strictness, however, only to professional and not to trading incomes, and I should be glad, if it were possible, to see a distinction made between trading and professional incomes. The claims of professional incomes, and all incomes derived entirely from personal exertions, seem to me to be the strongest possible. The claims of incomes from trade are less strong; because so far as the income consists of the interest of capital, it properly comes into the first class, and, being of a permanent character, is not entitled to exemption. If it were possible to tax traders on the interest of their capital at one rate, and on the remainder of their profits at another, as you do propose to tax the incomes of the capital that they borrow at one rate, and their profits at another; if it were possible to extend this to the interest of the whole of their capital, and tax it at a higher rate, and the surplus profits at a lower rate, I should be very glad to do it; but whether it can be done or not is a point upon which I am entirely in the hands of those who can judge better than I can.

Are you not now alluding to a distinction which requires you to deviate rather from what you have hitherto taken as the main guide to the discrimination which you require, namely, savings; do you suppose that the proportion of the savings which are effected out of professional earnings is larger, or as large, as those which are made out of the earnings of trades and manufactures, and other industrial employments which contain capital as one of their requisites? No doubt the mass of saving comes from traders; that is, a much greater absolute mass comes from them than from professional incomes; but whether, generally speaking, as large a proportion may not be saved from professional incomes I have no means of judging. Professional incomes I take to amount, on the whole, to much less than the aggregate of trading incomes, and therefore if they saved on the whole as large a proportion of their incomes, their savings would still bear a much smaller proportion to the entire savings of the country. There is one reason, however, which inclines me to think that very likely the savings from professional incomes may in reality be somewhat less in proportion than from trading incomes, namely, that perhaps a larger proportion of traders than of professional men are aiming at making fortunes. The great mass of professional men are aiming probably at little except a moderate provision for their children and for their old age, while successful traders are mostly aiming at making fortunes, and passing into a superior class altogether. That establishes a certain degree of probability that traders save in a larger ratio than professional men, but how far this is really the case it is not in my power to estimate.

Without venturing, therefore, to assert that traders or manufacturers save a larger proportion, you would probably admit that they certainly save as large a proportion as professional men do out of their earnings? Yes.

And, therefore, if you look to that test alone, there would be no plea for drawing a line of discrimination between them as regards the assessment on their earnings? Just so. If it were possible to carry out the principle of the tax, and to ascertain actual savings, I should have no objection whatever to any degree of favour which that principle might extend to traders. But since it is impossible to carry out that principle, the next principle that you can follow is that of the necessities or obligations for saving, and those are greater in the case of professional men than in the case of traders, for two reasons. One reason is, that the great majority of traders have capital of their own, which, being left to their children, may be sufficient to fulfil their obligation; since nobody is obliged to save, so as to leave his descendants as rich as himself. The obligation to save does not extend that far; it may be often sufficiently satisfied by leaving the capital only. But the capital only is not always the whole of what is left. Many businesses are in fact almost as hereditary as properties. In almost every very successful business it happens that if there is a son, who has been brought up to the business, and who is capable of it, he continues to carry it on, and thus inherits not only the interest on the capital, but that additional profit which is the reward of ability and industry.

Supposing that it were found impracticable to draw the line of separation between trades and incomes, from their merging into each other in many instances, so that it is impossible always to ascertain the amount of capital engaged in trade, which would be indispensable in order to carry out the discriminating assessment of trades, do you think that it would meet the justice and necessity of the case to involve both trades and professions in one common measure of relief? I should regret the necessity, but I would rather do that than not give relief at all. If I could not make the distinction, I would give to both, instead of withholding from both. And what would reconcile me mainly, if I could be reconciled, to making no distinction, would be the fact which you have mentioned, that the great mass of the actual saving of the country is made by the trading classes. If one-third or any other proportion of income may be considered to be actually saved by the trading classes, I should see no injustice in adopting that average, and taxing them only upon two-thirds.

Are you aware that in the paper which you have before you, the one-third is not stated to have been arrived at by any definite calculation, but it is rather a proportion inferentially derived from other great facts which are patent to those who have inquired into the subject; it is in itself rather an arbitrary figure? It is no doubt impossible to get any perfectly accurate statement, but some rough estimate may be made, and as far as I know, that may be a just one.

You see no reason yourself to question the propriety of that proportion? None whatever. I observe it assumes that more than one-third is actually saved by the trading classes, because one-third, in the plan before me, represents the excess of their proportional saving above that which is supposed to be made by the first class.

May the Committee infer from what you have now stated, that your wish would be to carry out a theory which would consider the amount of saving in individual cases, to be estimated from the nature of their tenure in the cases of incomes in the first schedule, but that failing the power of making that inquiry and that concession, you think it would be desirable to make the concession which is proposed for the second class alone, and in the proportion which is there stated? I would do so, so far as my information extends. I cannot speak positively as to the proportion, I must leave that to be judged of by others; but I am quite clear about this, that even if it were practically impossible to make the concession to any one else, the classes in the second table in this memorandum ought to have it.

W. GLADSTONE: *You have stated that you exclude from your view the class of difficulties, in any reconstruction of the income tax, which may be termed administrative, and deal with the question on abstract and scientific principles; may I ask you whether you also exclude from your view another class of difficulties, which may be termed political difficulties?* It is hardly my province to consider political difficulties, these being, I presume, the difficulties of carrying the question through Parliament.

I mean the difficulties of carrying the question through Parliament, and of making the measure acceptable to the country, which of course, as we know very well, would not depend upon the degree of its scientific accuracy, but in a much greater degree upon the feelings of men with regard to the relative mode of treatment? That last consideration I do feel bound to enter into.

You despair, do not you, of any mode of adaptation or of reconstruction of the income tax to the principles of justice, and you look to what you have fairly termed a rough estimate? Yes.

Those rough estimates, coming as they would, with all the disadvantages of novelty, in the matter of taxation, and aiming at supplanting a system which is old, and has been long established, is there not some danger that those rough estimates might give rise to very great differences of opinion as between those classes who were to receive remissions and those classes who were to undergo augmentations, in order to enable the others to receive remissions, and that the political difficulties to which that might give rise would be so considerable, that in all probability they would be insurmountable? If the system which is proposed to be interfered with were one that gave general satisfaction, and could be considered a popular system, I cannot deny that the new inequalities which might be introduced, or those which might be left unredressed, might be very severely criticised. But there is such dissatisfaction with the plan as it now is, that I think there could hardly be so much with any new one; at least if the cases in which redress was given by the new plan, were on the whole those which presented the strongest claims to it, as I think would be the case under the Honourable Chairman's plan. It seems to me, that any plan giving a relief of one-third to the whole mass of industrial incomes, would not only cover the greatest number of cases that have any claim, but also the strongest cases; and I should therefore anticipate that the complaint and dissatisfaction which might be excited by the impossibility of carrying the relief quite so far as the principle would go, would not be very great. I think that almost all the cases which would be left unrelieved, would be cases in which the claim to relief, if properly explained, would be seen to be not nearly so strong as in the cases of industrial incomes.

I wish to call your attention particularly to the circumstance that, as we must assume for the purpose of argument, one class of cases being relieved, another class of cases would not merely be left unrelieved, but they would necessarily be subjected to an additional tax, in order to make up the vacuum in the Exchequer which is caused by the relief granted to the other cases; and it is with reference to the dissatisfaction that might attend the positive increase of the taxation in the unrelieved cases that I wished to present to your mind the view of the political difficulties. That is a case which must arise in every attempt to redress the inequalities of taxation. If you relieve some of the payers, the Exchequer must either do without the money or must raise it in some other way. Those who have to make up the deficiency may complain, but that is not an objection to redressing a grievance, when the cases you are able to relieve are those in which the claim is strongest. Very much will depend upon the clearness and authority with which the real grounds for making the exemption were presented to the public mind, and with which, I think, they would perfectly well admit of being presented; the present Chancellor of the Exchequer, if he had to do it, would be perfectly competent to it. I think that they would admit of being so presented to the public, as to be made intelligible to reasonable people. To unreasonable people they would never be intelligible.

A great deal would depend, would it not, upon the practicability of drawing broad and clear lines of demarcation at the point where you pass over from one rate of tax to the other? Yes, and it is a very strong argument in favour of the Chairman's plan that it does so; that it draws the line very markedly and definitely. My desire would be, if possible, to run the risk of making the line of demarcation a little less definite, in order to include a still greater number of the cases to which the principle applies; but I speak entirely under correction, in regard to the administrative difficulties that would arise in making those distinctions, especially in reference to a very important consideration, the possible introduction of fresh frauds.

It would be necessary, would it not, for any body of persons charged with the responsibility of conducting public affairs, to look carefully through, and to test all the various forms of difficulty that might be raised, and it would not be sufficient for them to say that they had prepared a plan of which the general outlines were so sound, that they felt assured that it would be carried, but they must be prepared to give an answer to every difficulty that might be stated? Yes.

Have you ever felt yourself to be in the same predicament, and to be bound to go through the various forms of difficulty, and to deal with them definitively on that principle, and to consider whether the result is, to leave those clear demarcations which might be made intelligible and satisfactory to the public? I cannot pretend that I have considered it so fully, and with so much knowledge of the subject as those have done whose business it is, but I have paid some attention to it.

With regard to what I understand to be your principle of a perfectly just income tax, namely, that there should be an exemption of all savings, if it were attainable; am I right in supposing that you state the ground of that principle to be this, that if any other course is adopted, the income is twice taxed? Yes; a portion of the income is twice taxed.

Would you kindly point out particularly in what mode it is twice taxed? Suppose that out of an income of 1,000*l.* a year, I save 300*l.*, and spend 700*l.*; on that 700*l.* I pay the tax once; we will suppose it for the sake of simplicity to be 10 per cent. I pay, therefore, on the 300*l.* 30*l.*, and I have only 270*l.* remaining; those 270*l.* I make no other use of except to lay them out and receive what they produce, and that produce I expend, and pay the income tax again on its amount. The produce has thus been doubly reduced; in the first place by a reduction of the capital, and in the second place by a tax upon the returns. If there had been no income tax I should not merely have escaped the income tax on the new revenue, but that new revenue would have been one-tenth greater than it is, and therefore I say that I have been taxed twice. A parallel case would, perhaps, serve for illustration. Supposing there were a tax on stockings, intended to be 10 per cent.: if a tax were also laid upon the machinery by which they were made (supposing for simplicity the machinery to include all the expense of making them) will not the stockings be in reality taxed 20 per cent.? It may be replied that the stockings bear one part, and the machinery the other part of the tax; that you have got the machinery and you have got the stockings too. That is true, but the machinery is of no use except to produce the stockings. The stockings are to be the whole of your remuneration; you have paid 20 per cent. before you sell them, and you will not get back the tax unless you raise their price 20 per cent. In the same manner, I say, that on that part of any person's income which he saves and invests, and pays income tax on the returns, he is paying the tax twice. He cannot both spend the income and save it; but he is taxed as if he did both; he is taxed on it in the first instance just as if he spent it, and he is rated again on what he does spend, namely, its produce. He is taxed as if he used it for both purposes; but he can only use it for one, though he may use it for either. Therefore, I think you cannot claim the tax more than once.

Practically, the state of facts which you consider glaringly unjust in this respect, as I understand this, that a man with 1,000l. a year saving 300l., is liable to pay an income tax of 10 per cent. (that is 30l. upon the 300l. that

he saves) while that 300l. is in its transition state from income to capital?
Just so.

And that subsequently, he is also liable to pay income tax upon the fruits of the remaining 270l.? Yes, for he pays it at both ends; he has the amount reduced by the amount of income tax, in the first place; and then he pays a second income tax upon it when he gets it.

Do you consider the injustice of such a state of things, as I described in my question (if that was a true description of it) to be patent and self-evident? I consider that on the principles of equality it is so. If a person is taxed on one part of his income once, and on another part twice, that is contrary to what is universally received as the just principle of taxation; and contrary to public policy too, because the portion which is taxed twice is just the portion employed in a way in which it would rather be public policy to encourage its employment. In fact, it is liable to the same objection, in some degree, which applies to a graduated property tax. The great injustice of a graduated property tax is that, by sparing the prodigal and taxing the saving, it is a punishment for economy and a reward for the reverse. So is the present income tax; since, whoever saves part of his income, pays on that part double the tax that he would have paid if he had spent it.

If I understand your objection, it goes to the root of the principle of a tax upon income, and what you contend that justice requires is, that there should be no tax upon income as such, but a tax upon expenditure? Precisely: but seeing that levying it upon income is the only way in which it can be practically done, I would levy it in such a manner as to make it approximate as closely as possible to a tax upon expenditure.

The great bulk of our taxation already lies upon expenditure, does it not? Yes.

Do you think that all taxation ought to be placed upon expenditure, and that every tax which is not placed upon expenditure, sins against first principles? I think that every tax, in so far as it is levied upon anything but expenditure, does sin against first principles. The most advantageous manner of levying it may often be on income; but still I think in its practical incidence it ought to fall on expenditure.

Therefore, with respect to the principle of the tax, making all due allowance for the difficulty of its application, you are not prepared to go the length of saying that those taxes which are directly laid upon capital are indefensible upon principle? No; not the succession tax, for instance. Those who advocate a graduated property tax, I think, have thus much ground for their opinion: they feel instinctively that the State, in its taxation, ought to give some advantage to those whose income is the result of labour, above those to whom it comes without any exertion of their own; but the only way in which, as it seems to me, this distinction can be made financially, is on the occurrence of a vacancy by death, or the passage of property from one person to another; because as long as the income is in the hands of the person in whose hands it originated, the presumption is, that he earned it, and if you tax him at a greater proportion because the amount is greater, it is taxing him either because he has earned more, or because he has saved more; either of which seems to me to be unjust and impolitic.

Still, if I understand the matter rightly, the objection which you have taken to the present income tax, namely, that it begins by limiting capital, and then taxes the produce of the remaining capital, and therefore may be said to tax incomes twice over, that objection applies just as much in the case of a succession tax, inasmuch as a man who comes into an inheritance of the value of 10,000l., and has a succession tax of 1,000l. laid upon it, is liable, in the first instance, to have the capital diminished by the tax on the succession, and then on the current rent, which is taxed by the income tax, or in whatever form the tax may be, on the fruits of the capital itself? Perfectly true. But I do not think that the principle of equality of taxation has any application to the case of taxes on succession. It seems to me that taxes on succession stand on a different foundation from all other taxes, and that the State is entitled, in reference to them, to consider public policy and general morality, abstractedly from the special rule of equality of taxation. If a person is allowed by the State to succeed to that which he has not earned, but has obtained without any exertion, that is a privilege which he owes to the existence of law and society, to which the State is entitled to annex conditions, and if those conditions are just, when tried by a higher principle of morality, no general principle of equality of taxation has any application to them.

You assume that there is a peculiarity in the case of the tax upon succession, by its amount; would you condemn other taxes upon capital in its transfer? I would; I think them always indefensible.

Do you think that the principle which you have laid down as adverse to the taxation of capital, with the single exception of taxes on succession, is of so high an order that it can be really treated, not merely as one of policy, but as one which is imperative upon grounds of justice? When one speaks of any principle as imperative upon grounds of justice, one must speak with reference to its operation on the position and feelings of individuals; and I should say, therefore, that in so far as the feelings of individuals can receive what is due to them without adopting this principle, it is not absolutely imperative. But the exemption of savings would fully satisfy and cover all just claims of individuals; and if it were practicable, there would be no need to consider anything else; you would have a perfectly just tax, since, by exempting all savings, all claims on the ground of the necessity of saving would be satisfied. But since this principle cannot be practically carried out, the next thing is to consider what are the diversities of obligation upon different classes in respect to saving, and whether in the main, and as classes, they do fulfil those obligations; and if they do, I then think that the obligation of giving them a consideration for it, by leaving untaxed, as far as possible, the savings which they are bound to make, and which, as a class, they practically do make, is an imperative obligation of justice.

Supposing it were practicable to adjust the tax exactly upon the principle of exempting savings from charge, would not that state of the law be exceedingly favourable to the richer as compared with the poorer members of society; is it not a very much easier thing for the wealthier classes to save than for the poorer ones? Undoubtedly it is.

Then does not it seem that the question is raised in point of equity and justice as to the advantages in principle of a system of law which should adopt that basis, and should say to all classes of society, under the notion of equality and fairness, we will exempt all savings from taxation; it being at the same time admitted that it is a comparatively easy thing for those who live in abundance to save, and a very difficult thing for those who live in penury, and whose absolute wants press hardly upon their means? That is perfectly true; but I think it is an objection which applies to all the received maxims of taxation. For instance, it is a received maxim to tax persons in proportion to their means; but supposing that there is an income tax of 10 per cent., it is a much easier thing, apart from conventions, from social necessities or social follies, for a rich person to bear a deduction of 10 per cent. from his income than for a poor person. I do not see how you can allow for this consideration. I would allow for it in the case of a person who succeeds to property which he had not earned, and I have no objection even to graduation in the case of a succession tax; but I do not see how you can, either with justice or policy, tax a person more heavily because he earns more, or because, after having earned more, he saves more. I do not think that you can lay a tax upon energy, or industry, or prudence. It seems to me that even upon the question of justice, apart from policy, there is no stronger or more valid principle than that of not giving any advantage to self-indulgence over industry and economy, even though the effect may be to give some advantage, or rather, not to interfere with the natural advantage of the rich over the poor.

You have just stated that if you levy an equal income tax on all classes of the community amounting to 10 per cent., from the nature of things that tax of 10 per cent. would bear harder upon the poorer classes than upon the richer; but is it not also the case that if, instead of having that equal income tax of 10 per cent. upon all classes, you modify the principle of that tax, by saying, I will exempt from the charge of 10 per cent. a certain amount

which I estimate to be the proper savings of each person; the practical effect
of that change in the frame of the income tax would be to leave what
remains bearing still harder upon the poorer members of the community
than it did when the rate was equal? Not, I apprehend, if you took a fixed
proportion from each of them on the principle of averages; one-third, for
instance, as is proposed.

What I want to present to your mind is this; I understood you to set out
with the proposition that savings ought not to be taxed; and I understood
you at once frankly to admit that saving is much more difficult for the
poorer members of society than for the richer; that is to say, in other words,
that savings cannot be effected to the same amount, or that they cannot save
the same proportion of their respective incomes? Yes.

That being so, if it be true that we propose to deviate from an equal
income tax, by introducing the principle that savings are not to be taxed;
and if it be true that a greater proportion of savings will and can be made
by the rich than will or can be made by the poor, is it not true that the
adoption of your principle that savings shall not be taxed, does tend upon
the whole certainly to aggravate the burden of the tax upon the poorer as
compared with the richer classes? I should say not, because the relief that
you give in the case of the poor, is the relief of a much greater necessity.
Though they save less, still what they do save costs them a much greater
effort, and therefore to have that effort alleviated, is a greater advantage to
them. And in regard to the rich, though it is true that they can save more
without any substantial mischief to themselves, it does not follow that they
will. Those whose income is permanent, seldom do so. And if they do, I am
not sure that the fact that by doing so, they confer a special benefit on the
poor by adding to the capital of the country, is not a sufficient reason in
one way to overrule the reason in the other.

But the savings of the poor man are just as good as those of the rich, are
they not, so far as they go, in adding to the capital of the country? So far
as they go, no doubt.

Let us suppose that society is divided into two classes, the rich and the
poor; that all the poor men have 50l. a year each, and that all the rich men
have 1,000l. a year each; that the poor men can by effort and industry and
forethought save 5l. a year out of their 50l., and that the rich men can, by
a similar exercise of industry and forethought, save 200l. a year out of their
1,000l.; in that state of things, would not an equal income tax, levied upon
the gross income, be far more favourable to the interests of the poor class
as compared with the rich class, than an income tax which taxes the poor
man on 45l., and the rich man on 800l. a year? That, so far as it goes, may
be a reason for taxing people according to their necessities of saving, rather
than according to the saving which they actually make. It is, no doubt, an

THE INCOME AND PROPERTY TAX

important question of principle, how far the importance of not taxing twice ought to prevail over other considerations. But this is not the question to be decided practically, since we cannot exempt people on what they actually do save. A tax which was proportioned, not to people's actual savings, but to their necessities and obligations of saving, would not be liable to the objection which you have stated, whatever the force of that objection may be.

If a large allowance be made upon the assumption that it is an approximation to what persons may and should save, does not the same principle that this saving is a consideration altogether more applicable to persons in easy circumstances, than to persons in poorer circumstances, apply as much as if we could precisely measure the actual amount of saving in each case? But then the average that would be taken on the principle of having untaxed what people were bound to save, would of itself exclude the greater portion of the opulent classes from the benefit; it would exclude all but those who were obliged to save in order to fulfil a real necessity.

I quite understand the force of your argument as between one portion of the upper classes, and the other portion, that is to say, the distinction that you have so clearly and admirably stated between the owners of permanent and terminable incomes, and the owners of precarious and certain incomes; but then I wish to draw your attention to quite another division, the next division of society, not according to the source of income, nor according to the tenure of income, but according to the quantity of income relatively to the wants of human nature for subsistence and for comfort, and to ask whether it did not appear, that upon the whole, the adoption of this principle, that savings are not to be taxed (setting aside the degree in which you may be able to give it a precise application), and the attempt to frame a law upon that principle, would not be a change in our law favourable to the condition of the poorer classes of society as compared with the wealthier? I think it would be favourable to the saving classes, whether poor or rich, compared with the spending classes; and that consideration I think is even paramount to the other. If the rich are to be subject to a greater proportionate amount of taxation than the poor, I think it ought to be done in some other way. A succession duty is the most unobjectionable mode of doing it, because in that way it is confined to hereditary wealth. I think you must allow people to retain the full advantage for their lives of what they have acquired; but the State may deal with it on the occasion of succession. I certainly do think it fair and reasonable that the general policy of the State should favour the diffusion rather than the concentration of wealth, but not, I think, by taxing people twice on the same portion of their income, or by taxing people for the fact of their saving. Taxing people on what they save, and not taxing them on what they spend, or taxing people on a larger proportion of their income, because they are better off, does not hold the balance fairly between saving and spending; it is contrary to the canon of equity, and contrary to it in the worst way, because it makes that mode of employing income which it is public policy to encourage, a subject of discouragement.

You have just stated, that this would be in favour of the saving classes, as compared with the spending classes, but is it not true, that upon the whole the poorer classes are, and must be spending classes, and not saving classes, in comparison with the richer classes, relatively to the rich; and is it not also true that the change would be, so far as it goes, a change in favour of the richer classes of society as against the poorer? In one sense it would.

I think I have understood you to say, that you adopt generally the schedules of the Honourable Chairman, not as being perfect, but as being a great improvement upon the present structure of the income tax? Exactly.

There is one more point on which I should wish very much to have your opinion with as much exactitude as you can give it, and that is the point with regard to life incomes; but, first of all, are you prepared, according to the schedules of the Chairman, to adopt the principle, that all life income, as such, shall be charged with the full tax? I am not prepared to adopt that part of the Honourable Chairman's plan. I would exempt as many of the life incomes as could be got at without very inconvenient consequences.

I quite understand that your desire would be to give exemption to life incomes in a certain form; the form which I think you suggested was that an exemption should be laid down generally, and then a long list of exceptions should be made, which perhaps might contain a great proportion of them; but what I wish now to put specifically to you is this, whether you would be ready, rather than to retain the present income tax, to adopt the Chairman's plan as it stands in that important and vital point, namely, that it puts all life incomes whatever under the full tax? Yes; life incomes in the first class, life incomes from property: for I think that the Chairman's second class, taking it as a class, has a much stronger claim than almost any in the first class have; and that is a great object to exempt the second class, even if it were not possible to do justice to any in the first class. The only case that I would positively take out of the first class is pensions. I do not see any reasonable ground for refusing them exemption. There is another class, a class essentially professional, which, because the income is derived from land, the Chairman includes in his first class; it is the case of clergymen, holders of tithe rent-charge, or glebe with cure of souls. These I think in principle ought to be in the second class. It is quite true, however, that the Chairman's allowance of 100*l.* a year untaxed to each of them, does on the average satisfy the claim of the entire class, but it operates very unequally in individual cases.

Are you aware that the plan of the Honourable Chairman makes an allowance to a life interest in the case where it is founded upon a life annuity purchased with money? I am aware of that allowance.

And you would adopt that as part of your plan, would you? I have no doubt whatever, that in the case of what are called terminable annuities, the Chairman's plan is right, because a terminable annuity is not wholly income, but partly a replacement of capital; and it may be said of life annuities too, that they are a replacement of capital, so far as regards those by whom they have been bought. There is this difference, however, between the two cases, taken as classes, that in the case of terminable annuities, the capital is actually replaced, because it hardly ever answers the purpose of anybody to hold them, except persons in business, who hold them as investments; whereas, a very large proportion of life annuities are meant to be entirely consumed; the capital is sunk; and just as I think that when income is converted into capital, it should be exempted from the income tax, so I think that when capital is reconverted into income, and employed in expenditure, on the same principle it ought to become again subject to the tax. I therefore do not see, in the case of the great mass of life annuities, that there is any real ground for their being exempted; but I am aware that cases may be shown in which there is ground. So many practical difficulties would attend the attempt to make the distinction, that I will not venture to say it ought to be made. Still I think that in principle the case of terminable annuities, and that of the great bulk of life annuities, are not similar. An annuity which a person holds on his own life is usually intended to be consumed during his life, and the capital is not intended to be, and is not, saved and replaced; therefore, there is not the same injustice in subjecting life annuities to the entire income tax, as there is in the case of terminable annuities. I do not mean that the deduction (say of one-third) ought not to be made from them as from other life incomes; I mean that no special deduction ought to be made for the replacement of capital, such as is proposed in the case of terminable annuities. The proposition in the case of terminable annuities is not to deduct one-third, and charge the tax only upon two thirds; it is to separate what is replacement of capital, and to tax only the interest. That reason, I think, does not exist in the majority of life annuities that are held by persons for their own lives; still I am aware that if it were attempted to make a distinction, there might be means of evading it, and therefore I hesitate to give any opinion practically on the point.

In asking you those questions upon the Chairman's schedules, the form of question which I wish to put is this; are there any improvements which you think it vital as a matter of principle, to make in those schedules, in order to reconcile your mind to this plan, as a plan in substitution for the present income tax. I do not want merely to ask you what you think might be an improvement, but with respect to the point of pensions, I should like to know whether you think it vital to carry them over into the second class, or whether you are ready to admit that you cannot get anything better than a reconstruction of the income tax, which shall still continue to tax pensions upon their full annual amount? Yes; but at the same time I own that it is of very great importance to carry the principle on to all cases to which it may be found practicable to apply it, in order to diminish as much as possible, the number of those on whom, as has been justly remarked by yourself, an additional burden would be thrown by an exemption given to others.

You think, therefore, with regard to the question whether pensions shall be charged in full, though your plan would not charge them in full, yet you do not think it inadmissible to charge them in full as a part of a plan of reconstruction? If it were found impossible to make any other reform of the tax than just that which the Chairman has proposed, I would adopt his plan.

If pensions are to be charged in full, we should stand, should we not, in this predicament, that while aiming at equalising substantially the incidence of the tax, we should continue to levy the tax at the same rate upon a pension, which, in a multitude of cases, would not represent more than four or five years' purchase, and upon incomes from land, which, under the most favourable circumstances, would represent 30 or 35 years' purchase? The number of years purchase, though the ground taken by one class of reformers of the income tax is not, in my opinion, a tenable ground, I should consider only the necessity under which the holder might be of saving, and the means which his income afforded him of doing so: and certainly if the income were nearly expired, it would not afford him much means, but also those means would not be much crippled by the tax, as it would be for a short time only.

Therefore, you would not be staggered or alarmed by the fact, as it would be, that pensions being often worth four or five years' purchase, and rarely worth more than six or eight years' purchase, would be taxed at the same rate upon the net income as incomes arising from land, being worth in capitalised value four, or five, or six times as much? I should not consider the difference in capitalised value as any test of the injustice, but I should think that there was injustice. Still, as there must be some injustice in any income tax, and as the thing to be aimed at is to make that injustice the least possible, if it were shown to me, or if there were a general conviction, that other distinctions could not be made without involving consequences that it would not do to incur, I would then do as much justice as I could, and take the second class as the Chairman leaves it.

In respect to this particular case, what I understand is, that supposing A.B. were to object to the reconstituted income tax, that a pension worth five years' purchase was taxed as much as an income from land worth 35 years' purchase, your answer would be, if I understand you rightly, that you put that aside as not relevant to the matter in hand, because that is not the principle upon which you found that reconstruction? That is not the principle, but still I should admit that the pensioner was not justly treated.

The exemptions which you would desire to secure for pensions, you would desire to secure upon other grounds? Yes.

You do not think it absolutely vital in the plan for reconstruction that pensions should have any relief? I think it highly desirable in every plan of approximating taxation to justice, that a just principle should be carried out so far as it can go, that is, to the point at which it is stopped by insurmountable obstacles; but if other means fail, and it is thought that there are insurmountable obstacles to doing absolute justice in a particular case, I am forced to give way to them, but not for that reason to relax my support of what I consider justice in cases in which it is practicable.

Then, with respect to annuities for life, I understand you to consider that they ought to have an exemption? I think that the greater number of annuities for life have no real claim to peculiar exemption as annuities, but they have a claim to the general exemption on life incomes of one-third. I conceive that they have not, generally speaking, a claim to the exemption due to terminable annuities, of deducting the replacement of capital, because, as a general rule, the capital invested in them is not intended to be replaced, and is not replaced.

You have noticed, have you not, the mode in which the plan of the Chairman deals with the case of life annuities? Yes; he deals with life annuities in the same way as with terminable annuities, except that the calculations of course are somewhat different, because they depend upon the age and not solely upon the value.

You do not approve of this particular mode of dealing with them. You think that they are entitled to exemption, but not in that form? I find it difficult to make up my mind upon that subject, because it depends very much upon practical considerations. I have no doubt whatever as to their being entitled to the exemption of one-third, or whatever it is that is given to life incomes generally, because there is no class of persons on whom the obligations to save are more imperative than on a large proportion of life annuitants. But, on the other hand, the Chairman proposes that they should be allowed a deduction, not of this one-third, but the much larger deduction which is implied in exempting from taxation what is required to replace the capital. This I quite agree is a proper principle in the case of terminable annuities, that is, in the case of all annuities in which the capital is really intended to be replaced; and there is a class of life annuities, as the Honourable Chairman has had the goodness privately to point out to me, to which it applies. For instance, if a person receives money from an insurance office, paying for it by an annuity on his own life, that is a similar case to an annuity for a term of years; and there are just the same reasons for leaving untaxed the portion which is repayment of capital.

On the whole, I think that you have considered that life annuities ought to be treated on the general principle of life incomes, and ought to receive the same amount of exemption as life incomes? Just so.

But are you aware that is not the principle upon which the Chairman's plan deals with them? He deals with them as terminable annuities.

I presume that you do not consider it vital, or of first-rate importance to deal with them in that form? I do not attach first-rate importance to that distinction; I do not pretend to decide positively whether life annuities should or should not be treated like terminable annuities.

Do you consider it of first-rate importance that terminable annuities should receive the same exemptions as life incomes? I think that it is of importance, but not of such importance, that unless it could be done it would be a fatal objection to the Chairman's plan; I do not in that sense think it of first-rate importance.

Do you think that a plan could be said to conform in your view sufficiently to the interest of justice which levied upon all life annuities the full tax? As it would not do what I consider full justice, my opinion would depend upon whether the practical difficulties were such as satisfied me, or satisfied better judges than I can pretend to be, that it was not practicable to get nearer to complete justice. If you have got as near to justice as you can get, every reasonable person must be satisfied.

You are not satisfied in your own mind that this plan, which leaves all life interests subject to the full tax, with the exception of life interests in annuities purchased by money, is the nearest practicable approximation to justice? I am not satisfied, because life annuities and pensions, and even charges upon landed estates, and other settled property, in favour of collaterals who would not come into the property ultimately, or whose descendants would not benefit by it, might, so far as I can see, receive an exemption; it would be just to give it to them, and it is still to be proved to my satisfaction that it would be practically impossible.

Should I be justly representing your idea of the plan in this way, that you would accept it in carrying you so far on the road towards justice, but not as reaching it, and that consequently you would accept it, in the hope of effecting whatever further amendments experience might suggest? I should hope that if the alteration were to be made at all, it would be carried as far as practical difficulties permit. But if those who have the thing to do, find that the practical objections are insuperable to carrying it further, that would be a sufficient presumption that in the opinion of the best judges, this is the point at which it is necessary to stop, and if so, I would stop at this point.

At the same time, your respect for the opinions of those who have the thing to do is not sufficient to lead you to acquiesce in that conclusion if they say that they cannot do it at all? Not unless they tell me the grounds upon which they go, and then I might possibly be convinced. If they tell me what the difficulties are, I might possibly think that they were sufficient; or I might possibly think that they were better judges than I am of their sufficiency.

SIR S. NORTHCOTE: *I think I understood you to state that in apportioning taxation you should look to the circumstances of the person taxed, and not to the nature of the property from which the income is derived?* Yes, except in so far as it affects the circumstances of the person.

And persons should, you say, be taxed in proportion to their means? That is a proposition which requires some explanation before I can assent to it. I should say they should be taxed proportionally to their means of personal expenditure, their means of expenditure as contrasted with saving.

And you consider that their means are to be ascertained by taking the average of classes? That is one of the elements which must be ascertained in that way, because it can be ascertained in no other way. The incomes may be ascertained as they now are from individuals, but neither their actual savings nor their necessities for saving can be ascertained by inquiring into individual cases, but must be taken on the average of the class.

What do you mean by a class? I mean any number of persons who are in a situation capable of being clearly specified and defined, which situation places them in a different position as to their necessities for saving, from that of any other set of people.

Then, in classifying for the purpose of taxation, you must classify upon some principle which will distinguish one class from another class? Yes.

And which will be common to all individuals contained in that class? Certainly.

You might take many different principles of classification, might you not? I do not think you could take many that would be relevant to this point.

You might take, for instance, the case as to the tenure which persons have; you might distinguish persons according to their having life interests, or more than life interests? Yes.

Then, again, you might classify them according to the amount of their wealth, or according to their being above or below a certain rate of income? Yes.

Then you might classify them again, might you not, according to the circumstances of their families, as has been done in old times, when persons with large families were taxed at a lower rate; that would be another principle of taxation? Yes; it would be a possible principle, but an objectionable one.

You might classify them according to the nature of their property, or other source from which their incomes arise? That, also, is one of the elements.

Would it be possible to take more than one of those principles, and combine them for the purpose of classifying, or must you classify them upon one principle, rejecting all the others? I do not think it would be just to disregard any consideration which is relevant to the real principle, that is, the necessity for saving. You must, I think, make the classification, so as to allow for the greatest number possible of the circumstances that make it necessary for one person to save more than another, with the single exception of those circumstances which depend upon his own will. For instance, I would not admit large families as a ground, because it is not a necessity for anybody to have a large family; it is his choice, and I do not think any allowance should be made for that.

Is it not necessary in adopting any classification for any purpose whatsoever, as a scientific principle, that you should lay down some principle of classification, and adhere to that one principle? It does not seem to me always necessary to adhere to one principle; the best classification is sometimes grounded on a combination of principles.

Supposing you were going to classify books, for instance; you might classify them according to their size, or according to their language, or according to the subject-matter with which they dealt, but you must adopt one or other of those principles, must you not, and not mix up one or two of them together? That depends upon what your object is. If your object is to arrange them in a library, you often proceed upon more than one of those principles; for instance, you may proceed partially upon size, and partially upon subject; on the same shelf, it is necessary, in some degree, to place books of the same size, and yet you may place upon the same shelf, as far as possible, those which are upon the same subject. I mention this, to show that it is not necessary to adhere to one principle exclusively, and that you should take into consideration as many as are relevant to the purpose which you have in view.

Would you call putting books on shelves classifying them? That is the end for which I am supposing them to be classified; but if you are classifying them for any other end, of course the principle would be different.

Looking at it as a mere question of scientific principle, you do not think it necessary in forming a class, that you should take any one principle which distinguishes that class from all other classes, and which is common to all the individuals in it, and distinguishes them from individuals in other classes? I think you very seldom do anything practically on one principle only. It is almost always necessary to consider more than one principle.

Then, in fact, the classification ceases to be scientific, and becomes arbitrary in that case, does it not? Not necessarily; because all the elements of it may be scientific, and because each of them may only be allowed the weight which it derives from its scientific relation to the end which you have in view.

I understand you to say, that persons are to be classed for the purpose of taxation, according to their means, and that their means are to be ascertained by taking the average means of the class to which they belong, however that class is to be ascertained? Their means are to be ascertained in the same manner as at present, from their returns, or otherwise.

But with regard to the higher or lower rate of taxation to be placed upon one class or another class, do you not place people in the one class or the other class before you get their returns of the amount of their incomes? The necessity of classifying incomes before you receive the returns, arises from the fact that all incomes are not ascertained in the same way. You are obliged to have different schedules, because the income tax is levied from different classes in different ways, and upon different evidences. If the classification needed to be adopted to some other purpose, such as that of making allowances of the kind which this Committee are considering, it would probably be necessary to make some change in the principle of classification.

You stated a little while ago, did you not, that the savings of classes depend more on tenure than on anything else;[*] *what did you mean by tenure?* If I said that, I said what I cannot stand to. I am not aware that I said it; I think I may say that the word "tenure" is not my own word at all.

I do not mean to say that you stated that savings depended on tenure, but that the necessity of savings depended on it? I would not say that the necessity for savings depends entirely upon it, because in individual cases it does not; but it is very much affected by the fact of the tenure being permanent or temporary, and also by the fact of the income being fixed or precarious.

Then the income being fixed or precarious, has relation to the source of the income, has it not? It is very much affected by it; incomes from some sources are necessarily unfixed, while those from other sources may be, and generally are, fixed.

Upon what else does it depend, if it is not upon the nature and source of the income? In individual cases, it depends upon many things; for

[*See pp. 554 ff. above.]

instance, the most certain income from land may be affected by a bad year; the rents may not be collected, and in that way all incomes are precarious in some degree; but certain incomes are much more precarious than others, owing to their source. Incomes which are earned by continued labour, are liable to the contingencies of health, while all incomes that are earned at all, are subject to termination by death.

Is the income which a man receives from a ship, of which he is the owner, a precarious income? It is precarious in the sense in which all trading incomes are; that is, it may be a great deal one year, and very little another, or he may become a bankrupt, and have none at all.

Is the income which a man derives from the possession of a house precarious or not? No doubt it is precarious in some degree, but the precariousness of it depends upon circumstances which can be in a certain degree averaged.

Supposing a man to own a certain number of houses, and to make an income by letting them, is it not uncertain from year to year what he may make by the rent of those houses? Yes, it is uncertain; there is a character of precariousness in it, which applies to many more cases in some degree. For instance, in another case, which is in the Honourable Chairman's first class, namely, shares in public companies, the income from them is no doubt liable to vary from year to year, and therefore in that case the element of precariousness exists to a certain degree, but it exists much less than it does in many other cases.

At the present time the man who owns a ship and the man who owns a house pay at the same rate upon the incomes which they respectively derive from them; it is now proposed to diminish by one-third the amount which the owner of the ship has to pay, and to increase by some sensible proportion, the amount which the owner of the house has to pay; do you think that that is a fair arrangement to make? I think it is hardly fair to say that the tax on the income from the house will be increased, because it is proposed to make an allowance of 15 per cent. in the way of reduction. That, however, is on a different ground, undoubtedly, but I think there is one very considerable difference between the two cases (although they are border cases, as it were). The income of the shipowner is one in which he may make very large receipts at one time, and none at all at another. In the case of the owner of houses, the maximum we know; the maximum is the rental of the houses; more he cannot receive, and his liability to receive less is a moderate liability only. It is not likely that any person who only owns house property will have the bulk of his property generally unlet for many years, or will have much of it unlet at one time.

The owner of house property is, however, subject to some dangers which are peculiar to him; for instance, fashion may change, and his houses may become less valuable on that account, may they not? They may so, certainly.

And certain burthens may be thrown upon house property in respect of rates and taxes, from which other property, shipping property, for instance, is exempt? Yes, but you may set against that that the burthens may be diminished as well as increased.

But, as a matter of fact, is it not the case that taxes are laid upon house property which are not laid upon shipping property? Yes.

Are you aware that house property is subject to many disadvantages and burthens, and restrictions in its transfer from hand to hand, which do not apply to shipping property? That is perfectly true; none of which, I think, should exist.

But, nevertheless, while there are those differences between the two which make for the ship and against the house, you consider that there is a principle which would induce you to put the ship in the lower class and the house in the higher class? There arises, then, a question which not unfrequently does arise, namely, whether certain personal situations are to be considered as trades or not. There are undoubtedly persons holders of houses, and living by the rent of houses, who may be considered as approaching to the character of traders; and if they were all so, if all were in the situation in which some holders of a good deal of small house pro-perty really are, they might come with propriety into the Chairman's second class. They do not now, because, I suppose, the great majority of house property has not connected with it that amount of difficulty and liability to loss, and consequent precariousness.

You adopt a classification, do you not, which places the house in the higher taxed class, and the ship in the lower taxed class? Yes; I adopt that classification subject to any correction which justice may be found to require; but so far as I can see, it is not a clear case for making a distinction.

As you adopt this classification, I want to know what is the principle of classification which is applicable to the one case and not the other? The classification in the Chairman's schedules I do not consider to be a matter of principle, but of convenience: but the principle which in my mind would decide the question would be, whether the income from the ship was really more precarious and really more dependent upon personal exertion than the income from the house. If it is not, if the income from houses generally, or from any class of houses which can be distinctly defined, required as much personal exertion, and therefore, on that ground had as much of the element of non-permanency, and also was subject to as great risk, as the situation of the shipowner, I should say that there would be sufficient reason for putting it in the same class as the shipowner.

Supposing that this scheme were to become law, and that after it had become law any considerable number of persons were to come to the Chancellor of the Exchequer, and were to represent that they were owners of house property which they were in the habit of letting, and were to point out in what a disadvantageous position they were placed, and were to make out a case of hardship upon them, do you think it would be fair that the tax should be amended for the purpose of giving relief to such persons if they could clearly define their position? The consideration in that case would be whether their position represented that of any class which could be distinctly separated from all other classes; if it did, then you might separate them, but if it did not, they must go with their class, although the individual case may make it a hardship.

Have you ever been able yet to get at what the principle of the class is; because when you say that the one is rather more precarious than the other, would you not say that there are incomes included within this second class in the Chairman's schedule of which some are rather more precarious than others? Yes, certainly.

For instance, the income of a physician is rather more precarious than the income of a brewer, is it not? Yes; and if I could, I would make a distinction, as I have already said, between the case of traders and that of purely professional persons.

But you find it impossible to draw that distinction, and therefore you give the relief in common to all those classes? I do not know that it is impossible; I am inclined rather to think that it might be drawn, but I find there is a general opinion that it is impossible.

You think, do you not, that it ought to be drawn? I think it ought to be drawn, if it can be.

At what point would you propose to draw it? At the point where there is the broadest distinction, namely, the distinction between trading and professional incomes; between incomes derived from labour and capital, and incomes derived from labour only, except inasmuch as there may have been capital expended in education.

If the income is derived entirely from labour with no possible capital, you would treat it upon one footing; but if from capital, and not at all from labour, upon another footing; how would you deal with it if capital entered to a small extent, and labour to a large extent into the production of the income? It would very often happen in the case of a small trader, for instance, that the capital would be so small a proportion as not to be worth considering, and if so, I would give him the full benefit in the same manner as professional persons; but in the cases in which the capital was anything considerable, anything that would be much worth taxing, I should think it just, if it were practicable, to tax the interest on capital at one rate, and the profits above the interest at another and a less rate.

Do you think that it would be possible to distinguish each man's case, or must you settle it according to classes? On that point I cannot presume to have an opinion.

You are prepared, however, are you not, to adopt a scheme which would include in one class a number of cases which are shading off the one from the other? I am, because I think that must be the case in all classifications; you can very seldom draw a line so accurately as to include exactly everything that you would like to include, and exclude everything that you would like to exclude; you are obliged to take into consideration the intelligibility of the line.

Supposing that persons owners of house property made such a case as I have represented, and that the Chancellor of the Exchequer and Parliament were to let them into the favoured class, would not such an alteration probably be followed by applications from other classes of persons who would consider that they also had claims? No doubt it would; and you must stop at some point.

Do you think it possible to draw the line in such a way that all persons who were taxed at the higher rate, or at all events the greater bulk of them, would be satisfied to remain at the higher rate, or would there not be a continual pressure to get below the line? Yes; but I think there would be a smaller amount of pressure than there is now. By having an indiscriminating rule and granting no exemption to any one, you do not avoid drawing the line; all that you do is, you draw it in the worst place possible; you draw it by making no distinctions at all; whereas in any other place that you might draw it, you would at any rate be nearer to doing average justice than by drawing it at one extremity.

Take the case of a manufacturing business carried on, in the first place, by an individual, and, in the second place, by several individuals, forming a private partnership together; and, in the third place, by a joint stock company, all the three being in competition the one with the other; do you think that those three sets of trading persons should be taxed equally or unequally? I think the line should in this case be drawn exactly where the Honourable Chairman draws it; to tax the shareholders in the joint stock company at the higher rate, and the two others at the lower.

Why? Because the reasons for exemption are stronger in the other two cases than they are in that. The only reason that could be urged for exemption in the case of the shareholder, is the slight shade of precariousness that there is about his income, which is not usually great in those cases. Where the shareholder is poor, the property is usually in the funds, or in some comparatively secure and steady investment, and where he is not poor, it will generally be so divided that the risks will be an insurance against one another; therefore I think the claim is at its lowest point in the case of the shareholder in a company; it is at the lowest point that can be, where there is any precariousness at all. But in the other two cases, not merely the interest or profit on capital, but also the reward of industry and talent forms part of the income; and this element of the income, besides being more precarious, terminates with the life of the person.

As a matter of fact, do you believe that persons with very small incomes, who have small savings to invest, do invest them in very safe investments, or do they not very commonly invest them in very precarious securities? It is their own fault if they do, because very small savings can, in any case, be invested in the savings bank, or Government annuities.

There is no doubt that that may be, but you lay down as a reason, do you not, for excluding from view, the precariousness of those businesses, that the shareholders in them will be rich people, because poor people would invest in safe investments? The case of very poor people is otherwise provided for, by not taxing anybody who has not 100*l.* a year.

When you say that the precariousness in those cases is very slight, do you mean to say that there are not a very considerable number of those undertakings which become utter failures, and in which persons who have embarked in them are losers to a very great extent, of the amount of their investments? No doubt, these things happen, but you cannot provide against all cases of individual imprudence. It is necessary to be content with considering the general situation of individuals as to what they are obliged to do, or what they may reasonably do. It may reasonably be supposed that persons whose means are of importance to them, will not invest the whole of them in some very precarious undertaking; if they do, they must take the consequence.

But you do not mean to say that the precariousness of the income in those public companies is very slight and inappreciable? Taking public companies as a whole, taking any average of them, I should suppose that they are among the most secure investments, though of course there are many of them which are not secure.

I will put to you one case, which I have put to other witnesses; suppose you take the case of a widow's jointure; I understand you to say that you would not exempt that widow from any portion of taxation in respect of her income being a life income? I think not; after some consideration, I have come to the conclusion that it is not entitled to exemption.

That is to say, if her jointure arose out of land? Or out of settled property; and on this ground, that it may fairly be presumed that if she has children, they are provided for by the same instrument which gives her the jointure.

Supposing the case of a man who has a substantial business, and leaves his business to his children, and settles a jointure for his widow upon that

business, do you consider that she ought to have any remission or not?
I think not in that case, because she is under no peculiar obligation to save.

SIR F. HEYGATE: *You stated, did you not, that some annuities were meant to be consumed?* Yes.

Were what were called the Long Annuities[*] intended to be consumed in your opinion; the annuities which expired in 1860? No, I should think they could never have been held, except as a matter of investment. They could not have been held for the purposes of provision for the individual who held them, because an annuity that expires at a certain time is one of the most inconvenient forms in which such provision could be made, either by a person for himself, or by somebody else for him; it would be too much if he died before it expired, and too little if he did not die till after. Nobody wanting to provide, for himself or another, something which is to be his sole mode of support, would choose that mode.

Do you think that the capitalists who tendered for the late issue of Long Annuities did not make that calculation as the basis of their tenders? I do not know.

You think that they did not take it into consideration in offering a price to the Government? No doubt they took them as investments; they did not take them for a provision for themselves.

You also stated, did you not, that the daughters of individuals who have life interests in property, who married in their own class, were generally provided for by such marriages? They may be.

Will you explain what you mean by that? I was endeavouring to show that those who hold life annuities issuing from land or other settled property, though they have a claim to exemption, have not so strong a claim as industrial incomes, because the majority of them have not the average amount of motive or necessity to save which the owners of other life incomes have; either they have nobody to save for, or they have considerable chances of not needing to save for them. With regard to those latter cases, as in the case of a widow's jointure, in all probability she has no necessity to save for her children. That completeness of reason does not exist in the case of younger children, but there are reasons which make their claim less strong than that of industrial incomes, one of which I mentioned in the case of daughters, that there are many chances of their acquiring by marriage a position in which their separate income will not be so far of importance to their descendants as that they should be obliged to save a part of it.

Who would have to maintain those daughters if they were unmarried? As I observed some time since, they may not marry, or if they do, they may marry some one to whom their income is important: I therefore think

[*See 2 George III, c.10.]

them entitled to the concession; but still I do not think that the claim is as strong as the claim of industrial incomes; and if the concession could only be obtained upon industrial incomes, it would not be sacrificing people whose claim is greater to people whose claim is less; that is the sole object with which I alluded to the subject.

You consider that they have a claim, but not so strong a claim as the other class? Yes, that is so.

R. LOWE: *Upon what principle do you consider that the Chairman has divided those incomes into two classes?* Upon the principle I should say of not disturbing the existing classifications; that is the principle most apparent in it.

Is there not the principle of division into spontaneous and industrial incomes; does not that appear to pervade his division? It does; but it seems to me that the reason for making a distinction between spontaneous and industrial incomes is one of practicability rather than of principle.

He puts it as a matter of principle does he not? Of both, I think.

It is pretty logically carried out into first class and second class with some slight alterations; that is pretty much the way in which they are divided, is it not? Yes.   ·

He says, "The characteristic of all those incomes is that, consequent on the possession of the property from which they arise, they accrue spontaneously, and require no exercise of labour on the part of the owners."[*] *Your principle on the other hand is the necessity of savings, as I understand?* Yes.

And that arises mainly in your view as to whether the income be precarious or not? Whether the income be precarious, and whether it be only temporary.

Then the two schemes coincide in this, that you both would place professional incomes in the favoured class? Yes.

I suppose you would both agree in placing, for instance, incomes in fee or absolute ownership in a different class? Yes.

When we have established those two poles, the identity between you seems to end, does it not? It goes considerably further than that, because I should agree with the Chairman in subjecting to the entire tax the great mass of what are nominally life incomes, when they are in the first class, because though by law they are only incomes for life, still practically the possessor of them has the power of expending the whole.

I understood that those life incomes where the estate was charged for younger children, for instance, were entitled to some deduction? I think so; that is a point in which I differ from the Chairman's plan; but it is a difference on the question of practicability; not on that of principle.

[*Parliamentary Papers, 1861, VII, p. 284.]

I am asking you rather with regard to the principle of the thing, and not so much with regard to considerations of expediency or practicability, as to what you consider to be the just principle? I think the just principle would be, to exempt charges in favour of younger children.

Then we come to a clergyman's income, which I understood you to state you would treat as a professional income? Yes.

With regard to mines, how would you treat them? I do not feel that I understand that subject. The difficult question is to know how far deductions should be allowed for exhaustibility, on the same principle on which the replacement of capital is deducted in the Chairman's plan in the case of terminable annuities; and on that question I do not feel that I can give any opinion worth hearing.

A mine is in pari materiâ very much what a life annuity is, that is to say, a mine has a certain life of its own, has it not? Yes; only that there are not so good tables for calculating the duration of mines as of lives.

The means of calculating it are not so eligible, but the principle upon which it would be calculated would be pretty much the same; that is, there would be a number of elements of saving in mines which there would not be in the case of an estate in fee? Yes.

If that class in this paper is adopted of taking the estimated annual depreciation, you would be inclined to say that there should be some reduction made for mines? Yes, when they get near exhaustion; I am not sure that I should make it before.

With regard to public companies, I think you agree with the Chairman, that you would make no exemption? I would make no exemption in their case.

Annuities for life, you would place, if I understand you, under the head of incomes where saving was required, and you would make some deduction for them? I would.

And pensions the same? Yes.

And with regard to trades generally, you think that there should be some difference between trades and professions? As the income from trade is partly dependent upon life and health, and partly on permanent property, I would, therefore, make a distinction if it could be done.

Taking things in the abstract and not troubling ourselves with details as to how it is to be worked out, your opinion, as a matter of justice in the theory of taxation would be, as I have said, that you would agree with the two poles of the Chairman's plan; but the intervening circumstances would almost all of them require, in your view, some sort of deduction? A great many of them, certainly would. I think, however, that if the line had to be drawn with great simplicity, it ought to be drawn where the Chairman draws it. If we are to be content with such an approximation as can be made by taking a great mass of cases, which present upon the whole stronger claims to exemption than any others, I think that the Chairman, as nearly as possible, hits the mark.

I am not speaking so much now of what you might be willing to accept, as the Chancellor of the Exchequer put it to you,[*] *but rather as a matter of abstract reasoning?* As a matter of abstract reasoning, I should certainly carry the principle further, and make more distinctions than the Chairman has done.

I suppose you would look to further considerations if those classes could show any subdivision that could be effective? Certainly.

As to your principle of exemption, as I understand you, it is to exempt all savings, if that can possibly be done? Yes.

I do not quite understand what we mean by savings in that sentence; is it what a man does save, is it what a man can save, or is it what he ought to save? In principle, I should say that the remission should be on what he does save, neither more nor less; but as this cannot be carried out, I think you must consider, taking people in classes, what difference exists between them as to the necessity or obligation that they are under of saving, with some consideration also of how far you have reason to believe that, practically, as a matter of fact, they do, as a class, save up to the mark of obligation.

That is to say, we are to take a thing compounded of what a man does save and what he ought to save? You cannot practically enter into the consideration of what he does save, you must consider what the class ought to save, and then if you think that, on the whole, they do save an equivalent amount, you should exempt them. If you thought that, on the whole, they did not fulfil that obligation, but saved a great deal less than what they ought to save, it would be right to consider what they do save, rather than what they are bound to save; but as a matter of fact, I think that the classes who pay income tax do save, on the whole, up to their obligations.

We may take it as your view, that it is what men do save? What men ought to save, provided they do save it.

If a man saves more than he ought to save, what then? If a man saves more than he is bound to save, I think him entitled in principle to an allowance on it, because otherwise, he would be taxed twice. What a man does save is the best principle of exemption, but I am obliged to give up that as impracticable; and I take the other, and am willing to exempt people by considering what they are peculiarly bound to save.

Then, it comes to this, that the abstract principle is what a man ought to save? The principle upon which you are obliged to act, is what he ought to save; the perfect principle is what he does save, and that covers all other

[*See p. 574 ff. above.]

principles. If that is satisfied, all other principles are satisfied with it; but as you cannot get at that, then, if you adopt the principle of what he ought to save, and go upon that, I think you are right, provided you have fair reason to think that the exempted class, as a class, in the main fulfil that obligation; of course, if you thought that they did not, they would forfeit the privilege.

Then you do not agree with this opinion which I will read to you, out of your own book, in which you say this: "The principle therefore of equality of taxation interpreted in its only just sense, equality of sacrifice, requires that a person who has no means of providing for old age, or for those in whom he is interested, except by saving from income, should have the tax remitted, on all that part of his income which is really and bonâ fide *applied to that purpose"?*[*] If you could do that I should certainly think it right; the only question is as to the mode of doing it. As you cannot get at individual cases, you must go upon the general presumption drawn from the obligations of his position.

I understand you that this principle is introduced by you in order to ascertain the fact whether a man does save, and that you inquire what he ought to save as a means of getting at what he does save; is that so? Not as a means of getting at what he does save, because I know it does not correspond with what he does save; but in order to bear fairly upon one person as compared with another: I think you are bound to take into consideration, on the principle of justice between them, the difference in the necessity. That principle I should not need if I had the other, because the other covers it, and provides for everything which is included in it; but as I cannot have the other, I am obliged to be satisfied with this. I think they are both important principles.

But one or the other I suppose is the ultimate principle, and I understand the ultimate principle to be what a man does save? What a man does save, if you can get at it.

You think it is easier to get at what he ought to save than at what he does save? Yes; because you can take the average of classes.

And you take what he ought to save in order to get at what he does save? Yes; what he is to be considered as saving, when you cannot ascertain it otherwise.

I suppose you would not adhere to what you stated just now, that the rule is what a man ought to save, provided he does save it? In principle I do, but in practice you cannot tell what he does save. What he ought to save is not the only thing that you would have to consider if you knew what he did save; if you knew that he did not save what he ought to save, you could not defend making the allowance. But in the absence of this knowledge, you are not entitled to presume that he does not do his duty.

[*Principles of Political Economy, *in* Collected Works, *III, p. 815.]

What use will this be to me unless I found some presumption by which I may arrive at the fact of what he does save; why should I interpose the consideration at all, if I am to presume nothing either way from it? You only presume that which there is always sufficient proof of, namely, that his needs are different from those of another person. He may choose to sacrifice those needs to something else, but you cannot help that.

I can understand that if I am at liberty to presume from the fact that he ought to save, that he does save, but you say that I must not presume that? The only purpose for which we need to consider what he does save, is to justify us in taking into consideration what he ought to save.

Therefore, the ultimate principle is what he ought to save, and not what he does save? The ultimate principle is hardly an expression which I should apply to it. There are two principles, one is the principle of not taxing incomes twice over, and the other, which is a totally different principle, and is strictly one of justice, is that of showing equal consideration to the necessities of different people. Both of these are principles, and if you could satisfy them both you ought to do so. If you could satisfy the principle of not taxing income twice, the satisfaction due to the other principle would be included in that, because if you taxed everybody according to what he did save, you would by that very circumstance show the indulgence due to the necessities of the person who is obliged to save. If he himself has shown that he cares about these necessities, and if he has fulfilled the duty, he gets the advantage which you intend for him, and not otherwise. But as you cannot get at what he actually does save, you are obliged to found your system upon the other principle solely, only considering that former principle so far as to ascertain for your more complete justification, whether the ground on which you grant the exemption really exists; whether on the whole (since you cannot enter into individual cases) the class of persons whom you exempt have fulfilled the proper condition.

What is the principle upon which it solely rests? That which I propose as practicable rests upon the consideration of what a person is bound to save.

Then the thing rests upon that, and the inquiry for us is, what a man is bound as a moral duty to save, is that so? Yes.

If you mean by saving on your principle that regard should be had to money laid by, or incomes invested in something else; supposing a man is heavily in debt, and is paying off the debt by instalments, is that saving? Yes; that is saving, certainly.

However the debt may be contracted, whether it is a gambling debt or any other debt, you call that saving? Yes, I call that saving.

A man goes to a gambling house and spends a large sum of money, and pays off the debt by instalments; you would say that that was a saving within the meaning of the principle? Yes.

When does the income become taxed; because it is very important if it is to be exempted from taxation to fix upon the exact period of the transition taking place; when are we to call income savings? That is a practical rather than a theoretical question.

The income tax on the income of a landowner is levied on the tenant, and it is paid by the tenant before he pays his landlord, is it not? Yes.

And upon that the income tax is paid? Yes.

I want to know whether that part of the income in the tenant's hands is to be considered as saved for the purpose of this principle? It cannot, while in the tenant's hands, be dealt with as saving.

But the tax is levied upon it in the tenant's hands, is it not? Yes; but when we are entering into considerations such as that of the hands through which it passes, we are coming to a question of practical arrangement, and not to a question of principle.

I do not want to put it as a matter of practical arrangement, but merely to test the principle and to know when you would fix upon it the mark of saving which is to exempt it from taxation. The only difficulty that will arise is a difficulty of practice and not one of theory. In theory the principle is that whatever he does take from his personal consumption, and add to his capital, shall be exempted.

I find that it is laid down in the quotation which I read from your own book, that on the contrary a man "should have the tax remitted on all that part of his income which is really bonâ fide *applied to that purpose;" that I can quite understand, but now we have not to decide the question of what he does save, but what he ought to save; when is that to be decided for the purpose of collecting the tax?* It seems to me, that you are now upon the question of practicability, and not upon the question of principle; when you ask how it is to be ascertained, I am not obliged to show any mode of ascertaining it; I say that it cannot be ascertained, and that all you can do is, to consider the situation of the classes, and all the peculiarities of their situation which affect their obligation to saving, and then to make them an allowance.

Then it is by their being of that class, that you determine the question; you have no means of fixing upon the precise point when it becomes saving? No; the actual saving cannot be considered as a practical principle at all, but only as a sort of ultimate test by which you may, in some degree, measure the approximation to justice in any other system.

May I assume this as a principle, that it is a safe ground of solution to presume that men will do what they ought to do, and to remit the taxes to them accordingly? I think that you are never entitled to suppose that men will not do what they ought to do, for the purpose of doing something to them which would be an injustice if they did do what they ought to do.

Is it a safe ground of exception from a tax, that a man should be presumed to do what he ought to have done? I think it is a safe ground for taxation, that a person is not to be taxed in such a way, as would render it impossible or more difficult for him to do what he ought to do.

Of course, upon that principle, if a man could be shown to be deeply in debt, he ought not to be taxed at all, because it would render it more difficult for him to pay his debts? It might make it more difficult for him to pay his debts no doubt, and if you taxed a person so that it should make it more difficult for him to fulfil his duties, while other people were taxed in a way that had not that effect on them, he would suffer injustice, but not otherwise.

I will put the case of a person, we will say who is a fundholder, with an absolute interest; it is computed by a professional witness before this Committee, that this scheme would require 2,000,000l. to be made up somehow or other;[*] *that I presume must be levied by a fresh assessment on a new principle?* Yes.

What do you say with regard to the fundholder or tenant in fee? Do you think that he will be impressed by the doctrine of equal sacrifice, if he were saddled with a heavier tax, merely because it was presumed that some other persons had saved some portions of their incomes? What a person might do where he was himself interested, I cannot say, but I think that a person should not put it to himself in that way, but in this way; that persons whose circumstances require them to save, ought to have a concession made to them, such as shall make it possible for them to fulfil their duty without making a sacrifice to which others are not subject.

If they do not fulfil the duty, they are to have the concession all the same, are they not? That is one of the inconveniences which arise from the impossibility of going into individual cases. I would most gladly go into them if I could.

Say that a man does more than his duty, he will not have a remission for the excess? No, and so much the worse.

So that the man who does his duty, will not get remission upon all that he does; and the man who does not, will get a remission for what he does not do? But the result is a greater approximation to accurate justice than if you either gave a remission to all, or refused it to all.

We have it in evidence that very considerable frauds are practised under Schedule D.; one gentleman who is in the habit of acting as a consulting doctor for people in difficulties, has stated to the Committee that he never saw a schedule of a certain class of traders that he described, that was otherwise than incorrect in regard to income tax; and another gentleman thought that at 1d. in the 1l., it had been 50,000l. for the last 12 years in the City of London, which could only be correct upon the supposition that

[*Pressly, Charles, "Evidence," *Parliamentary Papers*, 1861, VII, p. 43.]

the trade income of London has not increased during that period; do those considerations make any difference to you in recommending the reduction? They make a difference in the question of imposing an income tax at all, and except in a case of absolute necessity, and as an extraordinary resource, I should be decidedly against it; but if there is to be an income tax, the frauds make, in my estimation, no difference in the reasons for reduction: because in the first place if you were to refuse the reduction on this ground, it would be punishing the honest man for what the rogues do; because if you announce that you must tax people in a higher ratio, because they defraud the revenue; if in fixing their taxation you assume that they are going to evade a part of it, you in fact license them for doing it.

You think, then, that this income tax tends to demoralise them? Yes, thoroughly.

Could you imagine anything more demoralising than for a man to have been successful for 20 years in cheating the Government of a large proportion of the tax, and then by a claim on the ground of morality, getting a remission of the tax? Certainly; one would be sorry that the remission should be granted to rogues; but I do not think it would do to assume that people are rogues, for the purpose of refusing to them what they would be entitled to if they were honest.

W. POLLARD-URQUHART: *In short, you would do them this justice, that you would take away from them all reasonable excuse for roguery?* Yes, I would do that; but I do not attach so much importance as some do to this, as a practical consequence of the reduction.

That would be one reason, would it not? Yes, certainly.

Because some people are rogues, it is no reason why others should not do the thing which is just? Just so; and the more so because to refuse people on the ground that they are going to be rogues, a concession which would be due to them if they were honest, is licensing them to be rogues, because you are recognising their roguery as a fact, and as a compensation necessary to make things just.

In short, to refuse a readjustment of the income tax because a great many people make false returns under Schedule D. is licensing those people to make false returns for the future? Certainly.

You were speaking of the income tax being highly immoral except as it is considered as a mere temporary tax for temporary purposes; do you not think that the obligation to make some adjustment of the income tax is much greater when it is likely to become a permanent law than when it was a mere temporary tax for temporary purposes? I think so.

Was not it regarded as a mere temporary tax when it was levied by Mr. Pitt[*] for 10 years, to the end of the war? Probably; and it is also to be considered that in the use of a national emergency, there is not so

[*39 George III, c. 13.]

much danger of fraud. People only grow fraudulent by degrees; they commit a great fraud at first; or at least not to the same extent.

The very circumstance mentioned by Mr. Lowe just now, that the income tax on traders had remained stationary in the City of London, shows, does it not, that people only get rogues by degrees? Yes. Besides, at a time when there is great national excitement, there is a strong feeling that there is a great public object which requires the tax, and people have both more feeling of their own against defrauding the Government, and are more restrained from it by each other's opinion.

When the income tax was first imposed by Sir Robert Peel,[*] *for the sake of trying a great experiment in taxation, it was to continue only five years, and it might be regarded as levied for a temporary purpose?* It might.

In that case it was quite fair to ask people to give money wherever they could get it, on the same principle that the Carthaginian ladies cut off their hair in the third Punic war? It was.

Whereas, now that it can no longer be considered as a temporary tax, you think that the obligation of readjustment is much stronger than in 1842, when it was first imposed since the war? Certainly; the nearer the approach to the prospect of permanency, the more reason exists for its being readjusted.

Do you not think that the prospect of its being permanent is much greater than it appeared to be in 1842? Yes.

You stated that you thought the people ought not to be taxed upon savings; do you not think that that principle applies with much greater force to the case where those savings are absolutely necessary, in order to keep the capital at the same point at which it was the year before? Yes; anything that goes to the replacement of capital ought not to be taxed.

Under the present tax it is considered as income, is it not? Yes; for instance, in the case of terminable annuities, which is the strongest of all.

Is not the case almost equally as strong where a person has spent his whole capital for his education, and for the purpose of maintaining himself in the many years that are necessary in almost every profession before realising any considerable income, that a part of his earnings, after he begins to derive a considerable income from his profession, ought generally to go to replace the capital so spent? No doubt that is one of the circumstances which plead in favour of his exemption.

Do you not think it a very strong circumstance? It is a circumstance among others.

In short, that part of his professional earnings which goes to the replacement of the capital spent in his education ought not in strictness to be considered income? But, on the other hand, if that capital belonged to him,

[*5 & 6 Victoria, c. 35.]

and if it was spent by himself, you may say, on that principle, that the interest on it becomes subject to the full taxation, and justly so.

You were asked, whether raising the number of pence in the pound, levied in order to make this readjustment, would excite discontent;[*] *would it excite more discontent than when 4d. in the pound was added to the income tax to pay for the extra expenses two years ago, when, for State reasons, the income tax was raised from 5d. to 9d. in the pound, without any readjustment; would it excite much more indignation to have it raised from 5d. to 7d. in the pound, in order to allow of a readjustment?* It is very difficult to say; but I think, generally speaking, that anything which is just, or which is as near as it is practicable to get to justice, and the grounds of which are laid clearly before the public, does, in time, command their approbation.

On the whole, you think that the fear of any dissatisfaction which might be caused by raising the income tax slightly, in order to admit of any equitable readjustment of it, would not be such as to constitute any valid objection against any scheme that might appear just? I think that the dissatisfaction would be chiefly at first, and that as soon as people were convinced that it really was not possible to carry the adjustment of the tax further, they would either turn themselves to getting rid of the tax itself, or they would gradually reconcile themselves to what remained of inequality.

Supposing the circumstances of the country would admit of a slight lowering of the tax, would it not be better to retain the income tax at the same poundage, at the same time giving a readjustment of the income tax, than lowering it 1d. or 2d. in the pound, as might be required? Decidedly.

Do you think that it would excite any very great dissatisfaction throughout the country if it was retained at its present rate, but at the same time readjusted according to the plan proposed by the Honourable Chairman, or according to any plan which seemed to be equitable? Of course, the occasion when the State could do without part of the produce of the tax, would be a particularly convenient opportunity for making this adjustment, and it would excite less dissatisfaction than if it implied an increase of the poundage.

You think that it would create much less dissatisfaction if it was done at the time when the State had an opportunity of taking off some amount of taxation, than if you were obliged to raise the whole general rate in order to readjust it? No doubt.

Do you think that such an opportunity occurring might certainly obviate any objection that might be raised against the readjustment on the ground of causing dissatisfaction? I think it would mitigate the dissatisfaction very much.

[*See pp. 562–3 above.]

On the whole, do you not think that the system proposed by the Chairman is much less unjust than the present system? Much less unjust in many respects.

Would it not be much better for the country to submit to the system proposed by the Chairman, even supposing it raised 1d. or 2d. more in the pound higher than at present, rather than to have it in its present shape? I think so; but I should be very anxious to carry the principle as much further as it could be carried without being stopped by obstacles, the nature of which could be made tolerably clear and intelligible to the public.

W. BUCHANAN: *Does your recommendation of a remission of one-third on professional and industrial incomes proceed upon the principle that there ought to be a saving of one-third, or does it arise from the consideration of the precariousness of those incomes?* It is their precariousness, combined with their temporary nature, which constitutes the obligation to make savings from them. It is because the incomes may end sooner, from loss of health and other causes, that professional persons are under a much stronger necessity of saving, than people who derive their incomes from property.

Then it is a consideration of the combined influence of those two principles? It is a consideration of the greater obligation to save on precarious and terminable incomes.

And not upon the principle that a merchant who has made a profit which enables him to lay by one-third more than he expends, and reinvests it, pays double tax? That is the principle that I would apply if I could; but inasmuch as I cannot apply it, I take another standard, to satisfy that which I consider to be the criterion of justice between one tax-payer and another, namely, the difference in their necessities.

And also the difference of the certainty of income? Yes, the difference of the certainty of income constitutes the difference in their necessities; because we are supposing the incomes to be equal; but one of those incomes is precarious, and the possessor cannot depend upon its continuance; and as he knows that it will cease with his life, he is obliged to save, whereas the other could dispense with saving.

Do not you consider that a professional income, when established, is a more certain income than a commercial or a trading income? I do not think it is so always; no doubt it is in some cases; but professional persons, for instance, lawyers who are making a large income by their practice occasionally, lose it by some of their juniors getting on, and making a more brilliant success in their profession.

But a man gaining his living by being a shipowner is exposed to every wind that blows, and he has certainly a much more precarious income than a professional man, has he not? But then, on the other hand, there is a portion of it dependent upon capital.

But the capital is involved in the success of the ship, is it not? He is under the necessity, no doubt, of insurance, but that enters into the expenses of his business.

He cannot insure against the adventure miscarrying? He cannot insure against a miscalculation of the markets, no doubt.

You propose, do you not, to introduce a preference in the tax in favour of professional incomes? I should prefer to do so, certainly; and it occurs to me that it ought to be so.

J. HUBBARD: *You are aware that the scheme which is before you is not a stereotyped one, and that it is of course open to any amendments which the course of evidence may suggest; the Committee, therefore, are naturally interested in hearing your comments upon it, therefore I would ask you two or three questions more. It was put to you, in answer to your objection to the way in which the present tax taxes capital, first in its creation as earnings, and then in its fruits, that there are other taxes which do tax capital; but is there not a great difference between a tax which, like the legacy duty, or the probate duty, or the succession duty, professedly taxing capital, and one which, professedly taxing income, does partially and capriciously tax capital?* It was exceedingly well put by one of the witnesses before the Committee, Mr. Ansell, that the injustice depends upon the combined circumstances, that it professes to be an income tax and does tax capital, and, that taxing capital, it does not tax it equally. It only taxes some capitals, and not others; and is therefore unjust as a tax upon capital.[*]

You have expressed an opinion that life incomes, if possible, should be considered with reference to the amount of tax levied upon them, as contrasted with the amount which would be levied if the property was held in fee; and I think you suggested that you would make the exemption extend to life interests, with certain qualifications; will you allow me to put a case to you, and perhaps you will tell me whether it would come into the category of such cases as you would relieve. A nobleman has a son who is unmarried, and whom he does not trust, but he leaves by his will landed property to the extent of 120,000l. a year, to trustees in trust to pay 100,000l. a year as an annuity to his son for his life, and 20,000l. a year to a married nephew, to whom he leaves also, and as heir in reversion, the estate; there are two life annuities charged upon that estate; are those life annuities of a like nature with those which you would tax at a diminished ratio, or would you tax them at the full amount of the assessable tax upon the rental? If I understand the statement correctly, the bulk of the income is supposed to be given for life to a person whose descendants are not to have it, while the smaller share of the income for life is given to the person whose descendants are to

[*Parliamentary Papers, 1861, VII, p. 190.]

have the whole. It is plain that if you could enter into individual cases, the one who should pay in full should be the one whose descendants are to have the property, and not the one whose descendants are excluded from it; but still I do not think you could take into consideration cases of so great a rarity as these. Generally speaking, if the estate is entailed or settled in trust in favour of a son or any other person for life, the remainder is to descendants, to that son's children, and if you limit yourself to providing for that which is so much the commonest case, you do not do any injustice worth speaking of.

Are you prepared to state from your knowledge of legal arrangements, that it would be possible to draw an enactment which would make practicable, without raising doubts and litigation, the discrimination which you wish to propose? I do not consider myself competent to do it in the best way, or anything like the best way, nor can I foresee all the cases that would arise, but I think I could suggest modes of drawing it, which would provide for the objects desired. I should lay down the rule, that all life incomes should be exempted, except such and such; then I would enumerate all the cases in which the motive for saving clearly does not exist, or exists in a very inferior degree.

In all those cases you would not, as some of the schemes placed before the Committee at a former period proposed, charge the whole of the life estate to be taxed, but you would diminish the taxation to the extent of the concession to individual cases? I would, because it would clearly be unjust to charge the full tax on a life interest, and the idea does not seem to me admissible of imposing a present tax upon the future holder.

With regard to life annuities, you stated, did you not, that whether an annuity was a life annuity or an annuity for years, if granted, for instance, by a landowner as the means of repaying a loan, made for the purpose of building a house, or improving his estate, you would see in each of those cases the clear repayment of capital to the corporation from whom he took the loan? Yes.

Seeing that in all cases, whether of a life annuity or an annuity for years, granted to a borrower, it is only as regards the application of the money that you would make the discrimination of charging the whole annuity with the tax? Yes.

Upon the assumption that it is meant to be consumed? Exactly.

At least you differ in that respect from the scheme before you, upon that assumption? Yes.

It is an assumption, is it not, that it is meant to be considered as expenditure? It is.

Upon the other hand, you propose to make a rebate of the tax upon the savings of capital? Yes.

But that is only for the purpose of balancing the charge which you make upon capital when consumed, and if you were unable to do the one, you would not I suppose do the other? That does not necessarily follow; I think the income tax should as far as possible be a tax upon expenditure; I should like to bring all personal expenditure under it if I could; and whenever I could, I should like to get hold of it and tax it.

Your principle is (to follow this to a conclusion) that you would exempt all savings? Yes.

And it is the operation of the same rule which induces you to wish to see pensions placed also in a favoured position? Yes, because, the income terminating with life, there is, generally speaking, a greater necessity for saving from it.

May pensions, do you think, be so far considered as the result of deferred payment for services as to be brought in as a kind of accessory to industrial incomes and salaries? A large proportion of them might logically be classed with industrial incomes; but not all, because some pensions are merely the result of good-will, and are not payments for service at all.

Do you think that they might be discriminated in that way, that where they bear the character of being only a deferred payment for antecedent services, they may be fairly treated in the same way as salaries? I would treat them in that way in all cases.

You have been asked to consider the position of houses and ships as placed one in one schedule, and one in the other; but is not the precise matter to be assessed the rent of the houses and not the houses themselves? Yes.

On the other hand, did you ever hear of the rent of ships? No.

Ships are only a means of industrial occupation, are they not? Yes.

And ships, therefore, are only one of the means which tend to the commercial earnings of the owners of the ships? Yes.

But are you aware that there is any such thing as ship-rent? I am not.

Then, you can hardly call these two matters parallel? Not exactly.

The estimate that has been communicated to you of the probable defalcation in the Exchequer from the application of any such remedy as the one before you has been stated at 2,000,000l.;[*] *supposing, for the argument, that the complaints against the income tax with regard to its incidence are real, and that the remedy of those evils would have such a costly result; must not that be the logical consequence, that the 2,000,000l. represents the amount of injustice inflicted by the present law?* That follows decidedly.

T. ESTCOURT: *I understood you, in answer to a former question, to draw a distinction between precarious incomes and incomes of a limited duration; and I understood you to state, that in your view the fair course would be to*

[*See p. 590 above.]

grant a concession of some deduction from the amount of tax payable for incomes that are terminable with life, or a less term; and I understood you to state, that you would make a still further deduction in the case of those incomes which were precarious; did I rightly understand you? Not quite. I did not express any opinion as to the possibility of making more than one rate of exemption. I have not made up my mind, practically, as to whether it is better to have several scales, or only one. But what I brought forward those considerations for, was to point out that the claims were much stronger, the necessity for saving being much greater, in some cases than in others; and my object was, not so much to recommend the application of different scales to those different cases, of which I am not able to judge sufficiently to have a decided opinion, but rather to show that, provided you could relieve the cases in which the claims were strongest, you need not so much mind not being able to relieve those in which they were much weaker; that the fact that you would perhaps be obliged to demand a little more from those who still have some claim to exemption, is not a conclusive objection to giving relief to those whose claims are much stronger.

I understand you to assign as the reason why any concession should be made with regard to Schedule D. to be two-fold, first, because the income is limited, and secondly, because it is precarious? It is both precarious and also limited in duration.

Have your opinions, with regard to this particular subject which has been brought before you to-day, varied since you gave evidence before the Committee in 1852?[*] I am not aware that they have; I have considered the subject more minutely since, and perhaps I may have more of an opinion upon some points of practical execution than I then had; but on the question of principle, my opinions have not altered.

Are you still of opinion, as you were in 1852, that equality requires that in assessing precarious incomes and those of limited duration, some deduction ought to be allowed, which I think you put at one-third, before the assessment is imposed? Yes.

[*See 465–98 above.]

CURRENCY AND BANKING

1867

EDITOR'S NOTE

Enquête sur les principes et les faits généraux qui régissent la circulation monétaire et fiduciaire. Vol. V. Paris: Imprimerie impériale, 1867, 589–96. Signed; not republished. Original heading: "Réponses de M. John Stuart Mill, Membre du Parlement D'Angleterre." Identified in JSM's bibliography as "Answers, in French, to the Questionnaire of the Imperial Commission d'Enquête in Currency and Banking, printed with their Report" (MacMinn, 97). No copy in Somerville College.

In the text below the questions are inserted before JSM's answers.

Currency and Banking

DES CRISES MONÉTAIRES

1. *Quelles ont été les causes de la crise monétaire de 1863-1864?* Autant que je puis en juger, la crise monétaire de 1863-1864 a eu pour cause générale l'immense absorption des capitaux disponibles de la France: d'abord par de fortes dépenses improductives, comme celles de la reconstruction des grandes villes; secondement, par la rapide immobilisation des capitaux en entreprises productives à long terme seulement, telles que les chemins de fer en France et à l'étranger; en troisième lieu, par les énormes emprunts que les gouvernements de la plupart des pays n'ont cessé de faire. A tout cela est venue s'ajouter une grande exportation des métaux précieux en échange du coton brut que l'Europe a dû acheter de l'Inde, de l'Égypte et d'autres pays à un prix très-élevé.

2. *Quelles analogies et quelles différences cette crise a-t-elle présentées avec les crises antérieures?* Les crises antérieures ont souvent été provoquées par des importations exceptionnelles de blé à la suite de mauvaises récoltes, et surtout par des excès de spéculation mercantile. Ces causes n'ont pas existé en 1863-1864.

3. *Les crises monétaires tendent-elles à devenir plus fréquentes? Tendent-elles à devenir plus générales?* A regarder l'histoire commerciale des cinquante années antérieures à 1865, la comparaison des dates n'a pas indiqué jusqu'ici que les crises monétaires tendent à devenir plus fréquentes. Cependant la plus grande étendue des marchés et la plus vaste échelle des opérations commerciales semblent devoir accroître le domaine du hasard dans ces opérations; à quoi l'on peut ajouter que les grandes associations mercantiles, surtout à responsabilité limitée, étant, par leur nature, plus téméraires que les capitalistes, tendent par là à multiplier les chances de crise. D'un autre côté, la grande multiplication des relations commerciales entre les divers pays et l'extrême rapidité des communications ont créé une solidarité entre tous les marchés du monde civilisé, qui tend à généraliser, mais en même temps à adoucir, les crises qui doivent leur naissance à des causes locales. L'effet, étendu à un champ plus vaste, s'amoindrit sur un point donné, parce que les mouvements internationaux de valeurs qui servent de correctifs aux perturbations locales, et qui autrefois se faisaient avec lenteur, sont aujourd'hui presque instantanés.

4. *Quelles som, dans un pays, les causes régulatrices du taux de l'inté-rêt?* Le taux moyen de l'intérêt dans un pays dépend de deux causes générales, savoir: 1° le taux moyen du profit industriel; 2° la proportion qui existe dans ce pays entre la classe industrielle, qui fait valoir elle-même ses capitaux, et ce qu'on peut nommer la classe prêtante, comme aussi entre les capitaux dont ces deux classes disposent. Aux États-Unis par exemple, où la classe des rentiers vivant de l'intérêt de capitaux prêtés est extrême-ment restreinte, le taux de l'intérêt est naturellement beaucoup plus élevé, relativement au profit moyen du commerce et de l'industrie, que dans la plupart des pays de l'Europe. Je ne parle ici que du taux moyen et normal de l'intérêt. Ses variations passagères dépendent de toutes les vicissitudes de la production, de la consommation et de la spéculation.

5. *Quelles sont les causes qui ont agi depuis dix ans sur le cours des métaux précieux?*

6. *Quelles sont les causes qui ont pu récemment réduire la disponibilité des capitaux?*

7. *Y a-t-il eu ralentissement dans la formation des épargnes ou mauvaise direction donnée à ces épargnes?*

8. *Y a-t-il eu insuffisance de capitaux ou excès d'entreprises?*

9. *La constitution de plusieurs sociétés de crédit, sous forme de sociétés anonymes, a-t-elle exercé de l'influence sur les embarras monétaires?*

10. *L'existence et l'organisation de ces sociétés sont-elles de nature à éloigner ou à rapprocher les causes de crise?*

11. *Quelle influence a exercée sur le marché intérieur la participation des capitaux français aux entreprises étrangères?*

12. *Quels avantages ou quels inconvénients présente la cote, à la Bourse de Paris, des valeurs étrangères et des emprunts étrangers?*

13. *Quel a été, depuis dix ans, le mouvement d'entrée et de sortie des métaux précieux? Y a-t-il des indications qui permettent de compléter les renseignements recueillis par l'Administration des Douanes?*

[*Answers to 5–13:*] Tout ce que mes connaissances locales me permet-tent d'offrir en réponse à ces neuf Questions est compris dans les réponses précédentes.

14. *Le déplacement du numéraire a-t-il lieu dans de fortes proportions?*

15. *Quelles opérations donnent lieu à ce déplacement? Exerce-t-il une influence sensible sur les transactions et sur le loyer de l'argent? Existe-t-il des moyens de détruire ou de limiter cette action?*

[*Answers to 14 and 15:*] Le déplacement du numéraire par entrée ou sortie tient à deux sortes de causes. Je ne m'occuperai que du mouvement de sortie, le seul qu'on ait songé jusqu'ici à empêcher ou à limiter. La sortie du numéraire peut avoir lieu par suite d'événements pour ainsi dire fortuits, entraînant des payements extraordinaires au dehors, non balancés par les créances provenant du commerce ordinaire d'exportation. Tels sont les achats de grains à l'étranger à la suite d'une mauvaise récolte; tels furent encore les achats de coton en Asie et en Afrique pendant la guerre civile aux États-Unis; telles sont aussi les dépenses militaires au delà des frontières. Toutes ces diverses causes de payements à faire dans les pays étrangers, entraînant exportation de numéraire, dépendent des vicissitudes naturelles ou de celles de la politique. Cette exportation a pourtant une autre cause plus générale, qui a son origine dans l'imprudence mercantile. Lorsque des spéculations excessives ont lieu sur un point quelconque du monde commercial, ce point devient rapidement débiteur des autres régions. Les marchandises qui sont devenues matière à spéculation haussent démesurément de prix; cette hausse factice arrête les exportations et stimule les importations; la balance des créances internationales se dérange; les dettes à l'étranger viennent à dépasser les créances: de là, sortie du numéraire. Plus tard, les spéculateurs s'occupant de réaliser leurs gains, les prix surhaussés s'abaissent: alors tout le monde s'empressant de vendre avant la débâcle générale, les prix retombent beaucoup plus vite qu'ils ne s'étaient élevés, et la réaction les fait tomber très au-dessous de leur taux normal: c'est ce qu'on appelle une crise commerciale. Alors un mouvement se déclare en sens inverse, et la rentrée du numéraire ramène enfin l'état normal.

La sortie du numéraire, soit qu'elle provienne de l'une on de l'autre des causes que je viens d'indiquer, ne laisse pas d'exercer de l'influence sur le loyer de l'argent; car le numéraire exporté est pris sur les capitaux disponibles, destinés à alimenter le marché des prêts. Quant aux moyens de détruire ou de limiter cette action, il ne saurait y en avoir qu'un seul: ce serait de laisser agir la perte de numéraire sur l'encaisse des banques, sans essayer de l'arrêter en diminuant les avances au commerce par voie d'escompte ou autrement.

Ce moyen me semble applicable et utile, ou inefficace et nuisible, suivant que le déplacement du numéraire a son origine dans les causes que j'ai qualifiées de naturelles et fortuites ou dans les excès de la spéculation.

Dans le cas, par exemple, d'une mauvaise récolte, le déplacement du numéraire a une limite naturelle, et s'arrête de lui-même dès que cette limite est atteinte. L'importation extraordinaire du blé une fois liquidée, le commerce international reprend son assiette ordinaire. Pourvu donc que l'encaisse habituel de la Banque ou des banques soit en excès de la plus grande sortie de numéraire qui a jamais eu lieu par suite d'une mauvaise récolte, on n'a pas, dans ce cas, à se préoccuper de la conservation de l'encaisse: on peut, sans danger, le laisser s'écouler, sans prendre aucune mesure violente pour en arrêter la sortie. Il est vrai qu'après la crise il faudra toujours ramener l'encaisse à son montant normal; mais, pour cela, il suffira d'une hausse modérée de l'escompte, sans aucune secousse violente. Parfois même le numéraire est ramené par le mouvement du marché international, sans qu'il y ait besoin de s'en occuper spécialement.

Il en est tout autrement lorsque la sortie du numéraire est déterminée par une hausse des prix amenée par une spéculation exagérée. L'écoulement ainsi produit n'a pas de limite naturelle, et n'a aucune raison de s'arrêter avant la cessation des causes qui l'ont amené. Il ne cesse et ne peut cesser que lorsque les hauts prix qui lui ont donné lieu ont pris fin par un mouvement de baisse, c'est-à-dire lorsque la spéculation a cédé à une réaction. En ce cas, l'écoulement du numéraire est le remède naturel et indispensable de la maladie, et parvint-on à le retarder, on ne réussirait qu'à prolonger le mal et à aggraver la crise finale. Si, en ce cas, la Banque s'abstenait d'agir pour défendre son encaisse, si elle continuait d'escompter aussi largement qu'auparavant, en laissant s'écouler sa réserve métallique, les spéculateurs, trouvant à emprunter au cours ordinaire, ne seraient pas réduits à vendre: ils pourraient prolonger pendant quelque temps encore leur lutte contre les lois naturelles; les prix surhaussés ne baisseraient pas, et partant l'écoulement suivrait son cours jusqu'à ce que la réserve même la mieux fournie y eût passé tout entière. A l'approche de cette catastrophe, la Banque, pour ne pas faire faillite, serait dans la nécessité de produire d'un seul coup la réaction qu'elle aurait dû préparer graduellement. Une diminution des escomptes et une élévation du taux de l'intérêt, qui eussent suffi pour arrêter la spéculation dans les commencements de la sortie des métaux précieux, ne suffiraient plus: il faudrait une action non-seulement plus brusque, mais plus excessive et plus violente. De là, écoulement général du crédit, la panique et la peine, qui est loin de frapper seulement les spéculateurs dont l'imprudence a amené le mal.

Une banque dirigée par des hommes capables, dès que sa réserve commence à s'en aller, trouvera dans sa connaissance des antécédents commerciaux le moyen de reconnaître les causes particulières qui ont produit l'écoulement; elle saura si le numéraire tend à sortir en quantité indéfinie ou seulement en quantité définie. Si l'on a laissé à cette banque sa pleine liberté d'action, c'est seulement dans le premier cas qu'elle se hâtera de protéger sa réserve, qu'elle aura eu soin de tenir normalement à un montant suffisant pour faire face, sans aucune mesure spéciale, à tout écoulement probable à limite définie.

DE LA MONNAIE FIDUCIAIRE

16. *Quelle est l'utilité de la monnaie fiduciaire?* La monnaie fiduciaire est très-supérieure à la monnaie métallique pour la commodité du transport et pour celle des grands et moyens payements. Elle est aussi une économie

du capital collectif de la société, un remplaçant d'un instrument d'échange très-coûteux par un autre qui ne coûte rien.

17. *Le rôle de cette monnaie tend-il à devenir plus important?* Oui, le rôle de cette monnaie tend à devenir plus important, tant qu'il reste une partie, même peu considérable, de la population qui, par défiance, refuse le billet de banque et exige le numéraire. Mais, une fois que le billet de banque est parvenu à se faire accepter partout comme l'équivalent du numéraire, il ne semble pas que son rôle tende à s'accroître davantage. Car, si la monnaie fiduciaire arrive à dépasser en quantité la monnaie métallique qui circulerait à sa place si elle n'existait pas, elle se déprécie; la mesure commune des valeurs devient variable et incertaine, et l'on retombe dans les inconvénients et dans les injustices du papier-monnaie. Cependant cette dégénération de la monnaie fiduciaire ne saurait avoir lieu dans le système de la convertibilité en espèces, à volonté et sur place.

18. *Est-ce par les émissions de billets au porteur et à vue, ou à l'aide des compensations par virements, comptes courants, chèques, etc., que le crédit tend à se développer?* Dès que les billets de banque ont obtenu la confiance générale et sont parvenus à remplacer le numéraire dans tous les recoins de la circulation, le développement normal du crédit n'a plus lieu par la multiplication des billets de banque, mais principalement au moyen de comptes courants et de virements qui économisent la monnaie courante, soit fiduciaire, soit métallique.

19. *L'emploi de la monnaie fiduciaire peut-il prendre un développement indéfini? Si non, dans quelles limites doit-il être renfermé?* En répondant à la 17e Question, j'ai exprimé mon opinion sur cette Question.

DES CONDITIONS D'UNE BONNE MONNAIE FIDUCIAIRE

20. *A quelles conditions l'emploi de la monnaie fiduciaire est-il sans inconvénients?*

21. *La convertibilité constante des billets est-elle indispensable?*

[*Answers to 20 and 21:*] Sur la nécessité absolue de la convertibilité constante et immédiate des billets, il n'y a plus de différence d'opinion parmi les hommes compétents. Elle me paraît la seule condition indispensable. Avec cette convertibilité suffisamment garantie, il n'y a pas de mauvais système de banques d'émission. La convertibilité serait évidemment illusoire si des billets pouvaient être émis par tout le monde. Même dans le système de la pluralité, il faudrait imposer la condition d'un capital considérable et de la publicité la plus complète. On pourrait en outre, et peut-être on devrait, exiger un dépôt de rentes sur l'État, égal à la somme de tous les billets émis et destiné à leur servir de garantie spéciale.

22. *L'unité du billet de banque en favorise-t-elle la circulation?* Assurément, l'unité du billet de banque en favorise la circulation, en dispensant le public de se donner la peine d'apprécier la solidité relative de diverses banques. Cet avantage, cependant, est surtout sensible dans les commencements.

23. *Quels sont les inconvénients et les avantages de la pluralité des banques, soit générales, soit à circonscription limitée?* En examinant quels sont les inconvénients et les avantages de la pluralité des banques, soit générales, soit à circonscription limitée, je dois d'abord écarter l'expédient de banques locales, chacune unique dans sa circonscription. Ce système équivoque n'offre ni les avantages de l'unité ni ceux de la pluralité. Par la pluralité des banques, j'entends leur concurrence. Ainsi entendue, la question de l'unité ou de la pluralité des banques d'émission ne me paraît pas avoir, à beaucoup près, le degré d'importance qu'on lui attribue. Les partisans et les ennemis de la pluralité semblent s'accorder à croire que si elle existait, il y aurait une facilité de crédit beaucoup plus grande qu'à présent. Les uns applaudissent à cette facilité, la regardant comme un bienfait inappréciable pour le commerce, tandis que les autres trouvent que les dangers en dépassent les avantages, et qu'en provoquant les excès de la spéculation, elle rendrait les crises beaucoup plus fréquentes et plus graves. Je ne puis me persuader qu'aucune de ces opinions soit fondée. Je crois qu'après quelques tâtonnements, et peut-être quelques excès temporaires dans l'usage d'une liberté nouvellement acquise, la circulation des billets se trouverait partagée entre un certain nombre d'établissements solides et prudents, qui se conduiraient collectivement à peu près comme la banque unique se conduit, et qu'on n'éprouverait ni les bienfaits ni les inconvénients auxquels on s'attend. Les banques ne manqueraient pas d'établir, selon l'usage de celles de l'Écosse, un échange hebdomadaire, sinon journalier, de leurs billets respectifs. Il en arriverait qu'une banque qui chercherait à accaparer la circulation en donnant de plus grandes facilités de crédit que les autres, ne pourrait augmenter ses émissions que momentanément: elle verrait rentrer ses billets, présentés par les autres banques, en quantité supérieure aux billets de ces banques qu'elle-même aurait en caisse, et il lui faudrait liquider le surplus en numéraire. L'extension du crédit, que les uns appellent de leurs vœux et que les autres repoussent, n'aurait donc lieu que lorsqu'elle serait provoquée ou favorisée par des causes générales, agissant sur toutes les banques à la fois, et tendant à déterminer une baisse générale de l'intérêt. Mais, toutes les fois que ces causes existent, elles exercent, comme on le voit toujours, une influence exactement pareille sur une banque unique. En fait, la hausse et la baisse de l'escompte auraient toujours lieu à peu près simultanément chez toutes les banques, et, selon toute probabilité, par un accord, au moins tacite,

entre elles. Il n'y aurait donc, à mon avis, que très-peu de différence pratique entre les deux systèmes, une fois que les esprits et les habitudes s'y seraient accommodés.

DES ÉTABLISSEMENTS QUI ÉMETTENT DES MONNAIES FIDUCIAIRES

24. *La Banque de France satisfait-elle à toutes les conditions à exiger d'une banque d'émission; si non, quelles modifications seraient désirables dans son organisation?*

25. *Quels avantages ou quelle infériorité présente l'organisation de la Banque de France, relativement à l'organisation et au régime des banques, soit d'émission, soit de dépôt, des autres pays, notamment des banques d'Angleterre, des États-Unis, de Hambourg et de Hollande?*

[*Answers to 24 and 25:*] Dans le système d'une banque unique, l'organisation de la Banque de France n'a pas de défaut capital à moi connu. Pour en constater les avantages, il faudrait faire l'énumération des défauts de la plupart des autres banques nationales. On peut lui reprocher quelques erreurs de conduite, le plus souvent contraires à son propre intérêt de banque, et qu'on doit regarder comme des concessions faites aux opinions qui lui sont hostiles. Je parle surtout des grands achats d'or au-dessus de sa valeur qu'elle a cru devoir faire pour renouveler son encaisse.

26. *Y a-t-il intérêt ou inconvénient à séparer le département de l'émission et celui de l'escompte?* Cette séparation du département de l'émission de celui de l'escompte, si elle avait lieu, aurait pour but d'assujettir le département de l'émission à une règle semblable à celle de la loi anglaise de Sir Robert Peel (1844), en ne permettant l'émission de billets au-dessus d'une limite fixe qu'en échange d'une somme égale en numéraire. Cette règle me semble, à tout prendre, plus nuisible qu'utile. Elle contraindrait la Banque à traiter absolument de la même manière tout écoulement de numéraire, sans égard à la diversité des causes qui y donnent lieu. Une hausse de l'intérêt serait dès lors inévitable, non dans quelques cas seulement, mais dans tous, et même dès le commencement de l'écoulement, afin de protéger l'encaisse du département de l'escompte. Or, si ma réponse aux 14e et 15e Questions est bien fondée, cette hausse de l'intérêt serait indispensable ou nuisible, suivant la cause de l'écoulement. Laissée à son propre jugement, une banque bien dirigée pourrait tenir compte de la diversité des causes, et recourir à la hausse de l'intérêt là seulement où la hausse est le remède nécessaire d'une crise provoquée par des spéculations excessives, tout en s'abstenant de s'en servir dans le cas où l'écoulement, provenant de causes naturelles, tendrait à cesser de lui-même sans avoir englouti tout l'encaisse.

Au contraire, sous la règle absolue de la loi anglaise de 1844, le remède est obligatoire là même où il aggrave le mal. Les billets présentés pour être échangés contre le numéraire sont forcément supprimés, et ne peuvent plus être employés à l'escompte. Le département de l'escompte n'a plus à compter que sur sa propre réserve; il est tenu de faire face à toutes les crises avec une partie seulement de la réserve totale de la Banque, puisque le numéraire du département de l'émission lui est fermé. De là, nécessité pour lui de défendre sa propre réserve par des hausses d'intérêt beaucoup plus fréquentes et plus extrêmes que celles qu'on avait éprouvées en Angleterre avant la séparation des deux départements. Il pourrait même arriver que le département de l'escompte fût à sec, et devint incapable de remplir ses engagements envers ses créanciers en compte courant, tandis que l'autre département de la même banque regorgerait de fonds. C'est pour éviter ce résultat étrange, qui serait, du moins en Angleterre, une catastrophe beaucoup plus grave que même la suspension momentanée de la convertibilité des billets de banque, qu'on a déjà trois fois suspendu la loi restrictive de 1844.

27. *Le cours légal, tel qu'il existe en Angleterre, s'il était attribué aux billets de la Banque de France, aurait-il pour effet d'en mieux assurer la circulation?*

28. *Quel nombre de signatures une banque doit-elle exiger pour sa sécurité?*

[*Answers to* 27 *and* 28:] Ces deux Questions exigeraient, pour y répondre, des connaissances locales ou professionnelles que je ne possède pas.

29. *L'émission des billets doit-elle être limitée? Convient-il de proportionner l'émission à l'encaisse ou au capital?* Toute limitation de l'émission des billets, autre que la limite naturelle imposée par la convertibilité, me semble déplacée. Ce n'est pas l'émission qu'il faut proportionner à l'encaisse, mais bien l'encaisse à l'émission.

DU FONCTIONNEMENT DE LA BANQUE

30. *A quel niveau doit être maintenu l'encaisse de la Banque pour assurer la convertibilité des billets?* Pour assurer la convertibilité, l'encaisse moyen doit être maintenu sensiblement au-dessus de la plus forte somme de métaux précieux qui soit jamais sortie de la Banque d'émission dans aucune crise. Quand la crise survient, si elle est un effet de causes naturelles, et un effet naturellement limité, on peut sans scrupule laisser écouler l'encaisse, sauf à le renouveler après la crise. Dans l'autre cas, c'est-à-dire quand la crise est la débâcle à la suite d'un mouvement de spéculation, il

faut prendre, dès le commencement de l'écoulement, des mesures décisives pour défendre l'encaisse.

31. *Quelles sont les causes qui tendent à diminuer ou à augmenter l'encaisse et les moyens à employer pour en maintenir le niveau?* On peut dire en termes généraux que l'encaisse s'augmente par l'abondance des capitaux, combinée avec une timidité générale à l'égard des entreprises hasardeuses. Il atteint ordinairement son maximum dans la période qui succède à une grande crise. Il diminue ensuite, à mesure que la spéculation renaît. Cependant celle-ci n'agit pas sur l'encaisse dès le commencement, mais seulement quand le temps est venu de remplir les engagements pécuniaires qu'on a pris.

32. *Quel est le rôle et quelle est la destination du capital de la Banque? Le capital doit-il être accru? Quels seraient les effets de cet accroissement?*

33. *La Banque devrait-elle aliéner, en totalité ou en partie, les rentes qu'elle possède? Quels seraient les effets de cette aliénation?*

34. *Le capital des banques d'émission doit-il, en général, être un capital de garantie ou peut-il être employé utilement dans les affaires de la Banque?*

[*Answers to* 32–34:] C'est seulement comme garantie qu'une banque, soit de dépôt, soit d'émission, a besoin d'un capital propre. Ce capital peut être employé dans les affaires de la Banque sans manquer à sa fonction de garantie; mais en ce cas il a besoin d'être plus considérable, ayant à couvrir à la fois les risques des affaires que fait la Banque non-seulement avec des dépôts et avec des billets, mais aussi avec ses propres fonds. On pourrait exiger de la Banque de France qu'elle réalisât son capital pour pouvoir l'employer tout entier à l'escompte; mais une telle mesure ne donnerait, dans un pays où le crédit est un peu développé, aucun avantage réel au commerce; car les sommes que la Banque retirerait de la vente de ses rentes seraient normalement puisées dans les capitaux disponibles du pays, dans ceux qui déjà alimentent directement ou indirectement l'escompte. Il y aurait déplacement, il n'y aurait pas accroissement des fonds destinés à l'escompte. La Banque se mettrait à la place de quelque autre, comme prêteur au commerce, et cet autre se mettrait à la place de la Banque, comme créancier de l'État. La seule exception serait si les rentes cédées par la Banque étaient achetées par des paysans, par exemple, avec des sommes provenant de l'épargne et qui seraient restées enfouies improductivement chez eux.

35. *Quels sont pour les banques d'émission, et spécialement pour la Banque de France, les avantages et les inconvénients des avances sur dépôt?* Cette Question exigerait, pour y répondre, des connaissances locales que je ne possède pas.

36. *L'élévation de l'escompte est-elle le seul moyen efficace de maintenir*

ou de reconstituer l'encaisse? L'achat d'or à l'étranger ne pourrait se payer qu'en lettres de change existant sur le marché, ou tirées à long terme sans contre-valeur: dans le premier cas, on ferait monter le taux du change, et l'on amènerait ainsi une nouvelle exportation de métaux précieux; dans le second, on n'arriverait qu'à éloigner un peu la sortie de l'or, sans même l'ajourner jusqu'à l'échéance des billets; car l'élévation générale des prix restant la même, il n'y aurait rien de changé dans les circonstances qui avaient amené la crise, et une nouvelle sortie de numéraire ne tarderait pas à se déclarer. Tous les moyens proposés pour maintenir ou pour reconstituer l'encaisse, en dehors de l'élévation du taux de l'escompte, me paraissent illusoires. On a proposé l'achat par la Banque de lettres de change sur l'étranger, mais elle ne ferait par là que se mettre à la place d'autres acheteurs ayant des dettes à payer à l'étranger, dettes qu'il leur faudrait, par conséquent, acquitter en or. Ces divers expédients seraient donc inefficaces pour protéger l'encaisse. D'un autre côté, le refus de la Banque d'escompter et la limitation des bordereaux seraient infiniment plus graves pour le commerce, en temps de crise, que la hausse la plus extrême de l'intérêt. Dans celle-ci, il ne s'agit que de payer très-cher pendant quelques semaines le secours dont on a besoin; mais l'impossibilité d'obtenir un secours suffisant pourrait entraîner la faillite.

37. *Est-il possible de prévenir les variations de l'escompte ou de les renfermer dans de certaines limites?* Il est impossible de prévenir les variations du taux de l'intérêt, et par conséquent de l'escompte. Elles dépendent de l'offre et de la demande des capitaux disponibles. Il n'y a aucun moyen de les mitiger, mais on peut les aggraver, et c'est l'effet des règles restrictives comme celle de la loi anglaise de 1844.

38. *Est-il possible d'imposer à une banque privilégiée un taux fixe d'escompte ou même un maximum?* Imposer à une banque privilégiée soit un taux fixe, soit un maximum du taux de l'escompte, pourrait être licite en droit, mais ne saurait, à mon avis, être utile à l'intérêt générale. Si l'état du marché des capitaux, en dehors de la Banque, déterminait un taux d'intérêt au-dessus de ce maximum, alors, en défendant à la Banque de profiter de cette hausse, on ne ferait que créer un privilège en faveur de ceux dont on aurait fait escompter le papier à un taux exceptionnellement favorable. En supposant même, ce qui est difficile à concevoir, qu'on pût ménager un moyen de partager également ce bénéfice entre tous les commerçants, on ne voit pourtant pas pourquoi l'État s'occuperait de donner le capital aux commerçants au-dessous de sa valeur, plutôt que de donner le pain au-dessous de sa valeur aux classes laborieuses.

39. *Quels sont les avantages et les inconvénients des petites coupures, notamment au point de vue de la conservation de l'encaisse?* Les coupures ne devraient pas être assez petites pour passer communément entre les

mains de personnes qui, par défaut d'éducation et d'expérience, seraient facilement portées aux paniques.

40. *Quel est celui des moyens suivants de défendre l'encaisse qui présente le moins d'inconvénients pour le commerce: élever le taux de l'escompte, refuser un certain nombre de bordereaux, graduer le taux de l'escompte d'après les échéances?* Voir ma réponse à la 36e Question.

41. *Le développement actuel des relations internationales entraîne-t-il une certaine solidarité entre les encaisses de toutes les banques d'émission?*

42. *Quelles sont les conséquences de cette solidarité? Est-il possible de la faire cesser ou de la restreindre?*

[*Answers to 41 and 42:*] La solidarité entre les encaisses des banques d'émission, sans être complète, est réelle, et plutôt un bien qu'un mal. Si elle fait sentir à chaque pays, jusqu'à un certain degré, les crises des pays voisins, il est vrai aussi que le mal des crises d'origine locale s'atténue en s'étendant sur un plus grand espace.

ENDOWMENTS

1869

EDITOR'S NOTE

Fortnightly Review, n.s. V (Apr., 1869), 377–90. Headed: "Endowments."
Signed; republished without textual changes in *D&D*, IV (1875), 1–24. Identified in JSM's bibliography as "an article headed 'Endowments' in the Fortnightly Review of April 1. 1869" (MacMinn, 98). No copy in Somerville College.

The variant at 618^{a-a} derives from the one known MS fragment (Yale University Library), which forms part of the collection obtained from the Sotheby sale of 27 July, 1927. Although the wording is generally close to that of the final text, the fragment is given in full, except for cancellations. (One cancellation—"is an offence both against liberty & against property"—is restored in the final text at 618.22–3. The typographical error at 620.26 ("it it" for "it") is corrected in *D&D*, IV.

Endowments

A FEW YEARS AGO, the question which required to be argued on the subject of endowments, was the right of the State to interfere with them: not merely the right to bring them back to their original purpose when by the corruption or negligence of the managers it had been departed from, but the right to change altogether the application designed by the founder. This question now scarcely needs further argument. Discussion, and the progress of political thought, have done their work. We have well-nigh seen the last of the superstition which allowed the man who owned a piece of land or a sum of money five hundred years ago, to make a binding disposition determining what should be done with it as long as time or the British nation should last; which, after limiting an owner's power to tie up his property in favour of individuals to the term of a single generation, thinks it spoliation to disobey his orders after the lapse of centuries, when their apparent purpose is connected with religion or charity. These prejudices had nearly ceased to be formidable, even before they received their death-blow from the triumphant passage through the House of Commons of the proposal for disendowing the Irish Protestant Church.[*] Whoever voted, or would vote, for that great measure of justice and common sense, indicates his opinion that the jurisdiction of the State over Endowments extends, if need be, to an entire alteration of their purposes; and even those whose political or ecclesiastical partisanship ranges them on the other side, find it consistent with their principles to propose alternative plans, as subversive as disendowment itself of the legal rights vested by the endowment in collective or fictitious public persons. There is, as on all other great questions, a minority behind the age; which is as natural as that there should be minorities in advance of it. But with the bulk of the nation the indefeasibility of endowments is a chimera of the past; so much so, that those who fought hardest against this superstition when it was alive, are now likely to find themselves under the obligation, not of re-arguing a gained cause, but rather of checking the reaction to a contrary extreme, which so generally succeeds the defeat of an old error, when the conflict has been long.

[*32 & 33 Victoria, c.42.]

Such a reaction, in fact, is already commencing. Some of the most effective and valuable champions of State authority over Endowments are claiming assent to doctrines which go far beyond providing for the due application to public uses of funds given for the public benefit. Some go the length of maintaining that endowments, or certain great classes of them at least, even when their purposes have not ceased to be useful, are altogether an evil, as the purposes would be better attained without them. Others stop short of this, but recommend that it should be unlawful to make endowments for any public purpose, except through the medium, and subject to the discretion, of the Government for the time being, or of an authority responsible to Parliament, and to those by whom parliaments and governments are made. In a paper in all other respects deserving of high eulogium,* Mr. Fitch—one of the men whose personal investigations have most largely contributed to make known the abuses of endowments— is not content with calling on statesmen to "estimate the enormous mischief which is done in England under the name of benevolence," and to "see the need of a more energetic and organised supervision of all public charities," but urges them "to go a step farther, and, while permitting the free exercise of testamentary rights *as between persons and persons,* make it illegal to devote any money to public objects except through the agency of some recognised body, which is amenable to public control. Is it too much to expect," asks Mr. Fitch, "that we shall soon see the wisdom of restraining the power of private persons to tamper with any one of those great national interests such as education and the relief of the poor, which demand organisation and fixed principles, and which still more imperatively demand complete readjustment from time to time, in accordance with the supreme intelligence and will of the nation, as represented in Parliament?"

It would be both unfair and unreasonable to impute to Mr. Fitch, as a settled conviction, the doctrine here incidentally thrown out—a doctrine breathing the very spirit, and expressed in almost the words, of the apologies made in the over-centralised governments of the Continent for not permitting any one to perform the smallest act connected with public interests without the leave of the Government. But when such a maxim finds its way to the public under such auspices, it is time to enter a protest in behalf of those "private persons" whose power of public usefulness Mr. Fitch estimates so lightly, but whose liberty of making themselves useful in their own way, without requiring the consent of any public authority, has mainly contributed to make England the free country she is; and whose well-directed public spirit is covering America with the very institutions which her state of society most needs, and was least likely in any other manner

*[Fitch, Joshua Girling.] "Educational Endowments," *Fraser's Magazine* [LXXIX], for January, 1869, Pp. 11–12.

to get—institutions for the careful cultivation of the higher studies. Whether endowments for educational purposes are a good or an evil is a fair question for argument, and shall be argued presently. But the reason by which Mr. Fitch supports his doctrine—namely, that as education and the relief of the poor require organization and fixed principles, no tampering with them by private persons should be allowed—would avail equally against allowing any private person to set up and support a school, or to expend money in his lifetime on any plan for the benefit of the poor. Such doctrines lead straight to making education and beneficence an absolute monopoly in the hands of, at the best, a parliamentary majority; that is, of an executive government making itself habitually the organ of the prevalent opinion in the country, but liable to spasmodic fits of interference by the country's more direct representatives. It is hardly necessary to say that Mr. Fitch cannot intend this; but it is those who do not intend a bad principle, but only a particular consequence of it, that usually do the work of naturalising the principle, and making it one of the moving forces in society and government.

While there are few things more true, under due limitations, there are few which in the present day it does more mischief to speak unguardedly about, than the "organisation" and "fixed principles" required in every-thing which aims at producing a public benefit. It is desirable that every particular enterprise for education or other public objects should be organised; that is, its conductors should act together for a known object, on a definite plan, without waste of strength or resources. But it is far from desirable that all such enterprises should be organized exactly alike; that they all should use the same means for the attainment of exactly the same immediate ends. And Mr. Fitch himself, as we saw, reinforces his argument drawn from the necessity of "fixed principles," by another grounded on the importance of unfixing those fixed principles from time to time.

The truth needs reasserting, and needs it every day more and more, that what the improvement of mankind and of all their works most imperatively demands is variety, not uniformity. What is called tampering by private persons with great public interests, as if it meant obstructing the Govern-ment in what it thinks fit to do for public uses with the funds at its dis-posal, means trying to do with money of their own something that shall promote the same objects better. It is tampering as those tamper with the religion of the country who build nonconformist chapels. It is healthy rivalry. If the law duly protects these private establishments against inter-ested misappropriation of their funds, many of them will probably do better in some respects, some perhaps better on the whole, than institutions held to "fixed principles" laid down by an Act of Parliament, or by the opinion of the majority. At all events, whether they do or not, they are necessary for the just protection of minorities, whose portion in the public interest deserves the attention of majorities equally with their own, but is far less likely to obtain it.

All this, though its importance is seldom adequately felt but by those who are directly interested in it, is not likely to be called in question, so far as it affects men's employment of their property during their own lifetime. But there is no reason ªwhy respect for the free agency of individuals should stop there, unless the power of bequest itself is a nuisance, and ought to be abated. If it is right that people should be suffered to employ what is lawfully their own in acts of beneficence to individuals taking effect after their death, why not to the public? There is good reason against allowing them to do this in favour of an unborn individual whom they cannot know, or a public purpose beyond the probable limits of human foresight. But within those limits, the more scope that is given to the varieties of human individuality, the better. Since trial alone can decide whether any particular experiment is successful, latitude should be given for carrying on the experiment until the trial is complete. For the length of time, therefore, which individual foresight can reasonably be supposed to cover, and during which circumstances are not likely to have so totally changed as to make the effect of the gift entirely different from what the giver intended, there is an obvious propriety in abiding by his dispositions. To set them aside, unless at the command of a still higher principle, is an offence both against liberty and against property. And all that the higher

---

ª-ª620 MS why respect for the liberty of individuals should stop there, unless the power of bequest itself is an evil which ought to be abated. There is no reason why people should be prevented from employing what is lawfully their own, in acts of beneficence taking effect after their death, to the public as well as to individuals. There *is* reason for preventing them from doing this in favour of an unborn individual whom they cannot know, or a public purpose beyond the probable limits of human foresight. But within those limits the more scope that is given to the varieties of human individuality, the better. Since trial alone can decide whether any particular experiment is successful, liberty should be allowed of carrying on the experiment until the trial is complete. For the length of time, therefore, which individual foresight can reasonably be supposed to cover, & during which circumstances are not likely to have so totally changed as to make the effect of the gift altogether different from what the giver intended, it is an offence, both against liberty & against property, to set aside his dispositions, unless at the command of a still higher principle, and all that the higher principle requires is that a term, not too distant, should be fixed—I will not decide that it should be half a century, or a century nor even whether it should be the same for all kinds of endowments—at the expiration of which their appropriation should come under the control of the State, to be modified, or entirely altered, at its discretion; provided that the purpose to which they may be diverted shall be of a permanent character, to remove the temptation of taking such funds for the current expenses at a time of financial difficulty.

I am not maintaining that there should be no limit to the right of making foundations, even when only temporary. There are strong reasons against allowing them to be made in such a manner as to tie up land from alienation. It is a matter of course

principle requires is, that a term, not too distant, should be fixed—I will not decide that it should be half a century or a century, or even whether it should be the same for all descriptions of endowments—but a term at the expiration of which their appropriation should come under the control of the State, to be modified, or entirely changed, at its discretion; provided that the new purpose to which they may be diverted shall be of a permanent character, to remove the temptation of laying hands on such funds for current expenses in times of financial difficulty.

I am not contending that there should be no limit to the right of making endowments, except a limit of time. There are strong reasons against permitting them to be so made as to tie up land from alienation. It is a matter of course that they should not be permitted for any purpose definitely illegal. I say "definitely," because the English common law has a number of vague formulae under cover of which almost anything of which the judge disapproves may be declared unlawful. But there are also employments of money which have so mischievous an effect, that they would most likely be prohibited, if it could be done without improper interference with individual liberty; and such an application of funds, though the State may be obliged to tolerate, it may be right that it should abstain from enforcing, on the mandate of the owner, after his death. Of this sort are most of the so-called doles; indiscriminate distributions of sums of money among the poor of a particular place or class, the effect of which may be to pauperise and demoralise a whole neighbourhood. In such cases, until the expiration of the term during which testamentary directions in general

---

that they should not be permitted for any purpose definitely illegal. I say "definitely" because the English common law has a number of vague formulæ under cover of which nearly anything of which the Judge disapproves may be pronounced illegal. But there are also some employments of money which have so mischievous an effect that they would most likely be prohibited if it could be done without an improper amount of interference with individual liberty: & such an application of funds though the State may not prevent, it may be right that it should abstain from enforcing, on the mandate of their owner, after his death. Of this sort are most of the so-called doles; indiscriminate distributions of sums of money among the poor of a particular place or class, the effect of which may be to pauperize and demoralize a whole neighbourhood. In such cases, until the expiration of the term which the law may allow for the validity of testamentary directions, the intention of the testator should be respected so far as it is not mischievous; interference being limited to the choice of an unobjectionable mode of doing good to the persons, or the sort of persons, whose good he intended; as by appropriating to a school for children what was destined for alms. And it is important that even this minor degree of discretion should be exercised with extreme reserve. The State has no business to consider, so long as the fixed term is unexpired, what employment of the money would be the most useful, or whether money is more wanted for other purposes. No doubt this would often be the case, but the money was not given to the State, nor for general uses. Nothing ought to be regarded as a warrant for setting the owner's dispositions prematurely aside, but that to permit their execution would be a clear & positive public mischief. [*see headnote, p. 614 above*]

may be allowed to be valid, the intention of the testator should be respected so far as it is not mischievous; the departure from it being limited to the choice of an unobjectionable mode of doing good to the persons, or the sort of persons, whom he intended to benefit; as, for instance, by appropriating to a school for children what was destined for alms. And it is important that even this minor degree of interference should be exercised with great reserve. The State is not entitled to consider, so long as the fixed term is unexpired, what mode of employing the money would be most useful, or whether it is more wanted for other purposes. No doubt this would often be the case; but the money was not given to the State, nor for general uses. Nothing ought to be regarded as a warrant for setting the donor's dispositions prematurely aside, but that to permit their execution would be a clear and positive public mischief.[a]

What tempts people to see with complacency a testator's dispositions invalidated, is the case of what are called eccentric wills—bequests determined by motives, and destined for purposes, with which they do not sympathise. And this propensity to count the wishes of the owner of the property for little or nothing, when they are unlike those which we think we should ourselves have had in his place, does not stop at public endowments, but extends to any large bequest in favour of an individual, which departs ever so little from the common practice of the common world. But does not this genuine intolerance of the majority respecting other people's disposal of their property after death, show how great is the necessity for protection to the rights of those who do not make resemblance to the majority their rule of life? A case of bequest which has been much noticed in the newspapers, and of which it is still uncertain whether it will be allowed to take effect, strikingly exemplifies this need. A person[*] left a sum of money by will to found an hospital for the treatment of the diseases of the lower animals, particularly birds and quadrupeds. He made the mistake of appointing as trustee for the purposes of the endowment, the University of London—a body constituted for special objects, and which could not with propriety undertake a duty so remote from the ends of its appointment. But can it be pretended that an hospital such as was designed by the testator, would not be a highly useful institution? Even if no regard were due to the animals themselves, is not the mere value of many of them to man, and the light which a better study of their physiology and pathology cannot fail to throw on the laws of animal life and the diseases of the human species, sufficient to make an institution for that study not merely useful, but important? When one thinks of this, and then considers that no such institution has ever been established in Europe; that a person willing to employ part of his superfluities in that way, is not born once in

[*Thomas Brown, of Dublin.]

several centuries; and that, now when one has been found, the use he makes of what is lawfully his own is a subject of contemptuous jeering, and an example held up to show the absurdities of testators, and the folly of endowments; can one desire a more conclusive evidence of what would happen if donations for public purposes were only valid when the purposes are consonant to the opinion of the majority? Who knows if even the Cornell University, with its "eccentric" provision that every student attending the University must work bodily for his living, would at present have been more than a project, if its realisation had depended on the will of the Government, or of an authority accountable to the majority?

Because an endowment is a public nuisance when there is nobody to prevent its funds from being jobbed away for the gain of irresponsible administrators; because it may become worse than useless if irrevocably tied up to a destination fixed by somebody who died five hundred years ago; we ought not on that account to forget that endowments protected against malversation, and secured to their original purpose for no more than two or three generations, would be a precious safeguard for uncustomary modes of thought and practice, against the repression, sometimes amounting to suppression, to which they are even more exposed as society in other respects grows more civilised. The fifty or hundred years of inviolability which I claim for them, would often suffice, if the opinion or practice is good, to change it from an uncustomary to a customary one, leaving the endowment fairly disposable for another use. Even when the idea embodied in the endowment is not an improvement, those who think it so are entitled to the opportunity of bringing it to a practical test. The presence of such attempts to promote the general well-being by means diverging from the common standard, keeps discussion alive, and obliges the prevailing opinions and customs to seek support from their own merits, and not from a blind acceptance of existing facts.

Some further observations require to be made on educational endowments, which are in some respects a peculiar case. Of these it cannot be said, in the present day at least, that they provide what, but for them, would not be provided at all. Education there would still be, and the real question is one of quality. Neither, again, has the argument, so important in other cases, of the protection due to uncustomary opinions, more than a limited application here. A very small minority is able to support a private school suitable to its requirements; and it might even seem that minorities are never in so much danger of being left out, as in the case of endowed institutions for education, which are usually more or less bound to opinions widely prevalent, and which, when the time has come for bringing them under the control of the State, fall into the power of the majority. This danger is very serious, when State institutions, or endowments under State superintendence, have a monopoly of education, or when those who are there educated have, as they have usually had, legal preferences or advantages over other people. But if endowed institutions, originally of a national character, or which have become so by the expiration of the term of inviolability, are open to all alike; and open in the only true sense, that is, with full liberty to refuse one part of the teaching while accepting another part; minorities would enjoy all the benefits that the endowments could give, while retaining the full power of providing, at their own cost, any education which they may consider preferable.

The question of educational endowments resolves itself into this: Is education one of those marketable commodities which the interest of rival dealers can be depended on for providing, in the quantity and of the quality required? Is education a public want which is sufficiently met by the ordinary promptings of the principle of trade? I should be the last to speak with sentimental disparagements of trade or its achievements, or to imagine that the motives which govern it can safely be dispensed with in any great department of the service of mankind. But the question is not quite fairly stated in the disjunctive programme, "Endowment or Free-Trade." Endowment *and* Free-Trade is the thing contended for. That there should be free competition in education; that law, or the State, when it prescribes anything on the subject, should fix what knowledge should be required, but not from whom it shall be procured, is essential to civil and political freedom. But will this indispensable free-trade in education provide what is wanted, better without than with the help, example, and stimulus of education aided by endowments?

There are many things which free-trade does passably. There are none which it does absolutely well; for competition is as rife in the career of fraudulent pretence as in that of real excellence. Free-trade is not upheld, by any one who knows human life, from any very lofty estimate of its worth, but because the evils of exclusive privilege are still greater, and what is worse, more incorrigible. But the capacity of free-trade to produce even the humblest article of a sufficient degree of goodness, depends on three conditions: First, the consumer must have the means of paying for it; secondly, he must care sufficiently for it; thirdly, he must be a sufficient judge of it. All three conditions are signally wanting in the case of national education. The first case, that of inability to pay, now, happily, requires only a passing notice. That those who are too poor to pay for elementary instruction, should have it paid for by others for them, has, after a battle of above half a century, taken its place in opinion among admitted national necessities. But the concession of this is the concession of all the rest, at least in principle; for, if those whom poverty disables from obtaining instruction by themselves ought to be helped to it by others, either because it is the interest or the duty of those others to take care that they have it, why not also those in whose case the obstacle is not the poverty, but the ignorance or selfishness of parents? With respect to the other two requisites —that the customer should care for the commodity, and that he should be able to judge of it—the tale is soon told. As a general rule, subject to exceptions, the wishes of parents in regard to the instruction of their children are determined by two considerations. First, what will bring in a direct pecuniary profit. Of this they think themselves judges, though most of them judge even of this very incompetently, being unable to see how any studies, except the direct practice of a business, can conduce to business success. Of other kinds of instruction they neither are, nor consider themselves to be, judges; and on these their rule of action is that by which they are guided in most other things of which they are personally ignorant—the custom of their class of society. If we desire, therefore, that the education of those who are above poverty, but who are not, for their own bane and that of others, predestined to idleness, should have any better guide than an extremely narrow conception of the exigencies of a business life, we must apply ourselves to the other of the two levers by which those we seek to act upon can be moved; we must introduce a better custom. It must be made the fashion to receive a really good education. But how can this fashion be set except by offering models of good education in schools and colleges within easy reach of all parts of the country? And who is able to do this but such as can afford to postpone all considerations of pecuniary profit, and consider only the quality of the education; either because, like the English Universities, they are certain of sufficient customers, or because they have the means of waiting many years till the time comes which shall show that the pupils they have trained are more than ordinarily fitted for all the uses of life? The funds for doing this can only be derived from taxation or from endowments; which of the two is preferable? Independently of the pecuniary question, schools and universities governed by the State are liable to a multitude of objections which those that are merely watched, and, in case of need, controlled by it, are wholly free from; especially that most fatal one of tending to be all alike; to form the same unvarying habits of mind and turn of character.

The abuses of endowments are flagrant, monstrous, and wholly inexcusable. But what funds, public or private, would not be a prey to malversation if the law took no notice of it; or if, though the law was what it ought to be, there was no individual whose interest and no public officer whose duty it was to put the law in force? There is surely nothing visionary in imagining these things remedied. It cannot be impossible, where there is the will, to prevent public funds from being diverted to private pockets. Nor can it be doubted that the variety of endowed institutions, and the influence of the State exerted within its proper limits, would ensure adequate provision for including in the course of education (either everywhere or only somewhere, according to the necessities of the case) whatever has any just claim to form a part of it. What is feared is, that the teacher's duty will be idly and inefficiently performed if his remuneration is certain, and not dependent on pupils and their payments. The apprehension is well grounded. But where is the necessity that the teacher's pay should bear no relation to the number and proficiency of his pupils? In the case of an ordinary schoolmaster, the fees of pupils would always be a part, and should generally be the greatest part, of his remuneration. In an university, or a great public school, even if the fees go to the collective body, it is not a law of nature that every tutor or professor should be paid neither more nor less than a fixed sum. Could anything be easier than to make the whole, or a large part, of his remuneration proportional to the number of those who attended his teaching during an entire term, or during a year? And would it be impossible that he should receive an extra sum for each of his pupils who passes a creditable examination, on leaving the institution, in his particular department? The real principle of efficiency in teaching, payment by results, is easily applied to public teaching, but wholly inapplicable to private school speculations, even were they subject to a general system of public examinations; unless by special agreement between schoolmasters and parents, which also is a thing we have no chance of seeing until the fashion can be set.

And is there any one so blind to the realities of life as to imagine that the emoluments of a private schoolmaster have in general any substantial connection with the merit and efficiency of his teaching? In the first place, he has a direct pecuniary interest in neglecting all studies not cared for by the general public, or by the section of it from whom he hopes for patronage. In those which they do care for, a little trouble goes much farther in aiming at a mere appearance of proficiency, than at the reality. The persons whom he has to satisfy are not experienced examiners, who take pains to find out how much the pupil knows, and are judges of it; but parents, most of whom know little of what is taught at schools, or have forgotten what they knew; many of whom do not test their child's knowledge by a single question, it being enough for them that he has been at what is called a respectable school—and who desire no better than to take for granted that all is right, and that the certificates or prizes which the children bring home from the master are the earnings of desert, not bribes for the good word of parents. These are not the mere abuses, but the natural fruits, of the trading principle in education; accordingly, the disclosures of the Schools Enquiry Commission[*] have been as damning to the character of the private, as to

[*Parliamentary Papers, 1867–68, XXVIII, i–xvii.]

that of the endowed, schools. When the pupil himself reflects, too late, that his schooling has done him no good, the impression left upon him, if he is one of the common herd, is not that he was sent to a bad when he ought to have been sent to a good school, but that school altogether is a stupid and useless thing, and schoolmasters a set of contemptible impostors. It is difficult to see, in the operation of the trading principle, any tendency to make these things better. When the customer's ignorance is great, the trading motive acts much more powerfully in the direction of vying with one another in the arts of quackery and self-advertisement than in merit. Those parents who desire for their children something better than what the private schools afford, and do not find that something better in the endowed schools as at present conducted, sometimes combine to form the subscription schools commonly called proprietary. This private election, as it were, of a schoolmaster, by a rate-paying qualification, is an improvement, as far as it goes, for those who take part in it; but as it is only had recourse to by parents who have some perception of the badness of the private schools, it makes the case of these last, if anything, rather worse than before, by withdrawing that small portion of parental influence which would really be exercised, and probably exercised beneficially. And the worth even of the Proprietary Schools depends on that of the high public institutions which are the trainers of schoolmasters, and whose certificates or honours are the chief evidence, often the only tolerable evidence available, to guide the proprietors in their choice.

Those who make the vices of mere trading education an argument for supplementing it by something else, are charged with ignoring the tendency which schools have, in common with other things, to improve with the general progress of human affairs. But human affairs are seldom improving in all directions at once, and it is doubtful if much of the improvement that is now going on is taking the direction of trade morality. Even in commerce properly so called—the legitimate province of self-interest—where it is enough if the ruling motive is limited by simple honesty, things do not look at present as if there were an increasing tendency towards high-minded honour, conscientious abhorrence of dishonest arts, and contempt of quackery. Even there the vastness of the field, the greatness of the stakes now played for, and the increasing difficulty to the public in judging rightly of transactions or of character, are making the principle of competition bring forth a kind of effects, the cure of which will have to be sought somewhere else than in the corrective influence of competition itself. There is more hope, doubtless, on the side of the parents. An increasing number of them are probably acquiring somewhat better notions of what education is, and a somewhat greater value for it. But experience proves that, of all the modes of human improvement, this particular one is about the slowest. The progress of the bulk of mankind is not in any great degree a spontaneous thing. In a few of the best and ablest it is spontaneous, and the others follow in their wake. Where society must move all together, as in legislation and government, the slowest get dragged on, at the price of a deplorable slackening in the pace of the quickest movers; but where each has to act individually, as in sending his children to school, and the power of the more advanced is only that of their opinion and their example, the general mass may long remain sadly behind.

However this may be, those cannot be accused of ignoring the improvability of private schools, who propose the means by which their improvement may most effectually be accelerated. Schools on the trading principle will not be improved unless the parents insist on their improvement, nor even then if, all other schools that are accessible being equally bad, the dissatisfaction can have no practical effect. To make those parents dissatisfied who care but little for good schooling, or are bad judges, and at the same time to make it a necessity for schoolmasters to pay regard to their dissatisfaction, there is but one way; and this is, to give to those who cannot judge of the thing itself, an external criterion to judge by; such as would be afforded by the existence of a certain number of places of education with the *prestige* of public sanction, giving, on a large and comprehensive scale, the best teaching which it is found possible to provide.

But it is objected—and this is almost the staple of Mr. Lowe's vigorous pamphlet[*]—that injustice is done to private schools, and their improvement impeded, by subsidising their competitors—bribing parents by the pecuniary advantages of endowments, and enabling the endowed schools to undersell the unendowed. There would be a great deal in this if the endowed schools were sufficiently multiplied to supply the whole demand for schooling. But a political economist need scarcely be reminded that the price of a commodity is determined by that portion of the quantity required which is produced and brought to market under the least favourable circumstances. So long as private schools are wanted in addition to public ones, there is no more fear of their being undersold by them, than there is lest the owners and occupiers of the most fertile soils should undersell those of the less productive. It may be true that, under the present abuses of endowments, parents are sometimes bribed to accept a bad education gratis; but the reformers of those institutions do not propose that their funds should be employed in giving gratuitous instruction to the children of the well-off classes, or in enabling those who can pay for a good education to obtain it at less than its value. Such, certainly, are not the intentions of the Schools Enquiry Commissioners, who propose a far other application of the

[*Lowe, Robert. *Middle Class Education. Endowment or Free Trade.* London: Bush, 1868]

funds of endowments than that of artificially cheapening education to those who are able, and whose duty it is, to pay its full price.

The endowments destined by the founders for purely elementary education were not within the scope of the Commission: and respecting these there is no difficulty, as they evidently ought to be applied in aid of that general plan for making elementary instruction universal, which statesmen and the public almost unanimously agree that it has become a duty to provide. The endowments with which the Commissioners were concerned were those that were intended to give an instruction superior to the elementary. These they propose should be taken, large and small together, to form, not indeed one common fund, but funds common to each of the districts into which the country is divided for registration purposes; each of these funds to be managed as a whole, and made to go as far as it can in establishing good and large schools for that district. This most judicious proposal is in accordance with one of the great educational principles with which Mr. Chadwick has so perseveringly identified himself—that there cannot be good teaching at a moderate expense in small schools. In a small school the same master is obliged to teach too many things, and to teach the same thing simultaneously to scholars differing too much in their degree of advancement; to the detriment necessarily of some, and generally of all. The schools proposed by the Commissioners are of three different grades, adapted not to adventitious differences in the quarter from whence the pupils come, but to the number of years which their parents are able and willing to spare for their instruction before they enter into active life. But the most important of all the Commission's recommendations, showing an appreciation of the duties of society in the matter of education, the most enlightened that ever yet proceeded from any public authority in the United Kingdom, is that of which I have now to speak. The State does not owe gratuitous education to those who can pay for it. The State owes no more than elementary education to the entire body of those who cannot pay for it. But the superior education which it does not owe to the whole of the poorer population, it owes to the *élite* of them—to those who have earned the preference by labour, and have shown by the results that they have capacities worth securing for the higher departments of intellectual work, never supplied in due proportion to the demand. It is therefore proposed by the Commissioners that the principal use made of the endowments should be to pay for the higher education of those who, in the course of their elementary instruction, have proved themselves to be of the sort on whom a higher education is worth bestowing, but whose parents are not in a condition to pay the price. The fruits of such a proposal, under any tolerable arrangements for carrying it into effect, would be almost beyond human power to estimate. The gain to society, by making available for its most difficult work, not those alone who can afford to qualify themselves, but all those who would qualify themselves if they could afford it, would be but a part of the benefit. I believe there is no single thing which would go so far to heal class differences, and diminish the just dissatisfaction which the best of the poorer classes of the nation feel with their position in it. The real hardship of social inequalities to the poor, as the reasonable among them can be brought to see, is not that men *are* unequal, but that they are born so; not that those who are born poor do not obtain the great objects of human desire unearned, but that the circumstances of their birth preclude their earning them; that the higher positions in life, including all which confer power or dignity, can not only be obtained by the rich without taking the trouble to be qualified for them, but that even were this corrected (to which there is an increasing tendency), none, as a rule, except the rich, have it in their power to make themselves qualified. By the proposal of the Commissioners, every child of poor parents (for, of course, girls must sooner or later be included), would have that power opened to him, if he passed with real distinction through the course of instruction provided for all; and the feelings which give rise to Socialism would be in a great measure disarmed, in as much of them as is unreasonable or exaggerated, by this just concession to that in them which is rational and legitimate.

It is not with this express purpose that the Commissioners have made the recommendation; it is because they believe that in itself it would be the greatest improvement in national education to which the endowments provided for the superior departments of instruction could possibly be applied. The work would be further carried on by the endowments of the Universities; which are already partly expended in scholarships, to aid the maintenance of those who have shown themselves worthy, but would not otherwise be able, to pursue the studies of the University. There are other important uses, which need not here be discussed, to which University endowments may be, and to some extent are, very suitably applied: for instance, the maintenance of professors, and in some cases the encouragement of students, in kinds of knowledge never likely to be sought by more than a few, but which it is of importance to mankind that those few should have the means of finding; such as those ancient languages which are chiefly valuable philologically; comparative philology itself, which has of late years yielded such a harvest of interesting and valuable knowledge; historical erudition in many of its departments; and, it may be added, the highest branches of almost all sciences, even physical: for the speculative researches which lead to the grandest results in science are not those by which money can be made in the general market.

One more point is too important to be omitted. Common justice requires, and the Commissioners have urged—though their proposals in this respect are far short of what they themselves would probably desire—that in the employment of the endowments equal provision should be made for the education of both sexes. Many of the original endowments were for girls as well as boys; in the progress of abuse the boys have very often had their rights filched from them, the girls almost always. In one of the great endowed establishments of which the efficiency has been least impaired by neglect or malversation, Christ's Hospital, the foundation was for both sexes: at present those who benefit by it are eighteen girls and 1,192 boys. Considering that, in the eyes of the law and of the State, one girl ought to count for exactly as much as one boy, and that, as members of society, the good education of women is almost more important than even that of men, it is an essential part of a just scheme for the use of the means provided for education that the benefit of them should be given alike to girls and to boys, without preference or partiality.

THORNTON ON LABOUR AND ITS CLAIMS

1869

EDITOR'S NOTE

Part I, *Fortnightly Review*, n.s. V (May, 1869), 505–18; Part II, *ibid.* (June, 1869), 680–700. Signed; republished in *D&D*, IV (1875), 25–85. Original heading, "Thornton on Labour and its Claims," footnoted: *"On Labour, its Wrongful Claims and Rightful Dues, its Actual Present and Possible Future. By William Thomas Thornton*, Author of "A Plea for Peasant Proprietors," &c. London [: Macmillan], 1869. 14s." Identified in JSM's bibliography as "Two articles on Mr. Thornton's book 'On Labour' in the Fortnightly Review of May 1, and June 1, 1869" (MacMinn, 99). No copy in Somerville College.

JSM originally offered, 16 March, 1869, to write on Thornton's book for the *Edinburgh*, but withdrew the offer on 22 March when the editor, Henry Reeve, suggested that he combine his remarks on Thornton with a review of the Report of the Trades Union Commission. Four days before withdrawing, however, JSM wrote to Reeve, in part: "I shall have much pleasure in writing a notice of Mr. Thornton's book for the 'Edinburgh Review', and shall, of course, put what I have to say in a form somewhat different from that in which I should write for another publication. My own point of view does not exactly coincide either with that of Mr. Thornton or with that of the 'Edinburgh' Reviewer to whom he refers; and, of course, I must be free to express my own view, and that only." He then summarizes Thornton's views of the virtues and vices of trades unions, and adds: "In these various opinions I entirely agree, and I should feel bound to express them in anything I write on the subject. It is for you to decide whether they would be unsuitable for publication in the 'E. Review.'" (Copy in the British Library of Political and Economic Science.)

In the Preface to the 7th ed. (1871) of his *Principles*, JSM remarks that since 1865 "there has been some instructive discussion on the theory of Demand and Supply, and on the influence of Strikes and Trades Unions on wages, by which additional light has been thrown on these subjects. . ." (*Collected Works*, II, xciv), and goes on, in a footnote, to refer the reader to this article and to Thornton's reply in the 2nd ed. of his book, for a view "of the present state of the discussion."

In the following text three corrections are made on the basis of the text in *D&D*, IV; the readings in the *Fortnightly*, identified as "69", are given as variants (see 642, 660, 666). Also the change required in dispensing with the two-part division for the *D&D* republication is indicated as a variant (see 646). Two errors introduced into the text of *D&D*, IV, not noted below, occur at 643.16 and 664.34: in the former, "accepted" is substituted for "excepted"; in the latter, "worthless" is substituted for "worth less". The variant at 667 derives from the one known MS fragment of the article, in the Harvard University Library, which was bought by G. H. Palmer with other MSS (mostly fragments) at the sale (21 to 28 May, 1905) of JSM's literary effects by Ramanille, bookseller in Avignon, on Helen Taylor's returning to England. The fragment is given in full (except for cancellations), although some wordings overlap; a hypothetical "will" is added to give syntactical continuity.

Thornton on Labour and Its Claims

PART I

MR. THORNTON long ago gave proof of his competency to the treatment of some of the most important questions of practical political economy, by two works of great merit, "Over Population and its Remedy,"[*] and "A Plea for Peasant Proprietors."[†] Of the latter of these especially it may be said, that nothing but the total absence, at the time of its publication, of any general interest in its subject, can account for its not having achieved a high repute and a wide circulation. The lack of interest in the subject has now ceased; opinion is rapidly advancing in the direction which the author favours; and a new edition, with its facts brought down to the latest date, would be welcomed by advanced politicians, and would materially contribute to the formation of an enlightened judgment on one of the economical questions on which truth is most important, and prejudice still most rife.

The present work, though popular and attractive in style, is strictly scientific in its principles and reasonings; and is therefore, as might be expected, strictly impartial in its judgments. A considerable part of the volume is employed in refuting the principles on which it is usual to rest those claims and aspirations of the labouring classes, which nevertheless the author, on better grounds, supports. No blind partisan on either side of the feud of labour against capital, will relish the book; but few persons of intelligence and impartiality who read it through, will lay it down without having reason to feel that they understand better than before some of the bearings of the questions involved in that conflict.

To this great practical merit are to be added two of a more theoretic kind, to the value of which I am the more called upon to bear testimony, as on the particular points touched upon in this department I shall have to express more difference than agreement. First: it contains a discussion of one of the fundamental questions of abstract political economy (the

[*London: Longman, Brown, Green, and Longmans, 1846.]
[†London: Murray, 1848.]

influence of demand and supply on price), which is a real contribution to science, though, in my estimation, an addition, and not, as the author thinks, a correction, to the received doctrine. Secondly: in the attempt to go to the very bottom of the question, what are the just rights of labour on one side, and capital on the other, it raises the great issues respecting the foundation of right and wrong, of justice and injustice, in a manner highly provocative of thought. To lay down a definite doctrine of social justice, as well as a distinct view of the natural laws of the exchange of commodities, as the basis for the deductions of a work devoted to such a subject as the principles and practice of Trades-Unionism, was inseparable from the thoroughness with which the author has sought to do his work. Every opinion as to the relative rights of labourers and employers, involves expressly or tacitly some theory of justice, and it cannot be indifferent to know what theory. Neither, again, can it be decided in what manner the combined proceedings of labourers or of employers affect the interests of either side, without a clear view of the causes which govern the bargain between them—without a sound theory of the law of wages.

Indeed, a theory of wages obtrusively meets the inquirer, at the threshold of every question respecting the relations between labourers and employers, and is commonly regarded as rendering superfluous any further argument. It is laid down that wages, by an irresistible law, depend on the demand and supply of labour, and can in no circumstances be either more or less than what will distribute the existing wages-fund among the existing number of competitors for employment. Those who are content to set out from generally-received doctrines as from self-evident axioms, are satisfied with this, and inquire no further. But those who use their own understanding, and look closely into what they assent to, are bound to ask themselves whether or in what sense wages do depend on the demand and supply of labour, and what is meant by the wages-fund.

The author of this work has asked himself these questions; and while he is, as his writings give evidence, well versed in political economy, and is able to hold his ground with the best in following out economical laws into their more obscure and intricate workings, he has become convinced that the barrier which seems to close the entrance into one of the most important provinces of economical and social inquiry, is a shadow which will vanish if we go boldly up to it. He is of opinion that economists have mistaken the scientific law not only of the price of labour, but of prices in general. It is an error, he thinks, that price, or value in exchange, depends on supply and demand.

There is one sense, in which this proposition of Mr. Thornton would be assented to by all economists; they none of them consider supply and demand to be the *ultimate* regulators of value.* That character, they hold, belongs to cost of production; always supposing the commodity to be a product of labour, and natural or artificial monopoly to be out of the question. Subject to these conditions, all commodities, in the long run and on the average, tend to exchange for one another (and, though this point is a little more intricate, tend also to exchange for money) in the ratio of what it costs, in labour and abstinence, to produce the articles and to bring them to the place of sale. But though the average price of everything, the price to which the producer looks forward for his remuneration, must approximately conform to the cost of production, it is not so with the price at any given moment. That is always held to depend on the demand and supply at the moment. And the influence even of cost of production depends on supply; for the only thing which compels price, on the average, to conform to cost of production, is that if the price is either above or below that standard, it is brought back to it either by an increase or by a diminution of the supply; though, after this has been effected, the supply adjusts itself to the demand which exists for the commodity at the remunerating price. These are the limits within which political economists consider supply and demand as the arbiters of price. But even within these limits Mr. Thornton denies the doctrine.

Like all fair controversialists, Mr. Thornton directs his attack against the strongest form of the opinion he assails. He does not much concern himself with the infantine form of the theory, in which demand is defined as a desire for the commodity, or as the desire combined with the power of purchase; or in which price is supposed to depend on the *ratio* between demand and supply. It is to be hoped that few are now dwelling in this *limbus infantum*. Demand, to be capable of comparison with supply, must be taken to mean, not a wish, nor a power, but a quantity. Neither is it at any time a fixed quantity, but varies with the price. Nor does the price

*"It is, therefore, strictly correct to say, that the value of things which can be increased in quantity at pleasure, does not depend (except accidentally, and during the time necessary for production to adjust itself) upon demand and supply; on the contrary, demand and supply depend upon it. . . . . . Demand and supply govern the value of all things which cannot be indefinitely increased; except that, even for them, when produced by industry, there is a minimum value determined by the cost of production. But in all things which admit of indefinite multiplication, demand and supply only determine the perturbations of value, during a period which cannot exceed the length of time necessary for altering the supply. While thus ruling the oscillations of value, they themselves obey a superior force, which makes value gravitate towards cost of production, and which would settle it and keep it there, if fresh disturbing influences were not continually arising to make it again deviate."—J. S. Mill, Princ. of Pol. Econ., book iii. ch. iii. §2. [in *Collected Works*, III, 475–6.]

depend on any ratio. The demand and supply theory, when rightly under-stood—indeed when capable of being understood at all—signifies, that the ratio which exists between demand and supply, when the price has adjusted itself, is always one of equality. If at the market price the demand exceeds the supply, the competition of buyers will drive up the price to the point at which there will only be purchasers for as much as is offered for sale. If, on the contrary, the supply, being in excess of the demand, cannot be all disposed of at the existing price, either a part will be withdrawn to wait for a better market, or a sale will be forced by offering it at such a reduction of price as will bring forward new buyers, or tempt the old ones to increase their purchases. The law, therefore, of values, as affected by demand and supply, is that they adjust themselves so as always to bring about an *equation* between demand and supply, by the increase of the one or the diminution of the other; the movement of price being only arrested when the quantity asked for at the current price, and the quantity offered at the current price, are equal. This point of exact equilibrium may be as momen-tary, but is nevertheless as real, as the level of the sea.

It is this doctrine which Mr. Thornton contests: and his mode of com-bating it is by adducing case after case in which he thinks he can show that the proposition is false; most of the cases being, on the face of them, altogether exceptional; but among them they cover, in his opinion, nearly the whole field of possible cases.

The first case, which is presented as the type of a class, rather than for its intrinsic importance, is that of what is called a Dutch auction.

When a herring or mackerel boat has discharged on the beach, at Hastings or Dover, last night's take of fish, the boatmen, in order to dispose of their cargo, commonly resort to a process called Dutch auction. The fish are divided into lots, each of which is set up at a higher price than the salesman expects to get for it, and he then gradually lowers his terms, until he comes to a price which some bystander is willing to pay rather than not have the lot, and to which he accordingly agrees. Suppose on one occasion the lot to have been a hundred-weight, and the price agreed to twenty shillings. If, on the same occasion, instead of the Dutch form of auction, the ordinary English mode had been adopted, the result might have been different. The operation would then have commenced by some bystander making a bid, which others might have successively exceeded, until a price was arrived at beyond which no one but the actual bidder could afford or was disposed to go. That sum would not necessarily be twenty shillings; very possibly it might be only eighteen shillings. The person who was prepared to pay the former price might very possibly be the only person present prepared to pay even so much as the latter price; and if so, he might get by English auction for eighteen shillings the fish for which at Dutch auction he would have paid twenty shillings. In the same market, with the same quantity of fish for sale, and with customers in number and every other respect the same, the same lot of fish might fetch two very different prices. (Thornton, pp. 47–8.)

This instance, though seemingly a trivial, is really a representative one and a hundred cases could not show, better than this does, what Mr. Thornton has and what he has not made out. He has proved that the law of the equalisation of supply and demand is not the whole theory of the particular case. He has not proved that the law is not strictly conformed to in that case. In order to show that the equilisation of supply and demand is not the law of price, what he has really shown is that the law is, in this particular case, consistent with two different prices, and is equally and completely fulfilled by either of them. The demand and supply are equal at twenty shillings, and equal also at eighteen shillings. The conclusion ought to be, not that the law is false, for Mr. Thornton does not deny that in the case in question it is fulfilled; but only, that it is not the entire law of the phenomenon. The phenomenon cannot help obeying it, but there is some amount of indeterminateness in its operation—a certain limited extent of variation is possible within the bounds of the law; and as there must be a sufficient reason for every variation in an effect, there must be a supplementary law, which determines the effect, between the limits within which the principal law leaves it free. Whoever can teach us this supplementary law, makes a valuable *addition* to the scientific theory of the subject; and we shall see presently that in substance, if not strictly in form, Mr. Thornton does teach it. Even if he did not, he would have shown the received theory to be incomplete; but he would not have, nor has he now, shown it to be in the smallest degree incorrect.

What is more; when we look into the conditions required to make the common theory inadequate, we find that, in the case at least which we have now examined, the incompleteness it stands convicted of amounts to an exceedingly small matter. To establish it, Mr. Thornton had to assume that the customer who was prepared to pay twenty shillings for a hundredweight of fish, was the only person present who was willing to pay even so much as eighteen shillings. In other words, he supposed the case to be an exception to the rule, that demand increases with cheapness: and since this rule, though general, is not absolutely universal, he is scientifically right. If there is a part of the scale through which the price may vary without increasing or diminishing the demand, the whole of that portion of the scale may fulfil the condition of equality between supply and demand. But how many such cases really exist? Among a few chafferers on the beach of a small fishing port, such a case, though even there improbable, is not totally out of the question. But where buyers are counted by thousands, or hundreds, or even scores; in any considerable market—and, far more, in the general market of the world—it is the next thing to impossible that more of the commodity should not be asked for at every reduction of price. The case of price, therefore, which the law of the equalisation does not reach, is one which may be conceived, but which, in practice, is hardly ever realised.

The next example which Mr. Thornton produces of the failure of supply and demand as the law of price, is the following:—

Suppose two persons at different times, or in different places, to have each a horse to sell, valued by the owner at £50; and that in the one case there are two, and in the other three persons, of whom every one is ready to pay £50 for the horse, though no one of them can afford to pay more. In both cases supply is the same, viz., one horse at £50; but demand is different, being in one case two, and in the other three, horses at £50. Yet the price at which the horses will be sold will be the same in both cases, viz., £50. (P. 49.)

The law does fail in this case, as it failed in the former, but for a different reason; not, as in the former case, because several prices fulfil the condition equally well, but because no price fulfils it. At £50 there is a demand for twice or three times the supply; at £50. 0s. 0¼d. there is no demand at all. When the scale of the demand for a commodity is broken by so extraordinary a jump, the law fails of its application; not, I venture to say, from any fault in the law, but because the conditions on which its applicability depends do not exist. If the peculiarities of the case do not permit the demand to be equal to the supply, leaving it only the alternative of being greater or less, greater or less it will be; and all that can be affirmed is, that it will keep as near to the point of equality as it can. Instead of conflicting with the law, this is the extreme case which proves the law. The law is, that the price will be that which equalises the demand with the supply; and the example proves that this only fails to be the case when there is no price that would fulfil the condition, and that even then, the same causes, still operating, keep the price at the point which will most nearly fulfil it. Is it possible to have any more complete confirmation of the law, than that in order to find a case in which the price does not conform to the law, it is necessary to find one in which there is no price that can conform to it?

Again:—

When a tradesman has placed upon his goods the highest price which any one will pay for them, the price cannot, of course, rise higher, yet the supply may be below the demand. A glover in a country town, on the eve of an assize ball, having only a dozen pairs of white gloves in store, might possibly be able to get ten shillings a pair for them. He would be able to get this if twelve persons were willing to pay that price rather than not go to the ball, or than go ungloved. But he could not get more than this, even though, while he was still higgling with his first batch of customers, a second batch, equally numerous and neither more nor less eager, should enter his shop, and offer to pay the same but not a higher price. The demand for gloves, which at first had been just equal to the supply, would now be exactly doubled, yet the price would not rise above ten shillings a pair. Such abundance of proof is surely decisive against the supposition that price must rise when demand exceeds supply. (Pp. 51–2.)

Here, again, the author is obliged to suppose that the whole body of customers (twenty-four in number) place the extreme limit of what they are willing to pay rather than go without the article, exactly at the same point—an exact repetition of the hypothesis about the horse who is estimated at £50, and not a farthing more, by every one who is willing to buy him. The case is just possible in a very small market—practically impossible in the great market of the community. But, were it ever so frequent, it would not impugn the truth of the law, but only its all-comprehensiveness. It would show that the law is only fulfilled when its fulfilment is, in the nature of things, possible, and that there are cases in which it is impossible; but that even there the law takes effect, up to the limit of possibility.

Mr. Thornton's next position is, that if the equalisation theory were literally true, it would be a truth of small significance, because—

Even if it were true that the price ultimately resulting from competition is always one at which supply and demand are equalised, still only a small proportion of the goods offered for sale would actually be sold at any such price, since a dealer will dispose of as much of his stock as he can at a higher price, before he will lower the price in order to get rid of the remainder. (P. 53.)

This is only saying that the law in question resembles other economical laws in producing its effects not suddenly, but gradually. Though a dealer may keep up his price until buyers actually fall off, or until he is met by the competition of rival dealers, still if there is a larger supply in the market than can be sold on these terms, his price will go down until it reaches the point which will call forth buyers for his entire stock; and when that point is reached it will not descend further. A law which determines that the price of the commodity shall fall, and fixes the exact point which the fall will reach, is not justly described as "a truth of small significance" merely because the dealers, not being dead matter, but voluntary agents, may resist for a time the force to which they at last succumb. Limitations such as these affect all economical laws, but are never considered to destroy their value. As well might it be called an insignificant truth that there is a market price of a commodity, because a customer who is ignorant, or in a hurry, may pay twice as much for the thing as he could get it for at another shop a few doors farther off.

The last objection of Mr. Thornton to the received theory, and the one that he lays most stress upon, is, that it assumes "that goods are offered for sale unreservedly, and that dealers are always content to let them go for what they will fetch." This, however, he observes,—

Is scarcely ever—nay, might almost be said to be absolutely never—the fact. With one notable exception, that of labour, commodities are almost never offered unreservedly for sale; scarcely ever does a dealer allow his goods to go for what they will immediately fetch—scarcely ever does he agree to the price which would result from the actual state of supply and demand, or, in other words, to the price at which he could immediately sell the whole of his stock. Imagine the situation of a merchant who could not afford to wait for customers, but was obliged to accept for a cargo of corn, or sugar, or sundries, the best offer he could get from the customers who first presented themselves; or imagine a jeweller, or weaver, or draper, or grocer, obliged to clear out his shop within twenty-four hours. The nearest approach ever made to such a predicament is that of a bankrupt's creditors selling off their debtor's effects at a proverbially 'tremendous sacrifice;' and even they are, comparatively speaking, able to take their time. But the behaviour of a dealer under ordinary pressure is quite different from that of a bankrupt's assignees. He first asks himself what is the best price which is likely to be presently given, not for the whole, but for some considerable portion of his stock, and he then begins selling, either at that price or at such other price as proves upon trial to be the best obtainable at the time. His supply of goods is probably immensely greater than the quantity demanded at that price, but does he therefore lower his terms? Not at all, and he sells as much as he can at that price, and then, having satisfied the existing demand, he waits awhile for further demand to spring up. In this way he eventually disposes of his stock for many times the amount he must have been fain to accept if he had attempted to sell off all at once. A corn dealer who in the course of a season sells thousands of quarters of wheat at fifty shillings per quarter, or thereabouts, would not get twenty shillings a quarter if, as soon as his corn ships arrived, he was obliged to turn the cargoes into money. A glover who, by waiting for customers, will no doubt get three or four shillings a pair for all the gloves in his shop, might not get sixpence a pair if he forced them on his customers. But how is it that he manages to secure the higher price? Simply by not selling unreservedly, simply by declining the price which would have resulted from the relations between actual supply and actual demand, and by setting up his goods at some higher price, below which he refuses to sell. (Pp. 55–6.)

I confess I cannot perceive that these considerations are subversive of the law of demand and supply, nor that there is any ground for supposing political economists to be unaware that when supply exceeds the demand, the two may be equalised by subtracting from the supply as well as by adding to the demand. Reserving a price is, to all intents and purposes, withdrawing supply. When no more than forty shillings a head can be obtained for sheep, all sheep whose owners are determined not to sell them for less than fifty shillings are out of the market, and form no part at all of the supply which is now determining price. They may have been offered for sale, but they have been withdrawn. They are held back, waiting for some future time, which their owner hopes may be more advantageous to him; and they will be an element in determining the price when that time comes, or when, ceasing to expect it, or obliged by his necessities, he consents to sell his sheep for what he can get. In the meanwhile, the price has been determined without any reference to his withheld stock, and determined in such a manner that the demand at that price shall (if possible) be equal to the supply which the dealers are willing to part with at that price. The economists who say that market price is determined by demand and supply do not mean that it is determined by the whole supply which would be forthcoming at an unattainable price, any more than by the whole demand that would be called forth if the article could be had for an old song. They mean that, whatever the price turns out to be, it will be such that the demand at that price, and the supply at that price, will be equal to one another. To this proposition Mr. Thornton shows an undeniable exception in the case of a dealer who holds out for a price which he can obtain for a part of his supply, but cannot obtain for the whole. In that case, undoubtedly, the price obtained is not that at which the demand is equal to the supply; but the reason is the same as in one of the cases formerly considered; because there is no such price. At the actual price the supply exceeds the demand; at a farthing less the whole supply would be withheld. Such a case might easily happen if the dealer had no competition to fear; not easily if he had: but on no supposition does it contradict the law. It falls within the one case in which Mr. Thornton has shown that the law is not fulfilled—namely, when there is no price that would fulfil it; either the demand or the supply advancing or receding by such violent skips, that there is no halting point at which it just equals the other element.

Do I then mean to say that Mr. Thornton is entirely wrong in his interpretation of the cases which he suggests, and has pointed out no imperfection in the current theory? Even if it were so, it would not follow that he has rendered no service to science. "There is always a benefit done to any department of knowledge by digging about the roots of its truths."[*] Scientific laws always come to be better understood when able thinkers and acute controversialists stir up difficulties respecting them, and confront them with facts which they had not yet been invoked to explain. But Mr. Thornton has done much more than this. The doctrine he controverts, though true, is not the whole truth. It is not the entire law of the phenomenon; for he has shown, and has been the first to show, that there are cases which it does not reach. And he has, if not fully defined, at least indicated, the causes which govern the effect in those exceptional cases. If there is a fault to be found with him, it is one that he has in common with all those improvers of political economy by whom new and just views "have been promulgated as contradictions of the doctrines previously

[*Mill, J. S. "De Quincey's Logic of Political Economy," p. 394 above.]

received as fundamental, instead of being, what they almost always are, developments of them;"[*] the almost invariable error of those political economists, for example, who have set themselves in opposition to Ricardo.

Let us, by Mr. Thornton's aid, endeavour to fix our ideas respecting that portion of the law of price which is not provided for by the common theory. When the equation of demand and supply leaves the price in part indeterminate, because there is more than one price which would fulfil the law; neither sellers nor buyers are under the action of any motives, derived from supply and demand, to give way to one another. Much will, in that case, depend on which side has the initiative of price. This is well exemplified in Mr. Thornton's supposed Dutch auction. The commodity might go no higher than eighteen shillings if the offers came from the buyers' side, but because they come from the seller the price reaches twenty shillings. Now, Mr. Thornton has well pointed out that this case, though exceptional among auctions, is normal as regards the general ᵃcourseᵃ of trade. As a general rule, the initiative of price does rest with the dealers, and the competition which modifies it is the competition of dealers.* When, therefore, several prices are consistent with carrying off the whole supply, the dealers are tolerably certain to hold out for the highest of those prices; for they have no motive to compete with one another in cheapness, there being room for them all at the higher price. On the other hand, the buyers are not compelled by each other's competition to pay that higher price; for (since, by supposition the case is one in which a fall of price does not call forth an additional demand) if the buyers hold out for a lower price and get it, their gain may be permanent. The price, in this case, becomes simply a question whether sellers or buyers hold out longest; and depends on their comparative patience, or on the degree of inconvenience they are respectively put to by delay.

By this time, I think, an acute reader, who sees towards what results a course of inquiry is tending before the conclusion is drawn, will begin to perceive that Mr. Thornton's improvements in the theory of price, minute as they appear when reduced to their real dimensions, and unimportant as they must necessarily be in the common case in which supply and demand are but disturbing causes, and cost of production the real law of

[*"De Quincey's Logic of Political Economy," p. 394 above.]

*"This," says Mr. Thornton," in speaking of tangible commodities, seems to me a more accurate as well as a simpler way of stating the case, than to say that the competition of dealers makes price fall, and that competition of customers makes it rise. What the latter competition seems to me really to do is, to show the dealers that a higher price than they previously supposed is attainable, and to induce them consequently to relax their own competition so as to attain it." (P. 69n.)

ᵃ⁻ᵃ69   cause

the phenomenon, may be of very great practical importance in the case which suggested the whole train of thought, the remuneration of labour. If it should turn out that the price of labour falls within one of the excepted cases—the case which the law of equality between demand and supply does not provide for, because several prices all agree in satisfying that law; we are already able to see that the question between one of those prices and another will be determined by causes which operate strongly against the labourer, and in favour of the employer. For, as the author observes, there is this difference between the labour market and the market for tangible commodities, that in commodities it is the seller, but in labour it is the buyer, who has the initiative in fixing the price. It is the employer, the purchaser of labour, who makes the offer of wages; the dealer, who is in this case the labourer, accepts or refuses. Whatever advantage can be derived from the initiative is, therefore, on the side of the employer. And in that contest of endurance between buyer and seller, by which alone, in the excepted case, the price so fixed can be modified, it is almost needless to say that nothing but a close combination among the employed can give them even a chance of successfully contending against the employers.

It will of course be said, that these speculations are idle, for labour is not in that barely possible excepted case. Supply and demand do entirely govern the price obtained for labour. The demand for labour consists of the whole circulating capital of the country, including what is paid in wages for unproductive labour. The supply is the whole labouring population. If the supply is in excess of what the capital can at present employ, wages must fall. If the labourers are all employed, and there is a surplus of capital still unused, wages will rise. This series of deductions is generally received as incontrovertible. They are found, I presume, in every systematic treatise on political economy, my own certainly included. I must plead guilty to having, along with the world in general, accepted the theory without the qualifications and limitations necessary to make it admissible.[*]

The theory rests on what may be called the doctrine of the wages fund. There is supposed to be, at any given instant, a sum of wealth, which is unconditionally devoted to the payment of wages of labour. This sum is not regarded as unalterable, for it is augmented by saving, and increases with the progress of wealth; but it is reasoned upon as at any given moment a predetermined amount. More than that amount it is assumed that the wages-receiving class cannot possibly divide among them; that amount, and no less, they cannot but obtain. So that, the sum to be divided being fixed, the wages of each depend solely on the divisor, the number of participants. In this doctrine it is by implication affirmed, that the demand for

[*Cf. "Preface" to the 7th ed. of *Principles of Political Economy, Collected Works*, II, p. xciv, quoted in part in headnote, p. 632 above.]

labour not only increases with the cheapness, but increases in exact proportion to it, the same aggregate sum being paid for labour whatever its
price may be.

But is this a true representation of the matter of fact? Does the employer
require more labour, or do fresh employers of labour make their appearance, merely because it can be bought cheaper? Assuredly, no. Consumers
desire more of an article, or fresh consumers are called forth, when the
price has fallen: but the employer does not buy labour for the pleasure of
consuming it; he buys it that he may profit by its productive powers, and
he buys as much labour and no more as suffices to produce the quantity of
his goods which he thinks he can sell to advantage. A fall of wages does not
necessarily make him expect a larger sale for his commodity, nor, therefore,
does it necessarily increase his demand for labour.

To this it may be replied, that though possibly he may employ no more
labour in his own business when wages are lower, yet if he does not, the
same amount of capital will be no longer required to carry on his operations; and as he will not be willing to leave the balance unemployed, he will
invest it in some other manner, perhaps in a joint stock company, or in
public securities, where it will either be itself expended in employing labour,
or will liberate some other person's capital to be so expended, and the
whole of the wages-fund will be paying wages as before.

But is there such a thing as a wages-fund, in the sense here implied?
Exists there any fixed amount which, and neither more nor less than which,
is destined to be expended in wages?

Of course there is an impassable limit to the amount which can be so
expended; it cannot exceed the aggregate means of the employing classes.
It cannot come up to those means; for the employers have also to maintain
themselves and their families. But, short of this limit, it is not, in any
sense of the word, a fixed amount.

In the common theory, the order of ideas is this. The capitalist's
pecuniary means consist of two parts—his capital, and his profits or
income. His capital is what he starts with at the beginning of the year,
or when he commences some round of business operations: his income
he does not receive until the end of the year, or until the round of operations is completed. His capital, except such part as is fixed in buildings
and machinery, or laid out in materials, is what he has got to pay wages
with. He cannot pay them out of his income, for he has not yet received
it. When he does receive it, he may lay by a portion to add to his capital,
and as such it will become part of next year's wages-fund, but has nothing
to do with this year's.

This distinction, however, between the relation of the capitalist to his
capital, and his relation to his income, is wholly imaginary. He starts at

the commencement with the whole of his accumulated means, all of which is potentially capital: and out of this he advances his personal and family expenses, exactly as he advances the wages of his labourers. He of course intends to pay back the advance out of his profits when he receives them; and he does pay it back day by day, as he does all the rest of his advances; for it needs scarcely be observed that his profit is made as his transactions go on, and not at Christmas or Midsummer, when he balances his books. His own income, then, so far as it is used and expended, is advanced from his capital and replaced from the returns, *pari passu* with the wages he pays. If we choose to call the whole of what he possesses applicable to the payment of wages, the wages-fund, that fund is co-extensive with the whole proceeds of his business, after keeping up his machinery, buildings and materials, and feeding his family; and it is expended jointly upon himself and his labourers. The less he expends on the one, the more may be expended on the other, and *vice versâ*. The price of labour, instead of being determined by the division of the proceeds between the employer and the labourers, determines it. If he gets his labour cheaper, he can afford to spend more upon himself. If he has to pay more for labour, the additional payment comes out of his own income; perhaps from the part which he would have saved and added to capital, thus anticipating his voluntary economy by a compulsory one; perhaps from what he would have expended on his private wants or pleasures. There is no law of nature making it inherently impossible for wages to rise to the point of absorbing not only the funds which he had intended to devote to carrying on his business, but the whole of what he allows for his private expenses, beyond the necessaries of life. The real limit to the rise is the practical consideration, how much would ruin him, or drive him to abandon the business: not the inexorable limits of the wages-fund.

In short, there is abstractedly available for the payment of wages, before an absolute limit is reached, not only the employer's capital, but the whole of what can possibly be retrenched from his personal expenditure; and the law of wages, on the side of demand, amounts only to the obvious proposition, that the employers cannot pay away in wages what they have not got. On the side of supply, the law as laid down by economists remains intact. The more numerous the competitors for employment, the lower, *cæteris paribus*, will wages be. It would be a complete misunderstanding of Mr. Thornton to suppose that he raises any question about this, or that he has receded from the opinions enforced in his former writings respecting the inseparable connection of the remuneration of labour with the proportion between population and the means of subsistence.

But though the population principle and its consequences are in no way touched by anything that Mr. Thornton has advanced, in another of its bearings the labour question, considered as one of mere economics, assumes a materially changed aspect. The doctrine hitherto taught by all or most economists (including myself), which denied it to be possible that trade combinations can raise wages, or which limited their operation in that respect to the somewhat earlier attainment of a rise which the competition of the market would have produced without them,—this doctrine is deprived of its scientific foundation, and must be thrown aside. The right and wrong of the proceedings of Trades' Unions becomes a common question of prudence and social duty, not one which is peremptorily decided by unbending necessities of political economy.

I have stated this argument in my own way, which is not exactly Mr. Thornton's; but the reasoning is essentially his, though, in a part of it, I have only been anticipated by him. I have already shown in what I consider his exposition of the abstract question to be faulty. I think that the improvement he has made in the theory of price is a case of growth, not of revolution. But in its application to labour, it does not merely add to our speculative knowledge; it destroys a prevailing and somewhat mischievous error. It has made it necessary for us to contemplate, not as an impossibility but as a possibility, that employers, by taking advantage of the inability of labourers to hold out, may keep wages lower than there is any natural necessity for; and *è converso*, that if work-people can by combination be enabled to hold out so long as to cause an inconvenience to the employers greater than that of a rise of wages, a rise may be obtained which, but for the combination, not only would not have happened so soon, but possibly might not have happened at all. The power of Trades' Unions may therefore be so exercised as to obtain for the labouring classes collectively, both a larger share and a larger positive amount of the produce of labour; increasing, therefore, one of the two factors on which the remuneration of the individual labourer depends. The other and still more important factor, the number of sharers, remains unaffected by any of the considerations now adduced.

The most serious obstacle to a right judgment concerning the efficacy and tendencies of Trades' Unions, and the prospects of labour as affected by them, having thus been removed, the author has a free field for the untrammelled discussion of those topics. *b*But the due consideration of them as presented in his work, requires an article to itself.

PART II

In a former article it has been*b* seen how Mr. Thornton, in the first chapter of his First Book, disproved, on grounds of pure political economy, the

*b-b*75   We have

supposed natural law by which, in the opinion of many, the price of labour is as strictly determined as the motion of the earth, and determined in a manner unalterable by the will or effort of either party to the transaction. But whatever in the affairs of mankind is not peremptorily decided for them by natural laws, falls under the jurisdiction of the moral law. Since there is a certain range, wider than has been generally believed, within which the price of labour is decided by a conflict of wills between employers and labourers, it is necessary, as in every other case of human voluntary action, to ascertain the moral principles by which this conflict ought to be regulated. The terms of the bargain not being a matter of necessity, but, within certain limits, of choice, it has to be considered how far either side can rightfully press its claims, and take advantage of its opportunities. Or, to express the same ideas in other phraseology, it has to be decided whether there are any *rights*, of labour on the one hand, or of capital on the other, which would be violated if the opposite party pushed its pretensions to the extreme limits of economic possibility.

To this Mr. Thornton answers,—None. As a matter of mere right, both the employer and the labourer, while they abstain from force or fraud, are entitled to all that they can get, and to nothing more than what they can get. The terms of their contract, provided it is voluntary on both sides, are the sole rule of justice between them. No one being under any obligation of justice to employ labour at all, still less is any one bound in justice to pay for it any given price.

Except under the terms of some mutual agreement, the employer is not bound to give anything. Before joining in the agreement he was under no obligation to furnish the labourer with occupation. Either he might not have required his or any one else's services, or he might have preferred to employ some one else. But if he was not bound to furnish employment at all, *à fortiori* he was not bound to furnish it on any particular terms. If, therefore, he did consent to furnish it, he had a right to dictate his own terms; and whatever else those terms might be, however harsh, illiberal, exorbitant, or what you will, they could not, at any rate or by any possibility, be unjust. For they could only be unjust in so far as they deviated from some particular terms which justice might have exacted. But, as we have seen, there were no such terms, and it is manifestly absurd to condemn a thing merely because its limits do not coincide with those of an abstraction incapable of being realised or defined, incapable, that is to say, of having any limits at all. (Thornton, p. 111.)

The counter-theory, on which the labourer's side of the question is usually argued, "that every man who has not by crime forfeited the right, and who has no other means of living, has a right to live by labour," [p. 88] Mr. Thornton entirely rejects.

Although [he says] these pages have little other object than that of determining how the labouring classes may most easily and effectually obtain fully as much as they ever dreamt of asking, the writer is constrained, even in the interest of those classes, to protest against the theory set up in their behalf. No cause can be permanently maintained that is suffered to rest on fallacies; and one pervading fallacy, beginning at the very first link, runs through the whole chain of reasoning of which the theory consists.

The right of the poor to live by labour, affirmed as unhesitatingly as if it were a self-evident proposition beyond the possibility of dispute, is explained to mean not merely the right so to live if they can themselves find the means, but to have the means supplied by others if they cannot themselves obtain them, and to have them supplied, nominally by society at large, but really by the richer portion of it, the rich alone being in a position to furnish what is required. But right on the one side necessarily implies corresponding obligation on the other; and how can society, or how can the rich, have incurred the obligation of maintaining in the world those whom they were in no degree instrumental in bringing into it? Only, if at all, in one or other of two ways. Either mankind were placed in possession of the earth which they inhabit on condition, expressed or implied, that the wants of all the earth's human inhabitants should be provided for from its produce; or part of those inhabitants have, by some communal act or institution of the whole body, been dispossessed of the means of providing for themselves. But in the first of these hypotheses, in order that the supposed condition should be equitable, it would be necessary that the earth should be capable of producing enough for the wants of whatever number of inhabitants might obtain footing upon it; whereas it is demonstrable that population would infallibly everywhere speedily outrun subsistence, if the earth's produce were freely accessible to all who had need. Of the other supposition, it is to be remarked that the only institution that has ever been accused of producing the alleged effect is the institution of property; and very slight advocacy will suffice to absolve an institution from the charge of depriving people of that which, but for itself, could not have existed. Let it be admitted that the earth was bestowed by the Creator, not on any privileged class or classes, but on all mankind, and on all successive generations of men, so that no one generation can have more than a life interest in the soil, or be entitled to alienate the birthright of succeeding generations. Let this be admitted, and the admission is surely large enough to satisfy the most uncompromising champion of the natural rights of man. Still it is certain that those rights, if fully exercised, must inevitably have proved themselves to be so far worse than worthless, as to have prevented any but a very minute fraction of the existing number of claimants from being born to claim them. The earth, if unappropriated, must also have remained untilled, and consequently comparatively unproductive. Anything like the world's actual population could not possibly have been in existence, nor, if it had been, would a whole year's growth of the earth's natural produce have sufficed for the subsistence of the earth's inhabitants during a single day. The utmost of which the poor have been dispossessed by the institution of property is their fair proportion of what the earth could have produced if it had remained unappropriated. Compensation for this is the utmost which is due to them from society, and the debt is obviously so infinitesimally small, that the crumbs which habitually fall from the tables of the rich are amply sufficient to pay it.

If these things be so, a strict debtor and creditor account between rich and poor would show no balance against the former. Society cannot properly be said to owe anything to the poor beyond what it is constantly and regularly paying. It is not bound in equity, whatever it may be in charity, to find food for the hungry because they are in need, nor to find occupation for the unemployed because they are out of work. By withholding aid, it is not guilty of the smallest injustice. For injustice implies violation of a right; and not only can there be no breach of right without disregard of a corresponding obligation, but that only can be a right the breach or denial of which constitutes a wrong. But wrong is committed only when some good which is due is withheld, or when some evil which is not due is inflicted. Applying this test, we shall find that the poor, as such, have no unliquidated claim against the rich. The latter are doing them no wrong, are guilty of no injustice towards them in merely abstaining from paying a debt which, whether due to the poor or not, is, at any rate, not due to them from the rich. It was not the rich who placed the poor on the earth, and it is not the rich who owe them the means of living here. How far the poor may be forgiven for complaining, as of a grievance, of having been placed here without adequate means of living, may possibly be a question for the theologian. But the political economist may fairly content himself with showing that the grievance is, at any rate, not one with which they can reproach any of their fellow-creatures, except their own parents. No other portion of society was a party to the transaction, and no other portion can justly be responsible for its consequences.* (Pp. 91–94.)

It is unnecessary to quote the application of these principles to the particular case of contracts for labour.

*That those who have not yet read Mr. Thornton's book may not be even temporarily liable to the misunderstanding of his meaning, and of the whole spirit of his writings, which might be the effect of reading only the passage cited in the text, I will at once bring forward the other side of his opinion. Nothing, he says, can be further from his purpose "than to exculpate the existing social system, or to suggest an excuse for continued acquiescence in its enormities. . . . . . To affirm that those evils of the existing social polity which constitute the peculiar grievance of the poor are not the result of human injustice, is perfectly consistent with the most vehement denunciation both of the evils themselves and of the heartless indifference that would perpetuate them. It is perfectly consistent, even with the admission that the rich are bound to do what they can to alleviate those evils—with this proviso, however, that they are so bound, not by their duty to others, but by their duty to themselves. The obligation is imposed upon them not by injunctions of justice, but by the force of sympathy and the exhortations of humanity and charity. The sacrifices which it may thus become incumbent on the rich to make, the poor are not in consequence entitled to demand. If the sacrifices are withheld, the rich stand convicted indeed of brute selfishness, but they do not thereby lay themselves open to the additional charge of injustice. This distinction is not drawn for the sake of pedantic precision; it is one of immense practical importance. To all right reasoning, it is essential that things should be called by their right names; and that nothing, however bad, should receive a worse name than it deserves. The more glaring a sin, the less reason is there for exaggerating it; and, in the case before us, the use of an erroneous epithet has been a fruitful source of further error. Unless the present constitution of society had been arbitrarily assumed to be unjust, it would never have been proposed to correct its injustice by resorting to means which would

Here, then, are two theories of justice arrayed against each other in order of battle: theories differing in their first principles, markedly opposed in their conclusions, and both of them doctrines *à priori*, claiming to command assent by their own light—to be evident by simple intuition: a pretension which, as the two are perfectly inconsistent, must, in the case of one or other of them, be unfounded, and may be so in the case of both. Such conflicts in the domain of ethics are highly instructive, but their value is chiefly negative; the principal use of each of the contrary theories is to destroy the other. Those who cherish any one of the numerous *à priori* systems of moral duty, may learn from such controversies how plausible a case may be made for other *à priori* systems repugnant to their own; and the adepts of each may discover, that while the maxims or axioms from which they severally set out are all of them good, each in its proper place, yet what that proper place is, can only be decided, not by mental intuition, but by the thoroughly practical consideration of consequences; in other words, by the general interest of society and mankind, mental and bodily, intellectual, emotional, and physical, taken together. Mr. Thornton seems to admit the general happiness as the criterion of social virtue, but not of positive duty—not of justice and injustice in the strict sense: and he imagines that it is in making a distinction between these two ideas that his doctrine differs from that of utilitarian moralists. But this is not the case. Utilitarian morality fully recognises the distinction between the province of positive duty and that of virtue, but maintains that the standard and rule of both is the general interest. From the utilitarian point of view, the distinction between them is the following:—There are many acts, and a still greater number of

---

otherwise have been at once perceived to be themselves utterly unjustifiable. On no other account could it ever have been supposed that liberty demanded for its own vindication the violation of liberty, and that the freedom of competition ought to be fettered or abolished. For freedom of competition means no more than that every one should be at liberty to do his best for himself, leaving all others equally at liberty to do their best for themselves. Of all the natural rights of man, there is not one more incontestable than this, nor with which interference would be more manifestly unrighteous. Yet this it is proposed to set aside as incompatible with the rights of labour, as if those could possibly be rights which cannot be maintained except by unrighteous means. (Pp. 94–5.)

The heartiness of Mr. Thornton's devotion to the interest of the labouring classes (or, it should rather be said, to the interest of human nature as embodied in them), is manifested throughout the work; but nowhere so vividly as in the noble Introductory Chapter, where he depicts a state of things in which all the grosser and more palpable evils of their poverty might be extinct, and shows that with this they ought not, and we ought not, to be content. It is not enough that they should no longer be objects of pity. The conditions of a positively happy and dignified existence are what he demands for them, as well as for every other portion of the human race.

forbearances, the perpetual practice of which by all is so necessary to the general well-being, that people must be held to it compulsorily, either by law, or by social pressure. These acts and forbearances constitute duty. Outside these bounds there is the innumerable variety of modes in which the acts of human beings are either a cause, or a hindrance, of good to their fellow-creatures, but in regard to which it is, on the whole, for the general interest that they should be left free; being merely encouraged, by praise and honour, to the performance of such beneficial actions as are not sufficiently stimulated by benefits flowing from them to the agent himself. This larger sphere is that of Merit or Virtue.

The anxiety of moralists for some more definite standard of judgment than the happiness of mankind appears to them to be, or for some first principle which shall have a greater hold on the feeling of obligation than education has yet given to the idea of the good of our fellow-creatures, makes them eager to erect into an axiom of morals any one of the familiar corollaries from the principle of general utility, which, from the impressiveness of the cases to which it is applicable, has taken a deep root in the popular mind, and gathered round itself a considerable amount of human feeling. When they have made choice of any such maxim, they follow it out as if there were no others of equal authority by which its application ought to be limited; or with only as much regard to those limitations, as the amount of common sense possessed by the particular thinker peremptorily enforces upon him as a practical being. The two opposite theories of social justice set forth by Mr. Thornton—the Rousseau or Proudhon theory, and his own—are cases of this description. The former of these, according to which all private appropriation of any of the instruments of production was a wrong from the beginning, and an injury to the rest of mankind, there is neither room, nor is it necessary, here to discuss. But I venture to think that, on intuitional grounds, there is quite as much to be said for it as for the rival theory. Mr. Thornton must admit that the Rousseau doctrine, in its most absolute form, has charmed great numbers of human beings, including not merely those to whose apparent interests it was favourable, but many of those to whom it was hostile; that it has satisfied their highest conceptions of justice and moral right, and has the "note" of intuitive truth as completely as the principles from which his own system is a deduction. Still more may this be said of the more moderate forms of the same theory. "Justice is supposed"—erroneously in the author's opinion—"to require that a labourer's remuneration should correspond with his wants and his merits" (p. 111). If justice is an affair of intuition—if we are guided to it by the immediate and spontaneous perceptions of the moral sense—what doctrines of justice are there, on which the human race would more instantaneously and with one accord put the stamp of its recognition, than these—that it is just that each should have what he deserves, and that, in the dispensation of good things, those whose wants are most urgent should have the preference? In conscience, can it be expected that any one, who has grounded his social theories on these maxims, should discard them in favour of what Mr. Thornton tenders instead—viz., that no one is accountable for any evil which he has not produced by some violence, fraud, or breach of engagement of his own; and that, these things apart, no one has any ground of complaint for his lot on earth, against those who had no hand in placing him here? Mr. Thornton himself concedes so much, as not positively to deny the justice of the maxims which he practically repudiates; but regards their violation as a grievance (if grievance at all) against the general order of the universe, and not against society, or the employers of labour. But if there be in the natural constitution of things something patently unjust—something contrary to sentiments of justice, which sentiments, being intuitive, are supposed to have been implanted in us by the same Creator who made the order of things that they protest against—do not these sentiments impose on us the duty of striving, by all human means, to correct the injustice? And if, on the contrary, we avail ourselves of it for our own personal advantage, do we not make ourselves participators in injustice—allies and auxiliaries of the Evil Principle?

While the author's intuitive theory of right and wrong has thus no advantage in point of intuitive evidence over the doctrine which it is brought to contradict, it illustrates an incurable defect of all these *à priori* theories— that their most important applications may be rebutted without denying their premises. To point out in what manner this consequence arises out of the inherent nature of such theories, would detain us too long; but the examples afforded of it by the author's theory are numerous and remarkable.

Take, for instance, what seems the strongest point in his principal argument—viz., that the institution of property in land does not deprive the poor of anything except "their fair proportion of what the earth could have produced if it had remained unappropriated;" that is, little or nothing— since, if unappropriated, it would have been untilled, and its spontaneous produce would have yielded sustenance to only a very small number of human beings. This may be an answer to Rousseau, though even to him not a complete one;* but it is no answer to the Socialists of the present day. These are, in general, willing enough to admit that property in land was a

---

*By no means a complete answer; for there is a medium between private appropriation of land and denial of protection to its fruits. Is there not such a thing as temporary appropriation? As a matter of fact, even in countries of the most improved agriculture, the tillage is usually performed by persons who have no property in the soil—often by mere tenants at will.

necessary institution in early ages, and until mankind were sufficiently civilised to be capable of managing their affairs in common for the general benefit. But when this time has arrived—and according to them it has arrived—the legitimacy of private landed property, they contend, has ceased, and mankind at large ought now to re-enter on their inheritance. They deny the claim of the first possessors to impose fetters on all generations, and to prevent the species at large from resuming rights of which, for good but temporary reasons, it had suspended the exercise. Society made the concession, and society can at any moment take it back.

Again, the author, in his chapter on the Rights of Capital [pp. 124ff.], very truly and forcibly argues, that these are a portion of the rights of labour. They are the rights of past labour, since labour is the source of all capital; and are sacred, in the same sense, and in an equal degree, with those of present labour. From this he deduces the equal legitimacy of any contract for employment, which past labour may impose on the necessities of present labour, provided there is no taint of force or fraud. But is there no taint of force or fraud in the original title of many owners of past labour? The author states the case as if all property, from the beginning of time, had been honestly come by; either produced by the labour of the owner himself, or bestowed on him by gift or bequest from those whose labour did produce it. But how stands the fact? Landed property at least, in all the countries of modern Europe, derives its origin from force; the land was taken by military violence from former possessors, by those from whom it has been transmitted to its present owners. True, much of it has changed hands by purchase, and has come into the possession of persons who had earned the purchase-money by their labour; but the sellers could not impart to others a better title than they themselves possessed. Movable property, no doubt, has on the whole a purer origin, its first acquirers having mostly worked for it, at something useful to their fellow-citizens. But, looking at the question merely historically, and confining our attention to the larger masses, the doctrine that the rights of capital are those of past labour is liable even here to great abatements. Putting aside what has been acquired by fraud, or by the many modes of taking advantage of circumstances, which are deemed fair in commerce, though a person of a delicate conscience would scruple to use them in most of the other concerns of life— omitting all these considerations, how many of the great commercial fortunes have been, at least partly, built up by practices which in a better state of society would have been impossible—jobbing contracts, profligate loans, or other abuses of Government expenditure, improper use of public positions, monopolies, and other bad laws, or perhaps only by the manifold advantages which imperfect social institutions gave to those who are already rich, over their poorer fellow-citizens, in the general struggle of life? We may be told that there is such a thing as prescription, and that a bad title may become a good one by lapse of time. It may, and there are excellent reasons of general utility why it should; but there would be some difficulty in establishing this position from any *à priori* principle. It is of great importance to the good order and comfort of the world that an amnesty should be granted to all wrongs of so remote a date that the evidence necessary for the ascertainment of title is no longer accessible, or that the reversal of the wrong would cause greater insecurity and greater social disturbance than its condonation. This is true, but I believe that no person ever succeeded in reconciling himself to the conviction, without doing considerable violence to what is called the instinctive sentiment of justice. It is not at all conformable to intuitive morality that a wrong should cease to be a wrong because of what is really an aggravation, its durable character; that because crime has been successful for a certain limited period, society for its own convenience should guarantee its success for all time to come. Accordingly, those who construct their systems of society upon the natural rights of man, usually add to the word natural the word imprescriptible, and strenuously maintain that it is impossible to acquire a fee-simple in an injustice.

Yet one more example, to show the ease with which conclusions that seem to follow absolutely from an *à priori* theory of justice can be defeated by other deductions from the same premises. According to the author, however inadequate the remuneration of labour may be, the labourer has no grievance against society, because society is not the cause of the insufficiency, nor did society ever bargain with him, or bind itself to him by any engagement, guaranteeing a particular amount of remuneration. And, this granted, the author assumes (at p. 394 and elsewhere) as a logical consequence, that proprietors must not be interfered with, out of regard to the interests of labour, in the perfectly free use of their property conformably to their own inclination. Now, if this point were being argued as a practical question, on utilitarian grounds, there probably would be little difference between Mr. Thornton's conclusions and my own. I should stand up for the free disposal of property as strongly, and most likely with only the same limitations, as he would. But we are now on *à priori* ground, and while that is the case, I must insist upon having the consequences of principles carried out to the full. What matters it that, according to the author's theory, the employer does no wrong in making the use he does of his capital, if the same theory would justify the employed in compelling him by law to make a different use—if the labourers would in no way infringe the definition of justice by taking the matter into their own hands, and establishing by law any modification of the rights of property which in their opinion would increase the remuneration of their labour? And, on the author's principles, this right cannot be denied them. The existing social arrangements, and law itself, exist in virtue not only of the forbearance, but of the active support of the labouring classes. They could effect the most fundamental changes in the whole order of society by simply withholding their concurrence. Suppose that they, who being the numerical majority cannot be controlled except by their own tacit consent, should come to the conclusion (for example) that it is not essential to the benefits of the institution of property that wealth should be allowed to accumulate in large masses; and should consequently resolve to deny legal protection to all properties exceeding a certain amount. There are the strongest utilitarian reasons against their doing this; but on the author's principles, they have a right to do it. By this mere abstinence from doing what they have never promised nor in any way bound themselves to do, they could extort the consent of the rich to any modification of proprietary rights which they might consider to be for their advantage. They might bind the rich to take the whole burden of taxation upon themselves. They might bind them to give employment, at liberal wages, to a number of labourers in a direct ratio to the amount of their incomes. They might enforce on them a total abolition of inheritance and bequest. All this would be a very wrong use of their power of withholding protection; but only because the conditions imposed would be injurious, instead of beneficial, to the public weal. Nor do I see what arguments, except utilitarian ones, are open to the author for condemning them. Even the manifest obligation of making the changes with the least possible detriment to the interests and feelings of the existing generation of proprietors, it would be extremely difficult to deduce from the author's premises, without calling in other maxims of justice than his theory recognises.

It is almost needless for me to repeat that these things are said, not with a view to draw any practical conclusions respecting the rights of labour, but to show that no practical conclusions of any kind can be drawn from such premises; and because I think, with Mr. Thornton, that when we are attempting to determine a question of social ethics, we should make sure of our ethical foundation. On the questions between employers and labourers, or on any other social questions, we can neither hope to find, nor do we need, any better criterion than the interest, immediate and ultimate, of the human race. But the author's treatment of the subject will have a useful effect if it leads any of those friends of democracy and equality, who disdain the prosaic consideration of consequences, and demand something more high-flown as the ground on which to rest the rights of the human race, to perceive how easy it is to frame a theory of justice that shall positively deny the rights considered by them as so transcendent, and which yet shall make as fair a claim as theirs to an intuitive character, and shall command by its *à priori* evidence the full conviction of as enlightened a thinker, and as warm a supporter of the principal claims of the labouring classes, as the author of the work before us.

The author's polemic against the doctrines commonly preached by the metaphysical theorists of the Cause of Labour, is not without other points of usefulness. Not only are those theorists entirely at sea on the notion of right, when they suppose that labour has, or can have, a right to anything, by any rule but the permanent interest of the human race; but they also have confused and erroneous notions of matters of fact, of which Mr. Thornton points out the fallacy. For example, the working classes, or rather their champions, often look upon the whole wealth of the country as the produce of their labour, and imply, or even assert, that if everybody had his due the whole of it would belong to them. Apart from all question as to right, this doctrine rests on a misconception of fact. The wealth of the country is not wholly the produce of present labour. It is the joint product of present labour and of the labour of former years and generations, the fruits of which, having been preserved by the abstinence of those who had the power of consuming them, are now available for the support or aid of present labour which, but for that abstinence, could not have produced subsistence for a hundredth part the number of the present labourers. No merit is claimed for this abstinence; those to whose persevering frugality the labouring classes owe this enormous benefit, for the most part thought only of benefiting themselves and their descendants. But neither is there any merit in labouring, when a man has no other means of keeping alive. It is not a question of merit, but of the common interest. Capital is as indispensable to labour as labour to capital. It is true the labourers need only capital, not capitalists; it would be better for them if they had capital of their own. But while they have not, it is a great benefit to them that others have. Those who have capital did not take it from them, and do not prevent them from acquiring it. And, however badly off they may be under the conditions which they are able to make with capitalists, they would be still worse off if the earth were freely delivered over to them without capital, and their existing numbers had to be supported upon what they could in this way make it produce.

On the other hand, there is on the opposite side of the question a kind of goody morality, amounting to a cant, against which the author protests, and which it is imperative to clear our minds of. There are people who think it right to be always repeating, that the interest of labourers and employers (and, they add, of landlords and farmers, the upper classes and the lower, governments and subjects, &c.) is one and the same. It is not to be wondered at that this sort of thing should be irritating to those to whom it is intended as a warning. How is it possible that the buyer and the seller of a commodity should have exactly the same interest as to its price? It is the interest of both that there should be commodities to sell; and it is, in a certain general way, the interest both of labourers and employers that business should prosper, and that the returns to labour and capital should be large. But to say that they have the same interest as to the division, is to say that it is the same thing to a person's interest whether a sum of money belongs to him or to somebody else. The employer, we are gravely told, will expend in wages what he saves in wages; he will add it to his capital, which is a fine thing for the labouring classes. Suppose him to do so, what does the labourer gain by the increase of capital, if his wages must be kept from rising to admit of its taking place?

Workmen are solemnly adjured, [says Mr. Thornton (p. 260),] not to try to get their wages raised, because success in the attempt must be followed by a fall of profits which will bring wages down again. They are entreated not to better themselves, because any temporary bettering will be followed by a reaction which will leave them as ill off as before; not to try to raise the price of labour, because to raise the price is to lower the demand, and to lower the demand is to lower the price. As if a great demand for labour were of any other use to the labourer than that of raising the price of labour, or as if an end were to be sacrificed to means whose whole merit consists in their leading to that same end. If all the political economy opposed to trades' unions were like this, trades' unions would be quite right in opposing political economy.

What is true is, that wages might be so high as to leave no profit to the capitalist, or not enough to compensate him for the anxieties and risks of trade; and in that case labourers would be killing the goose to get at the eggs. And, again, wages might be so low as to diminish the numbers or impair the working powers of the labourers, and in that case the capitalist also would generally be a loser. But between this and the doctrine, that the money which would come to the labourer by a rise of wages will be of as much use to him in the capitalist's pocket as in his own, there is a con-siderable difference.

Between the two limits just indicated—the highest wages consistent with keeping up the capital of the country, and increasing it *pari passu* with the increase of people, and the lowest that will enable the labourers to keep up their numbers with an increase sufficient to provide labourers for the increase of employment—there is an intermediate region within which wages will range higher or lower according to what Adam Smith calls "the higgling of the market." In this higgling, the labourer in an isolated condi-tion, unable to hold out even against a single employer, much more against the tacit combination of employers, will, as a rule, find his wages kept down at the lower limit. Labourers sufficiently organised in Unions may, under favourable circumstances, attain to the higher. This, however, supposes an organisation including all classes of labourers, manufacturing and agricultural, unskilled as well as skilled. When the union is only partial, there is often a nearer limit—that which would destroy, or drive elsewhere, the particular branch of industry in which the rise takes place. Such are the limiting conditions of the strife for wages between the labourers and the capitalists. The superior limit is a difficult question of fact, and in its estimation serious errors may be, and have been, committed. But, having regard to the greatly superior numbers of the labouring class, and the inevitable scantiness of the remuneration afforded by even the highest rate of wages which, in the present state of the arts of production, could possibly become general; whoever does not wish that the labourers may prevail, and that the highest limit, whatever it be, may be attained, must have a standard of morals, and a conception of the most desirable state of society, widely different from those of either Mr. Thornton or the present writer.

The remainder of the book is occupied in discussing the means adopted or which might be adopted by the operative classes, for obtaining all such advantages in respect of wages, and the other conditions of labour, as are within the reach of attainment: a subject comprehending all the questions respecting the objects and practices of Trades' Unionism, together with the whole theory and practice of co-operative industry. And here I am nearly at the end of my disagreements with Mr. Thornton. His opinions are in every respect as favourable to the claims of the labouring classes as is consistent with the regard due to the permanent interest of the race. His conclusions leave me little to do but to make a *résumé* of them, though I may still dissent from some of his premises. For example, the same principles which lead him to acquit employers of wrong, however they may avail themselves of their advantage to keep down wages, make him equally exculpate Unionists from a similar charge, even when he deems them to be making a short-sighted and dangerous use of the power which combinations give them. But while I agree with the author that conduct may be "grovelling and sordid" [p. 180] without being morally culpable, I must yet maintain that if there are (as it cannot be doubted that there are) demands which employers might make from labourers, or labourers from employers, the enforcement of which, even by the most innocent means, would be contrary to the interests of civilisation and improvement—to make these demands, and to insist on them as conditions of giving and receiving employment, is morally wrong.

Again, the author most justly stigmatises the English law of conspiracy, that reserved weapon of arbitrary and *ex-post-facto* coercion, by which anything, that a court of law thinks ought not to be done, may be made a criminal offence if done in concert by more than one person—a law of which a most objectionable use has been made against Trades' Unions.

But I cannot go entirely with him when he lays it down as an absolute and self-evident truth, that whatever is lawful when done by one person, ought not to be an offence when done by a combination of several. He forgets that the number of agents may materially alter the essential character of the act. Suppose, merely for the sake of illustration, that the state of opinion was such as to induce legislators to tolerate, within certain limits, the prosecution of quarrels and the redress of injuries by the party's own hands; as is the case practically, though not legally, in all countries where duelling prevails. If, under cover of this license, instead of a combat between one and one, a band of assailants were to set upon a single person, and take his life, or inflict on him bodily harm, would it be allowable to apply to this case the maxim, that what is permitted to one person ought to be permitted to any number? The cases are not parallel; but if there be so much as one case of this character, it is discussable, and requires to be discussed, whether any given case is such a one; and we have a fresh proof how little even the most plausible of these absolute maxims of right and wrong are to be depended on, and how unsafe it is to lose sight, even for a moment, of the paramount principle—the good of the human race. The maxims may, as the rough results of experience, be regarded as *primâ facie* presumptions that what they inculcate will be found conducive to the ultimate end; but not as conclusive on that point without examination, still less as carrying an authority independent of, and superior to, the end.

My difference with Mr. Thornton is in this case only theoretical; for I do not know of anything that ought to be legally interdicted to workmen in combination, except what would be criminal if done by any of them individually, viz., physical violence or molestation, defamation of character, injury to property, or threats of any of these evils. We hear much invective against Trades' Unions on the score of being infringements of the liberty of those working men on whom a kind of social compulsion is exercised to induce them to join a Union, or to take part in a strike. I agree with Mr. Thornton in attaching no importance whatever to this charge. An infringement of people's liberty it undoubtedly is, when they are induced, by dread of other people's reproaches, to do anything which they are not legally bound to do; but I do not suppose it will be maintained that disapprobation never ought to be expressed except of things which are offences by law. As soon as it is acknowledged that there are lawful, and even useful, purposes to be fulfilled by Trades' Unions, it must be admitted that the members of Unions may reasonably feel a genuine moral disapprobation of those who profit by the higher wages or other advantages that the Unions procure for non-Unionists as well as for their own members, but refuse to take their share of the payments, and submit to the restrictions, by which those advantages are obtained. It is vain to say that if a strike is really for the good of the workmen, the whole body will join in it from a mere sense of the common interest. There is always a considerable number who will hope to share the benefit without submitting to the sacrifices; and to say that these are not to have ^{c} brought before them, in an impressive manner, what their fellow-workmen think of their conduct, is equivalent to saying that social pressure ought not to be put upon any one to consider the interests of others as well as his own. All that legislation is concerned with is, that the pressure shall stop at the expression of feeling, and the withholding of such good offices as may properly depend upon feeling, and shall not extend to an infringement, or a threat of infringement, of any of the rights which the law guarantees to all—security of person and property against violation, and of reputation against calumny. There are few cases in which the application of this distinction can give rise to any doubt. What is called picketing is just on the border which separates the two regions; but the sole difficulty in that case is one of fact and evidence—to ascertain whether the language or gestures used implied a threat of any such treatment as, between individual and individual, would be contrary to law. Hooting, and offensive language, are points on which a question may be raised; but these should be dealt with according to the general law of the country. No good reason can be given for subjecting them to special restriction on account of the occasion which gives rise to them, or to any legal restraint at all beyond that which public decency, or the safety of the public peace, may prescribe as a matter of police regulation.

Mr. Thornton enters into a minute examination of the limits to the efficacy of Trades' Unions—the circumstances in which increased wages may be claimed with a prospect of success, and, if successful, of permanence. These discussions I must content myself with recommending to the attention of the reader, who will find in them much matter of great value. In the present article there is only room for the most general considerations, either of political economy or of morals. Under the former aspect, there is a view of the question, not overlooked by the author, but hardly, perhaps, made sufficiently prominent by him. From the necessity of the case, the only fund out of which an increase of wages can possibly be obtained by the labouring classes considered as a whole, is profits. This is contrary to the common opinion, both of the general public and of the workmen themselves, who think that there is a second source from which it is possible for the augmentation to come, namely, prices. The employer, they think, can, if foreign or other competition will let him, indemnify himself for the additional wages demanded of him, by charging an increased price to the consumer. And this may certainly happen in single trades, and even in large branches of trade, under conditions which are carefully investigated

^{c}69 it

by Mr. Thornton. The building trade, in its numerous subdivisions, is one of the most salient instances. But though a rise of wages in a given trade may be compensated to the masters by a rise of the price of their commodity, a rise of general wages cannot be compensated to employers generally by a general rise of prices. This distinction is never understood by those who have not considered the subject, but there are few truths more obvious to all who have. There cannot be a general rise of prices unless there is more money expended. But the rise of wages does not cause more money to be expended. It takes from the incomes of the masters and adds to those of the workmen; the former have less to spend, the latter have more; but the general sum of the money incomes of the community remains what it was, and it is upon that sum that money prices depend. There cannot be more money expended on everything, when there is not more money to be expended altogether. In the second place, even if there did happen a rise of all prices, the only effect would be that money, having become of less value in the particular country, while it remained of its former value everywhere else, would be exported until prices were brought down to nearly or quite their former level. But thirdly: even on the impossible supposition that the rise of prices could be kept up, yet, being general, it would not compensate the employer; for though his money returns would be greater, his outgoings (except the fixed payments to those to whom he is in debt) would be increased in the same proportion. Finally, if when wages rose all prices rose in the same ratio, the labourers would be no better off with high wages than with low; their wages would not command more of any article of consumption; a real rise of wages, therefore, would be an impossibility.

It being obvious, from these accumulated considerations, that a real rise of general wages cannot be thrown on the consumer by a rise of prices; it follows also that a real rise even of partial wages—of wages in one or a few employments—when thrown on the consumer by an increased price of the articles produced, is generally a gain made, wholly or in part, at the expense of the remainder of the labouring classes. For, the aggregate incomes of the purchasing public not being increased, if more is spent on some articles of consumption, less will be spent on others. There are two possible suppositions. The public may either reduce its consumption of the articles which have risen, or it may retrench by preference in other articles. In the former case, if the consumption falls off in full proportion to the rise of price, there is no more money than before expended in the article, and no more, therefore, to be divided between the labourers and their employers; but the labourers may possibly retain their improved wages, at the expense of profits, until the employers, weary of having less profit than other people, withdraw part of their capital. But if the consumption does not fall off, or falls off in a less degree, so that more is really spent on the articles after than before the rise, the prices of some other things will fall from diminished demand; the producers of those other things will have less to divide, and either wages or profits must suffer. It will usually be wages; for as there will not be employment in those departments for so many labourers as before, some labourers will be thrown out of work. As Mr. Thornton remarks, the general increase of the incomes of the community through the progress of wealth may make up to the other branches of the productive classes for what they thus lose, and convert it from an absolute loss, to the loss of a gain—the gain which as a body they would have derived from the general increase of wealth, but of which the whole, or more than the fair share, has been drawn off by a single branch. Still, the rise of wages in any department is necessarily at the expense either of wages in other departments or of profits, and in general both will contribute to it. So long, at least, as there are any classes of labourers who are not unionised, the successes of the Unions will generally be a cause of loss to the labourers in the non-unionist occupations.

From the recognition of this fact arises a serious question of right and wrong, as between Unionists and the remainder of the labouring classes. As between themselves and their employers, they are under no obligations but those of prudence. The employers are quite capable of taking care of themselves. Unionists are under no moral duty to their employers which the conditions they may seek to impose on them can possibly violate. But they owe moral duties to the remainder of the labouring classes, and moral duties to the community at large; and it behooves them to take care that the conditions they make for their own separate interest do not conflict with either of these obligations.

However satisfactorily the question may admit of being answered, it still requires to be asked, whether Unionists are justified in seeking a rise of wages for themselves, which will in all probability produce a fall of wages, or loss of employment, to other labourers, their fellow-countrymen. Still more is this question raised by those restrictive rules, forbidding the employment of non-unionists, limiting the number of apprentices, &c., which many Unions maintain, and which are sometimes indispensable to the complete efficacy of Unionism. For (as Mr. Thornton recognises) there is no keeping up wages without limiting the number of competitors for employment. And all such limitation inflicts distinct evil upon those whom it excludes—upon that great mass of labouring population which is outside the Unions; an evil not trifling, for if the system were rigorously enforced it would prevent unskilled labourers or their children from ever rising to the condition of skilled. In what manner is a system which thus operates, to be reconciled either with the obligations of general morality, or with the special regard professed by labouring men for the interest of the labouring class? To the justification of Unionism it is necessary not only that a mode of reconciliation should exist, but that Unionists should know it and consider it; for if there is ever so good a defence of their conduct, and they do not know or care about it, their case is morally the same as if there were none. Unionists who do not concern themselves with these scruples are, in intention, sacrificing the interests of their fellow-labourers, the majority of the labouring classes, to their own separate advantage; they are making themselves into an oligarchy of manual labourers, indirectly supported by a tax levied on the democracy.

There are, however, two considerations, either of which, in the mind of an upright and public spirited working man, may fairly legitimate his adhesion to Unionism. The first is, by considering the Unions of particular trades as a mere step towards an universal Union, including all labour, and as a means of educating the *élite* of the working classes for such a future. This is well put by Mr. Thornton:—

Though, in the interests of universal labour, the formation of national and cosmopolitan unionism be clearly an end to be aimed at, the best, if not the only means to that end is the previous formation and bringing to maturity of separate trade unions. The thing is scarcely to be done, if done at all, in any other way. National unionism is only to be built up piecemeal. To begin by laying foundations coextensive with the area to be finally covered, would be a sure way of never getting beyond the foundations. The only plan at all feasible, is for separate sections of labourers to organise themselves independently, and for each separate organisation to confine its attention to its own affairs, wherein it would long find abundant occupation without troubling itself about those of its neighbours, until it and they, having grown strong enough to stand alone, should perceive it to be for their mutual advantage to coalesce and stand together. This is the plan which, unconsciously perhaps for the most part, trades' unions are at present following, each in obedience to its own selfish instinct, seeking only to do the best for itself, yet each doing thereby the best for the others also. That this or any other plan will ever really eventuate in the formation of a confederacy embracing the entire working population, may to most people appear an utterly chimerical notion, and no doubt the chances are great against its realisation. But the thing, however improbable, is not more improbable than some of the actual phenomena of unionism would not long since have appeared. Half a century back, while the marvellous organising aptitudes of working men lay dormant and unsuspected, it would have been quite as difficult for any one to look forward to the existing 'amalgamation' of little less than 50,000 engineers or 70,000 miners, as it is now to imagine that in another century or so—no very long period in a nation's life—a combination of these and of other associations may weld together the whole community of British workmen as one brotherhood. At the present rate of progress less than a hundred years would suffice for the operation. (Pp. 289–90.)

This prospect may appear too remote, and even visionary, to be an actuating motive with any considerable number of Unionists; but it is certainly not beyond the aspirations of the intelligent leaders of Unionism, and what is more, some great steps have already been made in the direction of its realisation. A generation ago all Unions were local, and in those days strikes were much more frequent, much oftener unreasonable, and much oftener attended with criminal excesses, than is the case at present. Since then, a number of the most important trades have been formed into Amalgamated Societies extending to the whole country, and a central council decides with a view to the interests of the entire trade, what conditions shall be imposed on employers, and in what cases strikes shall take place. And it is admitted that the rules of these Amalgamated Societies are much less objectionable than those of the local unions previously were, and that the central body prevents many more strikes than it sanctions. The immediate motive to the amalgamations was, of course, the experience that attempts in one town to obtain a rise of wages, only caused the transfer of the business to another. Concert having been at length substituted for competition between different towns, the Unions now aim at effecting the same substitution between different countries: and within the last few years there is a commencement of International Congresses of working people, to prevent the efforts made in one country from being frustrated for want of a common understanding with other countries. And there can be little doubt that these attempts to lay the foundation of an alliance among the artisans of competing countries, have already produced some effect, and will acquire increasing importance.

There is, however, another, and a less elevated, but not fallacious point of view, from which the apparent injustice of Unionism to the non-united classes of labourers may be morally vindicated to the conscience of an intelligent Unionist. This is the Malthusian point of view, so blindly decried as hostile and odious, above all, to the labouring classes. The ignorant and untrained part of the poorer classes (such Unionists may say) will people up to the point which will keep their wages at that miserable rate which the low scale of their ideas and habits makes endurable to them. As long as their minds remain in their present state, our preventing them from competing with us for employment does them no real injury; it only saves ourselves from being brought down to their level. Those whom we exclude are a morally inferior class of labourers to us; their labour is worth less, and their want of prudence and self-restraint makes them much more active in adding to the population. We do them no wrong by intrenching ourselves behind a barrier, to exclude those whose competition would bring down our wages, without more than momentarily raising theirs, but only adding to the total numbers in existence. This is the practical justification, as things now are, of some of the exclusive regulations of Trades' Unions. If the majority of their members look upon this state of things, so far as the excluded labourers are concerned, with indifference, and think it enough for the

Unions to take care of their own members, this is not more culpable in them than is the same indifference in classes far more powerful and more privileged by society. But it is a strong indication of a better spirit among them, that the operatives and artisans throughout the country form the main strength of the demand, rapidly becoming irresistible, for universal and compulsory education. The brutish ignorance of the lowest order of unskilled labourers has no more determined enemies, none more earnest in insisting that it be cured, than the comparatively educated workmen who direct the Unions.

The moral duties which Unionists owe to society at large—to the permanent interest of the nation and of the race—are still less regarded than the duties imposed by good feeling towards their own class. There is as little practical sense of such duties in the minds of workmen as in those of employers—and there can scarcely be less. Yet it is evident (for instance) that it cannot be right that a contest between two portions of society as to the terms on which they will co-operate, should be settled by impairing the efficacy of their joint action. There must be some better mode of sharing the fruits of human productive power than by diminishing their amount. Yet this is not only the effect, but the intention, of many of the conditions imposed by some Unions on workmen and on employers. All restrictions on the employment of machinery, or on arrangements for economising labour, deserve this censure. Some of the Unionist regulations go even further than to prohibit improvements; they are contrived for the express purpose of making work inefficient; they positively prohibit the workman from working hard and well, in order that it may be necessary to employ a greater number. Regulations that no one shall move bricks in a wheelbarrow, but only carry them in a hod, and then no more than eight at a time; that stones shall not be worked at the quarry while they are soft, but must be worked by the masons of the place where they are to be used; that plasterers shall not do the work of plasterers' labourers, nor labourers that of plasterers, but a plasterer and a labourer must both be employed when one would suffice; that bricks made on one side of a particular canal must lie there unused, while fresh bricks are made for work going on upon the other; that men shall not do so good a day's work as to "best their mates;" that they shall not walk at more than a given pace to their work when the walk is counted "in the master's time"—these and scores of similar examples which will be found in Mr. Thornton's book,[*] equally vexatious, and some of them more ridiculous, are all grave violations of the moral rule, that disputes between classes should not be so conducted as to make the world a worse place for both together, and ultimately for the whole of the community. I do not say that there are never

[*See pp. 322 ff.]

cases which justify a resort to measures even thus bad in principle. A portion of society which cannot otherwise obtain just consideration from the rest, may be warranted in doing a mischief to society in order to extort what it considers its dues. But when thus acting, that portion of society is in a state of war with the rest; and such means are never justifiable but as weapons of war, like the devastation of a country and the slaughter of its innocent inhabitants—things abominable in themselves, but which may unhappily be the only means of forcing a powerful adversary to consent to just terms of accommodation. It is palpably for the good of society that its means of production, that the efficacy of its industry, should be as great as possible, and it cannot be necessary to an equitable division of the produce to make that efficacy less. The true morality of the workmen would be to second zealously all means by which labour can be economised or made more efficient, but to demand their share of the benefit. In what shape they shall obtain it, is a matter of negociation between the parties, the difficulties of which may be greatly lightened by an impartial arbitration; and it is in such cases, above all others, that advantage might be expected from the Councils of Conciliation, which Mr. Mundella and Mr. Rupert Kettle have so forcibly advocated, and have carried so successfully into practice in their respective localities. The identification of the interest of the workmen with the efficiency, instead of the inefficiency of the work, is a happy result as yet only attained by co-operative industry in some [d] of its forms. And if it should prove, in the end, not to be attainable otherwise; if the claims of the workmen to share the benefit of whatever was beneficial to the general interest of the business, became an embarrassment to the masters from which no system of arbitration could sufficiently relieve them, and growing inconvenience to them from the opposition of interest between themselves and the workmen should stimulate the conversion of existing businesses into Industrial Partnerships, in which the whole body of workpeople have a direct interest in the profits of the enterprise; such a transformation would be the true euthanasia of Trades' Unionism, while it would train and prepare at least the superior portion of the working classes for a form of co-operation still more equal and complete.

It is to this feature in the futurity of labour that the whole of Mr. Thornton's argument leads up: and to this he looks forward as the true solution of the great economic problem of modern life. Nowhere will be found so compact and comprehensive an account of the various forms of co-operative industry which have been tried in this and other countries with such remarkable success, either by combinations of operatives uniting their small savings, or by capitalist employers admitting their workmen to a participation in profits. I will not weaken these most interesting statements

[d]69 one

by abridgment, nor is it necessary to prolong this article by disserting on a subject which *is every year commanding more of the attention of the best practical minds. The reader may be referred to Mr. Thornton for a conclusive answer to the hesitations concerning the probabilities of success of this great movement, as well as for an inspiring picture of the blessings to human society which may rationally be expected from its progressive realisation.* I will rather turn back to Unionism, and conclude with a passage embodying the author's ultimate moral judgment upon it. (Pp. 333–36.)

Sufficient note has not perhaps been taken of the educational office which unionism is silently and unconsciously performing, and of the softening and composing influence which it is insensibly exercising over its constituents. Mere union, quite irrespectively of any special object, is of itself beneficial discipline. The mere act of association is of itself a wholesome subordination of the individual to the general. Merely to combine for some common object, causes people to take pride and pleasure in that object, whatever it be, and renders them ready to make sacrifices for its furtherance. And if the object be mutual defence and mutual support, then, for the associates to take an interest in it and in each other, is one and the same thing. Among trades' unionists accustomed to look to each other for assistance in sickness, in distress, and in old age, the sense of mutual dependence begets mutual attachment. In their official intercourse they speak of each other as 'brothers;' and the word is not an empty sound, but indicates the sort of relationship which they at least desire should subsist between them, and which, because they do desire it, is sure to grow up. So far their sympathies have already widened, and it is characteristic of all moral expansion never to cease expanding. Those who, from caring for none but themselves, have got so far as to care for their fellow-workmen, will not stop till they have learned to care for all their fellow-men. Love of their class will prove to have been only an intermediate stage between self-love and love of their kind. Nor is it only indirectly that unionism is qualified to contribute towards this moral development. Certain of its arrangements are calculated to lead straight towards the same result. Hitherto, protection against material evil and acquisition of material good have been its chief care, but higher objects are beginning to claim attention, and intellectual and moral improvement are coming in for a share of solicitude. In the lodges of the London bricklayers, drunkenness and swearing are expressly interdicted. Under the auspices of the Amalgamated Carpenters, industrial schools are being established. These are straws on the surface, showing how the current of unionist opinion is flowing. The day may not be very distant when increasing *esprit de corps* will make Amalgamated Engineers and Carpenters as proud individually of their respective societies, as jealous of their honour, and as unwilling to disgrace them, as the officers of the old Bengal Engineers used to

*–*MS [will] deservedly occupy an increasing place in public discussion. I therefore for the present refer the reader to Mr Thornton's paper not only for a most interesting collection of facts respecting the cooperative movement but for a most conclusive answer to all that has been said against the probability of its final success, & for a most inspiring picture of the blessing to human society which may rationally be expected from its progressive realization. [*see headnote, p. 632 above*]

be of their connection with that pre-eminently distinguished corps; and in proportion as those feelings become general among unionists, in the same proportion may unionism be expected to divest itself of its offensive attributes, exchanging eventually past violence and extravagance for as much moderation as its nature will admit of.

Still, even when so modified and chastened, the necessity for its continuing to exist at all will continue to be an evil. The one constitutional vice, inherent in and inseparable from unionism, is its being a visible and a tangible embodiment of that antagonism between labour and capital, which has always been the curse of the one and a thorn in the flesh of the other. . . . The utmost successes of which it is capable can never be such as well-wishers of their fellow-men, with any catholicity of sympathy, will be much disposed to rejoice over. Its highest achievements must always fall very short indeed of the consummation to which speculative philanthropy loves to look forward, when labour and capital, no longer needing to keep each other's aggressiveness in check, shall cordially combine for mutual co-operation. . . . But until the alliance is effected, and as long as the antagonism subsists, trades' unionism will continue to be an indispensable auxiliary of labour, and the sooner it is so recognised, both by the legislature and by capitalists, the better for the public peace.

LESLIE ON THE LAND QUESTION

1870

EDITOR'S NOTE

Fortnightly Review, n.s. VII (June, 1870), 641–54. Signed; republished in *D&D*, IV (1875), 86–110. Original heading: "Professor Leslie on the Land Question," footnoted: *"Land Systems and Industrial Economy of Ireland, England, and Continental Countries. By T. E. Cliffe Leslie, LL.B. of Lincoln's Inn, Barrister-at-Law, Examiner in Political Economy in the University of London, and Professor of Jurisprudence and Political Economy in the Queen's University in Ireland, and Queen's College, Belfast. London: [Longmans, Green,] 1870."* Identified in JSM's bibliography as "A review of Professor Cliffe Leslie's work on the Land Systems of different countries, in the Fortnightly Review of June 1, 1870" (MacMinn, 99). No copy in Somerville College.

In answer to a letter from Leslie, JSM wrote from Avignon, 8 March, 1870, in part: "I have just seen the advertisement of your book in Longmans' list. It is not worth while sending any proofs here as we leave for England at the beginning of next week." (Draft in British Library of Political and Economic Science.)

In the *D&D* version, many mistakes in the quotations from Leslie are corrected. The corrections in punctuation are accepted silently; the substantive corrections are also accepted, and the readings in the *Fortnightly* are given as variant notes. In these notes, "70" refers to the version in the *Fortnightly*; "75" to that in *D&D*, IV.

Leslie on the Land Question

THE FOUNDERS of Political Economy have left two sorts of disciples: those who have inherited their methods, and those who have stopped short at their phrases; those who have carried on the work of the masters, and those who think that the masters have left them no work to do. The former follow the example of their teachers in endeavouring to discern what principles are applicable to a particular case, by analysing its circumstances; the latter believe themselves to be provided with a set of catch-words, which they mistake for principles—free-trade, freedom of contract, competition, demand and supply, the wages fund, individual interest, desire of wealth, &c. —which supersede analysis, and are applicable to every variety of cases without the trouble of thought. In the language of Mr. Leslie, himself one of the best living writers on applied political economy—

A school of economists of no small pretensions, strongly represented in Parliament, supposes itself to be furnished with a complete apparatus of formulas, within which all economic knowledge is comprised;—which clearly and satisfactorily expounds all the phenomena of wealth, and renders all further investigation of the causes and effects of the existing economy of society needless, and even mischievous as tending to introduce doubt and heresy into a scientific world of certainty and truth, and discontent and disturbance into a social world of order and prosperity.* (P. 89.)

Since the downfall of Protectionism made Political Economy a term of honour, and no longer, with the classes dominant in politics and society, one of opprobrium, this routine school of political economists have mostly had things their own way; the more easily, as they comprise in their ranks some men of more than ordinary talents and acquirements, but who share the common infirmity of liking to get their thinking done once for all, and be saved all further trouble except that of referring to a formula. The

*Mr. Leslie adds: "Political writers and speakers of this school have long enjoyed the double satisfaction of beholding in themselves the masters of a difficult study, and of pleasing the powers that be, by lending the sanction of 'science' to all established institutions and customs, unless, indeed, customs of the poor. Instead of a science of wealth, they give us a science *for* wealth." [P. 89.]

ascendancy, however, of this school has always been disputed by those who hold that general maxims should be helps to thought, not substitutes for it. And the progress of events is now thrusting into the front, not merely of theoretical discussion, but of practical statesmanship, problems which definitely separate these two kinds of political economists, and put in evidence the broad distinction between them. Such is, in a peculiar degree, the question of Land Tenure, in Ireland and in England.

The Irish land difficulty having shown, by painful experience, that there is at least one nation closely connected with our own, which cannot and will not bear to have its agricultural economy ruled by the universal maxims which some of our political economists challenge all mankind to disobey at their peril; it has begun to dawn upon an increasing number of understandings, that some of these universal maxims are perhaps not universal at all, but merely English customs; and a few have begun to doubt whether, even as such, they have any claim to the transcendent excellence ascribed to them. The question has been raised whether the administration of the land of a country is a subject to which our current maxims of free trade, free contract, the exclusive power of every one over his own property, and so forth, are really applicable, or applicable without very serious limitations; whether private individuals ought to have the same absolute control, the same *jus utendi et abutendi*, over landed property, which it is just and expedient that they should be permitted to exercise over movable wealth.

Once fairly raised, this question admits of but one answer. The distinction between the two kinds of property is fundamental.

In the first place, land is a monopoly, not by the act of man, but of nature; it exists in limited quantity, not susceptible of increase. Now it is an acknowledged principle that when the State permits a monopoly, either natural or artificial, to fall into private hands, it retains the right, and cannot divest itself of the duty, to place the exercise of the monopoly under any degree of control which is requisite for the public good.

This control, moreover, is likely to be peculiarly needful, when the State has allowed private persons to appropriate the source from which mankind derive, and must continue to derive, their subsistence. The community has too much at stake in the employment of the land as an instrument for the supply of human wants, to be entitled to recognise any right in individuals to make themselves an impediment to the most beneficial use of it for that end. Wherever might is not accepted as a sufficient basis of right, the justification of private property in land has rested on the theory that most is made of the land for the good of the community by giving that full play to the stimulus of self-interest which is given by private ownership. But this theory, though it has a foundation in truth, is by no means absolutely true; and the limits of its truth ought to be the limits of its practical application.

The self-interest of the owners of land, under perfect freedom, coincides with the general interest of the community up to a certain point, but not wholly; there are cases in which it draws in a totally opposite direction. Not even in the point of view of Production is there a complete coincidence between the private interest of landowners and the public interest. In that of Distribution, whether the institution of private property in land should include the concession, to enrich a class, of all that annual increase of wealth which the mere progress of capital and population, in a prosperous community, showers down upon landlords without any exertion or sacrifice of their own, is a question not raised by Mr. Leslie, and which, for the present, we are content to leave undiscussed. But the self-interest of land-lords is far from a sufficient security for their turning the land to the best account, even as to its productive powers.

It has been urged, [says Mr. Leslie,] even by economists of eminence, ... that the best security the public can obtain for the good management of land is the personal interest of its private holders. The desire of wealth, it is urged, must impel the possessors of land, like the owners of capital in trade, to make the best commercial and productive use they can of their possessions. Political economy, I must affirm, countenances no such assumption. The desire of wealth is far from being a productive impulse under all circumstances; it is, on the contrary, sometimes a predatory *a*one. And*a* the fundamental assumption of political economy with respect to it is, that men desire to get wealth with the least possible trouble, exertion, and sacrifice; that besides wealth, they desire ease, pleasure, social position, and political power; and that they will combine all the gratification they can of their other desires with the acquisition of wealth. The situation of the inheritor of a large landed estate is entirely different from that of the trader, of whom (trained to habits of business, exposed to com-petition, and influenced not only by the desire of gain, but by the fear of being driven from the market altogether by better producers) it is true that the best security the public can have for the good management of his capital is his own private interest. It is as contrary to political economy as to common sense to assume that a rich sinecure *b*tends to make*b* its possessor industrious and improving; and the landholders of this country are the holders, not only of rich sinecures, but of sinecures the value of which tends steadily, and often rapidly, to increase without any exertion on their part. . . . . The interest of the proprietors of land is, according to the assumption their own conduct com-pels us to make, to get as much, not only of money, but of amusement, social consideration, and political influence as they can, making as little sacrifice as they can in return for any of those advantages, in the shape of leases to their tenants, the improvement of their estates, or even residence upon them when other places are more agreeable. That they are frequently guided solely by their interest in this sense is borne out by notorious facts; by absenteeism, by the frequent absence of all improvement on the part of the landlord and the refusal of any security to the tenant, by the mischievous extent of the preservation of game and the extension of *c*deer-forests*c* over what once was cultivated land.

*a–a*70   one; and   *b–b*70   makes
*c–c*70   deer-parks

The single circumstance that tenancy from year to year, a tenure incompatible with good agriculture, is the commonest tenure both in England and Ireland, affords positive proof that the interest of the landlord is no security to the public for the good management of the land in the absence of all interference of law. (Pp. 123–6.)

Wealth, [the author says elsewhere (p. 88)] is not the predominant interest of the most powerful classes.

But though the self-interest of landlords frequently operates to frustrate, instead of promoting, the interest which the community has in the most effective use of the productive powers of the soil, there is another party concerned whose self-interest does work in that useful direction; and that is, the actual cultivator of the soil, if he be either a small proprietor, or a tenant on conditions which secure to him the full fruits of his labour and outlay:—

He is a farmer by profession, with the habits of one, and exposed to much competition; he has his livelihood to make, and he would of course ^{d}be glad^d to make his fortune too, by ^{e}his^e farming. The public can, therefore, count upon the tenant doing his best by the land, if he is sure of deriving the benefit. But if he has no prospect of doing so, it becomes, on the contrary, his interest to labour only for the present, and to employ his savings and leisure anywhere rather than upon the permanent improvement of his farm. And that he cannot obtain the requisite security from contract alone, is evident, both from what has been said of the interest and conduct of landlords in the matter, and from the fact . . . . . that the Courts and the Legislature have found it necessary to interpose law after law to secure the property in their own improvements to the tenants. (P. 126.)

It is a great step in advance, and a signal triumph of political necessity over inveterate prejudice, that Parliament is now passing a bill[*] which recognises that in Ireland at least, security of tenure is indispensable to enlist the self-interest of the occupier of land on the side of good cultivation, and that this security cannot, in Ireland, be trusted to the operation of contract, but must be provided by law. There is something amusingly *naïf* in the form in which this interference of legislation represents itself to the minds of many who, with considerable reluctance, find themselves forced to support it. According to them, it is a deeply to be regretted, but unavoidable, setting aside of what they call the principles of political economy, in consequence of insuperable difficulties. May I venture to suggest that there are no such principles of political economy as those which they imagine themselves to be violating? The principles of political economy, as of every other department of knowledge, are a different thing from its practical precepts. The same principles require different precepts, wherever different

[*See 33 & 34 Victoria, c. 46.]

d-d70   like e-e+75 means are required for the same ends. If the interest of landlords does not afford sufficient security to tenants, it is not contrary, but in the strictest conformity, to the teachings of political economy, to provide other security instead. The absolute power of landlords over the soil is what political economy really condemns; and condemns in England as well as in Ireland, though its economic mischiefs are not, in England, so flagrant and unqualified.

Mr. Leslie's volume is partly a republication of essays which have appeared during the last three years in periodicals. But they are as fresh, and as germane to the present state of the question, as if they had been written yesterday; and they are supplemented by others which bring up the information and discussion to the latest date. They all relate to some of the aspects of the question of Land Tenure, and may be classed under three heads: the land question as it is in Ireland, the land question as it is in England, and the agricultural economy of those continental countries which the author has had the means of personally observing. We cannot attempt to give an adequate view of the contents of the volume; but in the hope of directing readers to the work itself, we will touch cursorily on a few of the points on which most stress is laid.

The view which Mr. Leslie takes of the condition of Ireland—and Mr. Leslie is an Irishman, of Ulster, who has studied the operation of economic laws in that country at first hand, and on the spot—is at once unfavourable and encouraging. Encouraging as regards the capabilities of the country, agricultural and even manufacturing, and the capacity of the people for thriving under a more tolerable land system; but unfavourable, as he considers much of the improvement alleged to have taken place, and to be still in progress, under the present system, in consequence of the famine and the emigration, to be merely imaginary. He denies the virtue either of emigration, or of the other favourite English prescription—the consolidation of farms—as a cure, or even much of a palliation, for Irish poverty. As a matter of fact, he asserts that the increase of wages which has taken place, considerable as it appears in comparison with the former standard, is not much more than equivalent to the rise in the price of articles of consumption caused by the gold discoveries, and by the railways, which have everywhere so greatly increased the price of agricultural produce in what were once, from the inaccessibility of markets, the cheap regions of the world. As a matter of science, he justly criticises the sweeping generalisation which assumes that whatever reduces the supply of labourers must proportionally raise wages, without regard to the effect which, in certain economic conditions, even a small rise in the price of labour may produce on the demand. On this subject he has shown that there is room and need for a supplementary chapter or section in our treatises on political economy; and it is no blame to him if, in a volume of this character, he rather points out the want than supplies it.* As far as Ireland is concerned, his opinion is, that the extensive substitution of pasture for tillage which has been taking place during the whole period of the emigration, and has been greatly facilitated by it, has curtailed the demand for labour in a proportion fully equal to the diminution of the supply. And the facts adduced, not only by Mr. Leslie, but by Professor Lyon Playfair, in his essay in Recess Studies, "On the Declining Production of Human Food in Ireland,"[*] show that this transformation and, in fact, supersession of rural industry, which at first only diminished the produce of tillage, but greatly increased the products of grazing farms, has now for some years decreased even the number of cattle, "through the want of winter keep, and what is worse, through a positive deterioration of the depastured soil," its fertilizing elements,

---

*"The bargain of wages is a transaction between the individual employer and his men; what that employer can give depends on *his own* means *for* profits, and not on the sum of the funds in his own and other people's possession. . . . . The aggregate amount of the funds expendible as wages does not, given the number of labourers, determine the rate of wages at all. . . . . Were only one labourer left in the country, would he earn as much as all the former labourers put together? Clearly not; unless he did as much work, and worked for all employers at once; for how else could the money be forthcoming to pay him? . . . If a single employer, or a few who could combine, had the entire amount, all the labour in the country which could not emigrate might be hired for its bare subsistence, whatever the rate in the power of the employer to give. Again, if the whole amount were, as it really is, very unequally shared among employers, the price of labour might be immeasurably lower than if it were equally shared; just as, at an auction, the prices paid for things will probably be immensely higher if the purchasers have equal means, than if most of the money is in the hands of a few. If two bidders, for example, have each £50, one of them may have to spend his whole fifty to get half what he wants; but if one of them has but £5, and the other has £95, the latter may get all he wants for £5 5s." (Pp. 41, 87–8.) Hence a very large emigration might take place, and yet the rise of wages be stopped at what the bulk of the employers of labour— in Ireland a very poor class—could afford to pay. "Although emigration may force employers either to pay more for labour or to forego it, it cannot enable them to pay more for it, as higher prices of produce will do; . . . it may, on the contrary, compel or determine them to diminish their outlay upon it, may force or induce them to relinquish enterprises already on foot, to forsake tillage for pasture, to emigrate themselves, and in various other ways to withdraw funds from the labour market. It may actually disable them from paying the same rate of wages as formerly, by withdrawing the strongest and most skilful hands from their employment; and again, in place of being the cause of a rise in the rate of wages, it may be the consequence of a fall." (P. 97.)

[*Recess Studies, ed. Alexander Grant. Edinburgh: Edmonston and Douglas, 1870, pp. 241–60.]

*f–f*70   and [printer's error?]

instead of being restored to it, having been carried out of the country in the bodies of the exported cattle ([Leslie,] p. 65). The single exception to the decline in the number of animals is sheep, the only farm product which increases in a soil abandoned to nature, and which, accordingly, has greatly increased in Ireland. The "decay of husbandmen"[*] and diminution of the produce of agriculture has had its natural effect in the decay of the country town and the village; and Mr. Leslie draws a sad picture of the desolation of the poverty-stricken country towns, the eastern coast excepted, which has been saved by the trade with England. Even the rise of prices, seemingly so beneficial to the farmer, is, under the wretched land system of Ireland, often the very reverse. "Rising prices, in themselves, and unaccompanied by security, only imperil the position of the tenant farmer, by tempting the proprietor to sudden changes in the terms of the tenure, or in the tenancy itself." (P. 63.) And tenancy at will is more universally the rule at this moment than it has been for several generations. "The natural consequence has been that system of husbandry which so experienced a judge as Mr. Caird lately described as everywhere meeting his eye, save in Ulster and the eastern seaboard of the country. 'What the ground will yield from year to year at the least cost of time, labour, and money is taken from it.' "[†]

The consolidation of farms, from which so much was expected, and which so many Englishmen still honestly believe to be the panacea for Irish poverty, perversely resisted by a population which it would essentially benefit, has proved, no less than the emigration, a complete failure as regards the prosperity of the country.

Mr. Brodrick, in one of the essays which the Irish land question has elicited from distinguished Englishmen,[‡] mentions with something of surprise, as a fact of which his inquiries in the island have convinced him, that fifteen and ten-acre farmers in Ireland pay a higher rent than larger farmers, with at least equal punctuality. The truth is that they generally produce more; and that the consolidation of farms means the diminution of crops, the extension of grazing, and, sooner or later, the exhaustion of the soil. The table in the note, taken from the last volume of Irish agricultural statistics, affords conclusive evidence that cultivation decreases, and g'grass, bog, and waste'g increase, in exact proportion to the size of farms. It may be true that not a few of the small holdings which have disappeared in recent years were, soil and situation considered, too diminutive; but they were so because the best land has been generally given to large grazing farms; and because the same error which has made landowners look

[*See Leslie, p. 69.]

[†Leslie, p. 63, quoting Caird, James. *The Irish Land Question*. London: Longmans, Green, Reader, and Dyer, 1869, p. 19.]

[‡Brodrick, George. "The Irish Land Question," in *Recess Studies*, ed. Alexander Grant, pp. 1–53.]

g–g70 [*quotation marks omitted*]

with disfavour on small farms, has led them to drive them to the worst ground and the worst situations, and to limit unduly both the duration of their tenure and the amount of land left to them. The consolidation of farms, in place of being an advance, has involved a palpable retrogression in Irish husbandry and in its productiveness. (Pp. 67–9.)

Since the immense produce raised from the barrenest soil in the small farms of Belgium, and the higher rent they actually pay, compared with large farms, have been made generally known in England, attempts have been made by Lord Rosse, Lord Dufferin, and others, to make out that the experience of Flanders, from difference of climate and other causes, is not applicable to Ireland. Mr. Leslie maintains, on the contrary, that the success of the *petite culture* in Flanders has been attained in spite of great disadvantages, not only of soil but of climate; that the British islands have much greater natural advantages than Flanders, for the success of five-acre farms; that "there is hardly any part of Europe, save England, better fitted for farms of the smallest description than the greater part of Ireland, including its waste lands; and even its waste lands could be made highly productive by Flemish agriculture." (P. 18.) Nor are the Irish peasantry, under anything like fair play, incapable of the qualities necessary for doing the fullest justice to small holdings.

In a southern county on this side, not many years ago a backward one from its isolation, there is a locality comprising several large estates well known to the writer, which, within his remembrance, and chiefly within very recent years, has undergone a complete transformation. It was farmed as most other parts of Ireland were farmed in his childhood; it is now farmed as well as any part of England, and a single dealer in a small town within it sells artificial manure to the value of £25,000 a year, who could probably not have sold a pound's worth to a former generation. From this locality, a large proprietor, of English descent, himself the cause of much of the improvement he describes, and who used to define the Irish tenant as a creature to whom multiplication and subdivision come by nature, but to whom the art of man cannot communicate an idea of farming or forbearance from marriage, now reports:— 'The twenty-acre men are holding on well, farming far better than formerly, and not involving themselves, as formerly, with wives and families as a matter of course. The farming of this class—Roman Catholics and indigenous Irish— is exceedingly improved; their prudence in the matter of marriage still more remarkable; their sisters and younger brothers, too, remaining frequently unmarried, as they will not marry out of their class, unless to better themselves.' . . . . Other instances of a landlord's good example being followed by his tenants, where English markets have come within reach, and English improvements in farming have become known, fell under the writer's observation in a recent visit to other eastern counties; and from one that was not visited, a farmer, loud for tenant-right, writes:—'Farming in general is greatly improving in this district and the neighbouring ones. Here farmers are to some extent able to compete with the landed proprietors at agricultural shows and the like.' (Pp. 39–40.)

It is not, therefore, as so often idly pretended, from any original incapacity or inveterate habits in the Irish race, that production and prosperity are declining throughout the whole space contained between "a line from Dublin to the nearest point of Lough Swilly in the north, and another to Bantry Bay in the south" (p. 70), a space including nearly three-fourths of the island. But to say more at present on the Irish part of the land question is inconsistent with our limits.

The land question in England, as Mr. Leslie justly observes, is unlike the land question in Ireland; but the evils of the system are different in kind rather than inferior in degree. The land question in Ireland is a tenant's question; and what the case principally requires is reform of the conditions of tenure. The land question in England is mainly a labourer's question, though the tenants also suffer deeply from the same causes which have reduced the labourers to their present state. Mr. Leslie tells once again the sad history of the divorce of the peasantry from the land. In England, unlike many other countries, the descendants of serfs had risen into a yeomanry, regarded by cotemporary chroniclers as the main strength of the country, both in war and in peace. In the last quarter of the seventeenth century the number of these small landed proprietors still "exceeded that of the tenant-farmers, amounting at the most moderate estimate to not less than 160,000 proprietors, who with their families must have made more than a seventh of the whole population." (P. 164, and the passage of Macaulay therein quoted.[*]) But now—

The landed yeomanry, insignificant in number and a nullity in political power, are steadily disappearing altogether; the tenant-farmers have lost the security of tenure, the political *h*independence*h*, and the prospect of one day farming their own estate, which they formerly enjoyed; and lastly, the inferior peasantry not only have lost ground in the literal sense, and have rarely any other connection with the soil than a pauper's claim, but have sunk deplorably in other *i*economical aspects*i* below their condition in former centuries. Thus a soil eminently adapted by natural gifts to sustain a numerous and flourishing rural population of every grade, has almost the thinnest and absolutely the most joyless peasantry in the civilised world, and its chief end as regards human beings seems only to be a nursery of over-population and misery in cities. (P. 163.)

Every grade of the rural population has sunk; the landed yeomanry are almost gone; the tenant-farmers have lost their ancient independence and interest in the soil; the labourers have lost their separate cottages and plots of ground, and their share in a common fund of land; and whereas all these grades were once

[*Macaulay, Thomas Babington, *The History of England*. London: Longman, Brown, Green, and Longman, 1849, I, pp. 334–5.]

*h-h*70 dependence
*i-i*70 essential respects

rising, the prospect of the landed yeomanry is now one of total extinction; that of the tenant-farmers, increasing insecurity; that of the agricultural labourer, to find the distance between his own grade and that of the one above him wider and more impassable than ever, while the condition of his own grade is scarcely above *that of* the brutes. Once, from the meanest peasant to the greatest noble, all had land, and he who had least might hope for more; now there is being taken away from who *has* little even that which he has—his cottage, nay, his separate room. Once there was an ascending movement from the lowest grade towards the highest; now there is a descending movement in every grade below the highest. Once the agricultural class had a political representation, and a voice in legislation, which they dared to raise against the landed gentry and nobility; now the latter have the supreme command at once of the soil and of the suffrages of its cultivators. (P. 174.)

In fact, there is no longer a true rural population remaining, for the ends, political, social, and economic, which such a population ought to fulfil. [P. 162.]

The means by which these lamentable changes have been brought about may be found in Mr. Leslie's volume, or in Mr. W. T. Thornton's "Over-population and its Remedy." They are summed up by Mr. Leslie, so far as relates to the labourers, in the following catalogue (pp. 207–8):—

Briefly enumerated, the chief causes by which the peasantry—the really most important class—have been dispossessed of their ancient proprietary rights and beneficial interests in the soil are the following:—

(1) Confiscation of their ancient rights of common, which were not only in themselves of great value, but most important for the help they gave towards the maintenance of their separate lands.

(2) Confiscation to a large extent of their separate lands themselves, by a long course of violence, fraud, and chicane, in addition to forfeitures resulting from deprivation of their rights of common.

(3) The destruction of country towns and villages, and the loss, in consequence, of local markets for the produce of peasant farms and gardens.

(4) The construction of a legal system based on the principle of inalienability from the feudal line, in the interest of great landed families, and incompatible with either the continuance of the ancient or the rise of a new class of peasant landholders.

(5) The loss, with their lands and territorial rights, of all political power and independence on the part of the peasantry; and, by consequence, the establishment and maintenance by the great proprietors of laws most adverse to their interests.

(6) Lastly, the administration by the great landowners of their own estates in such a manner as to impoverish the peasantry still further, and to sever their last remaining connection with the soil.

These various headings are explained and expounded in the pages which follow; and the author concludes—

The Irish land question is of more importance politically than the English for the hour, but it is not so economically even for the hour; and it is so,

i–i+75   *k–k*70 had politically, for the hour only. Economically, the emergency is much greater at this moment in this than in the other island; the main land question here relates to a poorer class than even the Irish tenantry, and there is a much greater amount of material misery and actual destitution in England, traceable mainly to its own land system, though aggravated by that of Ireland and the consequent immigration of poverty.

The day is not distant when the supreme question of English as of Irish politics, will be whether the national territory is to be the source of power and luxury to a few individuals, or of prosperity and happiness to the nation at large? and whether those few individuals, or the nation at large, are to determine the answer? (P. 229.)

Thus complete has been the failure of the English agricultural economy, if we look, not to the prosperity of landlords, nor even to the amount of produce raised from the soil, but to the truest test—the condition of the mass of the population. But when we pass, in our author's pages, from the picture of the evils to the suggestion of remedies, we are struck by a sense of their inadequacy. We imagine Mr. Leslie himself would be the first to admit that he does little more than break ground on the subject.

The causes of evil, in Mr. Leslie's apprehension, are, that landed property is in too few hands; that the movement even towards large farms has been carried too far; and that tenants have not sufficient security of tenure. Remedial measures, he believes, will be efficacious, just in so far as they tend to increase the number of proprietors of land, and to give to tenants the security of a long lease. To attain the former object—

There are three different methods recorded in history to make choice from. One is the French law of partition of family property among all children alike —an expedient which deserves no higher commendation than that it is better than the feudal system of disinheriting all the children but one. A second method which suggests itself with higher reason on its side, is a limitation of the amount of land that any single individual shall take by inheritance. Such a measure, however shocking to present proprietary sentiments, *could* not diminish the real happiness, it may safely be asserted, of one human being in the next generation; nor can it be confidently pronounced that the mischief resulting from the long retention of a restriction of a different kind upon the possession of land may not yet be found such that some such measure will be of necessity adopted, to make room for the natural increase of *m* population. But it would be a remedy which only a violent revolution could at present accomplish. . . . . . And if neither the French system of partition nor the agrarian system of the Gracchi is to be our model, ... we may yet find a model in the general tendency of English law reform since the system was established which first limited property in land to a particular line of descent in a particular number of families; for that end depriving each successive proprietor of the chief uses of property itself. The feudal landowner forfeited the right to sell his own land, to leave it by will, to let it securely, to provide for his family out of it, to subject it to the payment of his debts; he forfeited, therefore, the chief rights of property, taking only in exchange a right to confiscate the property of his tenants. (Pp. 191–2.)

*l*70   would   *m*70   the

Mr. Leslie's proposal is to restore to him these legitimate rights, abolishing all restrictions which deprive the owner of land for the time being of the power of alienation.

To extinguish the force of settlements as binding and irrevocable instruments, save so far as a provision for a wife is concerned; to put family settlements, save as to a wife, on the same footing as wills, *ipso facto* void upon marriage, and revocable by any subsequent conveyance or will; to enact that each successive proprietor shall take the land he succeeds to, free from any restriction on his rights of proprietorship; and further, to make provision that all lands left burdened with any charges shall be sold immediately on the death of the owner to pay off the incumbrance; with the addition, of course, of assimilating the devolution of land, in case of intestacy, to that of personal property. (Pp. 198–200.)

In order to judge of these proposals, it is not necessary to have come to a positive conclusion on the rather difficult legislative question, whether and in what cases settlements should be permitted; in other words, whether and to what extent an owner of property should have power to bequeath to one person a life-interest, and to another or others the succession after the death of the first. It is evident that settlement of property may be permitted without permitting settlement of land. It would be sufficient to enact that testamentary dispositions which do not confer unrestricted ownership on the person in whose favour they are made, shall not be valid for the land itself, but only for the proceeds of its sale. There are not the same objections to tying up consols and similar representative wealth from alienation, which there are in the case of the actual sources of production; and if, without forbidding the landowner to regulate, within certain limits, the descent of his pecuniary means beyond his immediate successor, it were put out of his power to detain for this purpose any portion of the land of the country from general circulation, he would be obliged either to bequeath the land in full ownership, implying liberty of sale, or if he thought it indispensable to tie the hands of his successor, the land would be sold by operation of law at his decease, and the restriction would only apply to the proceeds. Mr. Leslie, as we saw, proposes a sale of land at every succession to the extent necessary for clearing the remainder from all existing incumbrances. Without pledging ourselves to this proposal, which requires mature discussion, we may remark that if it were adopted, the proprietor, being no longer able to charge the land beyond his own life with a provision for younger children, must choose between leaving them a portion of the land itself, and selling a portion to raise money for their benefit. These provisions combined would greatly restrict the power of keeping together large masses of land in a particular line of descent; and it might fairly be anticipated that a great increase would take place in the quantity of land which would annually be brought into the market.

But Mr. Leslie, we should think, must be as well aware as anybody, how little this would do towards making any great part of the land of this country the property of the actual cultivators. In France, and other countries of the Continent, the sale of land generally means its purchase by the poor; for the poor give the highest price, the rich being neither numerous, nor, in general, addicted to rural duties or pleasures. But in England the sale of land means generally its sale to the rich. The annual accumulation of fortunes in manufactures and commerce raises up a perpetual succession of rich families, eager to step into the place of landowners who are obliged to sell. Unless changes much more radical than an increase of the facilities of alienation are destined to take place in this country, nearly all the land, however it may change hands, is likely to remain the property of the rich; nor are the new proprietors more likely than the old to lease their lands on terms more encouraging to the industry and enterprise of their tenants. No doubt, the increased quantity of land in the market would cause a cheapening of its price, which would bring it within the reach of a somewhat greater number of purchasers; and it would occasionally fall into the hands of persons intending to cultivate instead of letting it, but seldom of those who cultivate with their own hands. If the greater marketableness of land is to be made a benefit to the labouring class, it must be in another manner entirely; as, for example, by buying from time to time on account of the public, as much of the land that comes into the market as may be sufficient to give a full trial to such modes of leasing it, either to small farmers with due security of tenure, or to co-operative associations of labourers, as without impairing, but probably even increasing, the produce of the soil, would make the direct benefits of its possession descend to those who hold the plough and wield the spade. Mr. Leslie has not included any measure of this sort among his proposals, but it is quite germane to his principles, and necessary, we think, to enable them to produce their best effects.

Meanwhile, the measures which he proposes would render possible a multitude of agricultural and industrial enterprises, beneficial to the national wealth, and giving great employment to labour, which at present the restrictions of family settlements make impracticable. We quote at the foot of the page some striking examples of the obstructive operation of these arrangements.*

We have not space remaining for an analysis of the third part of Mr.

*"About fifteen years ago (Dr. Hancock relates in his "Treatise on the Impediments to the ⁿProsperityⁿ of Ireland" [London: Simms and McIntyre, 1850, pp. 85–7]) an enterprising capitalist was anxious to build a flax mill in the North of Ireland, as a change had become necessary in the linen trade from hand-spinning to mill-spinning. He selected as the site for his mill a place in a poor but populous district, situated on a navigable river, and in the immediate vicinity of extensive turf bogs. The capitalist applied to the landlord for a lease of fifty acres for a mill site, labourers' village, and his own residence, and of

ⁿ⁻ⁿ70   Property

Leslie's Essays, relating to the land systems and agricultural economy of Continental states. They are, however, a valuable contribution to our knowledge of the subject, relating to regions which the author has himself visited, and has been assisted in his inquiries by high economical and agricultural authorities on the spot: in Westphalia and the Ruhr Basin by several persons; in Central France by the eminent M. Léonce de Lavergne; and in Belgium by M. Emile de Laveleye, whose important paper in the

fifty acres of bog, as it was proposed to use turf as the fuel for the steam-engines of the mill. The landlord was most anxious to encourage an enterprise so well calculated to improve his estate. An agreement was concluded; but when the flax-spinner consulted his legal adviser, he discovered that the law prevented the landlord from carrying out the very liberal terms he had agreed to. He was bound by settlement to let at the best rent only; the longest lease he could grant was for three lives, or thirty-one years. Such a lease, however, at the full rent of the land, was quite too short a term to secure the flax-spinner in laying out his capital in building; the statute enabling tenants to lease for mill sites only allowing leases of three acres. The mill was not built, and mark the consequence. Some twenty miles from the spot alluded to, the flax-spinner found land in which he could get a perpetual interest; there he laid out his thousands; there he has for the last fifteen years given employment to hundreds of labourers, and has earned money. The poor but populous district continues as populous, but, if anything, poorer than it was. During the past season of distress, the people of that district suffered much from want of employment, and the landlord's rents were worse paid out of it than from any other part of his estate." (Pp. 52–3.)

"Belfast, the only great manufacturing city in Ireland, owes its greatness to a fortunate accident which converted the ground on which it stands from feudal into commercial territory, by transferring it from a great noble to its own citizens. But the growth of Belfast itself, on one side, has been strictly circumscribed by the rival claims of two noble proprietors, who were in litigation respecting them for more than a generation; and in a step the inhabitant passes from new streets to a filthy and decaying suburb, into which the most enterprising capitalist in the neighbourhood has been prevented from extending his improvements. On the other side of the town is some ground which the capitalist just referred to bought three years ago for the purpose of building; but which remains unbuilt on, in consequence of difficulties in the legal title; although in equity the title is indisputable, and is not disputed. Some years ago the same capitalist contracted for the purchase of another plot of ground in the neighbourhood. It proved, however, that the vendor was precluded by his marriage settlement from completing ᵒtheᵒ contract, although it reserved to him the unusual power to grant leases for 999 years. That, however, did not answer the same purpose; in the first place, because (a consequence of the land system, with its distinction between real and personal property), the succession duties are heavier on leasehold than on freehold estates. What is more important, a tenant for years has not the rights of ownership, as was afterwards experienced in the very case before us. The capitalist accepted a lease for 999 years; although diverted from his original design with respect to the ground. In putting it to a different purpose, he proceeded to level an eminence, and to carry away the gravel for use elsewhere. But the Law of Landlord and Tenant says: If a tenant

o–o70   his

Cobden Club volume[*] has recently brought home to many English readers the lessons contained in his remarkable works on Belgium, Holland, and Lombardy. The essays on the Ruhr Basin and on La Creuse are most interesting reading, and the facts they contain, when first published by Mr. Leslie, were almost wholly new to English readers. But the most valuable, for the general purposes of the book, are those on Belgium. Mr. Leslie's paper in the Cobden Club volume[†] had shown, in opposition to a still strong, though diminishing, prejudice, the great success of peasant properties in France. The paper in the present volume on Belgium renders the same justice to the small farms as well as the small properties of that country. If we compare with the minute and well-considered statements of Mr. Leslie and M. de Laveleye, such as are given on the contrary side even by such an authority as Mr. James Howard, in his "Continental Farms and Peasantry"[‡] (though Mr. Howard is by no means absolutely hostile to small farms, but expresses a strong sense of the desirableness of a certain admixture of them), we see nothing in the latter which seriously diminishes the consideration due to the former. Everything in Mr. Howard's remarks which is matter of fact—everything which is the result of actual observation —may be admitted, without affecting the worth of Belgian example as evidence in favour of what the *petite culture* is capable of. There is not a single drawback pointed out by Mr. Howard, which is inseparable from *petite culture*; while even in Belgium the drawbacks are shown by Mr. Leslie and M. de Laveleye to be steadily diminishing.

---

open pits for the purpose of raising stone or waste [?] it will be waste. And this being the law, the landlord actually obtained an injunction to restrain the tenant's proceedings, and mulcted him in damages. Once more; in another county the very same capitalist opened an iron mine by arrangement with the lord of the soil, and commenced works on an extensive scale. The landlord then demanded terms to which he was not entitled by his contract; but the price of Irish iron has not been high enough of late years to defray the cost of a Chancery suit, in addition to the cost of production; and delay, worry, and anxiety are not inducements to industrial enterprise, so the iron works were suspended. Here are five cases within the author's knowledge, all happening in recent years, in which a single individual has been arrested in the course of town enterprise and improvement by the state of the law. . . . It is well known that there are no manufacturing establishments on the Companies' estates, because these London guilds persistently refuse to give perpetuity lease for mill purposes; while on the borders of the county [Londonderry], Cookstown, Bally-mena, Ballymoney, and Coleraine, where such leases are granted, manufactures have increased and prospered, and even in the county, where freehold sites can be procured, manufactures have taken root." [*JSM's square brackets in both cases*] (Pp. 76–9.)

[*"The Land System of Belgium and Holland," in *Systems of Land Tenure in Various Countries*. London: Macmillan, 1870, pp. 228–78.]

[†"The Land System of France," *ibid.*, pp. 328–52.]

[‡*Continental Farming and Husbandry*. London: Ridgway, 1870.]

LAND TENURE REFORM

1871

EDITOR'S NOTE

Programme of the Land Tenure Reform Association, with an Explanatory Statement by John Stuart Mill. London: Longmans, Green, Reader, and Dyer, 1871, 6–16. Republished, *D&D*, IV (1875), 239–50, as "Explanatory Statement of the Programme of the Land Tenure Reform Association," with a footnote giving the ten points of the Programme. The footnote is dated July, 1870, the date of the adoption of the Programme, not of the writing of the "Explanatory Statement." Identified in JSM's bibliography as "The Explanatory Statement published with the Programme of the Land Tenure Reform Association in March 1871" (MacMinn, 100). No corrections or variants in Somerville College copy.

During the preliminary organization of the Association, in autumn, 1869, JSM served as Chairman of the Provisional Committee but, as he informed Andrew Reid (eventually Secretary of the Association), he would not take on the leadership of the Association once it was established. He was, however, actively involved in drawing up the Programme (completed during April, 1870), and became Chairman. On 15 March, 1871, he wrote to Longmans asking them to publish the pamphlet containing the Programme and his Explanatory Statement; Longmans agreed, and the pamphlet, to cost sixpence, was ready for the press on 27 March. Within the next year the Association had taken 2100 copies, largely for distribution to the working classes, and 331 had been bought by the public. For a document issued by the Association, under JSM's name as Chairman, see Appendix D, 766–7 below.

In the following text the one substantive variant (see 689) derives from *D&D*, IV, which is identified as "75". The ten points of the Programme, which appear before JSM's explanation in the pamphlet, are introduced as footnotes where appropriate.

Land Tenure Reform

OF ALL OUR LEADING INSTITUTIONS, none are more unsuited than the Land Laws to the state of society of which the Reform Act of 1867[*] is the harbinger. Originating in an age when the landholders were masters of the country, it is no wonder that they should require alteration now, when the country belongs, at least in principle, to the whole of its inhabitants. Our laws relating to land are the remains of a system which, as history tells us, was designed to prop up a ruling class. They were made for the purpose of keeping together the largest possible possessions in the families which owned the land, and by means of it governed the country. So long as those families were not obliged to share power with any other class, or with the people, the Land Laws were in many respects considerably worse than they are now; but what is left of them has still the same object: to contrive that the land of the family shall descend unbroken to the eldest son, and that the owner for the time being shall not be at liberty to defeat this purpose by selling the land. By these means the land has been prevented, to a large extent, from passing out of the hands of the idle into those of the industrious, and its ownership has been retained ᵃasᵃ the privilege of a small and decreasing number of families.

The removal of these remains of feudality is the object aimed at in the first three articles of the Society's Programme.[†] They hope to be aided in its attainment by all real Liberals, not excepting those who demand changes much more drastic. An active and influential portion of the working classes have adopted the opinion, that private property in land is a mistake, and that the land ought to be resumed, and managed on account of the State, compensation being made to the proprietors. Some of these reformers look with jealousy on any relaxation of the land monopoly, thinking that an increase of the number of landed proprietors would strengthen the obstacles

[*30 & 31 Victoria, c. 102.]
[†"I. To remove all Legal and Fiscal Impediments to the Transfer of Land. II. To secure the abolition of the Law of Primogeniture. III. To restrict within the narrowest limits the power of Tying up Land." (*Programme*, p. 3.)]

ᵃ⁻ᵃ+75

to a general resumption of the land. But even from their point of view, there is another side to the question; since, (in a country like this, where there is not, as in Ireland and France, an intense competition among the labouring classes for land, raising it far above its reasonable value) whatever brings more land into the market tends to lower its price, and diminishes the amount of compensation which, if the views of these reformers were to prevail, the nation would have to pay to the landowners. Meanwhile, so long as land is private property, whatever facilitates its passing into new hands tends to increase its productiveness, and thereby its usefulness to the nation at large: since those among the owners who are least provided with skill, enterprise, and capital, are those who are under the strongest inducement to sell their land. The Society, therefore, venture to hope that even the most extreme section of land reformers will not reject this first part of their programme; while they are assured of the support, to this extent, of many whose ideas of Land Tenure Reform go no farther.

The Society, however, are not content to stop at this point. They are of opinion that much more is amiss in the present system of landed property than merely the restraints on its alienation. Whether the hitherto fundamental institution of property in land is destined to be permanent, or to disappear, they do not take upon themselves to decide. On this, as on other questions of the distant future, persons of both modes of thinking may consistently give the Society their support. The Society is formed to promote, not the abolition of landed property, but its reform, and the vindication of those rights of the entire community which need not be, and never ought to have been, waived in favour of the landlords. One of these is the right of laying peculiar taxation on land. Landed property enjoys a special advantage over other property, and for that special advantage it ought to pay. This is the purpose of the Fourth Article of the Programme.[*]

There are some things which, if allowed to be articles of commerce at all, cannot be prevented from being monopolized articles. On all such the State has an acknowledged right to limit the profits. Railways, for instance, are inevitably a monopoly, and the State, accordingly, sets a legal limit to the amount of railway fares. Now, land is one of these natural monopolies. The demand for it, in every prosperous country, is constantly rising, while the land itself is susceptible of but little increase. All such articles, when indispensable to human existence, tend irresistibly to rise in price, with the progress of wealth and population. The rise of the value of land, and of the

[*"IV. To claim, for the benefit of the State, the Interception by Taxation of the Future Unearned Increase of the Rent of Land (so far as the same can be ascertained), or a great part of that increase, which is continually taking place, without any effort or outlay by the proprietors, merely through the growth of population and wealth; reserving to owners the option of relinquishing their property to the State at the market value which it may have acquired at the time when this principle may be adopted by the Legislature." (*Programme*, p. 3.)]

incomes of landowners, during the present century, has been enormous. Part of it, undoubtedly, has been due to agricultural improvements and the expenditure of capital on the soil. Much of it, however, is merely the result of the increased demand for agricultural products, and for building land, and would have taken place even though no money had been laid out in increasing the productive powers of the soil. Such outlay, moreover, as there has been, was made, in a great proportion of cases, not by the landlord, but by the tenant, who may or may not have been indemnified by a temporary enjoyment of the profits; but, sooner or later, the increased return produced by the tenant's capital has become an unearned addition to the income of the landlord.

The Society are of opinion that in allowing the land to become private property, the State ought to have reserved to itself this accession of income, and that lapse of time does not extinguish this right, whatever claim to compensation it may establish in favour of the landowners. The land is the original inheritance of all mankind. The usual, and by far the best argument for its appropriation by individuals is, that private ownership gives the strongest motive for making the soil yield the greatest possible produce. But this argument is only valid for leaving to the owner the full enjoyment of whatever value he adds to the land by his own exertions and expenditure. There is no similar reason for allowing him to appropriate an increase of value to which he has contributed nothing, but which accrues to him from the general growth of society, that is to say, not from his own labour or expenditure, but from that of other people—of the community at large.

The Society do not propose to disturb the landowners in their past acquisitions. But they assert the right of the State to all such accessions of income in the future. Whatever value the land may have acquired at the time when the principle they contend for shall obtain the assent of Parliament, they do not propose to interfere with. If, rather than submit to be specially taxed on the future increase of his rent, a landowner prefers to relinquish his land to the State, the Society are willing that the State should pay for it at its selling value. By this provision, all his just claims will be fully satisfied, while the bargain will still be highly advantageous to the nation, since an individual never gives, in present money, for a remote profit, anything like what that profit is worth to the State, which is immortal. In this manner, that increase of wealth which now flows into the coffers of private persons from the mere progress of society, and not from their own merits or sacrifices, will be gradually, and in an increasing proportion, diverted from them to the nation as a whole, from whose collective exertions and sacrifices it really proceeds. The State will receive the entire rent of the lands voluntarily sold to it by their possessors, together with a tax on the future increase of rent on those properties whose owners have sufficient confidence in the justice and moderation of the State to prefer retaining them. These owners should be allowed at any future period to alter their minds, and give up their lands for the price first offered; or more, if they can show that they have made, during the intervening period, substantial improvements at their own cost. The option thus allowed would be a permanent security to the landowners against any unjust or excessive exercise of the right of taxation by the State.

Objections have been made to the taxation of a prospective increase of rent, on the ground of difficulties of execution; but those difficulties, fairly encountered, would not, it is conceived, be very serious. It is not necessary to enforce the right of the State to the utmost farthing. A large margin should be allowed for possible miscalculation. A valuation of all the land in the country would be made in the first instance, and a registration established of subsequent improvements made by the landlord. Taxation would not commence until there had been time for an increase of value to accrue, and should then be kept carefully within the amount of increase due to general causes. If a landowner could prove that, owing to special circumstances, his estate had not shared in the general rise of value, he would be exempt from the tax: and at all events, if the just limit was exceeded, the power of surrendering the land at its original valuation, augmented by a just compensation for subsequent improvements, would be a sufficient protection to the pecuniary interests of the landlords.

This reassertion of the right of the State to lay special taxation, within the limits now specified, on the rent of land, is the extent of the claim made by the Society, in behalf of the nation, upon the lands which have been permitted to become the patrimony of private families. But there is another large portion of the lands of the country which are not yet private property, and to these the Society demands that the right of the nation be henceforth maintained. As much of the original right of the whole people to the land as the nation has already parted with to individuals, the programme of the Association leaves to those who have it. But they decidedly object to parting with any more. They demand that the practice of converting public property into private should henceforth terminate.

There are, in the first place, what are called the common lands. These are said to belong to the lord of the manor. But they are not his like his private estate—to deal with as he pleases. They are not his for the principal purpose to which land is applicable—that of cultivation. Even their spontaneous produce does not belong to him exclusively. The game is his, and the game is nearly the only thing found on them that is his. The natural pasture, and the wood which grows wild on the land, he shares with those of his neighbours who have rights of common; and if he wants to bring the land into cultivation, he must apply to the Inclosure Commissioners,[*] who

[*See 8 & 9 Victoria, c. 118.]

obtain for him an Act of Parliament. This Act of Parliament divides the land between him and the adjacent landowners, who alone, in rural districts, except by special grant from the lord of the manor, are considered to have rights of common; and neither tenants nor cottagers, save in quite exceptional cases, obtain any compensation, unless that name is given to the miserable reservation of a few acres for recreation ground or cottage allotments. The Society regard this disposal of the common lands as an iniquity, and demand that it should entirely cease. The demand is no infringement of private property. Neither the lord of the manor nor the neighbouring landowners are entitled to a farthing more than the value of what the land yields to them in its wild state. The Society are willing to respect existing possession, but they protest against making a fresh gift from the nation to its wealthiest members. If free gifts are to be made at all, they should at least be reserved for those who need them.

When the State thinks fit to exercise its right to these waste lands, the lord of the manor should be compensated for his manorial rights, and the commoners for their rights of common, at the existing value, and the land either kept open for the enjoyment of the people or cultivated for their use. The Society attach great importance to keeping open extensive tracts in a state of wild natural beauty and freedom; and a large portion of the waste lands of the country are of too poor a quality to be worth much for any other purpose. When the land is worth cultivation, and the wants of society require that it should be cultivated, the mode of bringing it into cultivation should be principally determined by the interest of the labouring classes. Were it desirable to give any further extension to private property in land, those classes would have a paramount claim to be admitted to a share in it, by the grant of the land in small parcels to respectable agricultural labourers at a fixed rent. But if, as is, perhaps, more to be expected, the opinion prevails that any further permanent alienation of the land is undesirable, these lands will remain with the State, or with local authorities, as a means of trying, with the greatest advantage and under every variety of circumstances, the modes in which land can be most successfully managed on the public account—whether by capitalist farmers, with stipulations for the benefit of the labourers, or by long leases on proper conditions to small cultivators, or finally, by co-operative farming.[*]

[*See the 5th and 6th articles of the *Programme* (pp. 3–4): "V. To promote a policy of Encouragement to Co-operative Agriculture, through the purchase by the State, from time to time, of Estates which are in the market, and the Letting of them, under proper regulations, to such Co-operative Associations, as afford sufficient evidence of spontaneity and promise of efficiency. VI. To promote the Acquisition of Land in a similar manner, to be let to Small Cultivators, on conditions, which, while providing for the proper cultivation of the land, shall secure to the cultivator a durable interest in it."]

A still more valuable resource than the common lands consists of the land owned by public bodies and endowed institutions. These possessions are not, in any sense whatever, private property. No one of those who profit by them has more than a life interest, most have not so much, and their interests can be bought up, or suffered to expire. All enlightened reformers acknowledge the moral distinction between private property and public endowments; and it is now an admitted doctrine among Liberals, that endowments, after a certain length of duration, are at the disposal of the State, which from that time should fix their destination. Many endowments are positively mischievous, and ought to be extinguished. Others, especially educational endowments, are highly useful, and under better management will, it may be hoped, become more so; and many, now worthless from abuse, only require to be properly looked after. A portion of the lands of the country, much larger and more valuable than the public in general are aware of, is thus at the disposal of the State. It can keep those lands together, and administer them either for the objects to which they are appropriated, or for such other objects as may be considered preferable, and permit them to be leased or occupied on such terms as it thinks fit by individuals or associations. It may, without injustice or detriment to any one, make use of them for any well-considered social or philanthropic experiments. Among the lands thus disposable is the soil of large portions of our great towns, and particularly of London. It is obvious what facilities their possession would give for promoting every improvement that tends to raise the condition of the mass of the people: sanitary works, improved dwellings, public gardens, co-operative buildings, co-operative agriculture, useful public institutions of every kind.*

These important reforms are the object of the 7th, 8th, and 9th articles of the Programme.[*] But inasmuch as the waste lands, and the lands

*There are some who think it a useful provision for the public interest that individuals should have the power to buy land as an investment, with an express view to obtaining, through its rise in value, a future provision for their family at a comparatively moderate present expense. It is thought that this power, in the hands of individuals, causes an earlier use to be made, through private fore-sight, of situations advantageous for building or for industrial purposes, than would otherwise be the case; and that of this foresight it is just that the individuals should reap the benefit. But in answer to this it should be considered, that it would be the duty of the Land Department of the State to exercise for its benefit the foresight now exercised by individuals for theirs. Neither would the benefits of individual sagacity be lost to the community; since the person who first perceived the advantageous use to which a piece of land might be put, would, if he could not acquire the absolute property, have the resource of applying to the Land Department for a long lease; which there need be no doubt that in such cases it would be the policy of the State to grant.

[*"VII. Lands belonging to the Crown, or to Public Bodies, or Charitable

belonging to public bodies, are irregularly and unequally distributed through the country; and the means which they afford, as well for executing recognised improvements, as for bringing to an experimental test such as are yet untried, ought not to be confined to some neighbourhoods, but should exist in all parts of the country; it is therefore provided, by the 5th and 6th articles,[*] that the State should purchase from private owners estates which are in the market, when such purchase is necessary for giving a fair trial in any neighbourhood to co-operative agriculture, or to a properly regulated system of small farming.

The 10th article of the Programme requires no explanation.[†] It is contrary to all principle that private proprietors, who may be, and often are, liberal and enlightened, but who may, on the contrary, be the most ignorant and capricious of mankind, should have the power of destroying, or of closing from public view, natural curiosities, or monuments and historical relics, of the greatest value to science, to history, and to the instruction and enjoyment of every person in the country who has sufficient knowledge and intelligence to appreciate their value.

---

and other Endowments, to be made available for the same purposes, as suitable conditions arise, as well as for the Improvement of the Dwellings of the Working Classes; and no such lands to be suffered (unless in pursuance of the above mentioned ends, or for peculiar and exceptional reasons) to pass into Private hands. VIII. All Lands now Waste, or requiring an Act of Parliament to authorize their inclosure, to be retained for National Uses: Compensation being made for Manorial rights and rights of Common. IX. That while it is expedient to bring a large portion of the present Waste Lands under Cultivation for the purposes and on the principles laid down in the preceding articles, it is desirable that the less fertile portions, especially those which are within reach of populous districts, should be retained in a state of wild natural beauty, for the general enjoyment of the community, and encouragement in all classes of healthful rural tastes, and of the higher order of pleasures; also, in order to leave to future generations the decision of their ultimate uses." (*Programme*, pp. 4–5.)]

[*See p. 693n above.]

[†"X. To obtain for the State the power to take possession (with a view to their preservation) of all Natural Objects, or Artificial Constructions attached to the soil, which are of historical, scientific, or artistic interest, together with so much of the surrounding land as may be thought necessary; the owners being compensated for the value of the land so taken." (*Programme*, p. 5.)]

PROPERTY AND TAXATION

1873

EDITOR'S NOTE

Fortnightly Review, n.s. XIII (Mar., 1873), 396–8. Signed; republished in *D&D*, IV (1875), 231–6. Original heading, as first of the *Fortnightly* "Critical Notices," *"L'Avere et l'Imposta.* Per Constantino Baer. Roma, Torino, Firenze [: Loescher], 1872." Not mentioned in JSM's bibliography. No copy in Somerville College. The *D&D* text, which is headed "L'Avere e l'Imposta," does not differ substantively from that in the *Fortnightly*, except in correcting "et" to "e" in the title. The title here used is taken from the text of JSM's review.

Writing to Cairnes from Avignon, 9 Dec., 1872, JSM says in part: "Have you ever turned your attention to the merits and demerits of a tax on property, i.e. land and capital, realized and unrealized, as a substitute for an income tax? The pros and cons are tolerably obvious, the pros consisting rather in the demerits of other direct taxes than in the recommendations of this. My attention has been drawn to the subject by an Italian correspondent of mine, Constantino Baer by name, a clever and sensible man, well versed in the best English political economy, and who has published a little book recommending, as the best system of taxation, a tax on land and capital, of a percentage on their pecuniary value, combined with taxes on such modes of expenditure as may be a fair test of a person's general scale of unproductive expenses. I have written, for the small print of the Fortnightly, a short notice of this book, but I should much like to have your opinion on its main position." (Letter in the British Library of Political and Economic Science.)

Property and Taxation

THOSE WHO ARE APT TO FEEL DISCOURAGEMENT at the slow progress of mankind, both in the discovery of truth and in the application of it, may derive comfort from the fact that those nations which, from historical accidents or their own energy, precede others in either of these kinds of improvement, are found to have laboured not for themselves only, but for all the rest, and greatly abridge the task for those who have fallen behind. The European nations which have lately been freed from the hindrances that had retarded their development—Italy and Hungary—with the vigorous impulse which the awakening of liberty gives to the human faculties, have thrown themselves into serious study; and being able to resort at once to the latest and best products of thought in the more advanced countries, are attaining by strides the results which their teachers were only able to reach by slow and measured steps. Knowing that they have all to learn, they learn all at once, having no habit, authority, or prejudice to detain them halfway.

If an example is desired, one will be found in the work before us, the production of a distinguished Italian political economist. Political economy, it is true, is no new subject to Italian intellect; the study of it may almost be said to have originated in Italy: its early cultivators who have left a reputation behind them were generally Italians, and chiefly (we leave the explanation to historians) Southern Italians; indeed, the speculative movement of Italy had for centuries its chief seat in the southern portion of the peninsula, as the political, commercial, and artistic had theirs in the northern. Owing, however, to the general slackening of the intellectual movement in Italy, caused by her unfortunate political situation in the last three centuries, she was outstripped in this as in other departments by more fortunate nations, and it was left to them to originate all the great improvements in this branch of knowledge. But, since restored to freedom, active minds in Italy have not only revived the study of scientific economics, but have placed themselves at once at the most advanced point which that study has yet reached. The work of Mr. Constantine Baer on "Property and Taxation" shows not only a familiar knowledge of the best English, French, and German authorities, but a mastery of their most improved doctrines not often met with even in England; and along with it, no ordinary degree of the ability required for what is a very different thing from a knowledge of economic truths—the power of applying them. We say this, although we have to add that as regards the specific proposal which the book is written to recommend—a matter not of principle, but of application—we do not consider it to be successful. But we have seldom seen a greater amount of sound practical argument brought to the support of a conclusion that we think practically unsound. Like everything written on such subjects by a person thoroughly competent in knowledge and ability, whether right or wrong on the particular point in question, the discussion is highly instructive.

Mr. Baer's case is this. The primary requisite of just taxation is that every one should be taxed in proportion to his means (*avere*). There are other requisites, as that taxation should not interfere injuriously with the free employment of labour and capital, that it should give the least possible opening to fraud or arbitrary exaction, and so forth: but the first requisite of all is that it should be equal. Mr. Baer ably confutes the standards different from this which have been or are occasionally professed or acted on; particularly the doctrine, which has a considerable hold on many minds, that persons should be taxed more or less according as they are supposed to benefit more or less by the services of the Government, or according as the services they receive cost more or less to the State.

But the main question is, in what sense is equality of means to be understood? and what constitutes a person's means? They are, according to Mr. Baer, of two descriptions: productive (if he have any such) and unproductive. The former are capital, and land employed as a source of income; the latter is his income, such parts excepted as he saves and converts into capital. In order, therefore, to reach the whole of his means, we ought to tax his income, and also his land and capital. An income-tax Mr. Baer rejects, and some of the objections to it are stated by him with much force. Income, in his opinion, is best reached by taxes on consumption, imposed on such articles or modes of outlay as can be taxed without interfering with the channels of industry, and as may be considered fair tests of a person's general expenditure: houses, servants, horses, and carriages Mr. Baer considers to be among the best. Capital and land he would tax by a percentage on their money value, which (as he remarks) represents, in the case of capital, only such part of the income from it as is measured by the ordinary rate of interest, and spares all such part as is either compensation for extra risk, or a return for the skill and industry of the possessor. The tax is to extend to property not yielding income, if of a kind admitting of accumulation, such as houses, furniture, pictures, and sculptures,

The practical means of levying such a tax are discussed in some detail by Mr. Baer, and he succeeds to a great extent in showing that there are accessible criteria which would in most cases enable it to be assessed with little danger of fraud by the taxpayer, or undue exaction by the receiver, and without harassing inquisition into private affairs; while, at the worst, the evils of this sort would be many times less for a tax on capital, than they necessarily are for taxes on income.

The objection which we have to bring against Mr. Baer's scheme of taxation will easily be anticipated. The *avere*, or possessions, of any one, on which taxation is to be grounded, are estimated by a wrong standard. Taxation is to be proportioned to means; but a person's means of paying taxes, or of bearing any other burden of a pecuniary nature, do not consist of his capital *and* his income, but of his capital *or* his income. He possesses them both in the sense of legal control, but only one or other of them for the purposes of his own consumption. His capital, so long as it remains capital, is not consumed by himself, but by the workpeople whom he employs, and the producers of his machinery and material: if he diverts it from their use to his own, it ceases to yield him an income. He can consume either his capital or his income, but not both; and if he is taxed on both, he is taxed twice over on the same means of payment. The maxim that equal means should pay equal taxes has nothing to rest upon unless the means intended are those which are available to pay taxes from. What forms no part of a person's means of expenditure forms no part of his means of paying taxes: while, if he withdraws it from production and employs it as means of expenditure, it pays, while it lasts, additional taxes on expenditure, and so, even in that case, satisfies the claims of financial justice. It is true that though he has no other advantage from his capital while it remains capital, he has a sense of power and importance connected with it; and in consideration of this it may be thought equitable to make him pay something additional to the State. But this is departing from the principle of taxation in proportion to means, and introducing another principle, that of distributive justice; it is laying a tax on an advantageous social position—a measure which, if defensible, must be so on moral or political grounds, not on economical.

Notwithstanding, however, the well-grounded objections on the score of justice, in a merely pecuniary point of view, to which a tax on capital is liable, the subject cannot be altogether disregarded by economists and politicians. No tax is in itself absolutely just; the justice or injustice of taxes can only be comparative: if just in the conception, they are never completely so in the application: and it is quite possible that nations may some day be obliged to resort to a moderate tax on all property, as the least unjust mode of raising a part of their revenue. The many injustices of a direct income-tax are generally acknowledged; while perhaps the greatest of all is that which is the least complained of, that it is a tax on conscience, and a premium on deception and improbity. The increase of commercial dishonesty, so much complained of for many years past, was predicted by good judges as the certain effect of Sir Robert Peel's income-tax; and it will never be known for how much of that evil product the tax may be accountable, or in how many cases a false return of income was the first dereliction of pecuniary integrity. Nevertheless, an income-tax is felt to be indispensable on our present financial system, because without it there are actually no means, recognised by existing opinion, of making the richer classes pay their just share of taxation—a thing which cannot be done by any system of taxes on consumption yet devised. Succession duties are, no doubt, the least objectionable mode of making property, as distinguished from income, contribute directly to the State, and they should be employed as far as practicable; but unless the duty is very light, there is great difficulty in protecting it against evasion. The tax proposed by Mr. Baer may, therefore, some time or other, have to be taken into serious consideration: and should that time come, his remarks on the practical side of the question will be found well worth attending and referring to by those who have to deal with the subject.

CHAPTERS ON SOCIALISM

1879

EDITOR'S NOTE

Fortnightly Review, n.s. XXV (Feb., 1879), 217–37; *ibid.* (Mar., 1879), 373–82; *ibid.* (Apr., 1879), 513–30. Original heading (of all three instalments): "Chapters on Socialism. By John Stuart Mill." As unpublished and incomplete, not mentioned in JSM's *Autobiography* or bibliography (but identified by Ney MacMinn in his introduction, xiin). The best evidence concerning its composition is in the "Preliminary Notice" by Helen Taylor (JSM's step-daughter), which appeared with the first instalment, and is retained here. For an account of the missing manuscript, see the Textual Introduction, xlvii above.

The first instalment contained the first two chapters (including Introductory); the second contained the third chapter; and the third the final two chapters.

Chapters on Socialism

PRELIMINARY NOTICE

IT WAS IN THE YEAR 1869 that, impressed with the degree in which, even during the last twenty years, when the world seemed so wholly occupied with other matters, the socialist ideas of speculative thinkers had spread among the workers in every civilised country, Mr. Mill formed the design of writing a book on Socialism. Convinced that the inevitable tendencies of modern society must be to bring the questions involved in it always more and more to the front, he thought it of great practical consequence that they should be thoroughly and impartially considered, and the lines pointed out by which the best speculatively-tested theories might, without prolongation of suffering on the one hand, or unnecessary disturbance on the other, be applied to the existing order of things. He therefore planned a work which should go exhaustively through the whole subject, point by point; and the four chapters now printed are the first rough drafts thrown down towards the foundation of that work. These chapters might not, when the work came to be completely written out and then re-written, according to the author's habit, have appeared in the present order; they might have been incorporated into different parts of the work. It has not been without hesitation that I have yielded to the urgent wish of the editor of this Review to give these chapters to the world; but I have complied with his request because, while they appear to me to possess great intrinsic value as well as special application to the problems now forcing themselves on public attention, they will not, I believe, detract even from the mere literary reputation of their author, but will rather form an example of the patient labour with which good work is done.

HELEN TAYLOR

January, 1879

INTRODUCTORY

IN THE GREAT COUNTRY beyond the Atlantic, which is now well-nigh the most powerful country in the world, and will soon be indisputably so, manhood suffrage prevails. Such is also the political qualification of France since 1848, and has become that of the German Confederation, though not of all the several states composing it. In Great Britain the suffrage is not yet so widely extended, but the last Reform Act[*] admitted within what is called the pale of the Constitution so large a body of those who live on weekly wages, that as soon and as often as these shall choose to act together as a class, and exert for any common object the whole of the electoral power which our present institutions give them, they will exercise, though not a complete ascendancy, a very great influence on legislation. Now these are the very class which, in the vocabulary of the higher ranks, are said to have no stake in the country. Of course they have in reality the greatest stake, since their daily bread depends on its prosperity. But they are not engaged (we may call it bribed) by any peculiar interest of their own, to the support of property as it is, least of all to the support of inequalities of property. So far as their power reaches, or may hereafter reach, the laws of property have to depend for support upon considerations of a public nature, upon the estimate made of their conduciveness to the general welfare, and not upon motives of a mere personal character operating on the minds of those who have control over the Government.

It seems to me that the greatness of this change is as yet by no means completely realised, either by those who opposed, or by those who effected our last constitutional reform. To say the truth, the perceptions of Englishmen are of late somewhat blunted as to the tendencies of political changes. They have seen so many changes made, from which, while only in prospect, vast expectations were entertained, both of evil and of good, while the results of either kind that actually followed seemed far short of what had been predicted, that they have come to feel as if it were the nature of political changes not to fulfil expectation, and have fallen into a habit of half-unconscious belief that such changes, when they take place without a violent revolution, do not much or permanently disturb in practice the course of things habitual to the country. This, however, is but a superficial view either of the past or of the future. The various reforms of the last two generations have been at least as fruitful in important consequences as was foretold. The predictions were often erroneous as to the suddenness of the effects, and sometimes even as to the kind of effect. We laugh at the vain expectations of those who thought that Catholic emancipation would tranquillise Ireland, or reconcile it to British rule. At the end of the first ten years of the Reform Act of 1832, few continued to think either that it would remove every important practical grievance, or that it had opened the door to universal suffrage. But five-and-twenty years more of its operation have given scope for a large development of its indirect working, which

[*30 & 31 Victoria, c. 102.]

is much more momentous than the direct. Sudden effects in history are generally superficial. Causes which go deep down into the roots of future events produce the most serious parts of their effect only slowly, and have, therefore, time to become a part of the familiar order of things before general attention is called to the changes they are producing; since, when the changes do become evident, they are often not seen, by cursory observers, to be in any peculiar manner connected with the cause. The remoter consequences of a new political fact are seldom understood when they occur, except when they have been appreciated beforehand.

This timely appreciation is particularly easy in respect to the tendencies of the change made in our institutions by the Reform Act of 1867. The great increase of electoral power which the Act places within the reach of the working classes is permanent. The circumstances which have caused them, thus far, to make a very limited use of that power, are essentially temporary. It is known even to the most inobservant, that the working classes have, and are likely to have, political objects which concern them as working classes, and on which they believe, rightly or wrongly, that the interests and opinions of the other powerful classes are opposed to theirs. However much their pursuit of these objects may be for the present retarded by want of electoral organization, by dissensions among themselves, or by their not having reduced as yet their wishes into a sufficiently definite practical shape, it is as certain as anything in politics can be, that they will before long find the means of making their collective electoral power effectively instrumental to the promotion of their collective objects. And when they do so, it will not be in the disorderly and ineffective way which belongs to a people not habituated to the use of legal and constitutional machinery, nor will it be by the impulse of a mere instinct of levelling. The instruments will be the press, public meetings and associations, and the return to Parliament of the greatest possible number of persons pledged to the political aims of the working classes. The political aims will themselves be determined by definite political doctrines; for politics are now scientifically studied from the point of view of the working classes, and opinions conceived in the special interest of those classes are organized into systems and creeds which lay claim to a place on the platform of political philosophy, by the same right as the systems elaborated by previous thinkers. It is of the utmost importance that all reflecting persons should take into early consideration what these popular political creeds are likely to be, and that every single article of them should be brought under the fullest light of investigation and discussion, so that, if possible, when the time shall be ripe, whatever is right in them may be adopted, and what is wrong rejected by general consent, and that instead of a hostile conflict, physical or only moral, between the old and the new, the best parts of both may be combined in a renovated social fabric. At the ordinary pace of those great social changes which are not effected by physical violence, we have before us an interval of about a generation, on the due employment of which it depends whether the accommodation of social institutions to the altered state of human society, shall be the work of wise foresight, or of a conflict of opposite prejudices. The future of mankind will be gravely imperilled, if great questions are left to be fought over between ignorant change and ignorant opposition to change.

And the discussion that is now required is one that must go down to the very first principles of existing society. The fundamental doctrines which were assumed as incontestable by former generations, are now put again on their trial. Until the present age, the institution of property in the shape in which it has been handed down from the past, had not, except by a few speculative writers, been brought seriously into question, because the conflicts of the past have always been conflicts between classes, both of which had a stake in the existing constitution of property. It will not be possible to go on longer in this manner. When the discussion includes classes who have next to no property of their own, and are only interested in the institution so far as it is a public benefit, they will not allow anything to be taken for granted—certainly not the principle of private property, the legitimacy and utility of which are denied by many of the reasoners who look out from the standpoint of the working classes. Those classes will certainly demand that the subject, in all its parts, shall be reconsidered from the foundation; that all proposals for doing without the institution, and all modes of modifying it which have the appearance of being favourable to the interest of the working classes, shall receive the fullest consideration and discussion before it is decided that the subject must remain as it is. As far as this country is concerned, the dispositions of the working classes have as yet manifested themselves hostile only to certain outlying portions of the proprietary system. Many of them desire to withdraw questions of wages from the freedom of contract, which is one of the ordinary attributions of private property. The more aspiring of them deny that land is a proper subject for private appropriation, and have commenced an agitation for its resumption by the State. With this is combined, in the speeches of some of the agitators, a denunciation of what they term usury, but without any definition of what they mean by the name; and the cry does not seem to be of home origin, but to have been caught up from the intercourse which has recently commenced through the Labour Congresses and the International Society, with the continental Socialists who object to all interest on money, and deny the legitimacy of deriving an income in any form from property apart from labour. This doctrine does not as yet show signs of being widely prevalent in Great Britain, but the soil is well prepared to receive the seeds of this description which are widely scattered from those foreign countries where large, general theories, and schemes of vast promise, instead of inspiring distrust, are essential to the popularity of a cause. It is in France, Germany, and Switzerland that anti-property doctrines in the widest sense have drawn large bodies of working men to rally round them. In these countries nearly all those who aim at reforming society in the interest of the working classes profess themselves Socialists, a designation under which schemes of very diverse character are comprehended and confounded, but which implies at least a remodelling generally approaching to abolition of the institution of private property. And it would probably be found that even in England the more prominent and active leaders of the working classes are usually in their private creed Socialists of one order or another, though being, like most English politicians, better aware than their Continental brethren that great and permanent changes in the fundamental ideas of mankind are not to be accomplished by a *coup de main*, they direct their practical efforts towards ends which seem within easier reach, and are content to hold back all extreme theories until there has been experience of the operation of the same principles on a partial scale. While such continues to be the character of the English working classes, as it is of Englishmen in general, they are not likely to rush headlong into the reckless extremities of some of the foreign Socialists, who, even in sober Switzerland, proclaim themselves content to begin by simple subversion, leaving the subsequent reconstruction to take care of itself; and by subversion they mean not only the annihilation of all government, but getting all property of all kinds out of the hands of the possessors to be used for the general benefit; but in what mode it will, they say, be time enough afterwards to decide.

The avowal of this doctrine by a public newspaper, the organ of an association (*La Solidarité*, published at Neuchâtel), is one of the most curious signs of the times. The leaders of the English working men—whose delegates at the congresses of Geneva and Bâle contributed much the greatest part of such practical common sense as was shown there—are not likely to begin deliberately by anarchy, without having formed any opinion as to what form of society should be established in the room of the old. But it is evident that whatever they do propose can only be properly judged, and the grounds of the judgment made convincing to the general mind, on the basis of a previous survey of the two rival theories, that of private property and that of Socialism, one or other of which must necessarily furnish most of the premises in the discussion. Before, therefore, we can usefully discuss this class of questions in detail, it will be advisable to examine from their foundations the general questions raised by Socialism. And this examination should be made without any hostile prejudice. However irrefutable the arguments in favour of the laws of property may appear to those to whom they have the double prestige of immemorial custom and of personal interest, nothing is more natural than that a working man who has begun to speculate on politics, should regard them in a very different light. Having, after long struggles, attained in some countries, and nearly attained in others, the point at which for them, at least, there is no further progress to make in the department of purely political rights, is it possible that the less fortunate classes among the "adult males" should not ask themselves whether progress ought to stop there? Notwithstanding all that has been done, and all that seems likely to be done, in the extension of franchises, a few are born to great riches, and the many to a penury, made only more grating by contrast. No longer enslaved or made dependent by force of law, the great majority are so by force of poverty; they are still chained to a place, to an occupation, and to conformity with the will of an employer, and debarred by the accident of birth both from the enjoyments, and from the mental and moral advantages, which others inherit without exertion and independently of desert. That this is an evil equal to almost any of those against which mankind have hitherto struggled, the poor are not wrong in believing. Is it a necessary evil? They are told so by those who do not feel it—by those who have gained the prizes in the lottery of life. But it was also said that slavery, that despotism, that all the privileges of oligarchy were necessary. All the successive steps that have been made by the poorer classes, partly won from the better feelings of the powerful, partly extorted from their fears, and partly bought with money, or attained in exchange for support given to one section of the powerful in its quarrels with another, had the strongest prejudices opposed to them beforehand; but their acquisition was a sign of power gained by the subordinate classes, a means to those classes of acquiring more; it consequently drew to those classes a certain share of the respect accorded to power, and produced a corresponding modification in the creed of society respecting them; whatever advantages they succeeded in acquiring came to be considered their due, while, of those which they had not yet attained, they continued to be deemed unworthy. The classes, therefore, which the system of society makes subordinate, have little reason to put faith in any of the maxims which the same system of society may have established as principles. Considering that the opinions of mankind have been found so wonderfully flexible, have always tended to consecrate existing facts, and to declare what did not yet exist, either pernicious or impracticable, what assurance have those classes that the distinction of rich and poor is grounded on a more imperative necessity than those other ancient and long-established facts, which, having been abolished, are now condemned even by those who formerly profited by them? This cannot be taken on the word of an interested party. The working classes are entitled to claim that the whole field of social institutions should be re-examined, and every question considered as if it now arose for the first time; with the idea constantly in view that the persons who are to be convinced are not those who owe their ease and importance to the present system, but persons who have no other interest in the matter than abstract justice and the general good of the community. It should be the object to ascertain what institutions of property would be established by an unprejudiced legislator, absolutely impartial between the possessors of property and the non-possessors; and to defend and justify them by the reasons which would really influence such a legislator, and not by such as have the appearance of being got up to make out a case for what already exists. Such rights or privileges of property as will not stand this test will, sooner or later, have to be given up. An impartial hearing ought, moreover, to be given to all objections against property itself. All evils and inconveniences attaching to the institution in its best form ought to be frankly admitted, and the best remedies or palliatives applied which human intelligence is able to devise. And all plans proposed by social reformers, under whatever name designated, for the purpose of attaining the benefits aimed at by the institution of property without its inconveniences, should be examined with the same candour, not prejudged as absurd or impracticable.

SOCIALIST OBJECTIONS TO THE PRESENT ORDER OF SOCIETY

As in all proposals for change there are two elements to be considered—that which is to be changed, and that which it is to be changed to—so in Socialism considered generally, and in each of its varieties taken separately, there are two parts to be distinguished, the one negative and critical, the other constructive. There is, first, the judgment of Socialism on existing institutions and practices and on their results; and secondly, the various plans which it has propounded for doing better. In the former all the different schools of Socialism are at one. They agree almost to identity in the faults which they find with the economical order of existing society. Up to a certain point also they entertain the same general conception of the remedy to be provided for those faults; but in the details, notwithstanding this general agreement, there is a wide disparity. It will be both natural and convenient, in attempting an estimate of their doctrines, to begin with the negative portion which is common to them all, and to postpone all mention of their differences until we arrive at that second part of their undertaking, in which alone they seriously differ.

The first part of our task is by no means difficult; since it consists only in an enumeration of existing evils. Of these there is no scarcity, and most of them are by no means obscure or mysterious. Many of them are the veriest commonplaces of moralists, though the roots even of these lie deeper than moralists usually attempt to penetrate. So various are they that the only difficulty is to make any approach to an exhaustive catalogue. We shall content ourselves for the present with mentioning a few of the principal. And let one thing be remembered by the reader. When item after item of the enumeration passes before him, and he finds one fact after another which he has been accustomed to include among the necessities of nature urged as an accusation against social institutions, he is not entitled to cry unfairness, and to protest that the evils complained of are inherent in Man and Society, and are such as no arrangements can remedy. To assert this would be to beg the very question at issue. No one is more ready than Socialists to admit—they affirm it indeed much more decidedly than truth warrants—that the evils they complain of are irremediable in the present constitution of society. They propose to consider whether some other form of society may be devised which would not be liable to those evils, or would be liable to them in a much less degree. Those who object to the present order of society, considered as a whole, and who accept as an alternative the possibility of a total change, have a right to set down all the evils which at present exist in society as part of their case, whether these are apparently attributable to social arrangements or not, provided they do not flow from physical laws which human power is not adequate, or human knowledge has not yet learned, to counteract. Moral evils, and such physical evils as would be remedied if all persons did as they ought, are fairly chargeable against the state of society which admits of them; and are valid as arguments until it is shown that any other state of society would involve an equal or greater amount of such evils. In the opinion of Socialists, the present arrangements of society in respect to Property and the Production and Distribution of Wealth, are, as means to the general good, a total failure. They say that there is an enormous mass of evil which these arrangements do not succeed in preventing; that the good, either moral or physical, which they realise is wretchedly small compared with the amount of exertion employed, and that even this small amount of good is brought about by means which are full of pernicious consequences, moral and physical.

First among existing social evils may be mentioned the evil of Poverty. The institution of Property is upheld and commended principally as being the means by which labour and frugality are insured their reward, and mankind enabled to emerge from indigence. It may be so; most Socialists allow that it has been so in earlier periods of history. But if the institution can do nothing more or better in this respect than it has hitherto done, its capabilities, they affirm, are very insignificant. What proportion of the population, in the most civilised countries of Europe, enjoy in their own persons anything worth naming of the benefits of property? It may be said, that but for property in the hands of their employers they would be without daily bread; but, though this be conceded, at least their daily bread is all that they have; and that often in insufficient quantity; almost always of inferior quality; and with no assurance of continuing to have it at all; an immense proportion of the industrious classes being at some period or other of their lives (and all being liable to become) dependent, at least temporarily, on legal or voluntary charity. Any attempt to depict the miseries of indigence, or to estimate the proportion of mankind who in the most advanced countries are habitually given up during their whole existence to its physical and moral sufferings, would be superfluous here. This may be left to philanthropists, who have painted these miseries in colours sufficiently strong. Suffice it to say that the condition of numbers in civilised Europe, and even in England and France, is more wretched than that of most tribes of savages who are known to us.

It may be said that of this hard lot no one has any reason to complain, because it befalls those only who are outstripped by others, from inferiority of energy or of prudence. This, even were it true, would be a very small alleviation of the evil. If some Nero or Domitian were to require a hundred persons to run a race for their lives, on condition that the fifty or twenty who came in hindmost should be put to death, it would not be any diminution of the injustice that the strongest or nimblest would, except through some untoward accident, be certain to escape. The misery and the crime would be that any were put to death at all. So in the economy of society; if there be any who suffer physical privation or moral degradation, whose bodily necessities are either not satisfied or satisfied in a manner which only brutish creatures can be content with, this, though not necessarily the crime of society, is *pro tanto* a failure of the social arrangements. And to assert as a mitigation of the evil that those who thus suffer are the weaker members of the community, morally or physically, is to add insult to misfortune. Is weakness a justification of suffering? Is it not, on the contrary, an irresistible claim upon every human being for protection against suffering? If the minds and feelings of the prosperous were in a right state, would they accept their prosperity if for the sake of it even one person near them was, for any other cause than voluntary fault, excluded from obtaining a desirable existence?

One thing there is, which if it could be affirmed truly, would relieve social institutions from any share in the responsibility of these evils. Since the human race has no means of enjoyable existence, or of existence at all, but what it derives from its own labour and abstinence, there would be no ground for complaint against society if every one who was willing to undergo a fair share of this labour and abstinence could attain a fair share of the fruits. But is this the fact? Is it not the reverse of the fact? The reward, instead of being proportioned to the labour and abstinence of the individual, is almost in an inverse ratio to it: those who receive the least, labour and abstain the most. Even the idle, reckless, and ill-conducted poor, those who are said with most justice to have themselves to blame for their condition, often undergo much more and severer labour, not only than those who are born to pecuniary independence, but than almost any of the more highly remunerated of those who earn their subsistence; and even the inadequate self-control exercised by the industrious poor costs them more sacrifice and more effort than is almost ever required from the more favoured members of society. The very idea of distributive justice, or of any proportionality between success and merit, or between success and exertion, is in the present state of society so manifestly chimerical as to be relegated to the regions of romance. It is true that the lot of individuals is not wholly independent of their virtue and intelligence; these do really tell in their favour, but far less than many other things in which there is no merit at all. The most powerful of all the determining circumstances is birth. The great majority are what they were born to be. Some are born rich without work, others are born to a position in which they can become rich *by* work, the great majority are born to hard work and poverty throughout life, numbers to indigence. Next to birth the chief cause of success in life is accident and opportunity. When a person not born to riches succeeds in acquiring them, his own industry and dexterity have generally contributed to the result; but industry and dexterity would not have sufficed unless there had been also a concurrence of occasions and chances which falls to the lot of only a small number. If persons are helped in their worldly career by their virtues, so are they, and perhaps quite as often, by their vices: by servility and sycophancy, by hard-hearted and close-fisted selfishness, by the permitted lies and tricks of trade, by gambling speculations, not seldom by downright knavery. Energies and talents are of much more avail for success in life than virtues; but if one man succeeds by employing energy and talent in something generally useful, another thrives by exercising the same qualities in out-generalling and ruining a rival. It is as much as any moralist ventures to assert, that, other circumstances being given, honesty is the best policy, and that with parity of advantages an honest person has better chances than a rogue. Even this in many stations and circumstances of life is questionable; anything more than this is out of the question. It cannot be pretended that honesty, as a means of success, tells for as much as a difference of one single step on the social ladder. The connection between fortune and conduct is mainly this, that there is a degree of bad conduct, or rather of some kinds of bad conduct, which suffices to ruin any amount of good fortune; but the converse is not true: in the situation of most people no degree whatever of good conduct can be counted upon for raising them in the world, without the aid of fortunate accidents.

These evils, then—great poverty, and that poverty very little connected with desert—are the first grand failure of the existing arrangements of society. The second is human misconduct; crime, vice, and folly, with all the sufferings which follow in their train. For, nearly all the forms of misconduct, whether committed towards ourselves or towards others, may be traced to one of three causes: Poverty and its temptations in the many; Idleness and *désœuvrement* in the few whose circumstances do not compel them to work; bad education, or want of education, in both. The first two must be allowed to be at least failures in the social arrangements, the last is now almost universally admitted to be the fault of those arrangements— it may almost be said the crime. I am speaking loosely and in the rough, for a minuter analysis of the sources of faults of character and errors of conduct would establish far more conclusively the filiation which connects them with a defective organization of society, though it would also show the reciprocal dependence of that faulty state of society on a backward state of the human mind.

At this point, in the enumeration of the evils of society, the mere levellers of former times usually stopped: but their more far-sighted successors, the present Socialists, go farther. In their eyes the very foundation of human life as at present constituted, the very principle on which the production and repartition of all material products is now carried on, is essentially vicious and anti-social. It is the principle of individualism, competition, each one for himself and against all the rest. It is grounded on opposition of interests, not harmony of interests, and under it every one is required to find his place by a struggle, by pushing others back or being pushed back by them. Socialists consider this system of private war (as it may be termed) [*] between every one and every one, especially fatal in an economical point of view and in a moral. Morally considered, its evils are obvious. It is the parent of envy, hatred, and all uncharitableness; it makes every one the natural enemy of all others who cross his path, and every one's path is constantly liable to be crossed. Under the present system hardly any one can gain except by the loss or disappointment of one or of many others. In

[*Cf. Hobbes, Thomas. *Leviathan*, in *English Works*, ed. Molesworth. London: Bohn, 1839, III, p. 115.]

a well-constituted community every one would be a gainer by every other person's successful exertions; while now we gain by each other's loss and lose by each other's gain, and our greatest gains come from the worst source of all, from death, the death of those who are nearest and should be dearest to us. In its purely economical operation the principle of individual competition receives as unqualified condemnation from the social reformers as in its moral. In the competition of labourers they see the cause of low wages; in the competition of producers the cause of ruin and bankruptcy; and both evils, they affirm, tend constantly to increase as population and wealth make progress; no person (they conceive) being benefited except the great proprietors of land, the holders of fixed money incomes, and a few great capitalists, whose wealth is gradually enabling them to undersell all other producers, to absorb the whole of the operations of industry into their own sphere, to drive from the market all employers of labour except themselves, and to convert the labourers into a kind of slaves or serfs, dependent on them for the means of support, and compelled to accept these on such terms as they choose to offer. Society, in short, is travelling onward, according to these speculators, towards a new feudality, that of the great capitalists.

As I shall have ample opportunity in future chapters to state my own opinion on these topics, and on many others connected with and subordinate to them, I shall now, without further preamble, exhibit the opinions of distinguished Socialists on the present arrangements of society, in a selection of passages from their published writings. For the present I desire to be considered as a mere reporter of the opinions of others. Hereafter it will appear how much of what I cite agrees or differs with my own sentiments.

The clearest, the most compact, and the most precise and specific statement of the case of the Socialists generally against the existing order of society in the economical department of human affairs, is to be found in the little work of M. Louis Blanc, *Organisation du Travail*. My first extracts, therefore, on this part of the subject, shall be taken from that treatise.

Competition is for the people a system of extermination. Is the poor man a member of society, or an enemy to it? We ask for an answer.

All around him he finds the soil preoccupied. Can he cultivate the earth for himself? No; for the right of the first occupant has become a right of property. Can he gather the fruits which the hand of God ripens on the path of man? No; for, like the soil, the fruits have been *appropriated*. Can he hunt or fish? No; for that is a right which is dependent upon the government. Can he draw water from a spring enclosed in a field? No; for the proprietor of the field is, in virtue of his right to the field, proprietor of the fountain. Can he, dying of hunger and thirst, stretch out his hands for the charity of his fellow creatures? No; for there are laws against begging. Can he, exhausted by fatigue and without a refuge, lie down to sleep upon the pavement of the streets? No; for there are laws against vagabondage. Can he, flying from the cruel native land where everything is denied him, seek the means of living far from the place where life was given him? No; for it is not permitted to change your country except on certain conditions which the poor man cannot fulfil.

What, then, can the unhappy man do? He will say, 'I have hands to work with, I have intelligence, I have youth, I have strength; take all this, and in return give me a morsel of bread.' This is what the working men do say. But even here the poor man may be answered, 'I have no work to give you.' What is he to do then?

. . . .

What is competition from the point of view of the workman? It is work put up to auction. A contractor wants a workman: three present themselves.—How much for your work?—Half-a-crown: I have a wife and children.—Well; and how much for yours?—Two shillings: I have no children, but I have a wife.— Very well; and now how much for you?—One and eightpence are enough for me; I am single. Then you shall have the work. It is done; the bargain is struck. And what are the other two workmen to do? It is to be hoped they will die quietly of hunger. But what if they take to thieving? Never fear; we have the police. To murder? We have got the hangman. As for the lucky one, his triumph is only temporary. Let a fourth workman make his appearance, strong enough to fast every other day, and his price will run down still lower; then there will be a new outcast, a new recruit for the prison perhaps!

Will it be said that these melancholy results are exaggerated; that at all events they are only possible when there is not work enough for the hands that seek employment? But I ask, in answer, Does the principle of competition contain, by chance, within itself any method by which this murderous dispro- portion is to be avoided? If one branch of industry is in want of hands, who can answer for it that, in the confusion created by universal competition, another is not overstocked? And if, out of thirty-four millions of men, twenty are really reduced to theft for a living, this would suffice to condemn the principle.

But who is so blind as not to see that under the system of unlimited com- petition, the continual fall of wages is no exceptional circumstance, but a necessary and general fact? Has the population a limit which it cannot exceed? Is it possible for us to say to industry—industry given up to the accidents of individual egotism and fertile in ruin—can we say, 'Thus far shalt thou go, and no farther?' The population increases constantly: tell the poor mother to become sterile, and blaspheme the God who made her fruitful, for if you do not the lists will soon become too narrow for the combatants. A machine is invented: command it to be broken, and anathematize science, for if you do not, the thousand workmen whom the new machine deprives of work will knock at the door of the neighbouring workshop, and lower the wages of their com- panions. Thus systematic lowering of wages, ending in the driving out of a certain number of workmen, is the inevitable effect of unlimited competition. It is an industrial system by means of which the working classes are forced to exterminate one another.

. . . .

If there is an undoubted fact, it is that the increase of population is much more rapid among the poor than among the rich. According to the *Statistics of European Population*, the births at Paris are only one-thirty-second of the population in the rich quarters, while in the others they rise to one-twenty-sixth. This disproportion is a general fact, and M. de Sismondi, in his work on Political Economy,[*] has explained it by the impossibility for the workmen of hopeful prudence. Those only who feel themselves assured of the morrow can regulate the number of their children according to their income; he who lives from day to day is under the yoke of a mysterious fatality, to which he sacrifices his children as he was sacrificed to it himself. It is true the workhouses exist, menacing society with an inundation of beggars—what way is there of escaping from the cause? . . . . It is clear that any society where the means of subsistence increase less rapidly than the numbers of the population, is a society on the brink of an abyss. . . . . Competition produces destitution; this is a fact shown by statistics. Destitution is fearfully prolific; this is shown by statistics. The fruitfulness of the poor throws upon society unhappy creatures who have need of work and cannot find it; this is shown by statistics. At this point society is reduced to a choice between killing the poor or maintaining them gratuitously— between atrocity or folly.*

So much for the poor. We now pass to the middle classes.

According to the political economists of the school of Adam Smith and Léon Say, *cheapness* is the word in which may be summed up the advantages of unlimited competition. But why persist in considering the effect of cheapness with a view only to the momentary advantage of the consumer? Cheapness is advantageous to the consumer at the cost of introducing the seeds of ruinous anarchy among the producers. Cheapness is, so to speak, the hammer with which the rich among the producers crush their poorer rivals. Cheapness is the trap into which the daring speculators entice the hard-workers. Cheapness is the sentence of death to the producer on a small scale who has no money to invest in the purchase of machinery that his rich rivals can easily procure. Cheapness is the great instrument in the hands of monopoly; it absorbs the small manufacturer, the small shopkeeper, the small proprietor; it is, in one word, the destruction of the middle classes for the advantage of a few industrial oligarchs.

Ought we, then, to consider cheapness as a curse? No one would attempt to maintain such an absurdity. But it is the speciality of wrong principles to turn good into evil and to corrupt all things. Under the system of competition cheapness is only a provisional and fallacious advantage. It is maintained only so long as there is a struggle; no sooner have the rich competitors driven out their poorer rivals than prices rise. Competition leads to monopoly, for the same reason cheapness leads to high prices. Thus, what has been made use of as a weapon in the contest between the producers, sooner or later becomes a cause of impoverishment among the consumers. And if to this cause we add the others we have already enumerated, first among which must be ranked the inordinate increase of the population, we shall be compelled to recognise the impoverishment of the mass of the consumers as a direct consequence of competition.

[*Sismondi, J.-C.-L. Simonde de. *Nouveaux principes d'économie politique.* 2nd ed. 2 vols. Paris: Delaunay, 1827.]

*See Louis Blanc, "Organisation du Travail," 4me édition, pp. 6, 11, 53, 57. [4th ed. Brussels: Hauman, 1845, pp. 41–2, 43–5, 85–6, 88–9.]

But, on the other hand, this very competition which tends to dry up the sources of demand, urges production to over-supply. The confusion produced by the universal struggle prevents each producer from knowing the state of the market. He must work in the dark and trust to chance for a sale. Why should he check the supply, especially as he can throw any loss on the workman whose wages are so pre-eminently liable to rise and fall? Even when production is carried on at a loss the manufacturers still often carry it on, because they will not let their machinery, &c., stand idle, or risk the loss of raw material, or lose their customers; and because productive industry as carried on under the competitive system being nothing else than a game of chance, the gambler will not lose his chance of a lucky stroke.

Thus, and we cannot too often insist upon it, competition necessarily tends to increase supply and to diminish consumption; its tendency therefore is precisely the opposite of what is sought by economic science; hence it is not merely oppressive but foolish as well.

. . . .

And in all this, in order to avoid dwelling on truths which have become commonplaces and sound declamatory from their very truth, we have said nothing of the frightful moral corruption which industry, organized, or more properly speaking disorganized as it is at the present day, has introduced among the middle classes. Everything has become venal, and competition invades even the domain of thought.

The factory crushing the workshop; the showy establishment absorbing the humble shop; the artisan who is his own master replaced by the day-labourer; cultivation by the plough superseding that by the spade, and bringing the poor man's field under disgraceful homage to the money-lender; bankruptcies multiplied; manufacturing industry transformed by the ill-regulated extension of credit into a system of gambling where no one, not even the rogue, can be sure of winning; in short a vast confusion calculated to arouse jealousy, mistrust, and hatred, and to stifle, little by little, all generous aspirations, all faith, self-sacrifice, and poetry—such is the hideous but only too faithful picture of the results obtained by the application of the principle of competition.*

The Fourierists, through their principal organ, M. Considérant, enumerate the evils of the existing civilisation in the following order:—

1. It employs an enormous quantity of labour and of human power unproductively, or in the work of destruction.

In the first place there is the army, which in France, as in all other countries, absorbs the healthiest and strongest men, a large number of the most talented and intelligent, and a considerable part of the public revenue. . . . . The existing state of society develops in its impure atmosphere innumerable outcasts, whose labour is not merely unproductive, but actually destructive: adventurers, prostitutes, people with no acknowledged means of living, beggars, convicts, swindlers, thieves, and others whose number tends rather to increase than to diminish. . . . .

To the list of unproductive labour fostered by our state of Society must be

*See Louis Blanc, "Organisation du Travail," pp. 58–61, 65–66, 4me édition. Paris, 1845. [Brussels, 1845, pp. 90–3, 97–8.]

added that of the judicature and of the bar, of the courts of law and magistrates, the police, gaolers, executioners, &c.—functions indispensable to the state of society as it is.

Also people of what is called 'good society'; those who pass their lives in doing nothing; idlers of all ranks.

Also the numberless custom-house officials, tax-gatherers, bailiffs, excisemen; in short, all that army of men which overlooks, brings to account, takes, but produces nothing.

Also the labours of sophists, philosophers, metaphysicians, political men, working in mistaken directions, who do nothing to advance science, and produce nothing but disturbance and sterile discussions; the verbiage of advocates, pleaders, witnesses, &c.

And finally all the operations of commerce, from those of the bankers and brokers, down to those of the grocer behind his counter.*

Secondly, they assert that even the industry and powers which in the present system are devoted to production, do not produce more than a small portion of what they might produce if better employed and directed:—

Who with any good-will and reflection will not see how much the want of coherence—the disorder, the want of combination, the parcelling out of labour and leaving it wholly to individual action without any organization, without any large or general views—are causes which limit the possibilities of production and destroy, or at least waste, our means of action? Does not disorder give birth to poverty, as order and good management give birth to riches? Is not want of combination a source of weakness, as combination is a source of strength? And who can say that industry, whether agricultural, domestic, manufacturing, scientific, artistic, or commercial, is organized at the present day either in the state or in municipalities? Who can say that all the work which is carried on in any of these departments is executed in subordination to any general views, or with foresight, economy, and order? Or, again, who can say that it is possible in our present state of society to develop, by a good education, all the faculties bestowed by nature on each of its members; to employ each one in functions which he would like, which he would be the most capable of, and which, therefore, he could carry on with the greatest advantage to himself and to others? Has it even been so much as attempted to solve the problems presented by varieties of character so as to regulate and harmonize the varieties of employments in accordance with natural aptitudes? Alas! The Utopia of the most ardent philanthropists is to teach reading and writing to twenty-five millions of the French people! And in the present state of things we may defy them to succeed even in that!

And is it not a strange spectacle, too, and one which cries out in condemnation of us, to see this state of society where the soil is badly cultivated, and sometimes not cultivated at all; where man is ill lodged, ill clothed, and yet where whole masses are continually in need of work, and pining in misery because they cannot find it? Of a truth we are forced to acknowledge that if the nations are poor and starving it is not because nature has denied the means

*See Considérant, "Destinée Sociale," tome i. pp. 35, 36, 37, 3me éd., Paris [: Librairie phalanstérienne], 1848.

of producing wealth, but because of the anarchy and disorder in our employment of those means; in other words, it is because society is wretchedly constituted and labour unorganized.

But this is not all, and you will have but a faint conception of the evil if you do not consider that to all these vices of society, which dry up the sources of wealth and prosperity, must be added the struggle, the discord, the war, in short, under many names and many forms which society cherishes and cultivates between the individuals that compose it. These struggles and discords correspond to radical oppositions—deep-seated antinomies between the various interests. Exactly in so far as you are able to establish classes and categories within the nation; in so far, also, you will have opposition of interests and internal warfare either avowed or secret, even if you take into consideration the industrial system only.*

One of the leading ideas of this school is the wastefulness and at the same time the immorality of the existing arrangements for distributing the produce of the country among the various consumers, the enormous superfluity in point of number of the agents of distribution, the merchants, dealers, shopkeepers and their innumerable employés, and the depraving character of such a distribution of occupations.

It is evident that the interest of the trader is opposed to that of the consumer and of the producer. Has he not bought cheap and undervalued as much as possible in all his dealings with the producer, the very same article which, vaunting its excellence, he sells to you as dear as he can? Thus the interest of the commercial body, collectively and individually, is contrary to that of the producer and of the consumer—that is to say, to the interest of the whole body of society.

. . . .

The trader is a go-between, who profits by the general anarchy and the non-organization of industry. The trader buys up products, he buys up everything; he owns and detains everything, in such sort that:—

1stly. He holds both Production and Consumption *under his yoke*, because both must come to him either finally for the products to be consumed, or at first for the raw materials to be worked up. Commerce with all its methods of buying, and of raising and lowering prices, its innumerable devices, and its holding everything in the hands of *middle-men*, levies toll right and left: it despotically gives the law to Production and Consumption, of which it ought to be only the subordinate.

2ndly. It robs society by its *enormous profits*—profits levied upon the consumer and the producer, and altogether out of proportion to the services rendered, for which a twentieth of the persons actually employed would be sufficient.

3rdly. It robs society by the subtraction of its productive forces; taking off from productive labour nineteen-twentieths of the agents of trade who are mere parasites. Thus, not only does commerce rob society by appropriating an exorbitant share of the common wealth, but also by considerably diminishing the productive energy of the human beehive. The great majority of traders would

*See "Destinée Sociale," par V. Considérant, tome i., pp. 38–40.

return to productive work if a rational system of commercial organization were substituted for the inextricable chaos of the present state of things.

4thly. It robs society by the *adulteration* of products, pushed at the present day beyond all bounds. And in fact, if a hundred grocers establish themselves in a town where before there were only twenty, it is plain that people will not begin to consume five times as many groceries. Hereupon the hundred virtuous grocers have to dispute between them the profits which before were honestly made by the twenty; competition obliges them to make it up at the expense of the consumer, either by raising the prices as sometimes happens, or by adulterating the goods as always happens. In such a state of things there is an end to good faith. Inferior or adulterated goods are sold for articles of good quality whenever the credulous customer is not too experienced to be deceived. And when the customer has been thoroughly imposed upon, the trading conscience consoles itself by saying, 'I state my price; people can take or leave; no one is obliged to buy.' The losses imposed on the consumers by the bad quality or the adulteration of goods are incalculable.

5thly. It robs society by *accumulations,* artificial or not, in consequence of which vast quantities of goods, collected in one place, are damaged and destroyed for want of a sale. Fourier (Th. des Quat. Mouv., p. 334, 1st ed.) says: 'The fundamental principle of the commercial systems, that of *leaving full liberty to the merchants,* gives them absolute right of property over the goods in which they deal; they have the right to withdraw them altogether, to withhold or even to burn them, as happened more than once with the Oriental Company of Amsterdam, which publicly burnt stores of cinnamon in order to raise the price. What it did with cinnamon it would have done with corn; but for the fear of being stoned by the populace, it would have burnt some corn in order to sell the rest at four times its value. Indeed, it actually is of daily occurrence in ports, for provisions of grains to be thrown into the sea because the merchants have allowed them to rot while waiting for a rise. I myself, when I was a clerk, have had to superintend these infamous proceedings, and in one day caused to be thrown into the sea some forty thousand bushels of rice, which might have been sold at a fair profit had the withholder been less greedy of gain. It is society that bears the cost of this waste, which takes place daily under shelter of the philosophical maxim of *full liberty for the merchants.*'

6thly. Commerce robs society, moreover, by all the loss, damage, and waste that follows from the extreme scattering of products in millions of shops, and by the multiplication and complication of carriage.

7thly. It robs society by shameless and unlimited *usury*—usury absolutely appalling. The trader carries on operations with fictitious capital, much higher in amount than his real capital. A trader with a capital of twelve hundred pounds will carry on operations, by means of bills and credit, on a scale of four, eight, or twelve thousand pounds. Thus he draws from capital *which he does not possess,* usurious interest, out of all proportion with the capital he actually owns.

8thly. It robs society by innumerable *bankruptcies,* for the daily accidents of our commercial system, political events, and any kind of disturbance, must usher in a day when the trader, having incurred obligations beyond his means, is no longer able to meet them; his failure, whether fraudulent or not, must be a severe blow to his creditors. The bankruptcy of some entails that of others, so that bankruptcies follow one upon another, causing widespread ruin. And it is always the producer and the consumer who suffer; for commerce, considered as a whole, does not produce wealth, and invests very little in proportion to the wealth which passes through its hands. How many are the manufactures crushed by these blows! how many fertile sources of wealth dried up by these devices, with all their disastrous consequences!

The producer furnishes the goods, the consumer the money. Trade furnishes credit, founded on little or no actual capital, and the different members of the commercial body are in no way responsible for one another. This, in a few words, is the whole theory of the thing.

9thly. Commerce robs society by the *independence* and *irresponsibility* which permits it to buy at the epochs when the producers are forced to sell and compete with one another, in order to procure money for their rent and necessary expenses of production. When the markets are overstocked and goods cheap, trade purchases. Then it creates a rise, and by this simple manœuvre despoils both producer and consumer.

10thly. It robs society by a considerable *drawing off* of *capital*, which will return to productive industry when commerce plays its proper subordinate part, and is only an agency carrying on transactions between the producers (more or less distant) and the great centres of consumption—the communistic societies. Thus the capital engaged in the speculations of commerce (which, small as it is, compared to the immense wealth which passes through its hands, consists nevertheless of sums enormous in themselves), would return to stimulate production if commerce was deprived of the intermediate property in goods, and their distribution became a matter of administrative organization. Stock-jobbing is the most odious form of this vice of commerce.

11thly. It robs society by the *monopolising* or buying up of raw materials. 'For' (says Fourier, Th. des Quat. Mouv., p. 359, 1st ed.), 'the rise in price on articles that are bought up, is borne ultimately by the consumer, although in the first place by the manufacturers, who, being obliged to keep up their establishments, must make pecuniary sacrifices, and manufacture at small profits in the hope of better days; and it is often long before they can repay themselves the rise in prices which the monopoliser has compelled them to support in the first instance. . . . .'

In short, all these vices, besides many others which I omit, are multiplied by the extreme complication of mercantile affairs; for products do not pass once only through the greedy clutches of commerce; there are some which pass and repass twenty or thirty times before reaching the consumer. In the first place, the raw material passes through the grasp of commerce before reaching the manufacturer who first works it up; then it returns to commerce to be sent out again to be worked up in a second form; and so on until it receives its final shape. Then it passes into the hands of merchants, who sell to the wholesale dealers, and these to the great retail dealers of towns, and these again to the little dealers and to the country shops; and each time that it changes hands, it leaves something behind it.

. . . . One of my friends who was lately exploring the Jura, where much working in metal is done, had occasion to enter the house of a peasant who was a manufacturer of shovels. He asked the price. 'Let us come to an understanding,' answered the poor labourer, not an economist at all, but a man of common sense; 'I sell them for 8*d*. to the trade, which retails them at 1*s*. 8*d*. in the towns.

ESSAYS ON ECONOMICS AND SOCIETY

If you could find a means of opening a direct communication between the workman and the consumer, you might have them for 1*s*. 2*d*., and we should each gain 6*d*. by the transaction.'*

To a similar effect Owen, in the *Book of the New Moral World*, part 2, chap. iii.[*]

The principle now in practice is to induce a large portion of society to devote their lives to distribute wealth upon a large, a medium, and a small scale, and to have it conveyed from place to place in larger or smaller quantities, to meet the means and wants of various divisions of society and individuals, as they are now situated in cities, towns, villages, and country places. This principle of distribution makes a class in society whose business it is to *buy from* some parties and to *sell to* others. By this proceeding they are placed under circumstances which induce them to endeavour to buy at what appears at the time a low price in the market, and to sell again at the greatest permanent profit which they can obtain. Their real object being to get as much profit as gain between the seller to, and the buyer from them, as can be effected in their transactions.

There are innumerable errors in principle and evils in practice which necessarily proceed from this mode of distributing the wealth of society.

1st. A general class of distributers is formed, whose interest is separated from, and apparently opposed to, that of the individual from whom they buy and to whom they sell.

2nd. Three classes of distributers are made, the small, the medium, and the large buyers and sellers; or the retailers, the wholesale dealers, and the extensive merchants.

3rd. Three classes of buyers thus created constitute the small, the medium, and the large purchasers.

By this arrangement into various classes of buyers and sellers, the parties are easily trained to learn that they have separate and opposing interests, and different ranks and stations in society. An inequality of feeling and condition is thus created and maintained, with all the servility and pride which these unequal arrangements are sure to produce. The parties are regularly trained in a general system of deception, in order that they may be the more successful in buying cheap and selling dear.

The smaller sellers acquire habits of injurious idleness, waiting often for hours for customers. And this evil is experienced to a considerable extent even amongst the class of wholesale dealers.

There are, also, by this arrangement, many more establishments for selling than are necessary in the villages, towns, and cities; and a very large capital is thus wasted without benefit to society. And from their number opposed to each other all over the country to obtain customers, they endeavour to undersell each other, and are therefore continually endeavouring to injure the producer by the establishment of what are called cheap shops and warehouses; and to support their character the master or his servants must be continually on the watch to buy bargains, that is, to procure wealth for less than the cost of its production.

*See Considérant, "Destinée Sociale," tome i. pp. 43–51, 3me édition, Paris, 1848.

[*London: Home Colonization Society, 1842, pp. 20–3.]

The distributers, small, medium, and large, have all to be supported by the producers, and the greater the number of the former compared with the latter, the greater will be the burden which the producer has to sustain; for as the number of distributers increases, the accumulation of wealth must decrease, and more must be required from the producer.

The distributers of wealth, under the present system, are a dead weight upon the producers, and are most active demoralisers of society. Their dependent condition, at the commencement of their task, teaches or induces them to be servile to their customers, and to continue to be so as long as they are accumulating wealth by their cheap buying and dear selling. But when they have secured sufficient to be what they imagine to be an independence—to live without business—they are too often filled with a most ignorant pride, and become insolent to their dependents.

The arrangement is altogether a most improvident one for society, whose interest it is to produce the greatest amount of wealth of the best qualities; while the existing system of distribution is not only to withdraw great numbers from producing to become distributors, but to add to the cost of the consumer all the expense of a most wasteful and extravagant distribution; the distribution costing to the consumer many times the price of the original cost of the wealth purchased.

Then, by the position in which the seller is placed by his created desire for gain on the one hand, and the competition he meets with from opponents selling similar productions on the other, he is strongly tempted to deteriorate the articles which he has for sale; and when these are provisions, either of home producing to become distributers, but to add to the cost of the consumer all the quent comfort and happiness of the consumers, are often most injurious, and productive of much premature death, especially among the working classes, who, in this respect, are perhaps made to be the greatest sufferers, by purchasing the inferior or low-priced articles. . . . .

The expense of thus distributing wealth in Great Britain and Ireland, including transit from place to place, and all the agents directly and indirectly engaged in this department, is, perhaps, little short of one hundred millions annually, without taking into consideration the deterioration of the quality of many of the articles constituting this wealth, by carriage, and by being divided into small quantities, and kept in improper stores and places, in which the atmosphere is unfavourable to the keeping of such articles in a tolerably good, and much less in the best, condition for use.

In further illustration of the contrariety of interests between person and person, class and class, which pervades the present constitution of society, M. Considérant adds:—

If the wine-growers wish for free trade, this freedom ruins the producer of corn, the manufacturers of iron, of cloth, of cotton, and—we are compelled to add—the smuggler and the customs' officer. If it is the interest of the consumer that machines should be invented which lower prices by rendering production less costly, these same machines throw out of work thousands of workmen who do not know how to, and cannot at once, find other work. Here, then, again is one of the innumerable *vicious circles* of civilisation . . . . for there are a thousand facts which prove cumulatively that in our existing social system the introduction of any good brings always along with it some evil.

In short, if we go lower down and come to vulgar details, we find that it is the interest of the tailor, the shoemaker, and the hatter that coats, shoes, and hats should be soon worn out; that the glazier profits by the hail-storms which break windows; that the mason and the architect profit by fires; the lawyer is enriched by law-suits; the doctor by disease; the wine-seller by drunkenness; the prostitute by debauchery. And what a disaster would it be for the judges, the police, and the gaolers, as well as for the barristers and the solicitors, and all the lawyers' clerks, if crimes, offences, and law-suits were all at once to come to an end!*

The following is one of the cardinal points of this school:—

Add to all this, that civilisation, which sows dissension and war on every side; which employs a great part of its powers in unproductive labour, or even in destruction; which furthermore diminishes the public wealth by the unnecessary friction and discord it introduces into industry; add to all this, I say, that this same social system has for its special characteristic to produce a repugnance for work—a disgust for labour.

Everywhere you hear the labourer, the artisan, the clerk complain of his position and his occupation, while they long for the time when they can retire from work imposed upon them by necessity. To be repugnant, to have for its motive and pivot nothing but the fear of starvation, is the great, the fatal, characteristic of civilised labour. The civilised workman is condemned to penal servitude. So long as productive labour is so organized that instead of being associated with pleasure it is associated with pain, weariness and dislike, it will alway happen that all will avoid it who are able. With few exceptions, those only will consent to work who are compelled to it by want. Hence the most numerous classes, the artificers of social wealth, the active and direct creators of all comfort and luxury, will always be condemned to touch closely on poverty and hunger; they will always be the slaves to ignorance and degradation; they will continue to be always that huge herd of mere beasts of burden whom we see ill-grown, decimated by disease, bowed down in the great workshop of society over the plough or over the counter, that they may prepare the delicate food, and the sumptuous enjoyments of the upper and idle classes.

So long as no method of attractive labour has been devised, it will continue to be true that 'there must be many poor in order that there may be a few rich;' a mean and hateful saying, which we hear every day quoted as an eternal truth from the mouths of people who call themselves Christians or philosophers! It is very easy to understand that oppression, trickery, and especially poverty, are the permanent and fatal appanage of every state of society characterized by the dislike of work, for, in this case, there is nothing but poverty that will force men to labour. And the proof of this is, that if every one of all the workers were to become suddenly rich, nineteen-twentieths of all the work now done would be abandoned.†

In the opinion of the Fourierists, the tendency of the present order of society is to a concentration of wealth in the hands of a comparatively few immensely rich individuals or companies, and the reduction of all the rest

*Considérant, "Destinée Sociale," tome i., pp. 59–60.
†Ibid., pp. 60–1.

of the community into a complete dependence on them. This was termed by Fourier *la féodalité industrielle.*

This feudalism, [says M. Considérant,] would be constituted as soon as the largest part of the industrial and territorial property of the nation belongs to a minority which absorbs all its revenues, while the great majority, chained to the work-bench or labouring on the soil, must be content to gnaw the pittance which is cast to them.*

This disastrous result is to be brought about partly by the mere progress of competition, as sketched in our previous extract by M. Louis Blanc; assisted by the progress of national debts, which M. Considérant regards as mortgages of the whole land and capital of the country, of which "les capitalistes prêteurs" become, in a greater and greater measure, co-proprietors, receiving without labour or risk an increasing portion of the revenues.

THE SOCIALIST OBJECTIONS TO THE PRESENT ORDER OF SOCIETY EXAMINED

It is impossible to deny that the considerations brought to notice in the preceding chapter make out a frightful case either against the existing order of society, or against the position of man himself in this world. How much of the evils should be referred to the one, and how much to the other, is the principal theoretic question which has to be resolved. But the strongest case is susceptible of exaggeration; and it will have been evident to many readers, even from the passages I have quoted, that such exaggeration is not wanting in the representations of the ablest and most candid Socialists. Though much of their allegations is unanswerable, not a little is the result of errors in political economy; by which, let me say once for all, I do not mean the rejection of any practical rules of policy which have been laid down by political economists, I mean ignorance of economic facts, and of the causes by which the economic phenomena of society as it is, are actually determined.

In the first place, it is unhappily true that the wages of ordinary labour, in all the countries of Europe, are wretchedly insufficient to supply the physical and moral necessities of the population in any tolerable measure. But, when it is further alleged that even this insufficient remuneration has a tendency to diminish; that there is, in the words of M. Louis Blanc, *une baisse continue des salaires*; the assertion is in opposition to all accurate information, and to many notorious facts. It has yet to be proved that there

Ibid., p. 134.

is any country in the civilised world where the ordinary wages of labour, estimated either in money or in articles of consumption, are declining; while in many they are, on the whole, on the increase; and an increase which is becoming, not slower, but more rapid. There are, occasionally, branches of industry which are being gradually superseded by something else, and, in those, until production accommodates itself to demand, wages are depressed; which is an evil, but a temporary one, and would admit of great alleviation even in the present system of social economy. A diminution thus produced of the reward of labour in some particular employment is the effect and the evidence of increased remuneration, or of a new source of remuneration, in some other; the total and the average remuneration being undiminished, or even increased. To make out an appearance of diminution in the rate of wages in any leading branch of industry, it is always found necessary to compare some month or year of special and temporary depression at the present time, with the average rate, or even some exceptionally high rate, at an earlier time. The vicissitudes are no doubt a great evil, but they were as frequent and as severe in former periods of economical history as now. The greater scale of the transactions, and the greater number of persons involved in each fluctuation, may make the fluctuation appear greater, but though a larger population affords more sufferers, the evil does not weigh heavier on each of them individually. There is much evidence of improvement, and none, that is at all trustworthy, of deterioration, in the mode of living of the labouring population of the countries of Europe; when there is any appearance to the contrary it is local or partial, and can always be traced either to the pressure of some temporary calamity, or to some bad law or unwise act of government which admits of being corrected, while the permanent causes all operate in the direction of improvement.

M. Louis Blanc, therefore, while showing himself much more enlightened than the older school of levellers and democrats, inasmuch as he recognises the connection between low wages and the over-rapid increase of population, appears to have fallen into the same error which was at first committed by Malthus and his followers, that of supposing that because population has a greater power of increase than subsistence, its pressure upon subsistence must be always growing more severe. The difference is that the early Malthusians thought this an irrepressible tendency, while M. Louis Blanc thinks that it can be repressed, but only under a system of Communism. It is a great point gained for truth when it comes to be seen that the tendency to over-population is a fact which Communism, as well as the existing order of society, would have to deal with. And it is much to be rejoiced at that this necessity is admitted by the most considerable chiefs of all existing schools of Socialism. Owen and Fourier, no less than M. Louis Blanc, admitted it, and claimed for their respective systems a pre-eminent power of dealing with this difficulty. However this may be, experience shows that in the existing state of society the pressure of population on subsistence, which is the principal cause of low wages, though a great, is not an increasing evil; on the contrary, the progress of all that is called civilisation has a tendency to diminish it, partly by the more rapid increase of the means of employing and maintaining labour, partly by the increased facilities opened to labour for transporting itself to new countries and unoccupied fields of employment, and partly by a general improvement in the intelligence and prudence of the population. This progress, no doubt, is slow; but it is much that such progress should take place at all, while we are still only in the first stage of that public movement for the education of the whole people, which when more advanced must add greatly to the force of all the two causes of improvement specified above. It is, of course, open to discussion what form of society has the greatest power of dealing successfully with the pressure of population on subsistence, and on this question there is much to be said for Socialism; what was long thought to be its weakest point will, perhaps, prove to be one of its strongest. But it has no just claim to be considered as the sole means of preventing the general and growing degradation of the mass of mankind through the peculiar tendency of poverty to produce over-population. Society as at present constituted is not descending into that abyss, but gradually, though slowly, rising out of it, and this improvement is likely to be progressive if bad laws do not interfere with it.

Next, it must be observed that Socialists generally, and even the most enlightened of them, have a very imperfect and one-sided notion of the operation of competition. They see half its effects, and overlook the other half; they regard it as an agency for grinding down every one's remuneration—for obliging every one to accept less wages for his labour, or a less price for his commodities, which would be true only if every one had to dispose of his labour or his commodities to some great monopolist, and the competition were all on one side. They forget that competition is a cause of high prices and values as well as of low; that the buyers of labour and of commodities compete with one another as well as the sellers; and that if it is competition which keeps the prices of labour and commodities as low as they are, it is competition which prevents them from falling still lower. In truth, when competition is perfectly free on both sides, its tendency is not specially either to raise or to lower the price of articles, but to equalise it; to level inequalities of remuneration, and to reduce all to a general average, a result which, in so far as realised (no doubt very imperfectly), is, on Socialistic principles, desirable. But if, disregarding for the time that part of the effects of competition which consists in keeping up prices, we fix our attention on its effect in keeping them down, and contemplate this effect in reference solely to the interest of the labouring classes, it would seem that if competition keeps down wages, and so gives a motive to the labouring classes to withdraw the labour market from the full influence of competition, if they can, it must on the other hand have credit for keeping down the prices of the articles on which wages are expended, to the great advantage of those who depend on wages. To meet this consideration Socialists, as we said in our quotation from M. Louis Blanc,[*] are reduced to affirm that the low prices of commodities produced by competition are delusive, and lead in the end to higher prices than before, because when the richest competitor has got rid of all his rivals, he commands the market and can demand any price he pleases. Now, the commonest experience shows that this state of things, under really free competition, is wholly imaginary. The richest competitor neither does nor can get rid of all his rivals, and establish himself in exclusive possession of the market; and it is not the fact that any important branch of industry or commerce formerly divided among many has become, or shows any tendency to become, the monopoly of a few.

The kind of policy described is sometimes possible where, as in the case of railways, the only competition possible is between two or three great companies, the operations being on too vast a scale to be within the reach of individual capitalists; and this is one of the reasons why businesses which require to be carried on by great joint-stock enterprises cannot be trusted to competition, but, when not reserved by the State to itself, ought to be carried on under conditions prescribed, and, from time to time, varied by the State, for the purpose of insuring to the public a cheaper supply of its wants than would be afforded by private interest in the absence of sufficient competition. But in the ordinary branches of industry no one rich competitor has it in his power to drive out all the smaller ones. Some businesses show a tendency to pass out of the hands of many small producers or dealers into a smaller number of larger ones; but the cases in which this happens are those in which the possession of a larger capital permits the adoption of more powerful machinery, more efficient by more expensive processes, or a better organized and more economical mode of carrying on business, and thus enables the large dealer legitimately and permanently to supply the commodity cheaper than can be done on the small scale; to the great advantage of the consumers, and therefore of the labouring classes, and diminishing, *pro tanto*, that waste of the resources of the community so much complained of by Socialists, the unnecessary multiplication of mere distributors, and of the various other classes whom Fourier calls the parasites of industry. When this change is effected, the larger capitalists, either individual or joint-stock, among which the business is divided, are seldom, if ever, in any considerable branch of commerce, so few as that

[*Pp. 718–19 above.]

competition shall not continue to act between them; so that the saving in cost, which enabled them to undersell the small dealers, continues afterwards, as at first, to be passed on, in lower prices, to their customers. The operation, therefore, of competition in keeping down the prices of commodities, including those on which wages are expended, is not illusive but real, and, we may add, is a growing, not a declining, fact.

But there are other respects, equally important, in which the charges brought by Socialists against competition do not admit of so complete an answer. Competition is the best security for cheapness, but by no means a security for quality. In former times, when producers and consumers were less numerous, it was a security for both. The market was not large enough nor the means of publicity sufficient to enable a dealer to make a fortune by continually attracting new customers: his success depended on his retaining those that he had; and when a dealer furnished good articles, or when he did not, the fact was soon known to those whom it concerned, and he acquired a character for honest or dishonest dealing of more importance to him than the gain that would be made by cheating casual purchasers. But on the great scale of modern transactions, with the great multiplication of competition and the immense increase in the quantity of business competed for, dealers are so little dependent on permanent customers that character is much less essential to them, while there is also far less certainty of their obtaining the character they deserve. The low prices which a tradesman advertises are known, to a thousand for one who has discovered for himself or learned from others, that the bad quality of the goods is more than an equivalent for their cheapness; while at the same time the much greater fortunes now made by some dealers excite the cupidity of all, and the greed of rapid gain substitutes itself for the modest desire to make a living by their business. In this manner, as wealth increases and greater prizes seem to be within reach, more and more of a gambling spirit is introduced into commerce; and where this prevails not only are the simplest maxims of prudence disregarded, but all, even the most perilous, forms of pecuniary improbity receive a terrible stimulus. This is the meaning of what is called the intensity of modern competition. It is further to be mentioned that when this intensity has reached a certain height, and when a portion of the producers of an article or the dealers in it have resorted to any of the modes of fraud, such as adulteration, giving short measure, &c., of the increase of which there is now so much complaint, the temptation is immense on these to adopt the fraudulent practices, who would not have originated them; for the public are aware of the low prices fallaciously produced by the frauds, but do not find out at first, if ever, that the article is not worth the lower price, and they will not go on paying a higher price for a better article, and the honest dealer is placed at a terrible disadvantage. Thus the frauds, begun by a few, become customs of the trade, and the morality of the trading classes is more and more deteriorated.

On this point, therefore, Socialists have really made out the existence not only of a great evil, but of one which grows and tends to grow with the growth of population and wealth. It must be said, however, that society has never yet used the means which are already in its power of grappling with this evil. The laws against commercial frauds are very defective, and their execution still more so. Laws of this description have no chance of being really enforced unless it is the special duty of some one to enforce them. They are specially in need of a public prosecutor. It is still to be discovered how far it is possible to repress by means of the criminal law a class of misdeeds which are now seldom brought before the tribunals, and to which, when brought, the judicial administration of this country is most unduly lenient. The most important class, however, of these frauds, to the mass of the people, those which affect the price or quality of articles of daily consumption, can be in a great measure overcome by the institution of co-operative stores. By this plan any body of consumers who form themselves into an association for the purpose, are enabled to pass over the retail dealers and obtain their articles direct from the wholesale merchants, or, what is better (now that wholesale co-operative agencies have been established), from the producers, thus freeing themselves from the heavy tax now paid to the distributing classes and at the same time eliminate the usual perpetrators of adulterations and other frauds. Distribution thus becomes a work performed by agents selected and paid by those who have no interest in anything but the cheapness and goodness of the article; and the distributors are capable of being thus reduced to the numbers which the quantity of work to be done really requires. The difficulties of the plan consist in the skill and trustworthiness required in the managers, and the imperfect nature of the control which can be exercised over them by the body at large. The great success and rapid growth of the system prove, however, that these difficulties are, in some tolerable degree, overcome. At all events, if the beneficial tendency of the competition of retailers in promoting cheapness is foregone, and has to be replaced by other securities, the mischievous tendency of the same competition in deteriorating quality is at any rate got rid of; and the prosperity of the co-operative stores shows that this benefit is obtained not only without detriment to cheapness, but with great advantage to it, since the profits of the concerns enable them to return to the consumers a large percentage on the price of every article supplied to them. So far, therefore, as this class of evils is concerned, an effectual remedy is already in operation, which, though suggested by and partly grounded on socialistic principles, is consistent with the existing constitution of property.

With regard to those greater and more conspicuous economical frauds, or malpractices equivalent to frauds, of which so many deplorable cases have become notorious—committed by merchants and bankers between themselves or between them and those who have trusted them with money, such a remedy as above described is not available, and the only resources which the present constitution of society affords against them are a sterner reprobation by opinion, and a more efficient repression by the law. Neither of these remedies has had any approach to an effectual trial. It is on the occurrence of insolvencies that these dishonest practices usually come to light; the perpetrators take their place, not in the class of malefactors, but in that of insolvent debtors; and the laws of this and other countries were formerly so savage against simple insolvency, that by one of those reactions to which the opinions of mankind are liable, insolvents came to be regarded mainly as objects of compassion, and it seemed to be thought that the hand both of law and of public opinion could hardly press too lightly upon them. By an error in a contrary direction to the ordinary one of our law, which in the punishment of offences in general wholly neglects the question of reparation to the sufferer, our bankruptcy laws have for some time treated the recovery for creditors of what is left of their property as almost the sole object, scarcely any importance being attached to the punishment of the bankrupt for any misconduct which does not directly interfere with that primary purpose. For three or four years past there has been a slight counter-reaction, and more than one bankruptcy act has been passed, somewhat less indulgent to the bankrupt; but the primary object regarded has still been the pecuniary interest of the creditors, and criminality in the bankrupt himself, with the exception of a small number of well-marked offences, gets off almost with impunity. It may be confidently affirmed, therefore, that, at least in this country, society has not exerted the power it possesses of making mercantile dishonesty dangerous to the perpetrator. On the contrary, it is a gambling trick in which all the advantage is on the side of the trickster: if the trick succeeds it makes his fortune, or preserves it; if it fails, he is at most reduced to poverty, which was perhaps already impending when he determined to run the chance, and he is classed by those who have not looked closely into the matter, and even by many who have, not among the infamous but among the unfortunate. Until a more moral and rational mode of dealing with culpable insolvency has been tried and failed, commercial dishonesty cannot be ranked among evils the prevalence of which is inseparable from commercial competition.

Another point on which there is much misapprehension on the part of Socialists, as well as of Trades Unionists and other partisans of Labour against Capital, relates to the proportions in which the produce of the country is really shared and the amount of what is actually diverted from those who produce it, to enrich other persons. I forbear for the present to speak of the land, which is a subject apart. But with respect to capital employed in business, there is in the popular notions a great deal of illusion. When, for instance, a capitalist invests £20,000 in his business, and draws from it an income of (suppose) £2,000 a year, the common impression is as if he was the beneficial owner both of the £20,000 and of the £2,000, while the labourers own nothing but their wages. The truth, however, is that he only obtains the £2,000 on condition of applying no part of the £20,000 to his own use. He has the legal control over it, and might squander it if he chose, but if he did he would not have the £2,000 a year also. As long as he derives an income from his capital he has not the option of withholding it from the use of others. As much of his invested capital as consists of buildings, machinery and other instruments of production, are applied to production and are not applicable to the support or enjoyment of any one. What is so applicable (including what is laid out in keeping up or renewing the buildings and instruments) is paid away to labourers, forming their remuneration and their share in the division of the produce. For all personal purposes they have the capital and he has but the profits, which it only yields to him on condition that the capital itself is employed in satisfying not his own wants, but those of labourers. The proportion which the profits of capital usually bear to the capital itself (or rather to the circulating portion of it) is the ratio which the capitalist's share of the produce bears to the aggregate share of the labourers. Even of his own share a small part only belongs to him as the owner of capital. The portion of the produce which falls to capital merely as capital is measured by the interest of money, since that is all that the owner of capital obtains when he contributes nothing to production except the capital itself. Now the interest of capital in the public funds, which are considered to be the best security, is at the present prices (which have not varied much for many years) about three and one-third per cent. Even in this investment there is some little risk—risk of repudiation, risk of being obliged to sell out at a low price in some commercial crisis.

Estimating these risks at ⅓ per cent., the remaining 3 per cent. may be considered as the remuneration of capital, apart from insurance against loss. On the security of a mortgage 4 per cent. is generally obtained, but in this transaction there are considerably greater risks—the uncertainty of titles to land under our bad system of law; the chance of having to realise the security at a great cost in law charges; and liability to delay in the receipt of the interest, even when the principal is safe. When mere money independently of exertion yields a larger income, as it sometimes does, for example, by shares in railway or other companies, the surplus is hardly ever an equivalent for the risk of losing the whole, or part, of the capital by mismanagement, as in the case of the Brighton Railway, the dividend of which, after having been 6 per cent. per annum, sunk to from nothing to 1½ per cent., and shares which had been bought at 120 could not be sold for more than about 43. When money is lent at the high rates of interest one occasionally hears of, rates only given by spendthrifts and needy persons, it is because the risk of loss is so great that few who possess money can be induced to lend to them at all. So little reason is there for the outcry against "usury" as one of the grievous burthens of the working classes. Of the profits, therefore, which a manufacturer or other person in business obtains from his capital no more than about 3 per cent. can be set down to the capital itself. If he were able and willing to give up the whole of this to his labourers, who already share among them the whole of his capital as it is annually reproduced from year to year, the addition to their weekly wages would be inconsiderable. Of what he obtains beyond 3 per cent. a great part is insurance against the manifold losses he is exposed to, and cannot safely be applied to his own use, but requires to be kept in reserve to cover those losses when they occur. The remainder is properly the remuneration of his skill and industry—the wages of his labour of superintendence. No doubt if he is very successful in business these wages of his are extremely liberal, and quite out of proportion to what the same skill and industry would command if offered for hire. But, on the other hand, he runs a worse risk than that of being out of employment; that of doing the work without earning anything by it, of having the labour and anxiety without the wages. I do not say that the drawbacks balance the privileges, or that he derives no advantage from the position which makes him a capitalist and employer of labour, instead of a skilled superintendent letting out his services to others; but the amount of his advantage must not be estimated by the great prizes alone. If we subtract from the gains of some the losses of others, and deduct from the balance a fair compensation for the anxiety, skill, and labour of both, grounded on the market price of skilled superintendence, what remains will be, no doubt, considerable, but yet, when compared to the entire capital of the country, annually reproduced and dispensed in wages, it is very much smaller than it appears to the popular imagination; and were the whole of it added to the share of the labourers it would make a less addition to that share than would be made by any important invention in machinery, or by the suppression of unnecessary distributors and other "parasites of industry." To complete the estimate, however, of the portion of the produce of industry which goes to remunerate capital we must not stop at the interest earned out of the produce by the capital actually employed in producing it, but must include that which is paid to the former owners of capital which has been unproductively spent and no longer exists, and is paid, of course, out of the produce of other capital. Of this nature is the interest of national debts, which is the cost a nation is burthened with for past difficulties and dangers, or for past folly or profligacy of its rulers, more or less shared by the nation itself. To this must be added the interest on the debts of landowners and other unproductive consumers; except so far as the money borrowed may have been spent in remunerative improvement of the productive powers of the land. As for landed property itself—the appropriation of the rent of land by private individuals—I reserve, as I have said, this question for discussion hereafter; for the tenure of land might be varied in any manner considered desirable, all the land might be declared the property of the State, without interfering with the right of property in anything which is the product of human labour and abstinence.

It seemed desirable to begin the discussion of the Socialist question by these remarks in abatement of Socialist exaggerations, in order that the true issues between Socialism and the existing state of society might be correctly conceived. The present system is not, as many Socialists believe, hurrying us into a state of general indigence and slavery from which only Socialism can save us. The evils and injustices suffered under the present system are great, but they are not increasing; on the contrary, the general tendency is towards their slow diminution. Moreover the inequalities in the distribution of the produce between capital and labour, however they may shock the feeling of natural justice, would not by their mere equalisation afford by any means so large a fund for raising the lower levels of remuneration as Socialists, and many besides Socialists, are apt to suppose. There is not any one abuse or injustice now prevailing in society by merely abolishing which the human race would pass out of suffering into happiness. What is incumbent on us is a calm comparison between two different systems of society, with a view of determining which of them affords the greatest resources for overcoming the inevitable difficulties of life. And if we find the answer to this question more difficult, and more dependent upon intellectual and moral conditions, than is usually thought, it is satisfactory to reflect that there is time before us for the question to work itself out on an experimental scale, by actual trial. I believe we shall find that no other test is possible of the practicability or beneficial operation of Socialist arrangements; but that the intellectual and moral grounds of Socialism deserve the most attentive study, as affording in many cases the guiding principles of the improvements necessary to give the present economic system of society its best chance.

THE DIFFICULTIES OF SOCIALISM

Among those who call themselves Socialists, two kinds of persons may be distinguished. There are, in the first place, those whose plans for a new order of society, in which private property and individual competition are to be superseded and other motives to action substituted, are on the scale of a village community or township, and would be applied to an entire country by the multiplication of such self-acting units; of this character are the systems of Owen, of Fourier, and the more thoughtful and philosophic Socialists generally. The other class, who are more a product of the Continent than of Great Britain and may be called the revolutionary Socialists, propose to themselves a much bolder stroke. Their scheme is the management of the whole productive resources of the country by one central authority, the general government. And with this view some of them avow as their purpose that the working classes, or somebody in their behalf, should take possession of all the property of the country, and administer it for the general benefit.

Whatever be the difficulties of the first of these two forms of Socialism, the second must evidently involve the same difficulties and many more. The former, too, has the great advantage that it can be brought into operation progressively, and can prove its capabilities by trial. It can be tried first on a select population and extended to others as their education and cultivation permit. It need not, and in the natural order of things would not, become an engine of subversion until it had shown itself capable of being also a means of reconstruction. It is not so with the other: the aim of that is to substitute the new rule for the old at a single stroke, and to exchange the amount of good realised under the present system, and its large possibilities of improvement, for a plunge without any preparation into the most extreme form of the problem of carrying on the whole round of the operations of social life without the motive power which has always hitherto worked the social machinery. It must be acknowledged that those who would play this game on the strength of their own private opinion, unconfirmed as yet by any experimental verification—who would forcibly deprive all who have now a comfortable physical existence of their only present means of preserving it, and would brave the frightful bloodshed and misery that would ensue if the attempt was resisted—must have a serene confidence in their own wisdom on the one hand and a recklessness of other people's sufferings on the other, which Robespierre and St. Just, hitherto the typical instances of those united attributes, scarcely came up to. Nevertheless this scheme has great elements of popularity which the more cautious and reasonable form of Socialism has not; because what it professes to do it promises to do quickly, and holds out hope to the enthusiastic of seeing the whole of their aspirations realised in their own time and at a blow.

The peculiarities, however, of the revolutionary form of Socialism will be most conveniently examined after the considerations common to both the forms have been duly weighed.

The produce of the world could not attain anything approaching to its present amount, nor support anything approaching to the present number of its inhabitants, except upon two conditions: abundant and costly machinery, buildings, and other instruments of production; and the power of undertaking long operations and waiting a considerable time for their fruits. In other words, there must be a large accumulation of capital, both fixed in the implements and buildings, and circulating, that is, employed in maintaining the labourers and their families during the time which elapses before the productive operations are completed and the products come in. This necessity depends on physical laws, and is inherent in the condition of human life; but these requisites of production, the capital, fixed and circulating, of the country (to which has to be added the land, and all that is contained in it), may either be the collective property of those who use it, or may belong to individuals; and the question is, which of these arrangements is most conducive to human happiness. What is characteristic of Socialism is the joint ownership by all the members of the community of the instruments and means of production; which carries with it the consequence that the division of the produce among the body of owners must be a public act, performed according to rules laid down by the community. Socialism by no means excludes private ownership of articles of consumption; the exclusive right of each to his or her share of the produce when received, either to enjoy, to give, or to exchange it. The land, for example, might be wholly the property of the community for agricultural and other productive purposes, and might be cultivated on their joint account, and yet the dwelling assigned to each individual or family as part of their remuneration might be as exclusively theirs, while they continued to fulfil their share of the common labours, as any one's house now is; and not the dwelling only, but any ornamental ground which the circumstances of the association allowed to be attached to the house for purposes of enjoyment. The distinctive feature of Socialism is not that all things are in common, but that production is only carried on upon the common account, and that the instruments of production are held as common property. The *practicability* then of Socialism, on the scale of Mr. Owen's or M. Fourier's villages, admits of no dispute. The attempt to manage the whole production of a nation by one central organization is a totally different matter; but a mixed agricultural and manufacturing association of from two thousand to four thousand inhabitants under any tolerable circumstances of soil and climate would be easier to manage than many a joint stock company. The question to be considered is, whether this joint management is likely to be as efficient and successful as the managements of private industry by private capital. And this question has to be considered in a double aspect; the efficiency of the directing mind, or minds, and that of the simple workpeople. And in order to state this question in its simplest form, we will suppose the form of Socialism to be simple Communism, *i.e.* equal division of the produce among all the sharers, or, according to M. Louis Blanc's still higher standard of justice, apportionment of it according to difference of need, but without making any difference of reward according to the nature of the duty nor according to the supposed merits or services of the individual. There are other forms of Socialism, particularly Fourierism, which do, on considerations of justice or expediency, allow differences of remuneration for different kinds or degrees of service to the community; but the consideration of these may be for the present postponed.

The difference between the motive powers in the economy of society under private property and under Communism would be greatest in the case of the directing minds. Under the present system, the direction being entirely in the hands of the person or persons who own (or are personally responsible for) the capital, the whole benefit of the difference between the best administration and the worst under which the business can continue to be carried on accrues to the person or persons who control the administration: they reap the whole profit of good management except so far as their self-interest or liberality induce them to share it with their subordinates; and they suffer the whole detriment of mismanagement except so far as this may cripple their subsequent power of employing labour. This strong personal motive to do their very best and utmost for the efficiency and economy of the operations, would not exist under Communism; as the managers would only receive out of the produce the same equal dividend as the other members of the association. What would remain would be the interest common to all in so managing affairs as to make the dividend as large as possible; the incentives of public spirit, of conscience, and of the honour and credit of the managers. The force of these motives, especially when combined, is great. But it varies greatly in different persons, and is much greater for some purposes than for others. The verdict of experience, in the imperfect degree of moral cultivation which mankind have yet reached, is that the motive of conscience and that of credit and reputation, even when they are of some strength, are, in the majority of cases, much stronger as restraining than as impelling forces—are more to be depended on for preventing wrong, than for calling forth the fullest energies in the pursuit of ordinary occupations. In the case of most men the only inducement which has been found sufficiently constant and unflagging to overcome the ever-present influence of indolence and love of ease, and induce men to apply themselves unrelaxingly to work for the most part in itself dull and unexciting, is the prospect of bettering their own economic condition and that of their family; and the closer the connection of every increase of exertion with a corresponding increase of its fruits, the more powerful is this motive. To suppose the contrary would be to imply that with men as they now are, duty and honour are more powerful principles of action than personal interest, not solely as to special acts and forbearances respecting which those sentiments have been exceptionally cultivated, but in the regulation of their whole lives; which no one, I suppose, will affirm. It may be said that this inferior efficacy of public and social feelings is not inevitable—is the result of imperfect education. This I am quite ready to admit, and also that there are even now many individual exceptions to the general infirmity. But before these exceptions can grow into a majority, or even into a very large minority, much time will be required. The education of human beings is one of the most difficult of all arts, and this is one of the points in which it has hitherto been least successful; moreover improvements in general education are necessarily very gradual, because the future generation is educated by the present, and the imperfections of the teachers set an invincible limit to the degree in which they can train their pupils to be better than themselves. We must therefore expect, unless we are operating upon a select portion of the population, that personal interest will for a long time be a more effective stimulus to the most vigorous and careful conduct of the industrial business of society than motives of a higher character. It will be said that at present the greed of personal gain by its very excess counteracts its own end by the stimulus it gives to reckless and often dishonest risks. This it does, and under Communism that source of evil would generally be absent. It is probable, indeed, that enterprise either of a bad or of a good kind would be a deficient element, and that business in general would fall very much under the dominion of routine; the rather, as the performance of duty in such communities has to be enforced by external sanctions, the more nearly each person's duty can be reduced to fixed rules, the easier it is to hold him to its performance. A circumstance which increases the probability of this result is the limited power which the managers would have of independent action. They would of course hold their authority from the choice of the community, by whom their function might at any time be withdrawn from them; and this would make it necessary for them, even if not so required by the constitution of the community, to obtain the general consent of the body before making any change in the established mode of carrying on the concern. The difficulty of persuading a numerous body to make a change in their accustomed mode of working, of which change the trouble is often great, and the risk more obvious to their minds than the advantage, would have a great tendency to keep things in their accustomed track. Against this it has to be set, that choice by the persons who are directly interested in the success of the work, and who have practical knowledge and opportunities of judgment, might be expected on the average to produce managers of greater skill than the chances of birth, which now so often determine who shall be the owner of the capital. This may be true; and though it may be replied that the capitalist by inheritance can also, like the community, appoint a manager more capable than himself, this would only place him on the same level of advantage as the community, not on a higher level. But it must be said on the other side that under the Communist system the persons most qualified for the management would be likely very often to hang back from undertaking it. At present the manager, even if he be a hired servant, has a very much larger remuneration than the other persons concerned in the business; and there are open to his ambition higher social positions to which his function of manager is a stepping-stone. On the Communist system none of these advantages would be possessed by him; he could obtain only the same dividend out of the produce of the community's labour as any other member of it; he would no longer have the chance of raising himself from a receiver of wages into the class of capitalists; and while he could be in no way better off than any other labourer, his responsibilities and anxieties would be so much greater that a large proportion of mankind would be likely to prefer the less onerous position. This difficulty was foreseen by Plato as an objection to the system proposed in his Republic of community of goods among a governing class; and the motive on which he relied for inducing the fit persons to take on themselves, in the absence of all the ordinary inducements, the cares and labours of government, was the fear of being governed by worse men.[*] This, in truth, is the motive which would have to be in the main depended upon; the persons most competent to the management would be prompted to undertake the office to prevent it from falling into less competent hands. And the motive would probably be effectual at times when there was an impression that by incompetent management the affairs of the community were going to ruin, or even only decidedly deteriorating. But this motive could not, as a rule, expect to be called into action by the less stringent inducement of merely promoting improvement; unless in the case of inventors or schemers eager to try some device from which they hoped for great and immediate fruits; and persons of this kind are very often unfitted by over-sanguine temper

[*See *Republic*, Books III–IV, 416ff.]

and imperfect judgment for the general conduct of affairs, while even when fitted for it they are precisely the kind of persons against whom the average man is apt to entertain a prejudice, and they would often be unable to overcome the preliminary difficulty of persuading the community both to adopt their project and to accept them as managers. Communistic management would thus be, in all probability, less favourable than private management to that striking out of new paths and making immediate sacrifices for distant and uncertain advantages, which, though seldom unattended with risk, is generally indispensable to great improvements in the economic condition of mankind, and even to keeping up the existing state in the face of a continual increase of the number of mouths to be fed.

We have thus far taken account only of the operation of motives upon the managing minds of the association. Let us now consider how the case stands in regard to the ordinary workers.

These, under Communism, would have no interest, except their share of the general interest, in doing their work honestly and energetically. But in this respect matters would be no worse than they now are in regard to the great majority of the producing classes. These, being paid by fixed wages, are so far from having any direct interest of their own in the efficiency of their work, that they have not even that share in the general interest which every worker would have in the Communistic organization. Accordingly, the inefficiency of hired labour, the imperfect manner in which it calls forth the real capabilities of the labourers, is matter of common remark. It is true that a character for being a good workman is far from being without its value, as it tends to give him a preference in employment, and sometimes obtains for him higher wages. There are also possibilities of rising to the position of foreman, or other subordinate administrative posts, which are not only more highly paid than ordinary labour, but sometimes open the way to ulterior advantages. But on the other side is to be set that under Communism the general sentiment of the community, composed of the comrades under whose eyes each person works, would be sure to be in favour of good and hard working, and unfavourable to laziness, carelessness, and waste. In the present system not only is this not the case, but the public opinion of the workman class often acts in the very opposite direction: the rules of some trade societies actually forbid their members to exceed a certain standard of efficiency, lest they should diminish the number of labourers required for the work; and for the same reason they often violently resist contrivances for economising labour. The change from this to a state in which every person would have an interest in rendering every other person as industrious, skilful, and careful as possible (which would be the case under Communism), would be a change very much for the better.

It is, however, to be considered that the principal defects of the present system in respect to the efficiency of labour may be corrected, and the chief advantages of Communism in that respect may be obtained, by arrangements compatible with private property and individual competition. Considerable improvement is already obtained by piece-work, in the kinds of labour which admit of it. By this the workman's personal interest is closely connected with the quantity of work he turns out—not so much with its quality, the security for which still has to depend on the employer's vigilance; neither does piece-work carry with it the public opinion of the workman class, which is often, on the contrary, strongly opposed to it, as a means of (as they think) diminishing the market for labourers. And there is really good ground for their dislike of piece-work, if, as is alleged, it is a frequent practice of employers, after using piece-work to ascertain the utmost which a good workman can do, to fix the price of piece-work so low that by doing that utmost he is not able to earn more than they would be obliged to give him as day wages for ordinary work.

But there is a far more complete remedy than piece-work for the disadvantages of hired labour, viz. what is now called industrial partnership—the admission of the whole body of labourers to a participation in the profits, by distributing among all who share in the work, in the form of a percentage on their earnings, the whole or a fixed portion of the gains after a certain remuneration has been allowed to the capitalist. This plan has been found of admirable efficacy, both in this country and abroad. It has enlisted the sentiments of the workmen employed on the side of the most careful regard by all of them to the general interest of the concern; and by its joint effect in promoting zealous exertion and checking waste, it has very materially increased the remuneration of every description of labour in the concerns in which it has been adopted. It is evident that this system of indefinite extension and of an indefinite increase in the share of profits assigned to the labourers, short of that which would leave to the managers less than the needful degree of personal interest in the success of the concern. It is even likely that when such arrangements become common, many of these concerns would at some period or another, on the death or retirement of the chiefs, pass, by arrangement, into the state of purely co-operative associations.

It thus appears that as far as concerns the motives to exertion in the general body, Communism has no advantage which may not be reached under private property, while as respects the managing heads it is at a considerable disadvantage. It has also some disadvantages which seem to be inherent in it, through the necessity under which it lies of deciding in a more or less arbitrary manner questions which, on the present system, decide themselves, often badly enough, but spontaneously.

It is a simple rule, and under certain aspects a just one, to give equal payment to all who share in the work. But this is a very imperfect justice unless the work also is apportioned equally. Now the many different kinds of work required in every society are very unequal in hardness and unpleasantness. To measure these against one another, so as to make quality equivalent to quantity, is so difficult that Communists generally propose that all should work by turns at every kind of labour. But this involves an almost complete sacrifice of the economic advantages of the division of employments, advantages which are indeed frequently over-estimated (or rather the counter-considerations are under-estimated) by political economists, but which are nevertheless, in the point of view of the productiveness of labour, very considerable, for the double reason that the co-operation of employment enables the work to distribute itself with some regard to the special capacities and qualifications of the worker, and also that every worker acquires greater skill and rapidity in one kind of work by confining himself to it. The arrangement, therefore, which is deemed indispensable to a just distribution would probably be a very considerable disadvantage in respect of production. But further, it is still a very imperfect standard of justice to demand the same amount of work from every one. People have unequal capacities of work, both mental and bodily, and what is a light task for one is an insupportable burthen to another. It is necessary, therefore, that there should be a dispensing power, an authority competent to grant exemptions from the ordinary amount of work, and to proportion tasks in some measure to capabilities. As long as there are any lazy or selfish persons who like better to be worked for by others than to work, there will be frequent attempts to obtain exemptions by favour or fraud, and the frustration of these attempts will be an affair of considerable difficulty, and will by no means be always successful. These inconveniences would be little felt, for some time at least, in communities composed of select persons, earnestly desirous of the success of the experiment; but plans for the regeneration of society must consider average human beings, and not only them but the large residuum of persons greatly below the average in the personal and social virtues. The squabbles and ill-blood which could not fail to be engendered by the distribution of work whenever such persons have to be dealt with, would be a great abatement from the harmony and unanimity which Communists hope would be found among the members of their association. That concord would, even in the most fortunate circumstances, be much more liable to disturbance than Communists suppose. The institution provides that there shall be no quarrelling about material interests; individualism is excluded from that department of affairs. But there are other departments from which no institutions can exclude it: there will still be rivalry for reputation and for personal power. When selfish ambition is excluded from the field in which, with most men, it chiefly exercises itself, that of riches and pecuniary interest, it would betake itself with greater intensity to the domain still open to it, and we may expect that the struggles for pre-eminence and for influence in the management would be of great bitterness when the personal passions, diverted from their ordinary channel, are driven to seek their principal gratification in that other direction. For these various reasons it is probable that a Communist association would frequently fail to exhibit the attractive picture of mutual love and unity of will and feeling which we are often told by Communists to expect, but would often be torn by dissension and not unfrequently broken up by it.

Other and numerous sources of discord are inherent in the necessity which the Communist principle involves, of deciding by the general voice questions of the utmost importance to every one, which on the present system can be and are left to individuals to decide, each for his own case. As an example, take the subject of education. All Socialists are strongly impressed with the all-importance of the training given to the young, not only for the reasons which apply universally, but because their demands being much greater than those of any other system upon the intelligence and morality of the individual citizen, they have even more at stake than any other societies on the excellence of their educational arrangements. Now under Communism these arrangements would have to be made for every citizen by the collective body, since individual parents, supposing them to prefer some other mode of educating their children, would have no private means of paying for it, and would be limited to what they could do by their own personal teaching and influence. But every adult member of the body would have an equal voice in determining the collective system designed for the benefit of all. Here, then, is a most fruitful source of discord in every association. All who had any opinion or preference as to the education they would desire for their own children, would have to rely for their chance of obtaining it upon the influence they could exercise in the joint decision of the community.

It is needless to specify a number of other important questions affecting the mode of employing the productive resources of the association, the conditions of social life, the relations of the body with other associations, &c., on which difference of opinion, often irreconcilable, would be likely to arise. But even the dissensions which might be expected would be a far less evil to the prospects of humanity than a delusive unanimity produced by the prostration of all individual opinions and wishes before the decree of the majority. The obstacles to human progression are always great, and require a concurrence of favourable circumstances to overcome them; but an indispensable condition of their being overcome is, that human nature should have freedom to expand spontaneously in various directions, both in thought and practice; that people should both think for themselves and try experiments for themselves, and should not resign into the hands of rulers, whether acting in the name of a few or of the majority, the business of thinking for them, and of prescribing how they shall act. But in Communist associations private life would be brought in a most unexampled degree within the dominion of public authority, and there would be less scope for the development of individual character and individual preferences than has hitherto existed among the full citizens of any state belonging to the progressive branches of the human family. Already in all societies the compression of individuality by the majority is a great and growing evil; it would probably be much greater under Communism, except so far as it might be in the power of individuals to set bounds to it by selecting to belong to a community of persons like-minded with themselves.

From these various considerations I do not seek to draw any inference against the possibility that Communistic production is capable of being at some future time the form of society best adapted to the wants and circumstances of mankind. I think that this is, and will long be, an open question, upon which fresh light will continually be obtained, both by trial of the Communistic principle under favourable circumstances, and by the improvements which will be gradually effected in the working of the existing system, that of private ownership. The one certainty is, that Communism, to be successful, requires a high standard of both moral and intellectual education in all the members of the community—moral, to qualify them for doing their part honestly and energetically in the labour of life under no inducement but their share in the general interest of the association, and their feelings of duty and sympathy towards it; intellectual, to make them capable of estimating distant interests and entering into complex considerations, sufficiently at least to be able to discriminate, in these matters, good counsel from bad. Now I reject altogether the notion that it is impossible for education and cultivation such as is implied in these things to be made the inheritance of every person in the nation; but I am convinced that it is very difficult, and that the passage to it from our present condition can only be slow. I admit the plea that in the points of moral education on which the success of Communism depends, the present state of society is demoralising, and that only a Communistic association can effectually train mankind for Communism. It is for Communism, then, to prove, by practical experiment, its power of giving this training. Experiments alone can show whether there is as yet in any portion of the population a sufficiently high level of moral cultivation to make Communism succeed, and to give to the next generation among themselves the education necessary to keep up that high level permanently. If Communist associations show that they can be durable and prosperous, they will multiply, and will probably be adopted by successive portions of the population of the more advanced countries as they become morally fitted for that mode of life. But to force unprepared populations into Communist societies, even if a political revolution gave the power to make such an attempt, would end in disappointment.

If practical trial is necessary to test the capabilities of Communism, it is no less required for those other forms of Socialism which recognise the difficulties of Communism and contrive means to surmount them. The principal of these is Fourierism, a system which, if only as a specimen of intellectual ingenuity, is highly worthy of the attention of any student, either of society or of the human mind. There is scarcely an objection or a difficulty which Fourier did not foresee, and against which he did not make provision beforehand by self-acting contrivances, grounded, however, upon a less high principle of distributive justice than that of Communism, since he admits inequalities of distribution and individual ownership of capital, but not the arbitrary disposal of it. The great problem which he grapples with is how to make labour attractive, since, if this could be done, the principal difficulty of Socialism would be overcome. He maintains that no kind of useful labour is necessarily or universally repugnant, unless either excessive in amount or devoid of the stimulus of companionship and emulation, or regarded by mankind with contempt. The workers in a Fourierist village are to class themselves spontaneously in groups, each group undertaking a different kind of work, and the same person may be a member not only of one group but of any number; a certain minimum having first been set apart for the subsistence of every member of the community, whether capable or not of labour, the society divides the remainder of the produce among the different groups, in such shares as it finds attract to each the amount of labour required, and no more; if there is too great a run upon particular groups it is a sign that those groups are over-remunerated relatively to others; if any are neglected their remuneration must be made higher. The share of produce assigned to each group is divided in fixed proportions among three elements—labour, capital, and talent; the part assigned to talent being awarded by the suffrages of the group itself, and it is hoped that among the variety of human capacities all, or nearly all, will be qualified to excel in some group or other. The remuneration for capital is to be such as is found sufficient to induce savings from individual consumption, in order to increase the common stock to such point as is desired. The number and ingenuity of the contrivances for meeting minor difficulties, and getting rid of minor inconveniences, is very remarkable. By means of these various provisions it is the expectation of Fourierists that the personal inducements to exertion for the public interest, instead of being taken away, would be made much greater than at present, since every increase of the service rendered would be much more certain of leading to increase of reward than it is now, when accidents of position have so much influence. The efficiency of labour, they therefore expect, would be unexampled, while the saving of labour would be prodigious, by diverting to useful occupations that which is now wasted on things useless or hurtful, and by dispensing with the vast number of superfluous distributors, the buying and selling for the whole community being managed by a single agency. The free choice of individuals as to their manner of life would be no further interfered with than would be necessary for gaining the full advantages of co-operation in the industrial operations. Altogether, the picture of a Fourierist community is both attractive in itself and requires less from common humanity than any other known system of Socialism; and it is much to be desired that the scheme should have that fair trial which alone can test the workableness of any new scheme of social life.*

The result of our review of the various difficulties of Socialism has led us to the conclusion that the various schemes for managing the productive resources of the country by public instead of private agency have a case for a trial, and some of them may eventually establish their claims to preference over the existing order of things, but that they are at present workable only by the *élite* of mankind, and have yet to prove their power of training mankind at large to the state of improvement which they presuppose. Far more, of course, may this be said of the more ambitious plan which aims at taking possession of the whole land and capital of the country, and beginning at once to administer it on the public account. Apart from all consideration of injustice to the present possessors, the very idea of conducting the whole industry of a country by direction from a single centre is so obviously chimerical, that nobody ventures to propose any mode in which it should be done; and it can hardly be doubted that if the revolutionary Socialists attained their immediate object, and actually had the whole property of the country at their disposal, they would find no other practicable mode of exercising their power over it than that of dividing it into portions, each to be made over to the administration of a small Socialist community. The problem of management, which we have seen to be so difficult even to a select population well prepared beforehand, would be thrown down to be solved as best it could by aggregations united only by locality, or taken indiscriminately from the population, including all the malefactors, all the idlest and most vicious, the most incapable of steady industry, forethought, or self-control, and a majority who, though not equally degraded, are yet, in the opinion of Socialists themselves, as far as

*The principles of Fourierism are clearly set forth and powerfully defended in the various writings of M. Victor Considérant, especially that entitled *La Destinée Sociale*; but the curious inquirer will do well to study them in the writings of Fourier himself; where he will find unmistakable proofs of genius, mixed, however, with the wildest and most unscientific fancies respecting the physical world, and much interesting but rash speculation on the past and future history of humanity. It is proper to add that on some important social questions, for instance on marriage, Fourier had peculiar opinions, which, however, as he himself declares, are quite independent of, and separable from, the principles of his industrial system.

regards the qualities essential for the success of Socialism, profoundly demoralised by the existing state of society. It is saying but little to say that the introduction of Socialism under such conditions could have no effect but disastrous failure, and its apostles could have only the consolation that the order of society as it now exists would have perished first, and all who benefit by it would be involved in the common ruin—a consolation which to some of them would probably be real, for if appearances can be trusted the animating principle of too many of the revolutionary Socialists is hate; a very excusable hatred of existing evils, which would vent itself by putting an end to the present system at all costs even to those who suffer by it, in the hope that out of chaos would arise a better Kosmos, and in the impatience of desperation respecting any more gradual improvement. They are unaware that chaos is the very most unfavourable position for setting out in the construction of a Kosmos, and that many ages of conflict, violence, and tyrannical oppression of the weak by the strong must intervene; they know not that they would plunge mankind into the state of nature so forcibly described by Hobbes (*Leviathan*, Part I. ch. xiii.),[*] where every man is enemy to every man:—

In such condition there is no place for industry, because the fruit thereof is uncertain, and consequently no culture of the earth, no navigation, no use of the commodities that may be imported by sea, no commodious building, no instruments of moving and removing such things as require much force, no knowledge of the face of the earth, no account of time, no arts, no letters, no society; and, which is worst of all, continual fear and danger of violent death; and the life of man solitary, poor, nasty, brutish, and short.

If the poorest and most wretched members of a so-called civilised society are in as bad a condition as every one would be in that worst form of barbarism produced by the dissolution of civilised life, it does not follow that the way to raise them would be to reduce all others to the same miserable state. On the contrary, it is by the aid of the first who have risen that so many others have escaped from the general lot, and it is only by better organization of the same process that it may be hoped in time to succeed in raising the remainder.

THE IDEA OF PRIVATE PROPERTY NOT FIXED BUT VARIABLE

The preceding considerations appear sufficient to show that an entire renovation of the social fabric, such as is contemplated by Socialism, establishing the economic constitution of society upon an entirely new basis, other than that of private property and competition, however valuable as an

[*English Works*, ed. Molesworth, III, p. 113.]

ideal, and even as a prophecy of ultimate possibilities, is not available as a present resource, since it requires from those who are to carry on the new order of things qualities both moral and intellectual, which require to be tested in all, and to be created in most; and this cannot be done by an Act of Parliament, but must be, on the most favourable supposition, a work of considerable time. For a long period to come the principle of individual property will be in possession of the field; and even if in any country a popular movement were to place Socialists at the head of a revolutionary government, in however many ways they might violate private property, the institution itself would survive, and would either be accepted by them or brought back by their expulsion, for the plain reason that people will not lose their hold of what is at present their sole reliance for subsistence and security until a substitute for it has been got into working order. Even those, if any, who had shared among themselves what was the property of others would desire to keep what they had acquired, and to give back to property in the new hands the sacredness which they had not recognised in the old.

But though, for these reasons, individual property has presumably a long term before it, if only of provisional existence, we are not, therefore, to conclude that it must exist during that whole term unmodified, or that all the rights now regarded as appertaining to property belong to it inherently, and must endure while it endures. On the contrary, it is both the duty and the interest of those who derive the most direct benefit from the laws of property to give impartial consideration to all proposals for rendering those laws in any way less onerous to the majority. This, which would in any case be an obligation of justice, is an injunction of prudence also, in order to place themselves in the right against the attempts which are sure to be frequent to bring the Socialist forms of society prematurely into operation.

One of the mistakes oftenest committed, and which are the sources of the greatest practical errors in human affairs, is that of supposing that the same name always stands for the same aggregation of ideas. No word has been the subject of more of this kind of misunderstanding than the word property. It denotes in every state of society the largest powers of exclusive use or exclusive control over things (and sometimes, unfortunately, over persons) which the law accords, or which custom, in that state of society, recognises; but these powers of exclusive use and control are very various, and differ greatly in different countries and in different states of society.

For instance, in early states of society, the right of property did not include the right of bequest. The power of disposing of property by will was in most countries of Europe a rather late institution; and long after it was introduced it continued to be limited in favour of what were called natural heirs. Where bequest is not permitted, individual property is only a life interest. And in fact, as has been so well and fully set forth by Sir Henry Maine in his most instructive work on Ancient Law,[*] the primitive idea of property was that it belonged to the family, not the individual. The head of the family had the management and was the person who really exercised the proprietary rights. As in other respects, so in this, he governed the family with nearly despotic power. But he was not free so to exercise his power as to defeat the co-proprietors of the other portions; he could not so dispose of the property as to deprive them of the joint enjoyment or of the succession. By the laws and customs of some nations the property could not be alienated without the consent of the male children; in other cases the child could by law demand a division of the property and the assignment to him of his share, as in the story of the Prodigal Son. If the association kept together after the death of the head, some other member of it, not always his son, but often the eldest of the family, the strongest, or the one selected by the rest, succeeded to the management and to the managing rights, all the others retaining theirs as before. If, on the other hand, the body broke up into separate families, each of these took away with it a part of the property. I say the property, not the inheritance, because the process was a mere continuance of existing rights, not a creation of new; the manager's share alone lapsed to the association.

Then, again, in regard to proprietary rights over immovables (the principal kind of property in a rude age) these rights were of very varying extent and duration. By the Jewish law property in immovables was only a temporary concession; on the Sabbatical year it returned to the common stock to be redistributed; though we may surmise that in the historical times of the Jewish state this rule may have been successfully evaded. In many countries of Asia, before European ideas intervened, nothing existed to which the expression property in land, as we understand the phrase, is strictly applicable. The ownership was broken up among several distinct parties, whose rights were determined rather by custom than by law. The government was part owner, having the right to a heavy rent. Ancient ideas and even ancient laws limited the government share to some particular fraction of the gross produce, but practically there was no fixed limit. The government might make over its share to an individual, who then became possessed of the right of collection and all the other rights of the state, but not those of any private person connected with the soil. These private rights were of various kinds. The actual cultivators, or such of them as had been long settled on the land, had a right to retain possession; it was held unlawful to evict them while they paid the rent—a rent not in general fixed by agreement, but by the custom of the neighbourhood. Between the actual cultivators and the state, or the substitute to whom the state had transferred

[*London: Murray, 1861.]

its rights, there were intermediate persons with rights of various extent. There were officers of government who collected the state's share of the produce, sometimes for large districts, who, though bound to pay over to government all they collected, after deducting a percentage, were often hereditary officers. There were also, in many cases, village communities, consisting of the reputed descendants of the first settlers of a village, who shared among themselves either the land or its produce according to rules established by custom, either cultivating it themselves or employing others to cultivate it for them, and whose rights in the land approached nearer to those of a landed proprietor, as understood in England, than those of any other party concerned. But the proprietary right of the village was not individual, but collective; inalienable (the rights of individual sharers could only be sold or mortgaged with the consent of the community) and governed by fixed rules. In mediæval Europe almost all land was held from the sovereign on tenure of service, either military or agricultural; and in Great Britain even now, when the services as well as all the reserved rights of the sovereign have long since fallen into disuse or been commuted for taxation, the theory of the law does not acknowledge an absolute right of property in land in any individual; the fullest landed proprietor known to the law, the freeholder, is but a "tenant" of the Crown. In Russia, even when the cultivators of the soil were serfs of the landed proprietor, his proprietary right in the land was limited by rights of theirs belonging to them as a collective body managing its own affairs, and with which he could not interfere. And in most of the countries of continental Europe when serfage was abolished or went out of use, those who had cultivated the land as serfs remained in possession of rights as well as subject to obligations. The great land reforms of Stein and his successors in Prussia consisted in abolishing both the rights and the obligations, and dividing the land bodily between the proprietor and the peasant, instead of leaving each of them with a limited right over the whole. In other cases, as in Tuscany, the *metayer* farmer is virtually co-proprietor with the landlord, since custom, though not law, guarantees to him a permanent possession and half the gross produce, so long as he fulfils the customary conditions of his tenure.

Again, if rights of property over the same things are of different extent in different countries, so also are they exercised over different things. In all countries at a former time, and in some countries still, the right of property extended and extends to the ownership of human beings. There has often been property in public trusts, as in judicial offices, and a vast multitude of others in France before the Revolution; there are still a few patent offices in Great Britain, though I believe they will cease by operation of law on the death of the present holders; and we are only now abolishing property in army rank. Public bodies, constituted and endowed for public purposes, still claim the same inviolable right of property in their estates which individuals have in theirs, and though a sound political morality does not acknowledge this claim, the law supports it. We thus see that the right of property is differently interpreted, and held to be of different extent, in different times and places; that the conception entertained of it is a varying conception, has been frequently revised, and may admit of still further revision. It is also to be noticed that the revisions which it has hitherto undergone in the progress of society have generally been improvements. When, therefore, it is maintained, rightly or wrongly, that some change or modification in the powers exercised over things by the persons legally recognised as their proprietors would be beneficial to the public and conducive to the general improvement, it is no good answer to this merely to say that the proposed change conflicts with the idea of property. The idea of property is not some one thing, identical throughout history and incapable of alteration, but is variable like all other creations of the human mind; at any given time it is a brief expression denoting the rights over things conferred by the law or custom of some given society at that time; but neither on this point nor on any other has the law and custom of a given time and place a claim to be stereotyped for ever. A proposed reform in laws or customs is not necessarily objectionable because its adoption would imply, not the adaptation of all human affairs to the existing idea of property, but the adaptation of existing ideas of property to the growth and improvement of human affairs. This is said without prejudice to the equitable claim of proprietors to be compensated by the state for such legal rights of a proprietary nature as they may be dispossessed of for the public advantage. That equitable claim, the grounds and the just limits of it, are a subject by itself, and as such will be discussed hereafter. Under this condition, however, society is fully entitled to abrogate or alter any particular right of property which on sufficient consideration it judges to stand in the way of the public good. And assuredly the terrible case which, as we saw in a former chapter,[*] Socialists are able to make out against the present economic order of society, demands a full consideration of all means by which the institution may have a chance of being made to work in a manner more beneficial to that large portion of society which at present enjoys the least share of its direct benefits.

[*Pp. 711–12 above.]

APPENDICES

Appendix A

McCulloch's Discourse on Political Economy (1825)

Westminster Review, IV (July, 1825), 88–92. Unsigned; not republished. Original heading: "Art. VI. *A Discourse on the Rise, Progress, Peculiar Objects, and Importance of Political Economy. By J. R. M'Culloch, Esq. Second Edition.* pp. 117. Edinburgh [: Constable]. 1825." Running head: "M'Culloch's Discourse on Political Economy." Not mentioned in JSM's bibliography or *Autobiography*. Vol. IV of the *Westminster* is missing from the Mills' set in Somerville College. Identified as partly by JSM in Alexander Bain, *James Mill* (London: Longmans, Green, 1882), 292, where a letter from James Mill to McCulloch (18/8/25) is cited, reading in part: "I suppose you have seen by this time the review of your Discourse in the *Westminster*? John expresses great dissatisfaction with the behaviour of the editors. The whole was the joint production of him and [William] Ellis: but they say that several important things were left out, and the article, by that and other editorial operations, disfigured." (Cf. Edmund K. Blyth, *Life of William Ellis* [London: Kegan Paul, Trench, 1889], 35–6, 352.) There is no external evidence to indicate what part of this slight review is by JSM; if a guess is permissible, it seems likely that the sketch of the history of Political Economy is his.

IF THERE IS ONE SIGN OF THE TIMES upon which more than any other we should be justified in resting our hopes of the future progression of the human race in the career of improvement, that sign undoubtedly is, the demand which is now manifesting itself on the part of the public for instruction in the science of Political Economy. It is unnecessary for us to bring forward any evidence to prove the existence of this demand—the fact is sufficiently notorious. It is equally notorious, that considerable respect is now paid by the more enlightened portion of our administration to the great principles of the science; that many members of the House of Commons are beginning to be familiar with the demonstrations by which those principles are established; and that those who have inherited the ignorance of their ancestors with their estates, have of late been obliged, however ungraciously, on many occasions, by the force of public opinion, to bow down to others who have less reverence for the errors of the past. And yet, surprising as it may appear, it is no less notorious, that up to the year 1818, the science of political economy was scarcely known or talked of beyond a small circle of philosophers, and that legislation, so far from being in conformity with its principles, was daily receding from them more and more.

At that time all the most important principles contained in the science had been clearly demonstrated, and the *materiel* for the formation of a regular system was collected. A long interval elapsed after the publication of the Wealth of Nations, in 1776, without any thing worth mentioning being contributed to the science. In 1798 appeared Malthus's Essay upon the Principle of Population; in 1802, Mr. Say's work;[*] in 1815, two Essays upon the Nature of Rent;[†] and in 1817, Mr. Ricardo's profound work upon the Principles of Political Economy and Taxation; and finally, in 1821, Mr. Mill's Elements of Political Economy.

The attention of those who wish to see an amelioration in the condition of the great mass of mankind ought henceforward to be mainly directed to the means of communicating to *all* that which is now known only to a *few*. The principal difficulty is overcome—the road to happiness is discovered—no groping, no perplexing research, no hopeless, thankless toil is required—all that remains to be done is, to remove the obstacles which conceal that road from the view of those who are less fortunate than ourselves. The perfectibility of the human species has long been looked upon as a fit subject of speculation for castle-builders and Utopians; and certainly the schemes by which it has frequently been thought that this perfectibility might be brought about, were well calculated to excite a smile even on the countenance of the most benevolent. On the other hand, political economists, as a class, have often been held up to hatred because their doctrines were considered as adverse to the scheme of perfectibility. This hatred has, however, been extremely ill-placed. For, waiving any opinion as to the scheme of perfectibility, and as to the possibility of attaching any very precise idea to the term, it must be allowed that political economists have shown in what manner the condition of mankind may be considerably improved. It must be allowed, moreover, that, previous to their inquiries, unknown causes existed, by which all plans for improvement were checked and counteracted. Not only have they pointed out these causes of evil, but, fearlessly braving the prejudices of the ignorant and vulgar, they have brought to light a remedy by which that evil may be averted. If, therefore, they are of opinion that the perfectibility of the species is a mere vision, although bright and fascinating to dwell upon, they have, at all events,

[*Say, Jean-Baptiste, *Traité d'économie politique.* 2 vols. Paris: Deterville, 1803.]

[†Malthus, T. R. *An Inquiry into the Nature and Progress of Rent.* London: Murray, 1815; West, Edward. *Essay on the Application of Capital to Land.* London: Underwood, 1815.]

produced a plan by which a large addition may almost immediately be made to human happiness, and which will ultimately raise the species to a state at least approaching to the perfectibility which has been aimed at.

The readiness with which all the late discoveries in economical science have been received and assented to, and the success which has attended all the attempts that have been made to diffuse a knowledge of them, hold out the strongest encouragement to those who have already devoted either time or talent for the purpose of imparting useful information, to persevere in their course, and to others to follow their example. Of all who have hitherto been engaged in this meritorious employment, there is no one who has distinguished himself more than the author of the Discourse which we have before us. Were it possible to trace any portion of the improvement in the public mind within these few years to the labours of particular individuals, we think that much might be traced to those of Mr. McCulloch. In him are united a profound knowledge of the principles of the science, a most uncommon degree of skill in illustrating and expounding them, a complete mastery of all the errors and sophisms which have heretofore prevailed, and of the arguments by which they are to be met, with an apostolic zeal in communicating his knowledge to others. What other qualities can be required to entitle a man to the character of a perfect teacher?

In the early part of last year a Lectureship upon Political Economy was founded for a limited number of years in honour of the late Mr. Ricardo; a manner of commemorating the virtues and talents of that great philosopher, as consonant to what it might be supposed would be his wishes, as it was creditable to the judgment of his friends and admirers. The well-known qualifications of Mr. McCulloch pointed him out to these gentlemen as the fittest person to fill the lecturer's chair. Mr. McCulloch had already given some courses of lectures at his own private risk at Edinburgh; but doubts were entertained by many whether the public mind was yet ripe for such an institution. The success, however, which attended his first course far exceeded the most sanguine expectations of the most ardent friends of the science, and induced a number of public-spirited individuals to invite him to deliver a course of lectures in the city, in addition to the one which he was engaged to deliver as Ricardo lecturer.

The student who wishes to form an idea of what political economy really means, and to judge for himself whether the knowledge of the science would repay him for the time and application which he must necessarily sacrifice in order to obtain it, cannot do better than purchase this pamphlet. It does not contain more than 117 pages, and is written in a popular and pleasing style. In it he will find a general view of the principles on which the science is founded; the distinguishing features of the most celebrated theories that have been advanced to explain its various results; the distinction between it and politics; and some remarks illustrative of the utility of its study to all ranks and orders of the community.

Mr. McCulloch puts forth no pretensions to originality in this discourse. It was written evidently with a view to attract those who as yet are strangers to the science. In this he has more than succeeded. Whoever carefully peruses its contents cannot fail to be inspired with a wish to perfect himself in the science, since he will see the necessity of either ceasing to take a part in the discussion of public affairs, or of qualifying himself to discuss them philosophically. Our space will not permit us to indulge in many examples of the style and spirit of the work. We subjoin the following:

There is a peculiarity in the political and economical sciences which deserves to be noticed, inasmuch as it serves to show the superior necessity and importance of general instruction in their principles. The peculiarity in question originates in the circumstance of the politician or economist being extremely apt to be influenced by other considerations than a regard to the interests of truth and the public welfare. The cultivators of the mathematical and physical sciences, can very rarely have any motive to bias their judgments, or to induce them to conceal or pervert the truth. But such is not the case with those who discuss political or economical questions. Every abuse, and every vicious and unjust institution and regulation, operates as a bounty on the production of false theories; for, though injurious to the public, they are almost always productive of advantage to a greater or smaller number of individuals, who, to preserve this advantage, enlist a portion of the press into their service, and labour, by means of perverted and fallacious statements, to make the public believe that the abuse is really beneficial to them, and that they are interested in its support. These attempts to make the *worse* appear the *better* cause, or to make the most flagrant abuses be viewed as national benefits, have very often been attended with complete success. And there are plainly no means of obviating this evil, of correcting what is really disadvantageous in the influence of the press, and of preventing the public from being misled by the specious sophistry of those whose interest and object it is to delude them, except by making them generally acquainted with the elementary and fundamental truths of this science. . . . . . Ignorance is the impure and muddy fountain whence nine tenths of the vice, misery, and crime, to be found in the world are really derived. Make the body of the people once fully aware of the circumstances which really determine their condition, and you may be assured that an immense majority will endeavour to turn that knowledge to good account. If you once succeed in convincing a man that it is *for his interest* to abandon one line of conduct and follow another, the chances are ten to one that he will do so. (Pp. 85–87.)

Appendix B

Petition on Free Trade (1841)

Morning Chronicle, 17 June, 1841, 6. Unsigned; not republished. Original heading: "Kensington. The following is the petition agreed to at the meeting held at Kensington on Tuesday evening." Identified in JSM's bibliography as "The Kensington Petition for free trade, agreed to at a public meeting held on the 15th June 1841, and printed in the Morning Chronicle of June 17th" (MacMinn, 53). No copy in Somerville College.

JSM wrote to Albany Fonblanque (17 June, 1841), saying in part: "The Kensington petition, printed in the Chronicle today, is of my writing, & I had a great share in getting up the public meeting, which, though in a very unpromising neighbourhood, was a very striking demonstration" (*Earlier Letters, Collected Works*, XIII, 478).

TO THE HONOURABLE THE HOUSE OF COMMONS

The humble petition of the inhabitants of Kensington and its vicinity, in public meeting assembled, sheweth,

That protecting duties, or, in other words, duties imposed on foreign commodities, not to raise a revenue, but to keep up the price of similar articles produced at home, are a tax on the whole community for the pecuniary profit of some class or classes, and are therefore an abuse of the power of legislation.

That the argument frequently urged in defence of such duties, namely, that they encourage production and favour the national industry, is in the opinion of your petitioners, not only unfounded, but the very reverse of the truth, inasmuch as employments which would not be carried on without an artificial high price, are by this very circumstance proved to be employments yielding of themselves a less return than that which the same amount of labour and capital would realise if left to take its natural course. A smaller production is by this means obtained through the sacrifice of a greater, and thus, in addition to what these restrictions take from one portion of the community to bestow upon another, they cause a further and commonly a still greater loss of national wealth, without benefit to any one.

That nevertheless former Parliaments, partly influenced by the class interests of their several members, and partly by mistaken views of public policy now exploded, have imposed protecting duties on almost every article of foreign produce or manufacture which could possibly come into competition with anything produced in our own country or its dependencies, thus throwing upon the public, in the increased price of the articles of their expenditure, burdens which, according to the calculations of the best practical authorities, exceed the amount of all the taxes which the people of this country pay to the state, while of this vast sum a very small portion alone reaches the coffers of the various classes of producers whom the legislature intended to benefit.

That of these burdens, the most revolting in its principle, the largest in its amount, and the severest in its pressure, is the tax on food, imposed by the present corn and provision laws.[*]

That a tax on food is the only tax from which no degree of abject poverty is an exemption, but which in its very nature falls heaviest upon the poorest class, nearly the whole of whose consumption consists of food.

That whatever makes the poor poorer, tends in the same proportion to render them ignorant and vicious, by depriving them of the opportunities and means of good education, while it strengthens and multiplies the temptations to which their condition exposes them. That the corn-laws, as producing these effects, are, in the view of your petitioners, opposed both to the first principles of morality and to the spirit of the Christian religion, as well as to the direct precepts of Scripture, which expressly declares,

"He that withholdeth corn, the people shall curse him; but blessing shall be upon the head of him that selleth it."[†]

That, so far as your petitioners are able to observe, these evils originate for some time existed, in a considerable portion of the labouring classes, a deeply seated hostility to existing political institutions, and in the country generally a growing alienation among the different ranks of society, the causes of which, your petitioners humbly submit, demand the most serious consideration from your honourable house.

That, so far as your petitioners are able to observe, these evils originate in the persuasion openly entertained by large bodies of persons that the ruling principle in the government of this country is not the public good, but the particular interest of certain classes, who command a majority, both in the other house of Parliament and in your honourable house. Your petitioners respectfully express their conviction that nothing has so much contributed to give rise to this unfortunate impression, or has given so much colour of truth to it, as the existing commercial restrictions, and in particular

[*See 9 George IV, c. 60.]
[†Proverbs, 11:26.]

the corn-laws. That by whatever arguments the supporters of those laws may justify themselves to their own minds, their reasons are not of a nature to be convincing or intelligible to persons whose small loaf is made smaller for no purpose apparent to them but that of still further enriching the rich. A bread tax for the supposed benefit of the landlords, and a people well affected to the state, are two things which, in the opinion of your petitioners, cannot easily co-exist.

That, entertaining these opinions, your petitioners have hailed with joy the announcement by her Majesty's government of a general revision of the existing import duties, and the introduction into your honourable house of measures, by which some of the most oppressive of those duties, and particularly, the most oppressive of all, the corn-laws, are considerably relaxed.[*] That although in the article of food nothing but entire freedom from taxation would be satisfactory to your petitioners as a permanent arrangement; yet, as a means of transition, to prevent too sudden a shock to existing interests, your petitioners fully subscribe to the propriety of retaining, for the present, a moderate duty on imported corn. And your petitioners are strongly of opinion that the protection thus temporarily conceded should be in the shape of a fixed duty rather than of a sliding scale. Your petitioners can scarcely imagine any mode of regulating a great branch of commerce and industry more injurious to all parties than the present variable scale of duties, under which the home grower can never know what degree of protection he has to reckon upon, nor the importer what rate of duty he will be required to pay.

That although the measures recently promulgated by her Majesty's government would have commanded, under any circumstances, the warmest support of your petitioners, they derive an additional recommendation from the particular time at which they are proposed, namely, when the approaching revision of the duties levied on our productions by several of our largest customers threatens us with retaliatory measures most ruinous to our foreign trade, while the state of our own revenue leaves us no option but either to lower the tariff, or impose new and onerous taxes upon the property or the already overburthened industry of the country.

Your petitioners, therefore, earnestly entreat your honourable house to give your most serious consideration to these various circumstances, and to adopt the measures recently submitted to you by her Majesty's government with respect to the duties on imports, and especially on foreign corn.

And your petitioners will ever pray.

[*See 5 & 6 Victoria, Sess. 2, c. 14.]

Appendix C

Examination Paper in Political Economy Set by JSM (1872)

JSM's interest in higher education for women led to his being asked to set examination papers in Political Economy for The College, Hitchin, later Girton College, Cambridge. The following paper is reproduced from JSM's *Letters*, edited Hugh S. R. Elliot (London, 1910), II, 336–7, where it is dated 6 May, 1872.

1. What is the distinction between Productive and Unproductive Labour, and between Productive and Unproductive Consumption?

2. Does all Productive labour tend to increase the permanent wealth of the country?

3. State any causes, in general operation, which tend to increase the productive power of labour, and any which tend to diminish it.

4. Explain in what sense the value of a commodity depends on supply and demand, and in what sense on cost of production.

5. What cost of production is it which determines the exchange value of the products of agriculture?

6. A state of free trade being supposed, can a country permanently import a commodity from a place where its cost of production is greater than that at which it could be produced at home?

7. What are the effects, first on the national wealth, and secondly, on the wages of labour, of a large government expenditure? and does it make any difference what the expenditure is upon?

8. In what respect are the interest of the labouring classes and that of the employers of labour identical? and in what respects, if in any, opposed?

9. What is the meaning of depreciation of the currency? and what are the principal causes of such depreciation?

10. By what means can a currency be protected against depreciation?

11. What is meant by the terms, a favourable and an unfavourable exchange? and is there any well-grounded objection to that phraseology?

12. How far, and in what respects, is the discovery of new and rich deposits of the precious metals a benefit to the national wealth?

13. Mention the principal circumstances that tend to produce either a rise or a fall in the rent of land.

14. State what are the known modes in which the produce of land, or the proceeds of the sale of that produce, are shared among the different classes of persons connected with the land, and state briefly the advantages and disadvantages of each.

Appendix D

Land Tenure Reform Association: Public Lands and Commons Bill (1872)

JSM was in Avignon during the early part of 1872, when this sheet must have been distributed, and there is no evidence that he took part in its composition, though he would surely have approved it. No marks on Somerville College copy.

LAND TENURE REFORM ASSOCIATION

Chairman, MR. J. STUART MILL

Treasurer, MR. P. A. TAYLOR, M.P.   Hon. Secretary, COLONEL T. A. COWPER

Offices:—9, Buckingham Street, Strand

PUBLIC LANDS AND COMMONS BILL

The Second Reading of the Public Lands and Commons Bill will be moved by Sir C. DILKE, on Wednesday, July 3rd. The Bill is brought in by Sir C. Dilke, Mr. Morrison and Mr. P. A. Taylor, and applies only to Public Lands, or Lands held by Corporations, Charities, &c. for public uses, to Commons and Rights of Way. It not only provides for the more economical administration of public lands, but contains provisions calculated largely to promote the social and material well being of the industrial classes.

The Bill provides for the appointment of overseers of all public lands, commons, and rights of way; the salaries of such overseers to be defrayed out of the proceeds of the lands under their charge. Their duties in regard to public lands will be to manage them in the most economical and efficient manner, to let such lands by public tender, and when tenders are equal, to give the preference to that in which the largest number of persons are interested, thus affording facilities for co-operative agriculture and co-operative building.

The duties of the overseers in regard to public commons and rights of way will be to make enquiries into the nature and extent of public rights, report the result to the Home Secretary, and mark the extent of such commons and rights of way upon maps of their several districts, thus permanently securing the rights of the public.

All earnest Land Reformers are therefore urged to support the Bill for the following reasons:—

1—Because it is desirable that as large a number of persons as possible should have an interest in the soil.

2—Because there is a growing disposition on the part of the present administrators of public lands and others to dispose of them to private individuals, and invest the proceeds in other kinds of property.

3—Because it is to the public advantage that no lands over which the public have any rights should pass into the hands of individual proprietors.

4—Because it is notorious that the present administration of public lands (the value of which is estimated at £500,000,000) is often attended by gross abuses, which the Bill would render almost impossible.

5—Because, from the absence of constant supervision, lands formerly devised for public purposes, have been converted to private uses.

6—Because, although co-operative agriculture has been successfully tried, as at Rahaline, in Ireland, and Acrington, in Suffolk, opportunities for extending its operations are not afforded by private landowners.

7—Because the Bill would prevent the annexation by private persons of strips of common land, and the stoppage of rights of way, actions which are now often indulged in with impunity.

8—Because the effect of the Bill would be to make known the whole extent of the lands over which public rights exist, and to secure such public rights in the future.

The Executive Committee of the LAND TENURE REFORM ASSOCIATION trust that their friends in the various constituencies will use every effort in behalf of the Bill, especially by communicating with their parliamentary representatives, and by obtaining resolutions from associated bodies in its favor, which also should be forwarded to the local members.

Appendix E

Bibliographic Index of Persons and Works Cited in the *Essays,* with
Variants and Notes

Mill, like most nineteenth-century authors, is very cavalier in his approach
to sources, seldom identifying them with sufficient care, and frequently
quoting them inaccurately. This Appendix is intended to help correct these
deficiencies, and to serve as an index of names and titles (which are consequently omitted in the Index proper). Included also, at the end of the
Appendix, are references to British statute law, which are entered in order
of date under the heading "Statutes" (826), and references to parliamentary
reports and evidence, which are entered in order of date under "Parliamentary
Papers" (824). The material is arranged in alphabetical order, with an entry
for each author and work quoted or referred to in the text proper and in
Appendices A–D.

In cases of simple reference only surnames are given.

The entries take the following form:

1. Identification: author, title, etc., in the usual bibliographic form.
2. Notes (if required) giving information about JSM's use of the source,
indication if the work is in his library, and any other relevant information.
3. A list of the places where the author or work is quoted, and a separate
list of the places where there is reference only. Those works which are
reviewed are specially noted.
4. A list of substantive variants between JSM's text and his source, in this
form: Page and line reference to the present text. Reading in the present
text] Reading in the source (page reference in the source).

The list of substantive variants also attempts to place quoted remarks in their
contexts by giving the beginnings and endings of sentences. Omissions of two
sentences or less are given in full; only the length of other omissions is given.
In a few cases, following the page reference to the source, cross-references are
given to footnoted variants in the present text. Translated material is given
in the original language.

ACTS. See Statutes.

ANON. "The Bank Charter," *Tait's Edinburgh Magazine*, I (June, 1832),
291–314.

NOTE: the reference is in an editorial footnote.

REFERRED TO: 192n

ANON. "Mr. Thomas Tooke on the Currency Principle," *Examiner*, 13 Apr., 1844, 226–7; and "Currency Crochets," *ibid.*, 27 Apr., 1844, 259–60.
REFERRED TO: 343n

ANSELL, CHARLES. "Evidence taken before the Select Committee on Income and Property Tax," *Parliamentary Papers*, 1861, VII, 179–92.
REFERRED TO: 595

ARISTOTLE. Referred to: 212

ATTWOOD, MATTHIAS. Referred to: 185

ATTWOOD, THOMAS. Referred to: 275. See also *Mansell & Co's Report*.

———— "Evidence taken before the Committee of Secrecy on the Bank of England Charter," *Parliamentary Papers*, 1831–32, VI, 452–68.
NOTE: Attwood's "Evidence" is first cited on 185.
REVIEWED: 183–92

ARKWRIGHT. Referred to: 156–7

AUBIN. Referred to: 378n

BABBAGE, CHARLES. *On the Economy of Machinery and Manufactures.* 3rd ed. London: Knight, 1832 [1833].
NOTE: The reference is to JSM's quotation from Babbage, in *Principles of Political Economy,* in *Collected Works,* III, 770.

REFERRED TO: 414

BACON. Referred to: 328

BAER, CONSTANTINO. *L'avere e l'imposta.* Rome: Loescher, 1872.
REVIEWED: 699–702

BALL. Referred to: 500

BARING, ALEXANDER. Referred to: 105–6

———— Speeches in the House of Commons (10 and 13 Feb., 1826), quoted in *Parliamentary History* for 1826, 189–95, 225–7, 229.

QUOTED: 118   REFERRED TO: 117–20

118.3   "stood] Let it be recollected that, in spite of all eloquent speeches, the house stood (225)
118.5   gentlemen] gent. [i.e., gentleman; i.e., Canning] (225)
118.5   He did] He (Mr. Baring) did (225)
118.8   country . . . . . If] [*1½-column omission*] (225–6)

BARING, FRANCIS THORNHILL. Referred to: 464, 500

———— "Evidence taken before the Select Committee on the Bank Acts," *Parliamentary Papers*, 1857 (Sess. 2), X.i, 177–206.

NOTE: the "quotations" are questions asked by Baring, a member of the Committee.

QUOTED: 512, 517

BARNETT. Referred to: 432

BEAUMARCHAIS, PIERRE AUGUSTIN CARON DE. *Le Barbier de Séville.*

NOTE: the phrase occurs in a speech by Basile, not by Figaro. No edition is cited.

QUOTED: 206

206.10   *Qui trompe-t-on ici?* asks Figaro.] Basile, *à part.*—Qui diable est-ce donc qu'on trompe ici? Tout le monde est dans le secret. (III, xi)

BEHREND. Referred to: 55, 56n, 67–8

NOTE: no copy of Behrend's *Corn Circular* has been located.

BIBLE. Referred to: 377

———— Isaiah, 28:10–11.

NOTE: cf. *ibid.*, 28:13.

QUOTED: 47

47.15   "line . . . precept;"] For precept must be upon precept, precept upon precept; line upon line, line upon line; here a little, and there a little: For with stammering lips and another tongue will he speak to this people.

———— Luke, 15:11–32.

REFERRED TO: 751

———— Proverbs, 11:26.

QUOTED: 762

———— I Thessalonians, 5:21.

QUOTED: 457

457.9–10 "try . . . good"] Prove all things; hold fast that which is good.

BLACKBURN. Referred to: 500

BLACKWOOD. Referred to: 678

BLAKE, WILLIAM. *Observations on the Effects Produced by the Expenditure of Government during the Restriction of Cash Payments.* London: Murray, 1823.

NOTE: the passages on 5–6 from Blake's pp. 4–5 and 5–6 are contiguous, only the footnote (see 5.38 below) being omitted. The footnote quoted on 7 belongs to the end of the passage quoted in JSM's footnote to the quotation.

REVIEWED: 3–22

QUOTED: 3–7, 11–12, 14–19, 22n

5.26   of the currency] of currency (4)
5.30   I] [*no paragraph*] I (4)
5.38   by it.] by it*. [*footnote:*] *I do not pretend to ascertain that due proportion. There is some ratio which ought to subsist between the total amount of the currency, and the total value of the commodities to be circulated by it. If that ratio be constant, the value of the currency will remain unaltered. (5n)
7.n8   At] [*no paragraph*] At (31)
7.n11   charges in] charges on (31) [*printer's error?*]
7.n14–15   consumption.] consumption*. (31) [*see my note above*]
11.1   [*paragraph*] Mr. Ricardo] [*no paragraph*] Indeed Mr. Ricardo (26)
12.3   It is] I am quite at a loss how to reconcile such an exchange with the theory of Mr. Wheatley and Mr. Ricardo; for it is (29n)
12.15   impossible.] impossible. The contradiction arises from transferring that language to the currency which is only applicable to the bills. [*end of note*] (29n)
14.29   twenty] twenty-two (53)
15.14   The political . . . have endeavoured] This opinion of Adam Smith has been controverted by the political economists of the present day, who have endeavoured (58)
15.28   other.] other*. [*footnote:*] This argument has been most ably and adroitly conducted by Mr. Mill, in his Elements of Political Economy, and, granting that new tastes and new wants spring up with the new capital, appears to me unanswerable. (59n)
16.7   further] farther (60)
17.15   Whenever] Now, whenever (56)

———— *Observations on the Principles which Regulate the Course of Exchange; and on the Present Depreciated State of the Currency.* London: Lloyd, 1810.

REFERRED TO: 188

BLANC, JEAN-JOSEPH LOUIS. Referred to: 728, 739

———— *Organisation du travail.* 4me ed. Brussels: Hauman, 1845.

NOTE: no copy of the 4th ed., Paris, having been available, the edition cited above has been used. As the variant notes below show, the text cannot have been much altered. The passages which JSM actually translates are enclosed in square brackets.

QUOTED: 716–19, 727   REFERRED TO: 730

716.33–717.10   Competition . . . then?] [*translated from:*] [La concurrence est pour le peuple un système d'extermination.] [*title of Part 1, chap ii*] [*paragraph*] Le pauvre est-il un membre ou un ennemi de la société? Qu'on réponde.

Il trouve tout autour de lui le sol occupé.

Peut-il semer la terre pour son propre compte? Non, parce que le droit de premier occupant est devenu droit de propriété.

Peut-il cueillir les fruits que la main de Dieu a fait mûrir sur le passage des hommes? Non, parce que, de même que le sol, les fruits ont été *appropriés*.

Peut-il se livrer à la chasse ou à la pêche? Non, parce que cela constitue un droit que le gouvernement afferme.

Peut-il puiser de l'eau à une fontaine enclavée dans un champ? Non, parce que le propriétaire du champ est, en vertu du droit d'accession, propriétaire de la fontaine.

Peut-il, mourant de faim et de soif, tendre la main à la pitié de ses semblables? Non, parce qu'il y a des lois contre la mendicité.

Peut-il, épuisé de fatigue et manquant d'asile, s'endormir sur le pavé des rues? Non, parce qu'il y a des lois contre le vagabondage.

Peut-il, fuyant cette patrie homicide où tout lui est refusé, aller demander les moyens de vivre, loin des lieux où la vie lui a été donnée? Non, parce qu'il n'est permis de changer de contrée qu'à de certaines conditions, impossibles à remplir pour lui.

Que fera donc ce malheureux? Il vous dira: « J'ai des bras, j'ai une intelligence, j'ai de la force, j'ai de la jeunesse; prenez tout cela, et en échange donnez-moi un peu de pain. » C'est ce que] font et [disent] aujourd'hui [les prolétaires. Mais ici même vous pouvez répondre au pauvre : « Je n'ai pas de travail à vous donner. » Que voulez-vous qu'il fasse alors?] (41–2)

717.11–46   What . . . another.] [*translated from:*] [*no paragraph*] [Qu'est-ce que la concurrence relativement aux travailleurs? C'est le travail mis aux enchères. Un entrepreneur a besoin d'un ouvrier: trois se présentent. « Combien pour votre travail? — Trois francs: j'ai une femme et des enfants. — Bien. Et vous? — Deux francs et demi: je n'ai pas d'enfants, mais j'ai une femme. — A merveille. Et vous? — Deux francs me suffiront: je suis seul. — A vous donc la préférence. » C'en est fait: le marché est conclu! Que deviendront les deux prolétaires exclus? Ils se laisseront mourir de faim, il faut l'espérer. Mais s'ils allaient se faire voleurs? Ne craignez rien, nous avons des gendarmes. Et assassins? Nous avons le bourreau. Quant au plus heureux des trois, son triomphe n'est que provisoire. Vienne un quatrième travailleur assez robuste pour jeûner de deux jour l'un, la pente du rabais sera descendue jusqu'au bout: nouveau paria, nouvelle recrue pour le bagne, peut-être!

Dira-t-on que ces tristes résultats sont exagérés; qu'ils ne sont possibles, dans tous les cas, que lorsque l'emploi ne suffit pas aux bras qui veulent être employés? Je demanderai, à mon tour, si la concurrence porte par aventure en elle-même de quoi empêcher cette disproportion homicide? Si telle industrie manque de bras, qui m'assure que, dans cette immense confusion créée par une compétition universelle, telle autre n'en regorgera pas? Or, n'y eût-il, sur trente-quatre millions d'hommes, que vingt individus réduits à voler pour vivre, cela suffit pour la condamnation du principe.

Mais qui donc serait assez aveugle pour ne point voir que, sous l'empire de la concurrence illimitée, la baisse continue des salaires est un fait nécessairement général, et point du tout exceptionnel? La population a-t-elle des limites qu'il ne lui soit jamais donné de franchir? Nous est-il loisible de dire à l'industrie abandonnée aux caprices de l'égoïsme individuel, à cette industrie, mer si féconde en naufrages: « Tu n'iras pas plus loin? » La population s'accroît sans cesse: ordonnez donc à la mère du pauvre de devenir stérile, et blasphémez Dieu qui l'a rendue féconde; car, si vous ne le faites, la lice sera bientôt trop étroite pour les combattants. Une machine est inventée: ordonnez qu'on la brise, et criez anathème à la science; car, si vous ne le faites, les mille ouvriers que la machine nouvelle chasse de leur atelier iront frapper à la porte de l'atelier voisin et faire baisser le salaire de leurs compagnons. Baisse systématique des salaires, aboutissant à la suppression d'un certain nombre d'ouvriers, voilà l'inévitable effet de la concurrence illimitée. Elle n'est donc qu'un procédé industriel au moyen duquel les prolétaires sont forcés de s'exterminer les uns les autres.] (43–5)

717.47–718.17   If . . . folly.] [*translated from:*] [*no paragraph*] [S'il est un fait incontestable, c'est que l'accroissement de la population est beaucoup plus rapide dans la classe pauvre que dans la classe riche. D'après la *statistique de la civilisation européenne*, les naissances, à Paris, ne sont que du 1/32e de la population dans les quartiers les plus aisés; dans les autres, elles s'élèvent au 1/26e. Cette disproportion est un fait général, et M. de Sismondi, dans son ouvrage sur l'économie politique, l'a très-bien expliqué en l'attribuant à l'impossibilité où les journaliers se trouvent d'espérer et de prévoir. Celui-là seul peut mesurer le nombre de ses enfants à la quotité de son revenu qui se sent maître du lendemain; mais quiconque vit au jour le jour, subit le joug d'une fatalité mystérieuse à laquelle il voue sa race, parce qu'il y a été voué lui-même. Les hospices sont là, d'ailleurs, menaçant la société d'une véritable inondation de mendiants. Quel moyen d'échapper à un tel fléau? [*3-sentence omission*] Il est clair], cependant, [que toute société où la quantité des subsistances croît moins vite que le nombre des hommes est une société penchée sur l'abime. [*2½ page omission*]

La concurrence produit la misère: c'est un fait prouvé par des chiffres.

La misère est horriblement prolifique: c'est un fait prouvé par des chiffres.

La fécondité du pauvre jette dans la société des malheureux qui ont besoin de travailler et ne trouvent pas de travail: c'est un fait prouvé par des chiffres.

Arrivée là, une société n'a plus qu'à choisir entre tuer les pauvres ou les nourrir gratuitement: atrocité ou folie.] (85–9)

718.19–719.15   According . . . well.] [*translated from:*] [Le *bon marché*, voilà le grand mot dans lequel se résument, selon les économistes de l'école des Smith et des Say, tous les bienfaits de la concurrence illimitée. Mais pourquoi s'obstiner à n'envisager les résultats du *bon marché* que relativement au bénéfice momentané que le consommateur en retire? Le *bon marché* ne profite à ceux qui consomment qu'en jetant parmi ceux qui produisent les germes de la plus ruineuse anarchie. Le *bon marché*, c'est la massue avec laquelle les riches producteurs écrasent les producteurs peu aisés. Le *bon marché*, c'est le guetapens dans lequel les spéculateurs hardis font tomber les hommes laborieux. Le *bon marché*, c'est l'arrêt de mort du fabricant qui ne peut faire les avances d'une machine coûteuse que ses rivaux, plus riches, sont en état de se procurer. Le *bon marché*, c'est l'exécuteur des hautes œuvres du monopole; c'est la pompe aspirante de la moyenne industrie, du moyen commerce, de la moyenne propriété; c'est, en un mot, l'anéantissement de la bourgeoisie au profit de quelques oligarques industriels.

Serait-ce que le *bon marché* doive être maudit], considéré en lui-même [? Nul n'oserait soutenir une telle absurdité. Mais c'est le propre des mauvais principes de changer le bien en mal et de corrompre toute chose. Dans le système de la concurrence, le *bon marché* n'est qu'un bienfait provisoire et hypocrite. Il se maintient tant qu'il y a lutte: aussitôt que le plus riche a mis hors de combat tous ses rivaux, les prix remontent. La concurrence conduit au monopole: par la même raison, le *bon marché* conduit à l'exagération des prix. Ainsi, ce qui a été une arme de guerre parmi les producteurs, devient tôt ou tard pour les consommateurs] eux-mêmes [une cause de pauvreté. Que si à cette cause on ajoute toutes celles que nous avons déjà énumérées, et en première ligne l'accroissement désordonné de la population, il faudra bien reconnaître comme un fait né directement de la concurrence, l'appauvrissement de la masse des consommateurs.

Mais, d'un autre côté, cette concurrence, qui tend à tarir les sources de la consommation, pousse la production à une activité dévorante. La confusion produite par l'antagonisme universel dérobe à chaque producteur la connaissance du marché. Il faut qu'il compte sur le hasard pour l'écoulement de ses produits, qu'il enfante dans les ténèbres. Pourquoi se modérerait-il, surtout lorsqu'il lui est permis de rejeter ses pertes sur le salaire si éminemment élastique de l'ouvrier? Il n'est pas jusqu'à ceux qui produisent à perte qui ne continuent à produire, parce qu'ils ne veulent pas laisser périr la valeur de leurs machines,] de leurs outils, [de leurs matières premières,] de leurs constructions, [de ce qui leur reste encore de clientèle, et parce que l'industrie, sous l'empire du principe de concurrence, n'étant plus qu'un jeu de hasard, le joueur ne veut pas renoncer au bénéfice possible de quelque heureux coup de dé.

Donc, et nous ne saurions trop insister sur ce résultat, la concurrence force la production à s'accroître et la consommation à décroître; donc elle va précisément contre le but de la science économique; donc elle est tout à la fois oppression et démence.] (90–3)

719.16–31   And . . . competition.] [*translated from:*] [Je n'ai rien dit, pour éviter les lieux communs et les vérités devenues déclamatoires à force d'être vraies, de l'effroyable pourriture morale que l'industrie, organisée ou plutôt désorganisée comme elle l'est aujourd'hui, a déposée au sein de la bourgeoisie. Tout est devenu vénal, et la concurrence a envahi jusqu'au domaine de la pensée.]

Ainsi, [les fabriques écrasant les métiers; les magasins somptueux absorbant les magasins modestes; l'artisan qui s'appartient remplacé par le journalier qui ne s'appartient pas; l'exploitation par le charrue dominant l'exploitation par la bêche, et faisant passer le champ du pauvre sous la suzeraineté honteuse de l'usurier; les faillites se multipliant; l'industrie transformée par l'extension mal réglée du crédit en un jeu où le gain de la partie n'est assuré à personne, pas même au fripon; et enfin, ce vaste désordre, si propre à éveiller] dans l'âme de chacun [la jalousie, la défiance, la haine, éteignant peu à peu toutes les aspirations généreuses] et tarissant toutes les sources [de la foi, du dévouement, de la poésie . . . voilà le hideux et trop véridique tableau des résultats produits par l'application du principe de concurrence.] (97–8)

BRIGHT, HENRY. Speech in the House of Commons (15 Feb., 1826), quoted in *Parliamentary History* for 1826, 320.

QUOTED: 121–2   REFERRED TO: 123

122.28   "was] [*paragraph*] Mr. *Bright* was (320)

BRODRICK, GEORGE CHARLES. "The Irish Land Question," *Recess Studies.* Ed. Alexander Grant. Edinburgh: Edmonston and Douglas, 1870, 1–53.

REFERRED TO: 677

BROUGHAM, HENRY PETER. Referred to: 399

———— Speech in the House of Commons (13 Feb., 1826), quoted in *Parliamentary History* for 1826, 227–8.

QUOTED: 118

118.24 "experience] He had observed that the opinion of the theorists went in favour of a paper circulation convertible into gold, it being supposed by them (and he confessed that experience (228)

118.25 this theory.] the same theory) that a paper payable in gold by law, on demand, could never exist in excess. (228)

———— Speech on the Corn Laws, *Hansard*, 1 March, 1827, cols. 783–5.

REFERRED TO: 148

BROWN, THOMAS.

NOTE: for details concerning this case, see University of London *v.* Yarrow, 1857 (I De Gex and Jones, 72).

REFERRED TO: 620–1

BUCHANAN, WALTER. Referred to: 550

———— "Evidence taken before the Select Committee on Income and Property Tax," *Parliamentary Papers*, 1861, VII, 212–32.

NOTE: the "quotations" are questions asked by Buchanan, a member of the Committee.

QUOTED: 594–5

BURGESS, HENRY. *A Letter to the Right Hon. George Canning, to explain in what manner the industry of the people, and the productions of the country, are connected with, and influenced by, internal bills of exchange, country bank notes and country bankers, Bank of England notes, and branch banks.* London: Harvey and Darton, 1826.

REFERRED TO: 95n

———— "Minutes of Evidence before the Committee of the Lords, (1826) on the Circulation of Promissory Notes," *Parliamentary Papers*, 1826–27, VI, 558–61.

QUOTED: 94–5

94.39–40 THE . . . LANCASHIRE] The . . . Lancashire (559)
94.40 all the] all (559)
94.40–1 IS BILLS OF EXCHANGE] is bills of exchange (559)
94.48–9 *bills . . . exceeding*] [*not in italics*] (559)
94.49 AMOUNTED TO FOUR-FIFTHS] amounted to four fifths (559)
95.3–4 MORE . . . ONE] more . . . one (559)
95.4 bank] banker (559)
95.8 FIFTY] fifty (559)
95.10 these] those (559)
95.10 these] those (559)

95.11   in great] in a great (559)
95.11–12   *are . . . notes*] [*not in italics*] (559)

BURKE. Referred to: 115

BUTLER, SAMUEL. *Hudibras.* Ed. Zachary Grey. 2 vols. London: Bensley, 1801.

NOTE: copy in JSM's library, Somerville College.

QUOTED: 206

206.18–19   Where . . . fly,] He could reduce all things to acts, / And knew their natures by abstracts; / Where entity and quiddity, / The ghosts of defunct bodies, fly; / Where truth in person does appear, / Like words congeal'd in northern air. (I, 19; Part I, Canto i, ll. 143–8)

CAIRD, JAMES. *The Irish Land Question.* London: Longmans, Green, Reader, and Dyer, 1869.

QUOTED: 677

CANNING, GEORGE. Referred to: 118, 151

NOTE: in Baring's speech, quoted here, the reference to "the right hon. gent." is to Canning.

———— Speech in the House of Commons (13 Feb., 1826), quoted in the *Morning Chronicle*, 14 Feb., 1826, 3–4.

QUOTED: 128

———— Speech on the Corn Laws, *Hansard*, 1 March, 1827, cols. 758–75.

REFERRED TO: 144–5, 149–50

CARLYLE, THOMAS. *Chartism.* London: Fraser, 1840.

NOTE: copy formerly in JSM's library, Somerville College.

REFERRED TO: 370

———— *Past and Present.* London: Chapman and Hall, 1843.

NOTE: copy in JSM's library, Somerville College, inscribed: "To Mrs. Taylor / with kind regards. / T.C."

QUOTED: 372, 379   REFERRED TO: 370

NOTE: JSM attributes the phrase "a fair day's wages for a fair day's work" to "the operatives", into whose mouths Carlyle puts it.

372.36   "a . . . work;"] "A fair day's-wages for a fair day's-work:" it is as just a demand as Governed men ever made of Governing. (24)

379.32–3   "cash . . . man;"] That 'Laissez-faire,' 'Supply-and-demand,' 'Cash-payment for the sole nexus,' and so forth, were not, are not, and will never be, a practicable Law of Union for a Society of Men. (44)

CASH PAYMENTS, Act to restrict. See 37 George III, cc. 45, 91.

CAVE. Referred to: 550

CHADWICK. Referred to: 627

CHARLES I (of England). Referred to: 481

CHARLES II (of England). Referred to: 401, 479–80

CICERO. *De Divinatione.*

NOTE: JSM quotes the same passage in both places. The Latin reads: "nihil tam absurde dici potest, quod non dicatur ab aliquo philosophorum" (2.58.119). There are many editions in JSM's library, Somerville College.

QUOTED: 41, 344

CLEOPATRA. Referred to: 401

CLINTON. Referred to: 185

COBBETT, WILLIAM. Referred to: 185   See *Mansell & Co's. Report.*

COLERIDGE, SAMUEL TAYLOR. *On the Constitution of the Church and State, According to the Idea of Each; with aids towards a right judgment on the late Catholic Bill.* 2nd ed. London: Hurst, Chance, 1830.

NOTE: this edition is in JSM's library, Somerville College, as is the edition which adds the two *Lay Sermons* (London: Pickering, 1839).

REFERRED TO: 220–1

COMBINATION ACTS. See 6 George IV, c. 129.

CONSIDÉRANT, VICTOR PROSPER. *Destiné sociale.* Vol. I. 3me ed. Paris: Librairie phalanstérienne, 1848.

NOTE: JSM's references appear to derive from the reissue (1848) of Vol. I, called the 2nd ed., which in fact reprints the 2nd ed. (1847). The variant notes below give the original from which JSM translates, with square brackets enclosing the passages actually quoted.

QUOTED: 719–27   REFERRED TO: 748n

719.36–8   In . . . revenue. . . . . The] [*translated from:*] [Nous avons d'abord l'ARMÉE qui prélève en France et dans tous les autres pays l'élite de la population en force et en santé, une grande quantité d'hommes de talent et d'intelligence, et une part considérable des revenus publics] : — le tout employé *à ne rien faire de productif,* en attendant que cela soit appliqué *à détruire.* [*1-page omission*] [*paragraph*] [*see next variant*] (35–6)

719.38–43 The . . . diminish. . . . . To] [*translated from:*] [*paragraph*] B) Disons
encore que [la société actuelle fait éclore à son souffle impur d'innombrables
légions de SCISSIONNAIRES, êtres improductifs ou destructeurs: chevaliers d'industrie, prostituées, gens sans aveu, mendiants, prisonniers, filoux, brigands et
autres scissionnaires dont le nombre tend moins que jamais à décroître.] [*1-page
omission*] [*see next variant*] (36)
719.43–720.14 To . . . counter.] [*translated from:*] C) [Au tableau des opérations
improductives que nécessite notre société, il faut ranger celles de la MAGISTRA-
TURE et du parquet, des cours et tribunaux, gendarmes, police, geôliers, bourreaux, etc., fonctions toutes indispensables aujourd'hui à la sûreté de la société;
        D) Sont improductifs encore les OISIFS, gens dits *comme il faut*, passant leur
vie à ne rien faire,] lions et lionnes, tigres et panthères, [les flâneurs et les
fainéants de tous les étages;
        E) Sont improductives les LÉGIONS FISCALES de la douane, des contributions
directes et indirectes, des octrois;] les receveurs, percepteurs, porteurs de con-
traintes, garnisaires, gabeloups, rats de cave, [toute cette immense armée qui
surveille, verbalise et prend, mais qui ne crée pas;
        F) Improductives les élucubrations des SOPHISTES, philosophes, métaphysiciens,
politiques, engagés dans des voies fausses, qui ne font pas avancer la science et
ne produisent que des débats stériles ou des commotions; les verbiages des
avocats, plaideurs, témoins, etc.
        G) Improductives enfin les opérations du COMMERCE, depuis celles des ban-
quiers à la bourse jusqu'à celles de l'épicier derrière son comptoir.] (37)
720.19—721.13 Who . . . only.] [*translated from:*] [*paragraph*] Ce que j'annonce
ici sera démontré sans réplique dans le cours de cet ouvrage: mais [qui déjà,
avec un peu de bonne volonté et de réflexion, refuserait de comprendre combien
l'incohérence, le désordre, la non-combinaison,] le défaut d'association, [le
morcellement de l'industrie livrée aujourd'hui à l'action individuelle, dépourvue
de toute organisation, dépourvue d'ensemble, sont des causes qui rétrécissent la
puissance de la production, perdent ou gaspillent nos moyens d'action? Le
désordre n'enfante-t-il pas la pauvreté, comme l'ordre et la bonne gestion
enfantent la richesse? L'incohérence n'est-elle pas une cause de faiblesse, comme
la combinaison une cause de force? Or, qui peut dire que l'industrie agricole,
domestique, manufacturière, scientifique, artistique et les opérations commerciales, sont organisées aujourd'hui dans la Commune et dans l'État? Qui
peut dire que tous les travaux qui s'exécutent dans ces domaines, sont subordon-
nés à des vues d'ensemble et de prévoyance; qu'ils sont conduits avec économie,
ordre et entente? Oui peut dire encore que notre société a puissance de développer, par une bonne éducation, toutes les facultés que la nature a données
à chacun de ses membres; d'employer chacun d'eux aux fonctions qu'il aimerait,
qu'il saurait le mieux exercer, qu'il exercerait par conséquent avec le plus
d'avantage pour lui et pour les autres? A-t-on seulement pensé à poser le pro-
blème des caractères, de l'emploi social et régulier des aptitudes naturelles et des
vocations? Hélas, l'utopie des plus ardents philanthropes c'est d'apprendre à lire
et à écrire à vingt-cinq millions de Français! Encore peut-on dans les circonstances actuelles les mettre au défi de réussir. [*½-page footnote omitted*]
        N'est-ce pas une étrange chose aussi, et qui accuse bien haut, ce spectacle
d'une société où la terre n'est pas ou est mal cultivée, où l'homme est mal logé,
mal vêtu;] où mille travaux urgents sont à faire, [et où des masses d'individus
manquent à chaque instant de travail, et s'étiolent dans la misère ne pouvant en
trouver? En vérité, en vérité, il faut bien reconnaître que si les nations sont
pauvres et faméliques, ce n'est pas que la nature] et l'art [ne leur fournissent
les moyens de créer d'immenses richesses, mais c'est qu'il y a anarchie et
désordre dans l'emploi que nous faisons de ces éléments: autrement dit, c'est
que la société est piteusement faite, et l'industrie non organisée.
        Mais ce n'est pas tout, et vous n'aurez qu'une faible idée du mal, si vous

ne réfléchissez pas qu'à tous ces vices qui tarissent la source des richesses et du bien-être, il faut ajouter encore la lutte, la discorde, la guerre sous mille noms et mille formes, que notre société fomente et entretient entre tous les individus qui la composent. Et toutes ces luttes, et toutes ces guerres correspondent à des oppositions radicales, à de profondes antinomies de tous les intérêts. Autant vous pourrez établir de classements et de catégories dans la nation, autant vous aurez d'oppositions d'intérêts, de guerres patentes ou latentes, à n'envisager même que le système industriel.] (38–40)

721.20–6 It . . . society.] [*translated from:*] [*no paragraph*] Or, [il est évident que l'intérêt du commerçant est en lutte avec celui du consommateur et du producteur. Le même objet qu'il a intérêt à vous vendre cher, qu'il vous vend cher, en effet, et dont il vante, outre mesure, la qualité, n'a-t-il pas eu intérêt à l'acheter à bon marché au producteur qui l'a créé?] ne l'a-t-il pas déprécié dans leurs transactions? — [Ainsi, l'intérêt du corps commercial, collectivement et individuellement envisagé, est en opposition avec celui du producteur et du consommateur, c'est-à-dire du corps social tout entier.] (43)

721.27—723.44 The . . . it.] [*translated from:*] [Le commerçant est un entremetteur qui met à profit l'anarchie générale, et la non organisation de l'industrie. Le commerçant achète les produits, il achète tout, il est propriétaire et détenteur de tout, de telle sorte que:

1º Il tient *sous le joug* la Production et la Consommation: puisque toutes deux sont obligées de lui demander, soit les produits à consommer en dernier terme, soit les produits bruts qui doivent être encore travaillés, les matières premières. Le Commerce, avec ses menées d'accaparement, de hausse et de baisse, ses opérations sans nombre et la *propriété intermédiaire* des objets, rançonne à droit et à gauche: il fait durement la loi à la Production et à la Consommation, dont il devrait n'être que le commis subalterne.

2º Il spolie le corps social par ses *immenses bénéfices*, — bénéfices prélevés sur le consommateur et le producteur, et tout-à-fait hors de proportion avec des services que le vingtième des agents qu'il emploie suffirait à rendre.

3º Il spolie le corps social par la *distraction* des forces productives, en enlevant aux travaux de création les dix-neuf vingtièmes de ses agents, qui sont de purs parasites. C'est-à-dire, qu'il ne spolie pas seulement en s'appropriant des valeurs sociales à doses exorbitantes, mais encore en diminuant considérablement l'énergie productive de l'atelier social. La très-grande majorité de ses agents reviendront aux fonctions productives aussitôt qu'une organisation commerciale rationnelle sera substituée à l'inextricable état de choses actuel.

4º Il spolie le corps social par la *falsification* des produits, falsification qui se pratique aujourd'hui avec une fureur poussée au-delà de toutes bornes. En effet, quand cent épiciers se sont établis dans une ville où il n'y en avait antérieurement que vingt, on ne consomme pas, pour autant, plus de denrées épicières dans cette ville. Voilà donc ces cent vertueux marchands obligés de s'arracher le profit que faisaient honnêtement les vingt premiers: la concurrence les force à se rattraper aux dépens de la consommation, soit par l'élévation des prix, ce qui arrive quelquefois; soit par la falsification des produits, ce qui arrive toujours. Dans un pareil état de choses il n'y a plus ni foi ni loi. [Les denrées inférieures ou frelatées sont vendues comme denrées de bonne qualité toutes les fois que le chaland bénin n'est pas assez connaisseur pour y voir clair. Et quand elle a bien *attrapé* ledit chaland, la conscience mercantile se reconforte en se disant:— « Je fais mon prix, on est libre de prendre ou de ne pas prendre, je ne force personne à acheter. » — Les pertes dont la falsification et la mauvaise qualité des produits grèvent la consommation sont incalculables.

5º Il spolie le corps social par des *engorgements*, factices ou non, à la suite desquels d'immenses quantités de marchandises encombrées sur un point s'avarient et se détruisent faute d'écoulement. Écoutons Fourier: (*Th. des quat. mouv.*, p. 334, 1ʳᵉ éd.)

« Le principe fondamental des systèmes commerciaux, le principe *laissez une entière liberté aux marchands*, leur accorde la propriété absolue des denrées sur lesquelles ils trafiquent; ils ont le droit de les enlever à la circulation, les cacher et même les brûler, comme a fait plus d'une fois la compagnie orientale d'Amsterdam, qui brûlait publiquement des magasins de canelle pour faire enchérir cette denrée: ce qu'elle faisait sur la canelle, elle l'aurait fait sur le blé, si elle n'eût craint d'être lapidée par le peuple, elle aurait brûlé une partie des blés pour vendre l'autre au quadruple de sa valeur. Eh! ne voit-on pas tous les jours, dans les ports, jeter à la mer des provisions de grains que le négociant a laissés pourrir pour avoir attendu trop long-temps une hausse; moi-même j'ai présidé, en qualité de commis, à ces infâmes opérations, et j'ai fait, un jour, jeter à la mer vingt mille quintaux de riz, qu'on aurait pu vendre avec un honnête bénéfice, si le détenteur eût été moins avide de gain. C'est le corps social qui supporte la perte de ces déperditions qu'on voit se renouveler chaque jour, à l'abri du principe philosophique: *laissez faire les marchands.* »

6⁰ Le commerce spolie encore par les *pertes, avaries, coulages,*] etc., [qui proviennent de l'extrême dissémination des produits et denrées dans des millions de magasins de détail, et par la multiplicité et la complication des transports morcelés.

7⁰ Il spolie le corps social par une *usure* sans limite et sans vergogne, une usure effrayante.] En effet, [le commerçant opère toujours avec un capital fictif, très-supérieur à son capital réel. Tel commerçant, avec un fonds de 30 mille francs, agit, en émettant des billets, par des revirements et des paiements successifs, sur un fonds de 100, 200, 300 mille fr.; il tire donc de ce capital *qu'il n'a pas*] [*5-sentence footnote omitted*] [des intérêts usuraires sans proportion avec ce qu'il possède véritablement.

8⁰ Il spolie le corps social par des *banqueroutes* sans nombre: car les accidens journaliers de nos relations industrielles, les commotions politiques, les perturbations de toute espèce, amènent le jour où le négociant, qui a émis des billets au-delà de ses moyens, ne peut plus faire face à ses affaires; sa débâcle, frauduleuse ou non, porte de rudes coups à ses créanciers. La banqueroute des uns entraîne celle des autres, c'est un feu de file de banqueroutes, une dévastation. Et c'est toujours le producteur et le consommateur qui pâtissent, puisque le commerce, considéré en masse, ne crée pas les richesses et n'engage que des valeurs très-faibles par rapport à la richesse sociale qui passe tout entière entre ses mains. Aussi combien de fabriques sont écrasées sous ces contre-coups! combien de sources fecondes sont taries par ces menées et ces désastres!

Le producteur fournit les denrées; le consommateur, l'argent: le commerce, lui, fournit des billets non hypothéqués ou hypothéqués sur de faibles valeurs, sur un crédit imaginaire; et les membres du corps commercial ne sont pas *solidaires* et *garants* les uns pour les autres!—Voilà en peu de mots toute la théorie de la chose.

9⁰ Il spolie le corps social, par l'*indépendance et l'irresponsabilité* qui lui permettent de n'acheter qu'aux époques où les producteurs, par obligation de se procurer des fonds pour payer les loyers et les avances de la production, sont forcés de vendre et se font entre eux concurrence. Quand les marchés sont très-pourvus et les produits à vil prix, le commerce achète. Puis, il opère la hausse, et par cette manœuvre bien simple il dépouille le producteur et le consommateur.

10⁰ Il spolie le corps social par une considérable *soustraction de capitaux*, qui reviendront à l'industrie productive, quand le commerce jouera son rôle subordonné, ne sera plus qu'une *agence* opérant des transactions directes entre de grands centres de consommation, des Communes sociétaires, et des producteurs plus ou moins éloignés. Ainsi les capitaux engagés dans les spéculations du commerce,—quelque faibles qu'ils soient comparativement à l'immensité des richesses qui passent par ses mains,—n'en composent pas moins des sommes énormes, qui reviendraient féconder la production si la propriété intermédiaire des objets était enlevée au commerce, et la circulation des produits administrativement organisée. *L'agiotage* est la plus odieuse manifestation de ce vice.]

L'agiotage spolie le corps social, en détournant les capitaux pour les faire entrechoquer dans les tripotages de hausse et de baisse, qui fournissent d'énormes bénéfices aux joueurs les plus habiles. Dès-lors les cultures et les fabriques n'obtiennent qu'à un prix exorbitant les capitaux nécessaires à leur exploitation; et les entreprises utiles qui ne donnent qu'un bénéfice lent et pénible, sont dédaignées pour les jeux d'agiotage qui absorbent la majeure partie du numéraire.

(*Th. des quat. mouv.*, p. 359, 1re éd.)

[11º Il spolie le corps social par *l'accaparement*:

Car l'enchérissement d'une matière accaparée est supporté ultérieurement par les consommateurs, et auparavant par les manufacturiers, qui, obligés de soutenir un atelier, font des sacrifices pécuniaires, fabriquent à petits bénéfices, soutiennent, dans l'espoir d'un meilleur avenir,] l'établissement sur lequel se fonde leur existence habituelle, [et ne réussissent que bien tard à établir cette hausse que l'accapareur leur a fait si promptement supporter. (*Ibid.*)]

L'accaparement est le plus odieux des crimes commerciaux, en ce qu'il attaque toujours la partie souffrante de l'industrie: s'il survient une pénurie de subsistances ou denrées quelconques, les accapareurs sont aux aguets pour aggraver le mal, s'emparer des approvisionnements existants, arrher ceux qui sont attendus, les distraire de la circulation, en doubler, tripler le prix par des menées qui exagèrent la rareté et répandent des craintes qu'on reconnaît trop tard pour illusoires. Ils font dans le corps industriel l'effet d'une bande de bourreaux qui irait sur le champ de bataille déchirer et agrandir les plaies des blessés.» (*Quat. Mouv.*, p. 334.)

[Enfin, tous ces vices, et bien d'autres que je n'ai pas cités, se multiplient les uns par les autres dans l'extrême complication des filets mercantiles: car les produits ne passent pas qu'une fois dans les mains avides du Commerce; il en est qui entrent dans vingt et trente filières avant d'être livrés au consommateur. D'abord la matière brute passe par la griffe commerciale pour arriver au fabricant qui lui donne une première façon; puis elle retombe au Commerce; et revient à une fabrication qui lui donne une autre forme; et ainsi de suite, jusqu'aux dernières confections. Alors elle entre dans les grands comptoirs, qui vendent aux magasins en gros, qui vendent aux détaillants des villes, qui vendent aux bas détaillants et détaillants de village. Or, à chaque passage, le produit a laissé quelque chose dans les mains mercantiles.] (46–51)

723.45–724.3 [*paragraph*]. . . . One . . . transaction.] [*translated from:*] [Un de mes amis qui parcourait dernièrement les montagnes du Jura où il se fait,] comme on sait, [une quantité considérable de travaux sur métaux, eut occasion d'entrer chez un paysan qui fabriquait des pelles; il lui demanda le prix de ses pelles:— « Entendons-nous, » répondit le pauvre paysan, pas économiste du tout, mais homme de bon sens; « moi je les vends 16 sous au commerce, qui vous les fait payer 40 dans vos villes. Si vous trouviez moyen de mettre le fabricant en rapport direct avec le consommateur, vous les auriez à 28 sous, et nous y gagnerions 12 sous tous les deux. »] (*Note de la première Édition.*) (54n) [*this is a footnote to the sentence after the last one quoted*]

725.41–726.9 If . . . end!] [*translated from:*] [Si les producteurs de vins demandent l'abolition des douanes [½-*page footnote omitted*], et la liberté d'importation et d'exportation, cette liberté ruine les producteurs de blé, les fabricants de fer, de draps, de coton, et, il faut le dire encore,] puisque cela est, [les contrebandiers et les douaniers. S'il est de l'intérêt des consommateurs que des machines soient inventées qui produisent à moins de frais et baissent le prix des objets, ces machines cassent les bras à des milliers d'ouvriers qui ne savent, ni ne peuvent s'employer aussitôt à d'autres travaux. C'est encore là un des mille *cercles vicieux* de la Civilisation], qui demanderait un chapitre d'observations, d'analyse et de critique: [car il y a mille faits qui prouvent cumulativement que, dans le

Régime social actuel, la production d'un bien entraîne toujours la production d'un mal avec elle.

Enfin, si vous descendez encore plus bas, si vous en venez aux détails vulgaires, vous trouvez que le tailleur, le cordonnier, le chapelier, ont intérêt à ce que les vêtements, les chaussures et les chapeaux soient promptement usés; que le vitrier a intérêt à la grêle et aux orages qui brisent les vitres; le maçon et l'architecte aux incendies. L'avocat s'enrichit aux procès, le médecin aux maladies, le marchand de vin à l'ivrognerie, la fille de joie à la débauche. Et quel malheur pour la magistrature, les gendarmes, les geôliers, comme pour les avocats, les avoués et toute la basoche, si les crimes, les délits et les procès venaient tout à coup à disparaître!] (59–60)

726.11–42 Add . . . abandoned.] [*translated from:*] [Ajoutez à tout cela que la Civilisation, qui sème de tout côté la division,] la zizanie [et la guerre, qui emploie une grande partie de ses forces à faire de grands travaux improductifs, ou à détruire; qui diminue considérablement encore la richesse générale par les frottements sans nombre et le désordre de son industrie; ajoutez à tout cela, dis-je, que cette forme sociale a pour caractère de produire la *répugnance industrielle,* le dégoût du travail.

Partout vous entendrez le travailleur, ouvrier ou fonctionnaire, maudire son sort et son occupation, soupirer après la retraite qui le délivrera enfin du supplice que sa position lui impose. C'est le grand, le fatal caractère de l'industrie civilisée, d'être répugnante, de n'avoir pour mobile pivotal que la *peur de mourir de faim.* Le travailleur civilisé est un véritable forçat. Tant que le travail productif ne sera pas organisé de manière à se conjuguer sur *plaisir* au lieu de se conjuguer sur *peine, ennui* et *répugnance,* il arrivera toujours que ceux qui pourront s'y soustraire l'éviteront. Ceux-là seuls se livreront au travail qui y seront CONTRAINTS [par le dénuement] et la misère, [sauf rares exceptions. Dèslors, les classes les plus nombreuses, les artisans de la richesse sociale, les créateurs actifs et directs du bien-être et du luxe seront toujours condamnés à côtoyer la misère et la faim; ils seront toujours inféodés à l'ignorance et à l'abrutissement; ils seront toujours ce vaste troupeau d'*hommes de somme* que nous voyons déformés, décimés par les maladies, et courbés, dans le grand atelier social, sur le sillon ou sur l'établi, pour préparer la nourriture raffinée et les somptueuses jouissances des classes supérieures et oisives.

Tant qu'on n'aura pas réalisé un procédé d'INDUSTRIE ATTRAYANTE, il sera vrai « *qu'il faut beaucoup de pauvres pour qu'il y ait quelques riches;* » aphorisme hideux et lâche, que vous entendez chaque jour passer, comme un axiome d'éternelle nécessité, sur les lèvres de gens qui se disent chrétiens ou philosophes! Il est très-facile de comprendre que l'oppression, la fourberie, l'indigence surtout, seront l'apanage permanent et fatal de toute société caractérisée par la répugnance industrielle, puisque alors c'est l'indigence seule qui peut] condamner et [forcer l'homme au travail; — et la preuve] péremptoire, [c'est que si tous les ouvriers, si tout le monde devenait riche subitement, les dix-neuf vingtièmes des travaux seraient abandonnés !!] (60–1)

727.3–7 This . . . them.] [*translated from:*] [Cette Féodalité,] avons-nous vu, [serait constituée dès que la plus grande partie des propriétés industrielles et territoriales de la nation appartiendrait à une minorité qui en absorberait tous les revenus, pendant que l'immense majorité, attachée aux bagnes manufacturiers et courbée à la glèbe, rongerait le salaire qu'on voudrait bien lui laisser.] (134)

CORN LAWS, BILLS. Most of the references are general, but see 3 George IV, c. 60; 7 & 8 George IV, c. 57; 9 George IV, c. 60; and 5 & 6 Victoria, Sess. 2, c. 14.

COULSON, WALTER (?). "Silk Trade," *Parliamentary Review for 1826*, 710–18.

NOTE: in George Grote's copy of this volume (University of London Library) the article is marginally identified in the Table of Contents as by "W. C."; in the volume for 1825, a pasted-in sheet identifies Walter Coulson as author of the article on the Game Laws.

REFERRED TO: 258n

COWPER. Referred to: 764

CURTEIS, EDWARD JEREMIAH. Speech in the House of Commons, 21 May, 1824, quoted in the *Morning Chronicle*, 22 May, 1824, 2.

QUOTED: 48n

DAVENPORT, D. Speech in the House of Commons (15 Feb., 1826), quoted in *Parliamentary History* for 1826, 319–20.

QUOTED: 122

122.26 "called] He called (320)
122.27 bills."] bills, and to look to themselves in time, before a perseverance in error brought ruin upon the country. (320)

DAVISON, JOHN. "Evidence (brought from the Lords) Relative to Foreign Trade: (Silk and Wine Trade)," *Parliamentary Papers*, 1821, VII, 452–4.

NOTE: JSM may be quoting from Moreau's transcription (*Rise and Progress*, 16–7) of Davison's evidence.

QUOTED: 133

133.8 sea."] sea; the duty is very heavy. (453)

DE QUINCEY, THOMAS. *The Logic of Political Economy*. Edinburgh: Blackwood, 1844.

NOTE: JSM quotes two of the passages cited below in his *Principles*: cf. 396–8 with *Collected Works*, III, 462, 462–3, and the variants below with *ibid.*, 1107–8.

REVIEWED: 393–404

QUOTED: 393, 396–404

393.22–3 *the laxity . . . science.*] [*not in italics*] (iii)
393.23 *science.* If] science. For example, that one desperate enormity of vicious logic, which takes place in the ordinary application to price of the relation between supply and demand, has ruined more arguments dispersed through speeches, books, journals, than a long life could fully expose. Let us judge by analogy drawn from mathematics. If (iii–iv)
393.28 facts] parts (iv)
393.29 ruins . . . . . Such] ruins. That science, which now holds "acquaintance with the stars" by means of its inevitable and imperishable truth, would become as treacherous as Shakspeare's "stairs of sand:" or, like the fantastic architecture

784 APPENDIX E

which the winds are everlastingly pursuing in the Arabian desert, would exhibit phantom arrays of fleeting columns and fluctuating edifices, which, under the very breath that had created them, would be for ever collapsing into dust. Such (iv)

393.30 practical application] *practical* applications (iv)
395.34 "a] Here lies a (vii)
396.27 Epsilon and Omicron.] *Epsilon* and *Omicron*:— (14)
396.32 that?] [*in italics*] (14)
396.37 that] [*in italics*] (15)
397.2 "a] It is in the next step that a (15)
397.2 insurmountable . . . which] insurmountable. It is a difficulty which (16)
397.11 The] [*no paragraph*] The (23)
397.24–5 cases out of] cases of (24)
397.32 price. U] price: U (24)
397.34 reversed: you] reversed. You (24)
397.36 for the] for a (24)
397.46 guineas] [*18-sentence footnote omitted*] (25–7)
398.16 gradation] graduation (28)
398.30 Suppose] Now, suppose the case reversed: suppose (30)
398.30 become the] become suddenly the (30)
398.35 utmost height] [*not in italics*] (30)
398.35 height. The] [*3-sentence omission*] (30)
398.40 not] [*in italics*] (30)
399.9 People] [*no paragraph*] People (viii)
399.10 does] [*in italics*] (viii)
400.20 all the world] the whole world (127) [*cf.* 399.15]
400.23 Try] [*no paragraph*] Try (127)
400.30 the price] it (127)
401.8 "whilst] Consequently, whilst (ix)
401.8 natural price] "*natural* price" (ix)
401.9 market price] "*market* price" (ix)
401.10 supply and] Supply to (ix)
401.10 binomial,"] binomial. (ix)
401.29 sale of] sale in England of (61)
401.38 more] [*in italics*] (62)
401.39 why—] why? (62)
402.39 No] no (77)
402.43 as from] as (77)
403.12 rank . . . You] rank. Ricardo ought not to have overlooked a case so broad as this. You (84)
403.20 produced . . . producing] produc*ed* . . . produc*ing* (84)
404.4 "corn traitors"] And, on the other hand, by parity of reason, if, 1. through draining; 2. guano; 3. bone dust; 4. spade culture, &c., the agriculturists of this country should, (as probably they will, if not disturbed by corn traitors,) through the known antagonist movement to that of rent, translate the land of England within the next century to a higher key, so that No. 250 were to become equal in power with the present No. 210—and so regressively, No. 40 equal with the present No. 1—in that case all functions of capital (wages, rent, profit) would rise gradually and concurrently, though not equally. (245n)
404.4–5 "corn-law incendiaries"] The corn-law incendiaries here, as every where when they approach the facts or the principles of the question, betray an ignorance which could not be surpassed if the discussion were remitted to Ashantee or Negroland. (152)
404.15 Although] [*no paragraph*] To this next step, therefore, let us now proceed, after warning the reader that even Ricardo has not escaped the snare which is here spread for the understanding; and that, although (16)

404.17   yet errors] yet that errors (16)
404.21   happen that a] happen (as it *has* happened in the present case,) though a [*sic*] (16–7)

DESCARTES. Referred to: 212

DILKE. Referred to: 766

DISRAELI. Referred to: 464, 500

DOMITIAN. Referred to: 713

DRUMMOND. Referred to: 198

DUFFERIN, LORD. See Blackwood.

DUVEYRIER, CHARLES. *Lettres politiques.* 2 vols. Paris: Amyot, 1843.
REFERRED TO: 382n

The Economist (London). Referred to: 432

Edinburgh Review. Referred to: 47

ELDON, LORD. See Scott, John.

ELLIS, JOHN. "Evidence taken before the Select Committee on the Savings of the Middle and Working Classes," *Parliamentary Papers*, 1850, XIX, 253–66.
NOTE: the "quotations" are questions asked by Ellis, a member of the Committee.
QUOTED: 413–14   REFERRED TO: 406

ELLIS, WILLIAM. "McCulloch's Discourse on Political Economy," *Westminster Review*, IV (July, 1825), 88–92.
NOTE: Ellis was co-author of this review, which is printed at 757–60.
REFERRED TO: 757

ESTCOURT, THOMAS HENRY SOTHERON. Referred to: 464, 550
NOTE: in the original headnote to the 1852 Committee, Estcourt is called Mr. Sotheron.

———— "Evidence taken before the Select Committee on Income and Property Tax," *Parliamentary Papers*, 1861, VII, 212–32.

NOTE: the "quotations" are questions asked by Estcourt, a member of the Committee.

QUOTED: 597–8

EUCLID. *Elements*. Referred to: 35, 327

NOTE: as the references are general, no edition is cited.

EVIDENCE. See Parliamentary Papers.

EWART, WILLIAM. "Minutes of Evidence taken before the Select Committee on the Savings of the Middle and Working Classes," *Parliamentary Papers*, 1850, XIX, 253–66.

NOTE: the "quotations" are questions asked by Ewart, who is omitted from the list of members of the Committee.

QUOTED: 412, 414, 416–19   REFERRED TO: 406

FERDINAND VII (of Spain). Referred to: 49

FERGUS. Referred to: 500

FITCH, JOSHUA GIRLING. "Educational Endowments," *Fraser's Magazine*, LXXIX (Jan., 1869), 1–15.

QUOTED: 616–17

616.15   "estimate] [*paragraph*] Ere long it may be hoped that statesmen will try to estimate (11)
616.16   benevolence," and to "see] benevolence; and will see (11)
616.18   charities," but urges them "to] charities. When they do this, they will certainly be prepared to (11)
616.19   *persons*, make] *persons*, will make (11)

FONTENELLE, BERNARD LE BOVIER DE. *Digression sur les Anciens et les Modernes*, in *Œuvres*, Vol. IV. New edition. Paris: Libraires associés, 1766.

NOTE: copy of this edition in JSM's library, Somerville College; the quotation is indirect.

QUOTED: 366

366.11–12   mankind . . . error.] Telle est notre condition, qu'il ne nous est point permis d'arriver tout d'un coup à rien de raisonnable sur quelque matière que ce soit; il faut avant cela que nous nous égarions long-temps, & que nous passions par diverses sortes d'erreurs & par divers degrés d'impertinences. (177)

FOURIER, FRANÇOIS MARIE CHARLES. Referred to: 446, 727–8, 730, 737–8, 747, 748n

—————— *Théorie des Quatre Mouvements et des destinées générales,* Vol. I of *Œuvres Complètes.* 2nd ed. Paris: Bureaux de la Phalange, 1841.

NOTE: JSM is following Considérant, who quotes from the 1st ed., which has not been consulted; therefore no variants are recorded.

QUOTED: 722–3

Fox. Referred to: 115

GLADSTONE, JOHN. "Evidence before the Committee of the Lords, (1826) on the Circulation of Promissory Notes," *Parliamentary Papers,* 1826– 27, VI, 511–20.

QUOTED: 93

93.28 We] Do they [banking establishments] allow interest upon deposits?—Perhaps, if I was to state in detail the manner in which our business is conducted, it might save the trouble of putting further questions. We (511)
93.30 *bills on London*] [*not in italics*] (511)
93.31 these] those (511)
93.31 *pay . . . bankers*] [*not in italics*] (511)
93.31 *receive from them*] [*not in italics*] (511)
93.33 We have] Are you to be understood that the circulation of Lancashire is carried on by bills of exchange in part, with the exception of that part of the circulation which is destined to the payment of labourers wages and various expenses on merchandize?—Not altogether; we also have (513)
93.34 *payment of duties*] [*not in italics*] (513)
93.35 *remittance*] [*not in italics*] (513)
93.35–6 THE . . . EXCHANGE] the . . . exchange (513)
93.37 *charges of merchandize*] [*not in italics*] (513)
93.37 *duties, freights*] [*not in italics*] (513)
93.37 items. I] items; for such purposes a house carrying on business to any extent may require 500*l.* or 1,000*l.* weekly. [*paragraph*] Have you any notion of the proportion of the circulation of Lancashire carried on by bills of exchange, and by Bank of England notes and cash?—I would not venture to give an opinion upon that subject; I think it is quite impossible to ascertain the extent of the one or the other, we have no means of doing so. I (513)
93.39 limited.] limited; but I would not venture an opinion upon the proportions, having no data on which I could correctly found it. (513)

GLADSTONE, WILLIAM EWART. Referred to: 550, 586

—————— "Evidence taken before the Select Committee on Income and Property Tax," *Parliamentary Papers,* 1861, VII, 212–32.

NOTE: the "quotations" are questions asked by Gladstone (Chancellor of the Exchequer), a member of the Committee.

QUOTED: 562–75

GLYN. Referred to: 500

GORDON, R. Speech in the House of Commons (15 Feb., 1826), quoted in *Parliamentary History* for 1826, 320.

QUOTED: 122–3

123.1   "The] [*paragraph*] Mr. *R. Gordon* said, that the (320)
123.2   member.] member (Mr. Sykes).
123.3   assist the] assist the interests of the (320)
123.5   judge] best judges (320)

GRACCHI. Referred to: 681.39

GRAHAM. Referred to: 500

GREENE, THOMAS. "Evidence taken before the Select Committee on the Savings of the Middle and Working Classes," *Parliamentary Papers*, 1850, XIX, 253–66.

NOTE: the "quotation" is a question asked by Greene, a member of the Committee.

QUOTED: 414   REFERRED TO: 406

GREG, SAMUEL. *Two Letters to Leonard Horner, Esq., on the Capabilities of the Factory System*. London: Taylor and Walton, 1840.

QUOTED: 381–2

381.27 which can] to (26)
381.28 benevolence from] benevolence (26)
381.37 "get rid of his aborigines."] There were only three or four families at this time on the spot, and my first care was to get rid of these aborigines and start entirely *de novo*. (5)
381.37 "endeavoured] In doing this [collecting hands], I endeavoured (5)
381.38 we] I (5)
381.39 we] I (5)
381.40 home] [*in italics*] (6)
382.1   migratory] [*in italics*] (6)

GRENFELL, PASCOE. Speech in the House of Commons (13 Feb., 1826), quoted in *Parliamentary History* for 1826, 227.

QUOTED: 118

118.14 it.] it (cheers). (227)
118.17 circulation.] circulation (cheers). (227)

GREY. Referred to: 432

GROSVENOR. Referred to: 453n

GURNEY, HUDSON. Speech in the House of Commons (13 Feb., 1826), quoted in *Parliamentary History* for 1826, 218.

QUOTED: 117   REFERRED TO: 114n

117.26 "could not help] He could not, he said, help (218)

GURNEY, SAMUEL. "Evidence taken before the Committee of Secrecy on the Bank of England Charter," *Parliamentary Papers*, 1831–32, VI, 249–69.

REFERRED TO: 351

HALDIMAND, WILLIAM. "Evidence taken before the Select Committee on the Expediency of the Bank Resuming Cash Payments," *Parliamentary Papers*, 1819, III, 54–71.

QUOTED: 85

85.36   "the Paris bankers,] The Paris bankers, therefore, (56)
85.39   advance] advantage (56)

HALE, WILLIAM. "Evidence (brought from the Lords) Relative to Foreign Trade: (Silk and Wine Trade)," *Parliamentary Papers*, 1821, VII, 437–42.

NOTE: JSM may be quoting from Moreau's transcription (*Rise and Progress*, 15–6) of Hale's evidence.

QUOTED: 133

133.17   "I] Quite so; I (437)
133.21   now are] are now (437)
133.23   the kingdom] this kingdom (437)

HANCOCK, WILLIAM NEILSON. *Impediments to the Prosperity of Ireland.* London: Simms and McIntyre, 1850.

NOTE: as JSM is quoting Hancock from Leslie, *Land Systems*, 52–3, the (extensive) variants are not recorded.

REFERRED TO: 683n

HANKEY, THOMSON. Referred to: 500

——— "Evidence taken before the Select Committee on the Bank Acts," *Parliamentary Papers*, 1857 (Sess. 2), X.i, 177–206.

NOTE: the "quotations" are questions asked by Hankey, a member of the Committee.

QUOTED: 534–9

HAYS, JOHN. *Observations on the Existing Corn Laws.* London: Richardson, 1824.

NOTE: mentioned only in the title and at 63n.

REVIEWED: 47–70

HEATHCOTE. Referred to: 550

HELPS, ARTHUR. *The Claims of Labour. An Essay on the Duties of the Employers to the Employed.* London: Pickering, 1844.

NOTE: the quotations are not from "the introduction," as JSM says, but from the first chapter.

REVIEWED: 365–89

QUOTED: 365

365.12 "how] The inquiring historian will give these things [new modes of luxury, or new resources in art] their weight, but will, nevertheless, persevere in asking how (3)
362.12 are fed,] were fed, and (3)
362.13 corresponds] corresponded (3)

———— *Essays Written in the Intervals of Business.* London: Pickering, 1841.

REFERRED TO: 380

———— *Thoughts in the Cloister and the Crowd.* London: Wix, 1835.

REFFERED TO: 380

HENLEY, JOSEPH WARNER. Referred to: 464

———— "Evidence taken before the Select Committee on Income and Property Tax," *Parliamentary Papers*, 1852, IX, 284–95, 298–324.

NOTE: the "quotations" are questions asked by Henley, a member of the Committee.

QUOTED: 480–6, 492–4

HENRY VIII (of England). Referred to: 484. See also 26 Henry VIII, c. 1.

HEYGATE, FREDERICK WILLIAM. Referred to: 550

———— "Evidence taken before the Select Committee on Income and Property Tax," *Parliamentary Papers*, 1861, VII, 212–32.

NOTE: The "quotations" are questions asked by Heygate, a member of the Committee.

QUOTED: 583–4

HEYGATE, WILLIAM. Speech in the House of Commons (14 Feb., 1826), quoted in *Parliamentary History* for 1826, 236.

QUOTED: 117

117.23 "excepting] Excepting (236)

HILDYARD, ROBERT CHARLES. Referred to: 500

———— "Evidence taken before the Select Committee on the Bank Acts," *Parliamentary Papers*, 1857 (Sess. 2), X.i, 177–206.

NOTE: the "quotations" are questions asked by Hildyard, a member of the Committee.
QUOTED: 528–34

HOBBES, THOMAS. *Leviathan, or the Matter, Form, and Power of a Commonwealth, Ecclesiastical and Civil*, in *The English Works of Thomas Hobbes*, III. Ed. William Molesworth. London: Bohn, 1839.

NOTE: the quotation at 715 is indirect. Copy in JSM's library, Somerville College.
QUOTED: 715, 749

749.19   In] [*no paragraph*] In (113)
749.20   no use] nor use (113)

HORNER, FRANCIS. Referred to: 115, 117

HORNER, LEONARD. Referred to: 381

HORSMAN, EDWARD. "Evidence taken before the Select Committee on Income and Property Tax," *Parliamentary Papers*, 1852, IX, 284–95, 298–324.

NOTE: the "quotations" are questions asked by Horsman, a member of the Committee.
QUOTED: 478, 495–6

HOUSE TAX. See 14 & 15 Victoria, c. 36.

HOWARD, JAMES. *Continental Farming and Peasantry*. London: Ridgway, 1870.

REFERRED TO: 685

HOWITT, WILLIAM. *The Rural Life of England*. 2 vols. London: Longman, Orme, Brown, Green, and Longmans, 1838.

NOTE: Howitt is quoting from his own article in *Tait's Edinburgh Magazine*, Nov., 1835.

QUOTED: 387n–388n

387.n33   "are] [*paragraph*] There are, in the outskirts of Nottingham, upwards of 5000 gardens, the bulk of which are (II, 305)
387.n42   cleared] cleaned (II, 307)
388.n1   cleaning] clearing (II, 307)
388.n6   windows . . . . . The] windows, good cellars for a deposit of choice wines, a kitchen, and all necessary apparatus, and a good pump to supply them with water. Many are very picturesque rustic huts, built with great taste, and hidden by tall hedges in a perfect little paradise of lawn and shrubbery—most delightful spots to go and read in of a summer day, or to take a dinner or tea in with a pleasant party of friends. Some of these places which belong to the substantial

tradespeople have cost their occupiers from one to five hundred pounds, and the pleasure they take in them may be thence imagined; but many of the mechanics have very excellent summer-houses, and there they delight to go, and smoke a solitary pipe, as they look over the smiling face of their garden, or take a quiet stroll amongst their flowers: or to take a pipe with a friend; or to spend a Sunday afternoon, or a summer evening, with their families. The (II, 307–8)

388.n7–8   calculated . . . . . You] calculated—and then the health and the improved taste! You (II, 308)
388.n9   now carrying] now are carrying (II, 308)
388.n14   "What a contrast," . . . "the] And then to think of the (II, 308) [cf. 388.n16 below]
388.n15   politics-loving] politics-brawling (II, 308)
388.n16   attraction."] attraction,—to think of this, and then to see the variety of sources of a beautiful and healthful interest which they create for themselves here:—what a contrast!—what a most gratifying contrast! (II, 308)
388.n17   "seems] At Nottingham, as I have observed, the taste seems (II, 309)
388.n20   rent] rental (II, 310)
388.n21   are] they get (II, 310)
388.n21–2   fresh . . . . . These gardens let] fresh. [paragraph] There are, according to a personal examination made by myself, now, upwards of 5000 of these gardens, containing, as single gardens, 400 square yards each,—the general scale of a garden; though a good many are held as double, and even treble gardens. These let (II, 310)
388.n22   which,] but (II, 310)
388.n23   garden . . . . . Thus] garden, or a total of 6250l. [3-sentence omission] [paragraph] Thus, (II, 310)
388.n24   person] persons (II, 310)

HUBBARD, JOHN GELLIBRAND. Referred to: 550

———— "Evidence taken before the Select Committee on Income and Property Tax," Parliamentary Papers, 1861, VII, 212–32.

NOTE: the "quotations" are questions asked by Hubbard, Chairman of the Committee.

QUOTED: 551–61, 595–7

———— "Memorandum submitted by the Chairman, Appendix 1 to the Report from the Select Committee on Income and Property Tax," Parliamentary Papers, 1861, VII, 315–17.

QUOTED: 584   REFERRED TO: 554–98 passim

584.20   those] these (284)
584.22   owners."] owners; and I would add that I not only do not desire, but, on the contrary, condemn any proposition for treating incomes of this class differentially, in virtue of any artificial peculiarity in the tenure of the owners. (284)

HUME, DAVID. Referred to: 184

HUME, JOSEPH. "Evidence taken before the Select Committee on Income and Property Tax," *Parliamentary Papers,* 1852, IX, 284–95, 198–324.

NOTE: the "quotations" are questions asked by Hume, Chairman of the Committee.
QUOTED: 464, 466–9, 471–6, 478–9, 486–92, 498

HUSKISSON, WILLIAM. Referred to: 132

———— *The Question concerning the Depreciation of our Currency Stated and Examined.* London: Murray, 1810.
REFERRED TO: 188

———— Speech in the House of Commons (10 Feb., 1826), quoted in *Parliamentary History* for 1826, 199–203.
REFERRED TO: 119

———— Speech on Mr. Ellice's Motion for a Select Committee on the State of the Silk Trade, *Hansard,* 23 February, 1826, cols. 763–809.
REFERRED TO: 139

JACOB, WILLIAM. "Evidence taken before the Select Committee to whom the several Petitions complaining of the Depressed State of the Agriculture in the United Kingdom, were Referred," *Parliamentary Papers,* 1821, IX, 355–76.
QUOTED: 56n

JOHNSTONE. Referred to: 500

JONES, CHARLES. See *Mansell & Co's Report*

JONES, RICHARD. *An Essay on the Distribution of Wealth, and on the Sources of Taxation.* London: Murray, 1831.
REFERRED TO: 394

KETTLE. Referred to: 666

KING, PETER. Referred to: 158–9

———— *Speech of the Right Hon. Lord King, in the House of Lords, on Tuesday, July 2, 1811, upon the Second Reading of Earl Stanhope's Bill, respecting Guineas and Bank Notes.* London: Ridgway, 1811.
REFERRED TO: 188

———— *Thoughts on the Restriction of Payments in Specie at the Banks of England and Ireland.* London: Cadell and Davies, 1803.

REFERRED TO: 188

KNIGHT, CHARLES. *The Rights of Industry: Addressed to the Working-Men of the United Kingdom.* London: Knight, 1831.

NOTE: the quotation is not specific, so no variant is given, but see Knight, 56. The work appeared as part of *The Working Man's Companion* (Society for the Diffusion of Useful Knowledge).

QUOTED: 385

LANSDOWNE, MARQUESS OF. See Petty-Fitzmaurice.

LAVELEYE, EMILE DE. "The Land System of Belgium and Holland," in *Systems of Land Tenure in Various Countries. A Series of Essays published under the sanction of the Cobden Club.* London: Macmillan, 1870, 228–78.

REFERRED TO: 684–5

LAVERGNE. Referred to: 684

LAW. Referred to: 184

NOTE: reference is to "Law's Mississippi Scheme."

LAWSON, JAMES ANTHONY. *Five Lectures on Political Economy; delivered before the University of Dublin, in Michaelmas Term, 1843.* London: Parker, 1844.

REFERRED TO: 449

LECLAIR, EDMÉ-JEAN. *Des améliorations qu'il serait possible d'apporter dans le sort des ouvriers peintres en bâtiments, suivies des règlements d'administration et de répartition des bénéfices que produit le travail.* Paris: Bouchard-Huzard, n.d.

REFERRED TO: 415

———— *Répartition des bénéfices du travail en 1842.*

NOTE: no copy of this work has been consulted; JSM's reference is from Duveyrier's *Lettres politiques,* II, 258ff.

REFERRED TO: 382n–383n

LESAGE, ALAIN-RENÉ. *Gil Blas de Santillane.*

NOTE: as JSM mentions no edition, and there is none in Somerville College, none is specified.

REFERRED TO: 212

LESLIE, THOMAS EDWARD CLIFFE. "The Land System of France," in *Systems of Land Tenure in Various Countries. A Series of Essays published under the sanction of the Cobden Club.* London: Macmillan, 1870, 328–52.

REFERRED TO: 685

——— *Land Systems and Industrial Economy of Ireland, England, and Continental Countries.* London: Longmans, Green, 1870.

REVIEWED: 671–85

QUOTED: 671, 673–4, 676–82, 683n–685n

671.13 A] [*no paragraph*] And in virtue of these terms, and a few others of like generality, a (89)
673.14 has been] has, however, been (123)
673.14–15 of eminence, ... that] of the eminence of Mr. Lowe, that (123)
673.21 one; and] one. And (124) *see* 673*a–a*]
673.32 makes] tends to make (124) [*see* 673*b–b*]
673.35 part . . . . . The] [*ellipsis indicates 5-sentence omission, including quotations from JSM*] (124–5)
673.35 The] And the (125)
673.45 deer-parks] deer forests (125) [*see* 673*c–c*]
674.2 both in] in both (126)
674.6 Wealth . . . classes.] [*no paragraph*] 'The desire for wealth,' in the same way (which is by no means, as already observed, the same thing with private interest, for wealth . . . classes*), is really a name for a multiplicity of wants, passions, and ideas, widely differing from each other, both in their nature and in their effects on production—as the accumulation of land differs from the hunger for bread—yet it stands for one identical and industrious principle with many considerable speakers and writers. [*the footnote quotes from a speech by Lowe in the House of Commons, 14 March*] (88–9)
674.15 He] [*no paragraph*] He (126)
674.16 like] be glad (126) [*see* 674*d–d*]
674.17 by farming] by his farming (126) [*see* 674*e–e*]
674.24 fact . . . . . that] fact previously mentioned that (126)
676.n1 The] [*no paragraph*] But the (41)
676.n2 *his own*] [*no italics*] (41)
676.n2 and] or (41) [*printer's error? See* 676*f–f*]
676.n3 possession . . . . . The] possession; nor are his means augmented by the scarcity of labour. [*46-page jump*] Moreover, the (41, 87)
676.n5–8 all . . . . . Were . . . him? . . . If] all. [*jump back to passage previously quoted*] Were . . . him? [*return to later passage*] If (87, 41, 87)
676.n21 Although] It ought to be sufficiently clear to every professed economist that, although (97)
676.n23 do; . . . it] do; and that it (97)
676.12 "through] [*paragraph*] It is not meant that in every case the substitution of pasture for tillage is a change for the worse, for a good tillage farm should have a portion, if possible, in permanent grass properly supplied with manure; but that the total extent of cultivation, in place of decreasing ought to have largely increased, is not only agreed by the highest authorities on agriculture in the island, but shows itself in an actual diminution in cattle as well as of crops, through (64–5)
676.13 soil,"] soil. (65)
677.29 punctuality.] punctuality.* [*footnote:*] 'Irish Land Question.' By the Honourable George Charles Brodrick. 'Recess Studies.' (67n)

677.33   grass . . . waste] 'grass . . . waste' (67) [see 677g–g]

677.34   farms.] farms.† [footnote gives figures quoted from Brodrick] (67n–68n)

678.3   them.] them.* [footnote:] On this subject, as on many others which cannot be discussed with the same advantage in these pages, the reader is referred to the letters of Mr. Morris, Times Commissioner, on the 'Irish Land Question'. (68n)

678.15   "there] There (18)

678.17   including] excluding (18)

678.18   agriculture] cultivation (18)

678.21   In] [no paragraph] In (39)

678.38–9   themselves.' . . . . Other] themselves. The condition of the country here shows rapid amelioration.' [paragraph] Other (39)

679.3   "a] Draw a (70)

679.5   south"] south, and the angle contained by those lines between the capital and the Atlantic—covering about three-fourths of an island which ought to be studded with cities, fine country towns, and smiling villages—does not include one large or flourishing city, and includes hardly a town or village whose trade and population have not decreased in the last twenty years. (70)

679.19   "exceeded] In the last quarter of the seventeenth century their number exceeded (164)

679.20–2   to . . . population.] 'to . . . population.'* [footnote:] *Macaulay's 'History of England,' chap. iii. (164)

679.24   The] [no paragraph] Now the (163)

679.26   dependence] independence (163) [see 679h–h]

679.30   essential respects] economical aspects (163) [see 679i–i]

679.36   Every] [paragraph] Thus every (174)

680.2   insecurity;] insecurity;* [footnote:] *Caird's 'English Agriculture,' p. 505. (174n)

680.3   and that of the] and the (174)

680.5   above the] above that of the (174) [see 680j–j and previous variant]

680.7   had] has (174) [see 680k–k]

680.14   In] [paragraph] Paradoxical as it may be, especially in contrast with the progress of England in trade and manufactures, and the progressive rise of the cultivators of the soil in all other civilised countries, from the Southern States of America to Russia, it is strictly true, that the condition of the English rural population in every grade below the landed gentry has retrograded; and, in (162)

681.31   would] could (191) [see 681l–l]

681.36   of the population] of population (192) [see 681m]

681.37–8   accomplish . . . . . . And] accomplish, and what we want is a remedy which needs only an adequate reform of Parliament for its accomplishment. And (192)

681.39   model, ... we] model—if the feudal model is set before us only as a warning—we (192)

682.4   To] There is one way to remedy the old and new evils together, and at once to purge our jurisprudence, and to emancipate land from its burdens and trammels—and that is to (198)

682.11–12   incumbrance; with the addition, of course, of assimilating the devolution of land, in case] incumbrance. [1-page omission] [paragraph] To complete the emancipation of land from artificial restrictions on its distribution and use out of the feudal line of descent, it is necessary to assimilate its devolution in the case (199–200)

683.n1   "About] [no paragraph] 'About (52)

683.n2   Property] Prosperity (52) [see 683n–n]

684.n22   season] seasons (53)

684.n23   employment, and the] employment, the (53)

684.n25   Belfast] [no paragraph] Belfast (76)

684.n25   owes its] owes, as has been mentioned in a previous page, its (77)
684.n33   improvements.] improvements.* [*footnote:*] *See also on this subject the next article. (77)
684.n39   his contract] the contract (77) [*see* 684*o–o*]
685.n1   waste [?] it] waste, it (78)
685.n3   Once] [*paragraph*] Once (78)
685.n10   Here] [*paragraph*] Here (78)
685.n12–18 law . . . . It . . . root.] law. [*3-sentence omission*] 'It . . . root.' [*Leslie is quoting from Maclagan's* The Irish Land Question, 24] (78–9)
685.n14   mill] such [*printer's error?*] (79)
685.n15   county [Londonderry],] county (79)

LEWIS, GEORGE CORNEWALL. Referred to: 500

———— "Evidence before the Select Committee on the Bank Acts," *Parliamentary Papers*, 1857 (Sess. 2), X.i, 177–206.

NOTE: the "quotations" are questions asked by Lewis (Chancellor of the Exchequer), Chairman of the Committee.

QUOTED: 501–11

LOCKE. Referred to: 184

LOWE, ROBERT. Referred to: 550, 592

———— "Evidence taken before the Select Committee on Income and Property Tax," *Parliamentary Papers*, 1861, VII, 212–32.

NOTE: the "quotations" are questions asked by Lowe, a member of the Committee.

QUOTED: 584–91

———— *Middle Class Education: Endowment or Free Trade.* London: Bush, 1868.

REFERRED TO: 626

LOYD, LEWIS. "Evidence before the Committee of the Lords, (1826) on the Circulation of Promissory Notes," *Parliamentary Papers*, 1826–27, VI, 561–4.

QUOTED: 93–4

93.41—94.1 NINE . . . GOLD] It is difficult to answer that question [concerning the proportion of bills of exchange to gold and Bank of England notes in Lancashire] with any accuracy; I should say that they were at least nine parts out of ten; nine . . . gold (561)
94.2   *still greater*] [*not in italics*] (561)
94.2–3   proportion. [*paragraph*] The] proportion. [*paragraph*] You are in the habit of having deposit accounts with the manufacturers in Manchester, are you not?— Yes. [*paragraph*] The (562)
94.4   *wages,*] wages (562)

94.4   notes?] notes, are you not? (562)
94.6   account] accounts (562)
94.7–8   *bills . . . London*] [*not in italics*] (562)
94.15–6   *repeated . . . wages*] [*not in italics*] (562)
94.17   *could . . . him*] [*not in italics*] (562)
94.19–20   *the . . . exchange*] [*not in italics*] (562)
94.20–1   *we . . . account*] [*not in italics*] (562)
94.25   *it . . . endorsements*] [*not in italics*] (562)
94.26   *it . . . medium*] [*not in italics*] (562)
94.26–7   THE PRINCIPAL PART] The principal part (562)
94.29   *fifty . . . them*] [*not in italics*] (562)
94.29   *twice that number*] [*not in italics*] (562)
94.29   *number. I*] number; I (562)
94.31–2   that? [*paragraph*] Again: "Do] [*4 questions and answers omitted*] (562)

LOYD, SAMUEL JONES. "Evidence taken before the Select Committee on the Bank Acts," *Parliamentary Papers*, 1857 (Sess. 2), X.i, 339–431.

REFERRED TO: 542

———— *Thoughts on the Separation of the Departments of the Bank of England.* London: Richardson, 1844.

REFERRED TO: 344–7

LUSIGNAN. Referred to: 432

MABERLY. Referred to: 110

MACAULAY, THOMAS BABINGTON. *The History of England from the Accession of James II.* 5 vols. London: Longman, Brown, Green, and Longmans, 1849–61.

NOTE: JSM merely accepts Leslie's reference, in *Land Systems*, 164, to Macaulay's 3rd chapter in Vol. I.

REFERRED TO: 679

McCULLOCH, JOHN RAMSAY. Referred to: 32n, 260, 345

———— "Corn Laws and Trade," *Supplement to the 4th, 5th, and 6th Editions of the Encyclopaedia Britannica.* Edinburgh: Constable, 1824, III, 342–73.

REFERRED TO: 51

———— *A Discourse on the Rise, Progress, Peculiar Objects, and Importance, of Political Economy: containing an outline of a course of lectures on the principles and doctrines of that science.* 2nd ed. Edinburgh: Constable, 1825.

REVIEWED: 757–60

QUOTED: 760

760.32 science . . . . . .] science. Few can honestly say with the poet, *Video meliora proboque deteriora sequor!* (86) [Ovid, *Metamorphoses,* VII, 20–1]

————— "Labour," in Adam Smith, *An Inquiry into the Nature and Causes of the Wealth of Nations,* ed. J. R. McCulloch. Edinburgh: Black, Tait, 1828, IV, 73–80.

REFERRED TO: 166n

————— "Political Economy," *Supplement to the 4th, 5th, and 6th Editions of the Encyclopaedia Britannica.* Edinburgh: Constable, 1824, VI, 216–78.

NOTE: JSM is quoting McCulloch from Malthus' review of this article; see Malthus, "Political Economy," below, 38.21–4.

QUOTED: 38   REFERRED TO: 25, 40–2

————— "Price of Foreign Corn—Abolition of the Corn-Laws," *Edinburgh Review,* XLI (October, 1824), 55–78.

NOTE: McCulloch is reviewing the 1st ed. of the work (Whitmore, *A Letter . . .* [London: Hatchard, 1822]) of which JSM is reviewing the 2nd ed. in "The Corn Laws," 45–70 above.

QUOTED: 56   REFERRED TO: 53–4, 57–8, 68–9

56.11 port†] [*JSM's footnote*] (61)

————— *The Principles of Political Economy: with a sketch of the rise and progress of the science.* Edinburgh: Tait, 1825.

REFERRED TO: 280–2

————— "Profits," in Adam Smith, *An Inquiry into the Nature and Causes of the Wealth of Nations.* Edinburgh: Black, Tait, 1828, IV, 184ff.

REFERRED TO: 180

————— "Value," in Adam Smith, *An Inquiry into the Nature and Causes of the Wealth of Nations,* ed. J. R. McCulloch. Edinburgh: Black, Tait, 1828, IV, pp. 81–100.

REFERRED TO: 164

MAINE, HENRY JAMES SUMNER. *Ancient Law: Its Connection with the Early History of Society, and its Relation to Modern Ideas.* London: Murray, 1861.

NOTE: copy in JSM's library, Somerville College.

REFERRED TO: 751

MAKGILL, GEORGE. *Rent no Robbery: An Examination of some erroneous doctrines regarding property in land*. Edinburgh: Blackwood, 1851.
REFERRED TO: 452n–453n

MALTHUS, THOMAS ROBERT. Referred to: 25–34, 36–42, 449, 728
NOTE: the references from 25 to 42 are included, although the article being reviewed is by Malthus; references to "the Reviewer," also Malthus, which are found on almost every page of this article, are excluded by the usual rule that references to authors within reviews are not given.

——— *Essay on the Principle of Population, as it Affects the Future Improvement of Society. With Remarks on the Speculations of Mr. Godwin, M. Condorcet, and Other Writers*. London: Johnson, 1798.
NOTE: JSM mentions no specific edition, and there is no copy of the work in his library. He may have read the three-volume 5th ed. (London: Murray, 1817), the most recent prior to the first article here printed which mentions the work.
REFERRED TO: 35, 366–9, 758

——— *An Inquiry into the Nature and Progress of Rent, and the Principles by which it is Regulated*. London: Murray, 1815.
REFERRED TO: 174, 179–80, 758

——— *The Measure of Value Stated and Illustrated with an Appreciation of it to the Alterations in the Value of the English Currency since 1790*. London: Murray, 1823.
REFERRED TO: 28, 31

——— "Political Economy," *Quarterly Review*, XXX (January, 1824), 297–334.
REVIEWED: 25–43
QUOTED: 25–6, 29–35, 37–43

25.10 "new . . . economy"] Our chief object is to call the attention of the reader to some of the main principles which characterize what may be called the new . . . economy, as contradistinguished from that of Adam Smith. (305)
25.18–19 "altered . . . speculation"] They [the author's school] seem to have proceeded upon a principle just the very reverse of the position above laid down by the author [political economy is a science "not of speculation, but of fact and experiment"], and to have altered . . . speculation; and not because they do not accord with facts and experience. (297–8)
26.5 "Adam . . . Malthus"] It has been our object in this Article to point out to the reader the main characteristic differences which distinguish the new school of Political Economy from that of Adam . . . Malthus. (331)
29.25 "The main . . . which] We now proceed to consider the main principles which (307)
29.26 economy, appear] economy. These appear (307)
31.17 at about] at above (310)

31.27   worth about] worth above (310)
32.7–10   "the quantity . . . circulating:"] Of some other articles of exchange, particularly coppice-wood and timber, the proportion of the value resolvable into profits is much larger; while it is universally allowed that the quantity . . . circulating. (310)
32.11   acknowledged] allowed (310) [*cf. previous entry*]
33.8   "that demand] That the demand (307)
33.9   influence on] effect upon (307)
35.10   "only] It is, however, only (315)
35.12–13   *proportion . . . accumulated*] [*not in italics*] (315)
35.18–19   "the proportion] Of all the truths which Mr. Ricardo has established, one of the most useful and important is, that profits are determined by the proportion (315)
35.19   *goes to labour,*] goes to labour. (315)
35.25–6   "greater . . . labour,"] On this important point the present treatise is silent;* but the prevailing opinion is, that it depends upon the greater . . . labour. [*footnote:*] *The author says, 'The limits to which this Article has already extended prevent our entering into an investigation of the various circumstances which determine the market rate of wages.' (p. 269.) (315)
35.30   "The] And it will be found that the (315)
37.20   "that] That (308)
38.19   "The] [*no paragraph*] The (321)
38.21–4   cause; to . . . fertility of . . . taxation."] cause—" *to . . . fertility in taxation."* (321) [*In McCulloch the passage reads:*] cause–to A DIMINUTION . . . ADVANTAGE, *resulting . . . fertility of . . . taxation.* (269) [*Malthus erroneously refers to* p. 296]
39.6   "What] [*paragraph*] What (323)
39.8   obviously a] obviously and unquestionably a (323)
39.8   *value of produce!*] value of produce owing . . . [*as in* 39.9] (323)
39.9   capital!"] capital, which would necessarily occasion a different division of what was produced, and award a larger proportion of it to the labourer, and a smaller proportion of it to the capitalist. (323)
39.27   Innumerable] [*no paragraph*] But innumerable (325)
39.31   It] [*no paragraph*] As it is, it (324)
39.33   whom] which (325)
40.35   "and] Now, supposing this increase to have taken place, under the circumstances stated, in the funds specifically destined for the maintenance of labour, the necessary consequence would be, that, instead of an *unusually great demand* for labourers, there would be a *diminished demand*, and (326–7)
41.3   clear."] clear, and it only remains to be considered whether it is confirmed by experience. (327)
41.20   "For] Now (329)
41.31   bare . . . . We] bare. All people have not been in London, and could not therefore personally contradict such an affirmation; but on account of its extreme improbability none would believe it, and in justification of this disbelief they would naturally say that, if it were true, they must have heard more of it. Now we (330)
43.15–16   "sweeping generalizations," . . . "fatal to all clear explanation"] The sweeping generalizations which make no difference in the different parts of a work that co-operate to form a whole, appear to us, we confess, to be fatal to all clear explanation of the means by which the final result is attained. (306)

———— *Principles of Political Economy Considered with a View to Their Practical Application.* London: Murray, 1820.

REFERRED TO: 28

MANNERS. Referred to: 383

Mansell & Co's. Report of the Important Discussion held in Birmingham, August the 28th and 29th, 1832, between William Cobbett, Thomas Attwood, and Charles Jones, Esqrs. on the Question Whether it is best for the safety and welfare of the nation to attempt to relieve the existing distress "by an action on the Currency," *or* by an "Equitable Adjustment" of the Taxes, Rents, Debts, Contracts, and Obligations, which now strangle the industry of the Country? 2nd ed. Birmingham: Mansell, 1832.

NOTE: the 2nd ed. gives a fuller report than the 1st (extracted from the *Birmingham Journal*), Birmingham: *Journal* Office, 1832.

REFERRED TO: 185

MARTINEAU, HARRIET. "The Moral of Many Fables," *Illustrations of Political Economy*, No. XXV. London: Fox, 1834.

REVIEWED: 225–8

QUOTED: 228

228.9 "capitalists] As wages rise (without advantage to the labourer) in consequence of a rise in the value of food, capitalists (120)
228.10 Under] [*paragraph*] Under (120)
228.12–13 *under . . . extinction*] [*not in italics*] (120)
228.18 Productive] [*paragraph*] Productive (3)
228.19 Many] [*paragraph*] Many (3)
228.20 this; many] this. Many (3)
228.21 All] [*paragraph*] All (3)

MILL, JAMES. Referred to: 32n

——— *Elements of Political Economy*. London: Baldwin, Cradock, and Joy, 1821.

REFERRED TO: 16n, 758

——— 2nd ed., 1824.

QUOTED: 33, 65–6   REFERRED TO: 32n

33.27–8 *demand and suppy*] [*not in italics*] (89)
66.5 In] [*no paragraph*] In (198)

——— 3rd ed., 1826.

NOTE: cf. JSM's quotation of this passage, in slightly altered form, in his *Principles of Political Economy, Collected Works*, III, 589–90.

QUOTED: 234   REFERRED TO: 236

234.18 in importing] on importing (120)
234.28–9 labour. [*paragraph*] The] labour. If the exchange, however, was made in

this manner, the whole of the advantage would be on the part of England; and Poland would gain nothing, paying as much for the cloth she received from England, as the cost of producing it for herself. [*paragraph*] But the (121)

234.32 cloth." But "the] cloth. The (121) [*style altered in present text*]

———— "The State of the Nation," *Westminster Review*, VI (Oct., 1826), pp. 249–78.

NOTE: identified as by JM in the copy in JSM's library, Somerville College.

REFERRED TO: 144n

MILL, JOHN STUART. "The Corn Laws," *Westminster Review*, III (April 1825), 394–420.

NOTE: i.e., that printed at 45–70 above.

REFERRED TO: 136, 144n

———— "De Quincey's Logic of Political Economy," *Westminster Review*, XLIII (June, 1845), 319–31.

NOTE: i.e., that printed at 391–404 above; page references below are to this edition.

QUOTED: 641–2

641.42 "have] But for want of sufficiently careful habits of systematic thought, these new views have (394)

641.42 been promulgated] been too frequently promulgated (394)

642.2 developments] *developments* (394)

642.2 them;"] them; corollaries flowing from these fundamental principles, certain conditions of fact being supposed. (394)

———— "Evidence taken before the Select Committee on Income and Property Tax," *Parliamentary Papers*, 1852, IX, 780–91, 794–820.

NOTE: i.e., that printed at 463–98 above.

REFERRED TO: 598

———— *Principles of Political Economy with Some of their Applications to Social Philosophy. Collected Works*, II and III. Toronto: University of Toronto Press, 1965.

NOTE: for ease of reference, all notes specify the collated edition cited above, although, for example, the 1st ed. (1848) is referred to at 414. The quotation at 587, taken by Lowe presumably from the 4th ed. (1857), is repeated in part at 589 (again by Lowe); in its first appearance it contains a typographical error ("or all" for "on all") which is silently corrected in the text.

QUOTED: 415, 587, 589, 635n   REFERRED TO: 407, 414–16, 432, 452n, 465, 479, 486, 643

415.25 "the] Finally I must repeat my conviction, that the (III, 896)

415.27 receivers,] receivers of them, (III, 896)

415.27–8 not fit for indefinite duration."] neither fit for, nor capable of, indefinite duration: and the possibility of changing this system for one of combination without dependence, and unity of interest instead of organized hostility, depends altogether upon the future developments of the Partnership principle. (III, 896)

587.7   "The] [*paragraph*] The (815)

635.n4   it. . . . . . Demand] it. [*ellipsis indicates 5-sentence omission*] [*paragraph*] To recapitulate: demand (III, 475)

———— "War Expenditure," *Westminster Review*, II (July, 1824), 27–48.

NOTE: i.e., that printed at 1–22 above.

REFERRED TO: 41

MILTON, LORD. See Wentworth-Fitzwilliam.

MOREAU, CÉSAR. *Rise and Progress of the Silk Trade in England, from the earliest period to the present time (Feby. 1826,) Founded on official Documents.* London: Treuttel and Würtz, 1826.

NOTE: although the article is ostensibly a review of Moreau, neither he nor his book is mentioned throughout; the evidence of Hale and Davison before the Lord's Committee on Foreign Trade, and the Report of that Committee may, however, be quoted from Moreau's transcription. (The edition is lithographed from a holograph.)

REVIEWED: 127–39

Morning Chronicle. See Curteis; Smith, Henry; "T.G."

MORRISON. Referred to: 766

MUNDELLA. Referred to: 666

NAPOLEON I (of France). Referred to: 6, 10, 196

NAVIGATION ACTS. See 6 George IV, cc. 105, 109.

NERO. Referred to: 713

NEWCASTLE, FOURTH DUKE OF. See Clinton.

NEWDEGATE, CHARLES. "Evidence taken before the Select Committee on Income and Property Tax," *Parliamentary Papers*, 1852, IX, 284–95, 298–324.

NOTE: the "quotations" are questions asked by Newdegate, a member of the Committee.

QUOTED: 469–74

NEWMAN, FRANCIS WILLIAM. *Lectures on Political Economy*. London: Chapman, 1851.

REVIEWED: 441–57

QUOTED: 443–7, 449–54, 456n, 457

443.37   "by] By (32)
443.38   or to] or his to (32)
444.1–2   pleases, but] pleases; and if the State, in order to avoid the evil of each man arming for the defence of his own, has taken on itself to defend Property from the attack of violence, then it must equally defend the rights of the Legatee or Heir, as the rights of the Testator while he lived. But that is no reason in itself, why the State should enforce the Testator's desire to continue lord of his property even after he is dead. If he chooses to give it away and make another owner of it,—as completely owner of it as he was himself,—this is within his natural power and right. But (32)
444.2   limitations."] limitations:—to say, "this property shall belong to my wife, only so long as she does not marry again; this shall belong to my son, on condition that he does not change his religion; these rents shall be paid to a certain religious house, as long as it continues to observe the statutes and recognize the creed which I now dictate to it; and in order to enforce this my will, I forbid the selling and using of this property:—only the yearly fruits, rents, produce of it shall be enjoyed and used; I therefore vest the *nominal* ownership in certain Trustees, who shall secure the *beneficial* use of it to those others whom I have named." (32–3)
445.6   from the] from their (11)
445.7   would] could (11)
446.31   The] [*no paragraph*] The (12)
446.31–2   though, . . . nature,] though (. . . Nature) (12)
446.36–7   and, unless . . . respected,] and that (unless . . . respected) (12)
447.28   "it] In fact, it (153)
449.4   "when] My opinion is, that the Malthusian doctrine, when (107)
449.4   theory," it is "undeniably] theory, is undeniably (107)
449.12   "it] [*paragraph*] First, it (109)
449.20   "it] [*paragraph*] But farther, it (111)
449.25–6   test," . . . "is] test of the last, is (111)
449.28   portion] fraction (111)
450.22–3   improvement . . . . . . [*paragraph*] If] improvement.—Thus the occupants have a certain right in the land prior to Statute Law, which right ought to be confirmed by Law, when the time comes for enactments. [*paragraph*] If (134)
450.29   further] farther (135)
450.34   profit] *Profit* (135)
450.35–6   rent. . . . . . . [*paragraph*] Let] [*2-paragraph omission*] (135–7)
450.39   not . . . elsewhither?] [*in italics*] (137)
450.43   of the] for the (137)
450.44–5   the owner . . . soil] [*in italics*] (137)
450.48—451.1   yours.' . . . . . . [*paragraph*] But] [*3-sentence omission*] (137)
451.8   might] may (138)
451.21   the owner of the soil] [*in italics*] (138)
451.24   exacted] enacted (138) [*treated as printer's error*]
451.27   nothing] [*in italics*] (139)
451.39   Imagine] [*no paragraph*] Imagine (140)
451.40   , for the present,] *for the present* (140)
452.2–3   for water,] for the water; (141)
453.8   "disorganized"] [*see variant at 454.8 below*] (292)
453.8   "relapsing] Nearly the same [there is no fixed moral union] is true of all ranks

in London: hence a selfishness which barely extends beyond the family circle is a prevalent type of character; and this is a precursor of dissolution in society, which is relapsing (292)

453.23   He] [*no paragraph*] He (291)

453.27   wishes . . . We] wishes. [*3-sentence omission*] [*paragraph*] We (292) [*cf.* 454.6–7 *below*]

454.5   market or] market and (292)

454.6–7   life. . . . Marriage, with . . . it,] life. [*here follows the sentence partly quoted at* 453.8 *above; JSM then jumps back to the passage omitted at* 453.27 *above, which reads:*] It is a specific duty of the Ruler to promote moral unions, and, with a view to them, to sanction permanent relations in various ways. Of these, that with which all civilization begins, is Marriage. To be without this, is to be lower than the lowest savages now known: yet, marvellous to say, this (with . . . it) (292) [*see also* 456.n3–5 *below*]

454.8   disorganized] [*in italics*] (292)

454.16   "labour-leases,"] Such injurious proceedings [as strikes] ought to excite the masters to inquire, whether there is not some way of inducing the best men to enter into engagements for a longer series of time;—which might be called *Labour-leases.*" (327)

454.30   before the Church] *before the Church,* (305)

456.n3–5   "permanent . . . known,"] [*see* 454.6–7 *above*] (292)

457.16–17   "the . . . patriotism;"] Here it seems clear enough what is the primary cause of the nation becoming as a heap of sand, viz., *the loss of local patriotism,* which has followed on the decay of local liberties by the development of centralization. (293)

NEWTON. Referred to: 212

NORMAN, GEORGE WARDE. *Remarks upon Some Prevalent Errors, with Respect to Currency and Banking, and Suggestions to the Legislature and the Public as to the Improvement of the Monetary System.* London: Richardson, 1838.

REFERRED TO: 344–5

NORTHCOTE, STAFFORD HENRY. Referred to: 550

————— "Evidence taken before the Select Committee on Income and Property Tax," *Parliamentary Papers,* 1861, VII, 212–32.

NOTE: the "quotations" are questions asked by Northcote, a member of the Committee.

QUOTED: 575–83

OVERSTONE, LORD. See Loyd, Samuel Jones.

OWEN, ROBERT. Referred to: 446, 728, 737–8

————— *The Book of the New Moral World, Containing the Rational System of Society, Founded on Demonstrable Facts, Developing the*

Constitution and Laws of Human Nature and of Society. [Part First.] London: Wilson, 1836. *The Book of the New Moral World, explanatory of the Elements of the Science of Society or the Social State of Man.* Part Second. London: Home Colonization Society, 1842.

NOTE: the work was completed in seven parts, the last appearing in 1844. A copy of the work, "Complete in Seven Parts" (London: Watson, 1849), is in JSM's library, Somerville College.

QUOTED: 724–5   REFERRED TO: 373

724.15   as gain] or gain (21) [*printer's error?*]
724.21   individual] individuals (21)
724.27   and the] and (21)
724.29   easily] early (21) [*printer's error?*]
724.37   amongst] among (21)
725.11–12   independence—to . . . business—] independence to . . . business, (22)
725.18–19   costing to] costing (22)
725.29–30   articles. . . . . [*paragraph*] The] articles. A moment's reflection must now make it evident that the distribution of wealth under the present system of society, is most erroneous in principle and highly injurious in practice, to the producer, distributor, and consumer. [*paragraph*] The (22–3)

OXENSTIERNA, AXEL.

NOTE: source not located.
QUOTED: 113

PALEY, WILLIAM. *The Principles of Moral and Political Philosophy.* 15th ed. 2 vols. London: Faulder, 1804.

NOTE: this is the edition in JSM's library, Somerville College. The reference is to Vol. II, pp. 429 ff.
REFERRED TO: 474

Parliamentary History and Review; containing Reports of the Proceedings of the two Houses of Parliament during the Session of 1825:—6 Geo. IV. With Critical Remarks on the Principal Measures of the Session. 2 vols. London: Longman, Rees, Orme, Brown, and Green, 1826.

REFERRED TO: 106, 122

Parliamentary History and Review; containing Reports of the Proceedings of the two Houses of Parliament during the Session of 1826:—7 Geo. IV. With Critical Remarks on the Principal Measures of the Session. 2 vols. London: Longman, Rees, Orme, Brown, and Green, 1826. See Baring, Alexander; Bright; Brougham; Coulson; Davenport; Gordon; Grenfell; Gurney, Hudson; Heygate, William; Huskisson; Parnell; Peel, Robert; Smith, John; Tierney; Wilson, Thomas.

PARLIAMENTARY PAPERS. See 824.

PARNELL, HENRY BROOKE. Speech in the House of Commons 14 Feb.,
1826), quoted in *Parliamentary History* for 1826, 235–6.

QUOTED: 109   REFERRED TO: 119n

109.18   "a] A (236)
109.19   which," . . . "a] which, under similar circumstances, a (236)

PARSONS. Referred to: 678

PASTA. Referred to: 281, 285–6

PEEL, FREDERICK. "Evidence taken before the Select Committee on the
Savings of the Middle and Working Classes," *Parliamentary Papers,*
1850, XIX, 253–66.

NOTE: the "quotations" are questions asked by Peel, a member of the Committee.
QUOTED: 412–13   REFERRED TO: 406

PEEL, ROBERT. Referred to: 344–7, 356–7, 359n, 507, 530, 592, 607, 702.
See also: 59 George III, c. 49; 5 & 6 Victoria, c. 35; and 7 & 8
Victoria, c. 32.

———— Speech in the House of Commons (13 Feb., 1826), quoted in
Parliamentary History for 1826, 213–6.

QUOTED: 120

120.2   "It] He was of opinion, that if it were adopted, it (214)
120.6   silver.] silver (hear, hear). (214)

PESTALOZZI. Referred to: 215

PETTY-FITZMAURICE. Referred to: 110–11

PITT. Referred to: 115, 121, 474, 479, 486, 591. See also: 38 George III,
c. 60; 39 George III, c. 13.

PLATO, *Gorgias.* Referred to: 312

NOTE: the reference is to 463b. JSM renders the passage containing the terms thus:
"Of this pursuit [Adulation] there are many other branches [besides rhetoric],
and cookery is one, which is thought to be an art, but, in my opinion, is no
art, but a skill, and routine." "Notes on Some of the More Popular Dialogues
of Plato, No. III. The Gorgias," *Monthly Repository,* n.s. VIII (Oct., 1834),
700.

———— *Republic.* Referred to: 741

NOTE: the reference is primarily to 416ff.

Remarks on Mr. Malthus' Two Last Publications. London: Murray, 1815.

NOTE: at 179 the reference (by McCulloch?) is erroneously to 1817.
REFERRED TO: 174, 179

———— *The High Price of Bullion, a Proof of the Depreciation of Bank Notes.* London: Murray, 1810.

REFERRED TO: 188

———— *Observations on Some Passages in an Article in the Edinburgh Review, on the Depreciation of Paper Currency; also Suggestions for securing to the public a currency as invariable as gold, with a very moderate supply of that metal. Being the Appendix, to the Fourth Edition of "The High Price of Bullion,"* &c. London: Murray, 1811.

REFERRED TO: 188

———— *On the Principles of Political Economy and Taxation.* 3rd ed. London: Murray, 1821.

NOTE: the references at 393 and 758 are to the 1st ed. (London: Murray, 1817).
QUOTED: 31–2   REFERRED TO: 35, 152n, 174, 232–6, 241, 293–5, 297, 299, 393, 758

———— *Proposals for an Economical and Secure Currency; with observations on the profits of the Bank of England, as they regard the public and the proprietors of Bank stock.* London: Murray, 1816.

REFERRED TO: 188

———— *Reply to Mr. Bosanquet's Practical Observations on the Report of the Bullion Committee.* London: Murray, 1811.

REFERRED TO: 188

RICARDO, JOHN LEWIS. "Evidence taken before the Select Committee on Income and Property Tax," *Parliamentary Papers*, 1852, IX, 284–95, 298–324.

NOTE: the "quotations" are questions asked by Ricardo, a member of the Committee.
QUOTED: 472, 474, 496–8

ROBESPIERRE. Referred to: 737

ROBY. Referred to: 95

ROEBUCK, JOHN ARTHUR. "Timber Trade," *Westminster Review*, VII (Jan., 1827), 126–46.
REFERRED TO: 148

ROSSE, LORD. See Parsons.

ROTHSCHILD, NATHAN M. Referred to: 86, 184n

———— "Evidence taken before the Committee of Secrecy on the Bank of England Charter," *Parliamentary Papers*, 1831–32, VI, 381–93.
REFERRED TO: 351

ROTHWELL, RICHARD. "Evidence taken before the Select Committee to whom the several Petitions complaining of the Depressed State of the Agriculture of the United Kingdom, were Referred," *Parliamentary Papers*, 1821, IX, 87–9.
REFERRED TO: 19–20

ROUS, JOHN. "Evidence taken before the Select Committee to whom the several Petitions complaining of the Depressed State of the Agriculture of the United Kingdom, were Referred," *Parliamentary Papers*, 1821, IX, 178–80.
REFERRED TO: 19–20

ROUSSEAU. Referred to: 211, 651–2

RUSSELL. Referred to: 432

ST. ATHANASIUS. Referred to: 26

ST. AUGUSTINE. Referred to: 26

ST. DOMINIC. Referred to: 156

ST. JEROME. Referred to: 26

SAINT JUST. Referred to: 737

SAY, JEAN-BAPTISTE. *Traité d'économie politique, ou simple exposition de la manière dont se forment, se distribuent, et se consomment les richesses.* 2 vols. Paris: Deterville, 1803.
NOTE: JSM gives 1802 as the date of publication; a copy of the 4th ed. (2 vols., Paris: Deterville, 1819) in JSM's library, Somerville College.
REFERRED TO: 321, 758

SAY, LÉON. Referred to: 718

SCOTT, JOHN. Referred to: 151

SCOTT, WALTER ["Malachi Malagrowther"]. *Thoughts on the Proposed Change of Currency, and other late alterations, as they affect, or are intended to affect, the Kingdom of Scotland.* Edinburgh: Blackwood, 1826.

REFERRED TO: 116

SENIOR, NASSAU WILLIAM. "Report—On the State of Agriculture," *Quarterly Review*, XXV (July, 1821), 466–504.

REFERRED TO: 151n–152n

SHAKESPEARE. Referred to: 401

SILK ACT. See 5 George IV, c. 21.

SISMONDI, JEAN-CHARLES-LEONARDO SIMONDE DE. *Nouveaux principes d'économie politique, ou de la richesse dans ses rapports avec la population.* 2nd ed. 2 vols. Paris: Delaunay, 1827.

REFERRED TO: 718

SLANEY, ROBERT AGLIONBY. "Evidence taken before the Select Committee on the Savings of the Middle and Working Classes," *Parliamentary Papers*, 1850, XIX, 253–66.

NOTE: the "quotations" are questions asked by Slaney, Chairman of the Committee.

QUOTED: 407–16, 418–29   REFERRED TO: 406

SMITH, ADAM. Referred to: 25–7, 29–30, 32, 37, 149, 214–15, 395, 411, 718

———— *An Inquiry into the Nature and Causes of the Wealth of Nations. With a Commentary by the Author of "England and America"* [E. G. Wakefield]. 4 vols. London: Knight, 1835–9.

NOTE: for ease of reference this edition (the one cited in JSM's *Principles*) is used throughout, except at 27, where the 1st ed. is cited (2 vols. London: Strahan and Cadell, 1776), and 162–80, where the edition from which JSM's article derives is used (ed. J. R. McCulloch. 4 vols. Edinburgh: Black, Tait, 1828). The references to this edition at 178/179 may be found in Wakefield's edition at II, 4 and 39. The quotation at 300 is indirect. In Somerville College there are the 3-vol. 8th ed. (London, 1796), the 2-vol. edition ed. Rogers (Oxford, 1869), and a gift copy of McCulloch's edition, Vol. I inscribed: "To John Mill

Esq/This copy of the edition of a/work to the value of which/he has essentially contributed/is presented by his friend/the Editor".

QUOTED: 164, 238, 293, 300, 657

REFERRED TO: 26–7, 163–4, 168–9, 174, 177–8, 179–80, 301, 312, 367, 758

164.4 "There] [*paragraph*] There (ed. McCulloch, I, 241; ed. Wakefield, II, 4)
164.5–6 *demand . . . market*] [*not in italics*] (*ibid.*)
164.6 *market:*"] market; and there are others for which it either may or may not be such as to afford this greater price. (*ibid.*)
238.18 "the higgling of the market"] In exchanging indeed the different productions of different sorts of labour [employment] for one another, some allowance is commonly made for both [hardship and ingenuity]. It is adjusted, however, not by any accurate measure, but by the higgling and bargaining of the market, according to that sort of rough equality which, though not exact, is sufficient for carrying on the business of common life. (I, 102) [*1st square brackets Wakefield's; 2nd mine*]
293.3–4 "the . . . which has been paid for everything."] Labour was the first price, the . . . that was paid for all things. (I, 101)
300.22–3 much will . . . it.] It may be laid down as a maxim, that wherever a great deal can be made by the use of money, a great deal will commonly be given for the use of it. . . . (I, 211)
657.37–8 "the higgling of the market"] [*see variant at* 238.18 *above*]

SMITH, HENRY. Speech at a public meeting (30 Jan., 1826), reported in the *Morning Chronicle*, 6 Feb., 1826, 3.

NOTE: the quotation is indirect.

QUOTED: 129n

129.n3–4 that . . . manufacturer.] [*paragraph*] Mr. HENRY SMITH said, a duty of 100 per cent. would not protect the English manufacturer, and explained the circumstances connected with another Petition which had been drawn up, signed by a great many weavers, and sent to Sir Thomas Lethbridge for presentation. (3)

SMITH, JOHN. Speech in the House of Commons (15 Feb., 1826), quoted in *Parliamentary History* for 1826, p. 320.

QUOTED: 109

109.15 "knew] [*paragraph*] Mr. *John Smith* could state of his own personal knowledge, that during the panic in the money-market last December, enormous sums had been paid for pecuniary loans; indeed, he knew (320)
109.16 paid.] paid (hear, hear). (320)

SMITH, JOHN ABEL. "Evidence taken before the Select Committee on the Savings of the Middle and Working Classes," *Parliamentary Papers*, 1850, XIX, 253–66.

NOTE: the "quotations" are questions asked by Smith, a member of the Committee.
QUOTED: 416–20, 422–8 REFERRED TO: 406

SMITH, MARTIN TUCKER. Referred to: 500

——— "Evidence taken before the Select Committee on the Bank Acts,"
Parliamentary Papers, 1857 (Sess. 2), X.i, 177–206.

NOTE: the "quotations" are questions asked by Smith, a member of the Committee.
QUOTED: 516

SOCIETY FOR THE DIFFUSION OF USEFUL KNOWLEDGE. Tract on the
"claims of capital." See Knight, Charles.

La Solidarité (Neuchâtel). Referred to: 709

SOLLY, EDWARD. "Evidence taken before the Select Committee to whom the
several Petitions complaining of the Depressed State of the Agriculture
of the United Kingdom, were Referred," *Parliamentary Papers*, 1821,
IX, 315–19.

QUOTED: 54–5   REFERRED TO: 53, 56n

54.18   *constantly*] [*not in italics*] (316)
54.20   *It . . . England*] [*not in italics*] (316)
54.24–5   *Even . . . here*] [*not in italics*] (317)
55.9   They] I think, in the first instance, the price would be lowered; but that it
would ultimately recover; because it would have the effect of raising the value
of land, and the expense of cultivation on the continent, for they (317)
55.9   corn, for cattle] corn for cattle (317)

SOUTHEY, ROBERT. "Inquiry into the Poor Laws, &c.," *Quarterly Review*,
VIII (Dec., 1812), 319–56.

QUOTED: 27

27.1–3   "a . . . ability;"] Adam Smith's book is the code, or confession of faith of
this system; a . . . ability, for fifty pages would have comprised its sum and
substance as well as two Scotch quartos. (337)
27.3–4   "manufacturing animal," . . . from him;] That book considers man as a
manufacturing animal, a definition which escaped the ancients: it estimates his
importance, not by the sum of goodness and of knowledge which he possesses,
not by the virtues and charities which should flow towards him and emanate
from him, not by the happiness of which he may be the source and centre, not
by the duties to which he is called, not by the immortal destinies for which he
is created; but by the gain which can be extracted from him, or of which he
can be made the instrument. (337)
27.6–7   "plucked . . . virtues."] Pluck the wings of his intellect, strip him of the
down and plumage of his virtues, and behold in the brute, denuded, pitiable
animal, the man of the manufacturing system! (337)

SPOONER, RICHARD. Referred to: 500

———"Evidence taken before the Select Committee on the Bank Acts,"
Parliamentary Papers, 1857 (Sess. 2), X.i, 177–206.

NOTE: the "quotations" are questions asked by Spooner, a member of the Committee.
QUOTED: 540–2

STATUTES. See 826.

STEIN. Referred to: 752

STEWART, DUGALD. *Elements of the Philosophy of the Human Mind.* 3 vols. London: Strahan and Cadell, 1792.

REFERRED TO: 311

STUART, JAMES ("The Old Pretender"). Referred to: 210

STUART, JAMES. Referred to: 406

SWIFT, JONATHAN. *Gulliver's Travels,* in *Works,* XII. Ed. Walter Scott. Edinburgh: Constable, 1814.

NOTE: JSM is quoting Thompson at 155. The two indirect quotations are from the same passage in *Gulliver's Travels,* Voyage II, Chapter vii. This edition is the one in JSM's library, Somerville College.

QUOTED: 155, 186

155.22–3   That the man who made two blades of grass grow where there was one before, was always held to be a public benefactor.] And, he [the King of Brobdingnag] gave it for his opinion, 'That, whoever could make two ears of corn, or two blades of grass, to grow upon a spot of ground where only one grew before, would deserve better of mankind, and do more essential service to his country, than the whole race of politicians put together.' (176)

SYKES. Referred to: 122

"T. G." Letter to the Editor, *Morning Chronicle,* 28 Jan., 1826, 3.

QUOTED: 134n

134.n2   I] But I (3)
134.n2–3   myself for] myself to you for (3)

TAYLOR, HELEN. "Preliminary Remarks" to "Chapters on Socialism."

QUOTED: 705

TAYLOR, PETER ALFRED.

NOTE: the *Programme of the Land Tenure Reform Association* (above, 687–95) was issued over the names of JSM, Taylor, and Andrew Reid.

REFERRED TO: 764

THELUSSON, FREDERICK. Referred to: 119n

THELUSSON, PETER ISAAC. Referred to: 199. See also: 39 & 40 George III, c. 98

THOMPSON, THOMAS PERRONET. *A Catechism on the Corn Laws: with a List of Fallacies and the Answers.* 2nd ed. London: Ridgway, 1827.

NOTE: the actual review of Thompson begins on 151; he is first mentioned on 149. JSM's page references (and some variants) bear no relation to the 3rd ed. (London: Ridgway, 1827), the one he cites, but accurately reflect the 2nd ed. (cited above), which has therefore been used. Four of the "fallacies" on 156–7, however, do not appear in the 2nd ed.; they have been collated against the 3rd, although again the page references are not correct. Thompson (27) heads his questions "What is the answer to the fallacy", and places the answers in parallel columns with the fallacies, which are numbered. The fallacies quoted by JSM from the 2nd ed., in the order quoted, are: 11, 14, 16, 18, 23, 28, 29, 34, 35, 37, 38, 49, 50, 54, 59, 61, 86, 89, 90, 99, 104, 105, 106, 107, 115, 124, 127, 128, 130, 132, 134, 120, 119, and 135–50 (the final one in the 2nd ed.). From the 3rd ed., between 134 and 120 of the 2nd (156–7 above), he quotes 135, 136, 138, and 139.

REVIEWED: 143–59   QUOTED: 152–8

153.18   If] [*paragraph*] If (33)
153.37–8   delusion. [*paragraph*] A] delusion.—This, therefore, may be called the *halfpenny apiece* fallacy. [*paragraph*] A (33)
154.7   The] [*paragraph*] The (34)
154.23   The] [*paragraph*] The (35)
155.2   The] [*paragraph*] If (44)
155.19   The] [*paragraph*] The (47)
155.39   removed.] [*JSM omits the final paragraph of the answer*] (49)
156.2   it.] [*JSM omits the final paragraph of the answer*] (51)
156.17   lie] lies (55) [*treated as printer's error*]
156.21   The] [*paragraph*] The (55)
156.25   The] [*paragraph*] The (55)

———— *An Exposition of Fallacies on Rent, Tithes, &c. Containing an Examination of Mr. Ricardo's Theory of Rent and of the arguments brought against the conclusion that tithes and taxes on the land are paid by the landlords, the doctrine of the impossibility of a general glut, and other propositions of the modern school. With an inquiry into the comparative consequences of taxes on agricultural and manufactured produce. Being in the form of a Review of the Third Edition of Mr. Mill's Elements of Political Economy.* London: Hatchard; Rivington, 1826.

NOTE: JSM's long footnote is in effect a review of Thompson's work.

REFERRED TO: 151n–152n

THORNTON, HENRY. *An Enquiry into the Nature and Effects of the Credit of Great Britain.* London: Hatchard, 1802.

NOTE: copy of this work in JSM's library, Somerville College, with George Grote's bookplate.

QUOTED: 90–1   REFERRED TO: 188

91.6   kingdom.] kingdom*. [*5-sentence footnote omitted*] (40n–41n)

————— *Substance of Two Speeches in the Debate in the House of Commons, on the Report of the Bullion Committee, on the 7th and 14th of May, 1811*. London: Hatchard, 1811.

REFERRED TO: 188

THORNTON, WILLIAM THOMAS. *On Labour: Its Wrongful Claims and Rightful Dues, its Actual Present and Possible Future*. London: Macmillan, 1869.

REVIEWED: 633–68

QUOTED: 636, 638–40, 642n, 647–52, 657–8, 663, 665, 667–8

636.32   twenty shillings.] 20*s*.* [*footnote:*] *In point of fact, the fish are sold not by weight but by number—herrings usually by the hundred. On the beach at Brighton the price is sometimes as low as 1*s*. sometimes as high as 12*s*. the hundred—generally about 4*s*. or 5*s*. (48n)
636.36   price] sum (48)
638.6   Suppose] [*no paragraph*] Suppose (49)
638.34   When] [*no paragraph*] When (51)
639.19   Even] [*no paragraph*] Even (53)
639.22-3   price, before . . . remainder."] price. (53)
639.32   "a truth of small significance"] [*paragraph*] But further, not only is the orthodox theory not true—not only would it be of little significance if true—it is not even by its propounders believed to be true, except on certain conditions; and of these conditions there is one which, as will now be shown, is scarcely ever present. (55)
639.41   "that] Hitherto it has been throughout assumed that (55)
640.3   Is] [*no paragraph*] Such has hitherto been throughout the assumption, but such is (55)
640.12   weaver] mercer (55) [*printer's error?*]
640.22   all, and he] all: he (56)
642.n7   attain] obtain (69n) [*printer's error?*]
647.24   Except] [*no paragraph*] But, except (111)
647.39   "that] [*paragraph*] The basis on which the theory rests is the assumption that (88)
647.40   labour,"] labour. (88)
647.42   Although] Nevertheless, and although (91)
649.13   on the earth] on earth (94)
649.20   be responsible] be held responsible (94)
649.n5   "than] It may be prudent, therefore, to explain that nothing can be further from their [these remarks'] purpose than (94)
649.n6   enormities . . . . . . To] enormities. No one can be readier than the present writer to exclaim, in the words of Mr. Taylor's 'Philip Van Artevelde,'—/Where is there on God's earth that polity,/Which it is not by consequence converse/A treason against nature to uphold?/But to (94)
649.n19   precision; it] precision. It (95)
650.n10   means."] means.* [*1-page footnote, mentioning JSM by name, omitted*] (95n–97n)
651.37   is supposed] is very gratuitously supposed (111)
652.31-2   "their . . . unappropriated;"] [*see* 648.43-4 *above*]
657.12   adjured," . . . "not] adjured by them, in the name of political economy, not (260)
657.15   will] must (260)

657.21 end. If] end. Against such teaching, robust understandings of working men instinctively revolt. If (260)

658.30–1 "grovelling and sordid"] On the contrary, if anyone choose to stigmatise them ["all the views of Unionism"] as grovelling and sordid, I am not concerned to reply. (180)

663.16 Though,] [*no paragraph*] But though (289)

663.17 be clearly] be thus clearly (289)

665.35 "best their mates"] 'Not besting one's mates' has by several unions been made the subject of special enactment. (328)

665.36 "in the master's time"] Every reader may not have quite perceived what was meant when, a few sentences back, men were spoken of as not being allowed to sweat themselves if walking in their masters' time. (330) [*cf.* Thornton, 328]

667.10 Sufficient] [*no paragraph*] Sufficient (333)

668.8 and a tangible] and tangible (335)

668.10 other . . . . The] [*ellipsis indicates 5-sentence omission*] (335–6)

668.16 co-operation . . . . But] co-operation. What ground there is for hoping that such alliance will eventually displace existing antagonism, will be considered in the remaining division of this treatise; but (336)

———— *Over-Population and its Remedy; or, an Inquiry into the Extent and Causes of the Distress Prevailing among the Labouring Classes of the British Islands, and into the means of Remedying it.* London: Longman, Brown, Green, and Longmans, 1846.

NOTE: copy formerly in JSM's library, Somerville College.

REFERRED TO: 633, 680

———— *A Plea for Peasant Proprietors; with the Outlines of a Plan for their Establishment in Ireland.* London: Murray, 1848.

REFERRED TO: 633

TIERNEY, GEORGE. Speech in the House of Commons (17 Feb., 1826), quoted in *Parliamentary History* for 1826, 358–60.

QUOTED: 122

122.4 approved of] approved entirely of (259)

———— Speech in the House of Commons (26 May, 1826), quoted in *Parliamentary History* for 1826, 311–15.

NOTE: the quotation is indirect.

QUOTED: 117

The Times. Referred to: 371n

TITE, WILLIAM. Referred to: 500

———— "Evidence taken before the Select Committee on the Bank Acts," *Parliamentary Papers*, 1857 (Sess. 2), X.i, 177–206.

NOTE: the "quotations" are questions asked by Tite, a member of the Committee.

QUOTED: 512–16, 523, 541

TOOKE, THOMAS. Referred to: 61, 545

———— *Considerations on the State of the Currency.* 2nd ed. London: Murray, 1826.

QUOTED: 77, 92n   REFERRED TO: 86, 109, 111, 302

77.9   these] those (45)
77.14 speculation . . . . . The impulse to a rise having been] speculation. [*3-sentence omission*] [*paragraph*] The impulse, therefore, to a rise being (45)
77.21 Cotton] [*paragraph*] Cotton (46)
77.23 wool,] wool*, [*1-page footnote omitted*] (46n–47n)
77.24 subject] subjects (47)
77.25 occasion.] occasion, as the event proved, though not in so great a degree as cotton. (47–8)
92.n2 "The] [*paragraph*] The (48)
92.n8 of operators] of the operators (49)
92.n9 In] [*paragraph*] In (49)
92.n14 If] [*paragraph*] If (49)

———— "Evidence taken before the Select Committee to whom the several Petitions complaining of the Depressed State of the Agriculture of the United Kingdom, were Referred," *Parliamentary Papers,* 1821, IX, 224–40, 287–98, 344–55.

REFERRED TO: 56–7

———— *A History of Prices, and of the State of the Circulation, from 1793 to 1837; preceded by a brief sketch of the state of the Corn Trade in the last two centuries.* 2 vols. London: Longman, Orme, Brown, Green, and Longmans, 1838.

NOTE: the six volumes of the completed work are in JSM's library, Somerville College.
REFERRED TO: 343

———— *A History of Prices, and of the State of the Circulation, in 1838 and 1839, with Remarks on the Corn Laws, and on some alterations proposed in our Banking System. Being a continuation of the History of Prices, from 1793 to 1837.* London: Longman, Orme, Brown, Green, and Longmans, 1840.

QUOTED: 350–1   REFERRED TO: 343

350.28 "That] [*no paragraph*] That (273)
350.30 not self-evident] [*in italics*] (273)
350.30 consistent with experience] [*in italics*] (273)
350.31 therefore necessarily] [*in italics*] (273)
350.41 private. As] private; as (274)
351.1   capital] capitals (274)
351.2   bullion. The] bullion; the (274)

———— *An Inquiry into the Currency Principle; the Connection of the Currency with Prices, and the Expediency of a Separation of Issue from Banking.* London: Longman, Brown, Green, and Longmans, 1844.

REVIEWED: 343–61

QUOTED: 352, 357–61

352.10   "the] [*paragraph*] In a convertible state of the currency, given the actual and contingent supply of commodities, the greater or less demand will depend, not upon the total quantity of money in circulation, but upon the (71)

352.10   revenues of] revenues, valued in gold, of (71)

352.12   wages."] wages, destined for current expenditure. (71)

357.21   "That] It is probable, however, that Mr. Bosanquet, in his theory of high prices as a consequence of a low rate of interest, may be under the influence of the same opinion as that of Mr. Gilbart and many others—that (81)

357.22   the *stimulus*] *the stimulus* (82)

357.23   be] he [*i.e.,* Bosanquet] (82)

357.29   borrower. Such] borrower; such (82)

357.41   of."] of.* [*footnote:*] *See Appendix (B). (79)

357.42   "A] [*no paragraph*] What I mean to say is, that a (136) [*this passage is in "Appendix (B)," referred to in the variant above*]

358.3   "But why should this purchasing power be] A power of purchase might thus doubtless be created; but why should it be (79) [*this sentence immediately precedes that quoted at 357.39–41*]

358.5–6   resale? The] resale? The truth is . . . idea of. The (79) [*the omitted sentence is that quoted at 357.39–41*]

358.n6   speculators] speculations [*sic*] (137)

358.n17   prempt] prompt (137) [*treated as printer's error*]

358.n24   prempt] prompt (137) [*treated as printer's error*]

358.n27–8   realised, if] realised by sales, if (137)

359.3   "That] 17. That (124) [*this is the last of Tooke's list of "Conclusions"*]

360.6–9   "merchant, banker, or money dealer," . . . "Could for . . . cause.] [*paragraph*] Although there is no modern experience of such a state of things, if any merchant, banker, or money-dealer were to have the case laid distinctly before them, could any of them for . . . cause? (109)

360.11   irrevocably] inexorably (109)

360.15–16   in sufficient time] [*in italics*] (110)

360.19   "And] [*no paragraph*] And (111)

360.21–2   system of issuing] system of union of issuing (111)

361.1   "the] [*paragraph*] Now, without attaching such exaggerated importance as Mr. Bosanquet and Mr. Gilbart, and some others who oppose the currency principle do, to the effects of great variations in the rate of interest, I am inclined to think, that excepting the convertibility of the paper and the solvency of banks, which are and ought to be within the province of the legislature most carefully to preserve, the (105–6)

361.1   banking system] system of banking (106)

361.2   another," namely, "the] another, is the (106)

361.3   credit."] credit incidental to one as compared with the other; and a careful consideration of the various plans which have been submitted to the public for carrying out the currency principle, has led to a confirmation of the opinion which I have before expressed, that under a complete separation of the functions of issue and banking, the transitions would be more abrupt and violent than under the existing system; unless, and upon this, in my opinion, the question hinges, the deposit or banking department were bound to hold a much larger reserve than seems to be contemplated by any of the plans which I have seen. (106)

———— *On the Bank Charter Act of 1844, its Principles and Operation; with Suggestions for an Improved Administration of the Bank of England.* London: Longman, Brown, Green, and Longmans, 1856.

NOTE: copy in JSM's library, Somerville College, inscribed "Mr. [?] Stuart Mill Esqr./With the sincere regards/of his friend/the Author".

REFERRED TO: 501–2

———— *Thoughts and Details on the High and Low Prices of the Last Thirty Years.* 4 parts. London: Murray, 1823.

REFERRED TO: 4–5, 13

———— 2nd ed., 1824.

NOTE: at 8 JSM is probably not quoting Tooke (see variants below); they may be using a common source.

QUOTED: 8, 21, 97n.   REFERRED TO: 19–20, 74n

8. Table 34,954,845] 34,953,816
8. Table 34,566,571] 34,567,271
97.n7 "a great] I can recollect, moreover, that [in 1808–09] there was a great (73)
97.n9 credit," is "an] credit, which is an (73)

TORRENS, ROBERT. Referred to: 399–400

———— *The Budget. On Commercial and Colonial Policy. With an introduction in which the deductive method, as presented in Mr. Mill's System of Logic, is applied to the solution of some controverted questions in political economy.* London: Smith, Elder, 1844.

NOTE: an earlier version was issued in parts, 1841–42.

REFERRED TO: 231

———— *An Inquiry into the Practical Working of the Proposed Arrangements for the Renewal of the Charter of the Bank of England, and the Regulation of the Currency: With a refutation of the fallacies advanced by Mr. Tooke.* London: Smith, Elder, 1844.

REVIEWED: 343–61

QUOTED: 347, 353n, 360–1

347.28 "will] [*paragraph*] For the reasons set forth in the tract now submitted to the public, I am of opinion, that the proposed measures for the renewal of the Charter of the Bank of England, and for the regulation of the provincial banks of issue, are the most important and the most salutary, as regards the reform of our monetary system, which have been brought under the consideration of Parliament, since the Act of 1819, for the resumption of cash payments; that their adoption by the Legislature will preserve the circulating medium from any greater fluctuations than those which would take place were the currency exclusively metallic; and will (iv) [*see next variant*]

347.35   "the most] (iv) [*see variants above and below*]

347.36   has] have (iv) [*see variant at 347.28*]

347.38   payments."] (iv) [*see variant at 347.28*]

347.40   "the reform] The agricultural classes will, as I have attempted to show, reap the largest proportional advantage from the steadiness imparted to the currency by the proposed reform (iv) [*follows directly the sentence from which JSM has just quoted*]

349.12–13   "cycles . . . depression,"] [*see variants at 347.28–38 above. The second of these terms is also used by Tooke,* Inquiry, *55*]

353.n5–7   "consequently . . . 1,000,000*l.*,"] [*paragraph*] Under these circumstances, and so long as the banker did not advance his deposits in loans, or upon securities, the amount of checks which the inhabitants of Birmingham could draw upon the bank, in settling their pecuniary transactions with each other, could not exceed 1,000,000*l.*, being the amount of their deposits; and, consequently, . . . 1,000,000*l.* (10)

360.38–9   "cycles . . . depression,"] [*see variant at 349.12–13 above*]

361.9   "can] He can (55)

361.9–10   publication,"] publication; because, in his "History of Prices," he has a deposit and a book credit with the Bank of Fame, against which he can largely draw. (55)

TURGOT. Referred to: 139, 211–12, 335

TURNER. Referred to: 550

VANCE, JOHN. Referred to: 500

———— "Evidence taken before the Select Committee on the Bank Acts," *Parliamentary Papers,* 1857 (Sess. 2), X.i, 177–206.

NOTE: the "quotations" are questions asked by Vance, a member of the Committee.

QUOTED: 511–12

VANE. Referred to: 464

VANSITTART. Referred to: 100

VESEY, THOMAS. Referred to: 464

———— "Evidence taken before the Select Committee on Income and Property Tax," *Parliamentary Papers,* 1852, IX, 284–95, 298–324.

NOTE: the "quotations" are questions asked by Vesey, a member of the Committee.

QUOTED: 495

WAKEFIELD. Referred to: 394

WATT. Referred to: 157

824APPENDIX E

WOOD, CHARLES. Referred to: 464, 500

——— "Evidence taken before the Select Committee on the Bank Acts," *Parliamentary Papers*, 1857 (Sess. 2), X.i, 177–206.

NOTE: the "quotations" are questions asked by Wood, a member of the Committee.
QUOTED: 517.23

——— "Evidence taken before the Select Committee on Income and Property Tax," *Parliamentary Papers*, 1852, IX, 284–95, 298–324.

NOTE: the "quotations" are questions asked by Wood, a member of the Committee.
QUOTED: 469, 474–80, 484, 487, 491, 495

WOOL ACT. See 5 George IV, c. 47.

PARLIAMENTARY PAPERS

"Report from the Select Committee on the High Price of Gold Bullion," *Parliamentary Papers*, 1810, III, 1–232.

REFERRED TO: 188

"Minutes of Evidence Taken before the Select Committee on the Expediency of the Bank Resuming Cash Payments," *Parliamentary Papers*, 1819, III. See Haldimand.

"Second Report (brought from the Lords) Relative to Foreign Trade: (Silk and Wine Trade)," *Parliamentary Papers*, 1821, VII, 423–7. See Davison; Hale.

NOTE: JSM may be quoting from Moreau's transcription (*Rise and Progress*, 13–4) of the Report.

QUOTED: 133

133.28–9 *almost entirely carried on by machinery*] [*not in italics*] (425)

"Minutes of Evidence Taken before the Select Committee to whom the several Petitions complaining of the Depressed State of the Agriculture of the United Kingdom, were Referred," *Parliamentary Papers*, 1821, IX. See Jacob; Rothwell; Rous; Solly; Tooke.

"Minutes of Evidence before the Committee of the Lords, (1826) on the Circulation of Promissory Notes," *Parliamentary Papers*, 1826–27, VI. See Burgess; Gladstone, John; Loyd, Lewis.

"Minutes of Evidence Taken before the Committee of Secrecy on the Bank of England Charter," *Parliamentary Papers*, 1831–32, VI. See Attwood, Thomas; Gurney, Samuel; Rothschild.

STATUTES

26 Henry VIII, c. 1. An Acte concerning the kynges highness to be supreme head of the churche of Englande, and to have auctoritie to reforme and redresse all errours, heresies, and abuses in the same (1534).

REFERRED TO: 209n

I William & Mary, c. 20. An Act for a grant to their Majesties of an aid of twelve pence in the pound for one year, for the necessary defence of their realms (1688).

REFERRED TO: 480

2 George III, c. 10. An Act for raising by annuities, in manner therein mentioned, the sum of twelve millions, to be charged on the sinking fund; and for applying the surplus of certain duties on spirituous liquors, and also the monies arising from the duties on spirituous liquors, granted by an act of this session of parliament (1761).

REFERRED TO: 583

13 George III, c. 68. An Act to impower the Magistrates therein mentioned to settle and regulate the Wages of Persons employed in the Silk Manufacture within their respective Jurisdictions (1773).

REFERRED TO: 128

37 George III, cc. 45, 91. An Act for confirming and continuing, for a limited Time, the Restriction contained in the Minute of Council of the 26th February, 1797, on Payments of Cash by the Bank (3 May 1797); and An Act to continue, for a limited time, an Act, made in this present Session of Parliament, intituled, [as above] . . . , under certain Regulations and Restrictions (22 June, 1797).

REFERRED TO: 5–6, 184, 187–8

38 George III, c. 60. An Act for making perpetual, subject to redemption and purchase in the manner therein stated, the several sums of money now charged in Great Britain as a land tax for one year, from the 25th day of March 1798 (21 June, 1798).

REFERRED TO: 479–87

39 George III, c. 13. An Act to repeal the duties imposed by an act, made in the last session of parliament, for granting an aid and contribution for the prosecution of the war; and to make more effectual provision for the like purpose, by granting certain duties upon income, in lieu of the said duties (9 January, 1799).

REFERRED TO: 474, 479, 591

39 & 40 George III, c. 98. An Act to restrain all Trusts and Directions in Deeds or Wills, whereby the Profits or Produce of Real or Personal Estate shall be accumulated, and the beneficial Enjoyment thereof postponed beyond the Time therein limited (28 July, 1800).

NOTE: known as the Thelusson Act.

REFERRED TO: 199

59 George III, c. 49. An Act to continue the Restrictions contained in several Acts on Payments in Cash by the Bank of *England*, until the 1st May 1823, and to provide for the gradual Resumption of such Payments; and to permit the Exportation of Gold and Silver (2 July, 1819).

NOTE: JSM refers to the Act as "Peel's Bill."

REFERRED TO: 186, 347

3 George IV, c. 60. An Act to amend the Laws relating to the Importation of Corn (15 July, 1822).

NOTE: also relevant are 55 George III, c. 26; 1 & 2 George IV, c. 87, and (for 143–59), 9 George IV, c. 60.

REFERRED TO: 47–70 *passim*, 87, 109, 134–6, 143–59 *passim*

5 George IV, c. 21. An Act to Reduce the Duties on Importation of Raw and Thrown Silk, and to Repeal the Prohibition on the Importation of Silk Manufactures, and to Grant Certain Duties Thereon (12 April, 1824).

REFERRED TO: 70, 127–8, 132, 134

5 George IV, c. 41. An Act to repeal certain Duties on Law Proceedings in the Courts in *Great Britain* and *Ireland* respectively; and for better protecting the Duties payable upon Stamped Vellum, Parchment, or Paper (28 May, 1824).

REFERRED TO: 70

5 George IV, c. 47. An Act to alter the Laws relating to the Duties on the Importation of Wool, and of Hare and Coney Skins (3 June, 1824).

REFERRED TO: 70

5 George IV, c. 95. An Act to repeal the Laws relative to the Combination of Workmen; and for other Purposes therein mentioned (21 June, 1824).

REFERRED TO: 128, 427

6 George IV, cc. 105, 109. An Act to repeal the several Laws relating to the Customs (5 July, 1825), and An Act for the Encouragement of *British* Shipping and Navigation (5 July, 1825).

REFERRED TO: 70

6 George IV, c. 129. An Act to repeal the Laws relating to the Combination of Workmen, and to make other Provisions in lieu thereof (6 July, 1825).

REFERRED TO: 70

7 George IV, c. 6. An Act to limit, and after a certain Period to prohibit, the issuing of Promissory Notes under a limited Sum in *England* (22 Mar., 1826).

REFERRED TO: 78

7 George IV, c. 46. An Act for the better regulating Copartnerships of certain Bankers in *England* (26 May, 1826).

NOTE: the Act actually enabled banks with an unlimited number of partners to be established at a distance exceeding sixty-five miles from London.

REFERRED TO: 78–9, 105

7 & 8 George IV, c. 57. An Act to permit, until 1st May, 1828, certain Corn, Meal, and Flour to be entered for Home Consumption (2 July, 1827).

NOTE: superseded by 9 George IV, c. 60, and 5 & 6 Victoria, Sess. 2, c. 14. The reference is to the discussion eventually leading to the Act.

REFERRED TO: 143. See also Brougham, "Speech"; Canning, "Speech" (1827).

9 George IV, c. 60. An Act to amend the Laws relating to the Importation of Corn (15 July, 1828).

NOTE: repealed by 5 & 6 Victoria, Sess. 2, c. 14.

REFERRED TO: 762–3

10 George IV, c. 7. An Act for the Relief of His Majesty's Roman Catholic Subjects (13 April, 1829).

REFERRED TO: 196, 369, 706

2 & 3 William IV, c. 45. An Act to amend the Representation of the People in *England* and *Wales* (7 June, 1832).

REFERRED TO: 191, 195, 369–70, 706

4 & 5 William IV, c. 76. An Act for the Amendment and better Administration of the Laws relating to the Poor in *England* and *Wales* (14 August, 1834).

REFERRED TO: 371, 374, 437

2 & 3 Victoria, c. 37. An Act to amend, and extend until the First Day of *January* One thousand eight hundred and forty-two, the Provisions of an Act of the First Year of Her present Majesty for exempting certain Bills of Exchange and Promissory Notes from the Operation of the Laws relating to Usury (29 July, 1839).

NOTE: the laws repealed go back to 37 Henry VIII, c. 9 (1545); the Act of 1839 was extended from time to time, and then repealed by 17 & 18 Victoria, c. 90 (1854).

REFERRED TO: 422, 461, 531

5 & 6 Victoria, Sess. 2, c. 14. An Act to Amend the Laws for the Importation of Corn (29 April, 1842).

NOTE: the reference at 763 is to the introduction of the measures leading to the Act.

REFERRED TO: 383–4, 763

5 & 6 Victoria, c. 35. An Act for granting to Her Majesty Duties on Profits arising from Property, Professions, Trades, and Offices, until the Sixth Day of *April* One thousand eight hundred and forty-five (22 June, 1842).

NOTE: referred to as Peel's Income Tax Act.

REFERRED TO: 465–98 *passim*, 592, 702

7 & 8 Victoria, c. 32. An Act to regulate the Issue of Bank Notes, and for giving to the Governor and Company of the Bank of *England* certain Privileges for a limited Period (19 July, 1844).

NOTE: sometimes referred to by JSM as the "plan" or "measure" of Sir Robert Peel.

REFERRED TO: 343–61 *passim*, 501–47 *passim*, 607–8, 610

7 & 8 Victoria, c. 110. An Act for the Registration, Incorporation, and Regulation of Joint Stock Companies (5 September, 1844).

REFERRED TO: 407–29 *passim*

8 & 9 Victoria, c. 37. An Act to regulate the Issue of Bank Notes in *Ireland*, and to regulate the Repayment of certain Sums advanced by the Governor and Company of the Bank of *Ireland* for the Public Service (21 July, 1845).

REFERRED TO: 511

8 & 9 Victoria, c. 38. An Act to regulate the Issue of Bank Notes in Scotland (21 July, 1845).

REFERRED TO: 511

8 & 9 Victoria, c. 118. An Act to facilitate the Inclosure and Improvement of Commons and Lands held in common, the Exchange of Lands, and the Division of intermixed Lands; to provide Remedies for defective or incomplete Executions, and for the Nonexecution, of the Powers of general and local Inclosure Acts; and to provide for the Revival of such Powers in certain Cases (8 August, 1845).

REFERRED TO: 692

9 & 10 Victoria, c. 22. An Act to amend the Laws relating to the Importation of Corn (26 June, 1846).

REFERRED TO: 371, 384n

9 & 10 Victoria, c. 27. An Act to amend the Laws relating to Friendly Societies (3 July, 1846).

NOTE: the references may also be to 13 & 14 Victoria, c. 115, which was not actually enacted until 15 Aug., 1850.

REFERRED TO: 408–9, 426

14 & 15 Victoria, c. 36. An Act to repeal the Duties payable on Dwelling Houses according to the Number of Windows or Lights, and to grant in lieu thereof other Duties on Inhabited Houses according to their annual Value (24 July, 1851).

REFERRED TO: 485, 489–90, 496–7

15 & 16 Victoria, c. 31. An Act to legalize the Formation of Industrial and Provident Societies (30 June, 1852).

REFERRED TO: 407n

17 & 18 Victoria, c. 81. An Act to make further Provision for the good Government and Extension of the University of *Oxford*, of the Colleges therein, and of the College of *Saint Mary Winchester* (7 August, 1854).

REFERRED TO: 214n

19 & 20 Victoria, c. 88. An Act to make further Provision for the good Government and Extension of the University of *Cambridge*, of the Colleges therein, and of the College of King *Henry* the Sixth at *Eton* (29 July, 1856).

REFERRED TO: 214n

23 Victoria, c. 14. An Act for granting to Her Majesty Duties on Profits arising from Property, Professions, Trades and Offices (3 April, 1860).

NOTE: also relevant is 5 & 6 Victoria, c. 35.

REFERRED TO: 551–98 *passim*

30 & 31 Victoria, c. 102. An Act further to amend the Laws relating to the Representation of the People in England and Wales (15 August, 1867).

REFERRED TO: 689, 706–7

32 & 33 Victoria, c. 42. An Act to put an end to the Establishment of the Church of Ireland, and to make provision in respect of the Temporalities thereof, and in respect of the Royal College of Maynooth (26 July, 1869).

REFERRED TO: 615

33 & 34 Victoria, c. 46. An Act to amend the Law relating to the Occupation and Ownership of Land in Ireland (1 Aug., 1870).

REFERRED TO: 674

Index

in increased by Bank of England operations after 1844, 357–61, 502, 512, 518, 520–1, 524, 537–9; 3 per cent as minimum, 411; high in United States, 602; not foreseeable or controllable, 610
See also Bank of England, Profits
International Society, 708
International trade: Ricardo's theory of, 10–12, 30, 232–3; statistics of British (1782–1823), 21; utility of not measured by merchants' fortunes, 130–1; Britain gains most in, 260–1; between Britain and France, 260–1, 271; in securities, 526–7
  theory of: scientific, 232–3; restatement of, 233–4; calculating advantage for each nation under barter, 235–41, with money, 241–3; and cost of carriage, 243–5; uncertain effects of tax on exports, 245–8; inadvisable benefits of tax on imports, 248–51; inventions and export of machinery, 251–2; influence of exports on price of imports, 253–4; underselling in, 234, 254–7; restrictions on imports, 257–8; effects of payment of tribute or subsidy, 258–60
Inventions: effect of exporting in international trade theory, 251–2; encouraged by co-operation, 414
Ireland: banking in, 106, 107, 511–12; effect of absentee landlords on imports of, 260; cottier tenancy in, 226, 389n, 448; land debentures in, 428; emigration from, 574, 677; disendowment of Protestant church of, 615; agricultural economy of, 672, 675–9, 765; character of people of, 675, 678–9; outmoded land laws of, 683n–5n; price of land in, 690
Italy: silk manufacturing in, 131–3; Lombardy undersold, 256; métayer tenure in, 389n, 752; freedom and new intellectual growth in, 699

JACOBINS, 158
Jewish law: on master and servant, 454; on property, 751
Joint-stock companies: liability of, 421, 424; compared to co-operatives, 425; as banks in Ireland, 511;

taxation of 581–2. *See also* Partnership
Jura (France), 723
Justice, cost of, 408, 418–19, 685n

LABOUR: relative productivity of in agriculture and industry, 42; demand for depends on capital, 49–50; effect of economizing in agriculture, 180; employment of not increased by additional currency, 189–90; productive and unproductive, 228, 280–9; division of results in large proportion of capital idle, 268; benefits of employment of unproductive, 270–1; skill of as wealth, 281, 285; as primary means of production, 290, 293; freedom of, 453–7; and abstinence as bases of economic life, 714; Fourierist criticisms of wastefulness and boredom of, 719–21, 726; how made attractive under Fourierism, 747–8
  claims and rights of: growing sympathy towards, 365–6, sparked by Malthus' theory of population, 366–9, by Reform Bill (1832), 369, by Chartism, 369–70, and encouraged by Carlyle, 370–1; misguided philanthropy in regard to, 371–6; education sole solution to, 376–9; return to feudalism no answer to, 379–80; alienation in employer-employee relations, 380–2; possible legislation to meet, 383–7; in regard to bargaining for wages, 646–68, Thornton quoted on, 647–9; rights of capital supposedly rights of past labour, 653–4; must be based on interests of human race, 655; in regard to wealth and capital, 656–8; and trade unions, 658–68
See also Co-operation, Labouring Class, Partnership, Socialism, Trade unions, Wages
Labour Congresses, 708
Labourers' Friend Society, 372
Labouring class: need for prudence among, 368–9, 374–5, 379, 449; alienation and improvements in relations with employers, 378–82, 634; Mr. Greg's scheme for, 381–2; and gardening, 388n; and laws of partnership, 407–29; use of

not universal, 672; desire for wealth sometimes predatory, 673; in regard to land tenure, 673–5

definition of: (i) how nation is made rich, 312; (ii) laws of production, distribution, and consumption of wealth, 313–18; (iii) JSM's, 318, 323; as moral not physical science, 316–21; as social science, 319–21; Say's meaning of, 321; as part of science of society, 321–3; as abstract science, 325, 329, 333

method of: distinction between theory and practice, 323–5; *a posteriori* and *a priori*, 325–7; *a priori* only scientific method, 327–31; *a posteriori* for verification, 331–3; principles and disturbing causes, 330–1; use of "generalization" and "exception," 337–9

Politicians, unscientific training of, 110–17

Politics: reason replaces authority as standard in, 369; studied from labouring class's point of view, 707. *See also* Government, Parliament, Socialism

Population: discovery of principle of as raising political economy to science, 30, 40; and capital as regulating wages, 35–6, 40; increase of and wages and profit, 40–1, 299–300; necessary restriction of, 227, 374–5, 449–50, encouraged by trade unions, 664–5, and communism, 728–9; and poverty and poor laws, 227–8, 375, 449; corrected inferences from principle of, 366–7, 449–50, 728–9; and prudence in Ireland, 678; increase of among rich and poor in Paris, 717–18

Poor Laws: 227–8, 371, 375, 437, 449, 617

Poverty: considered inevitable, 367, before principle of population understood, 366–8, 449–50, 727–9; and socialism, 710–11; charity no way of remedying, 371–6, without restrictions on marriage, 374–5; education sole means of ending, 376–9; relief of through allotment system, 387n–9n

Practical men, ignorance of, 19 98, 112–14, 118, 121, 127, 130, 184,

190, in Parliament (1826), 110–18, compared with theorists, 324–5, 334–5; and philosophers in ancient world 334n; social rôle of practical philosopher, 334–7, 393; practical statesmanship, 333, and land tenure reform, 672

Prester John, 158

Préfet, role of in French government, 436

Price: Smith on causes of, 163–4, 168; how determined in socialist economy, 446; erroneous theory of demand and supply and, 448. *See also* Price level, Value

Price level: causes discussed of fluctuations in British (*c.* 1793–1824), 5–18, 99; supposedly lowered by competition of capital, 37; how determined by quantity of money, 37, 184–5, 350–6; effect on of small changes in price of necessities, 61; rise in and in wages, 661. *See also* Commercial crisis, Foreign exchange, Money

Production: diminishing returns in, 165–9; and capital and wages, 290–1; laws of and political economy, 314–15, 317–18

influence of consumption on: consumption must be as great as p., 42; all which is produced already consumed, 262–4; under division of labour, 264–5; effect of sojourners on use of capital, 265–7; full employment of capital not desirable, 274–5; periods of stagnation and briskness inevitable, 275–9

See also Consumption, Universal glut

Productive: labour relatively in agriculture and manufacturing, 42; and unproductive, defined, 280–9

Profits: rate of in war and peace, 18; erroneous theory of, 29, 34–5, 37–41; importance of high, 50–1; in silk manufacturing, 134–5; effect of additional demand on, 268–70; as composed of interest and wages of superintendence, 270, 300–2, 411, 735; rate of defined, 290–2; gross, 291–2; Ricardian theory of restated and corrected 293–7; and wages, 293–300; in North America, 293; and